Value at Risk and Bank Capital Management

Value at Risk and Bank Capital Management

Francesco Saita

AMSTERDAM • BOSTON • HEIDELBERG • LONDON
NEW YORK • OXFORD • PARIS • SAN DIEGO
SAN FRANCISCO • SINGAPORE • SYDNEY • TOKYO
Academic Press is an imprint of Elsevier

Academic Press is an imprint of Elsevier

30 Corporate Drive, Suite 400, Burlington, MA 01803, USA
525 B Street, Suite 1900, San Diego, California 92101-4495, USA
84 Theobald's Road, London WC1X 8RR, UK

This book is printed on acid-free paper.

Copyright © 2007, Elsevier Inc. All rights reserved.

Library of Congress Cataloging-in-Publication Data
APPLICATION SUBMITTED

British Library Cataloguing-in-Publication Data
A catalogue record for this book is available from the British Library.

ISBN 13: 978-0-12-369466-9
ISBN 10: 0-12-369466-3

For information on all Academic Press publications
visit our Web site at www.books.elsevier.com

Printed in the United States of America
07 08 09 10 9 8 7 6 5 4 3 2 1

Contents

Preface

About the Book

Risk management is at the heart of bank management and is one of the most fascinating fields for academic research. Developments in risk measurement techniques, risk management practices, and regulation have reinforced each other to increase the attention of a wider and wider public to a number of topics that in the mid-1990s would have reached the attention of only a few specialists. Understanding bank risk management is now recognized as a key requisite for most (if not all) of the managers working at a financial institution. The purpose of this book is to present risk measurement methodologies and to discuss their implications and consequences on the bank's decision-making process.

In fact, it would be limited to analyze and study risk management problems by focusing on risk measurement methodology issues only. While measurement methodologies are clearly very important and research in this field is crucial, a well-designed risk management process is also based on a clear and effective definition of risk control, performance evaluation, and capital allocation processes. The science of risk measurement and the art of management are both required, and this makes risk management an attractive topic not only for finance specialists but for human resource and organization specialists and researchers as well.

In my personal experience as a teacher in executive risk management seminars designed for different target audiences, as a researcher, and sometimes as a consultant, I have noted how important is to consider carefully not only the technical soundness of risk measurement methodologies, but also the consequences their application may have on human behavior. Measuring a trader's risk capital and including this number in his or her performance evaluation and compensation scheme sounds fine, but unintended consequences are always possible. Bankers Trust was among the pioneers in the development of risk management techniques and processes, but many think that lawsuits with some large customers in the mid-1990s and the subsequent reputational problems were mainly the result of a compensation scheme making the traders focus only on short-term profit, even if they were correctly measured in risk-adjusted terms.

The intent to link risk measurement methodologies with their impact on internal processes also explains the structure of this book. The first two chapters introduce the concept of value at risk and discuss the different types of capital that bank capital management has to consider (also discussing the main impacts of the Basel II Accord and the new IAS/IFRS accounting principles). The book then goes on to cover risk measurement. Besides dealing with "classic" market, credit, and operational risks (Chapters 3 to 5), it also discusses two crucial topics that have so far received less attention than they should: (1) how to measure business risk (Chapter 5) and (2) how to estimate overall economic capital through the aggregation of different risks (Chapter 6). The remainder of the book analyzes how a bank can structure risk control and risk-adjusted performance measurement processes, with the final chapter discussing the links between the capital allocation process and the budgeting and planning process.

Addressing all these issues while trying to keep the book as unifying as possible is not an easy task (even though suggestions for selected further reading are provided at the end of each chapter). Any reader can judge whether or not I have been able to find the right balance. In any case, I hope this book may give even nonspecialists a clear picture of key methodologies, their critical assumptions, and their implications for bank management while providing experienced readers with a useful critical discussion of a number of crucial topics that are still in their early stages of development, such as business risk, risk aggregation, and the definition of target returns for individual business units within the capital allocation process.

Acknowledgments

The people I am indebted to for this book are almost uncountable. On one hand there are all the people in academia whom I have had the chance to listen to or to discuss or work with since the early 1990s and who contributed to the development of my interest in all the different aspects of risk management. On the other hand, this book is also the result of a number of meetings, interviews, and discussions with many talented risk managers, regulators, and consultants while facing real-world problems.

Though the people I should thank are many, the first one, and not only in order of appearance, is Andrea Sironi, who first introduced me to value at risk in 1992 and who has since been fundamental in developing my research interest in this field. All the projects and executive seminars in which we have worked together have been an opportunity for endless, passionate discussions on risk management problems, some of which are reflected in this book. He has always been not only a friend, but also the most wonderful colleague one could hope to work with.

Also of great importance to me have been the research environment at Bocconi University and the many great colleagues there and its proximity to the real world of financial institutions. I would like to mention in particular Roberto Ruozi, who invited me to join Bocconi; Paolo Mottura, whose advice and example have always been precious; Luca Erzegovesi, who first introduced me to quantitative finance and who, together with Roberto Ruozi, Pier Luigi Fabrizi, and Giancarlo Forestieri, patiently supervised most of my first publications. For this book, I am especially grateful to Andrea Resti for a number of interesting discussions and for the comments he gave me on some specific parts of the book. Very useful comments on individual chapters also came from Leo Corvino and Mascia Bedendo, from Bocconi, and Mauro Senati and Maria Egle Romano, from Banca Intesa and UniCredit, respectively. I would like to thank them all, together with Giacomo de Laurentis, Giuseppe Lusignani, and Mario Masini, for the useful discussions on risk management topics we had in the past.

I am deeply indebted to many different people at New York University's Salomon Center for the period I spent there as a visiting scholar in 1994–95, when I started researching (and interviewing people) in the risk management field. The frequent opportunity to listen to and have discussions with people such as Ed Altman, Tony Saunders, Roy Smith, and Ingo Walter (just to name the people most relevant for this book) has been invaluable, as for any young researcher wishing to understand risk management and decision-making processes in large financial institutions. I am particularly grateful to Ed Altman for the kind advice he has given me a number of times since then. I must also thank the many different top managers I interviewed during that period from two of the largest New York–based international banks and the numerous risk managers from European banks I interviewed or held discussions with more recently. While almost all asked for anonymity (about which I will keep my promise), they know how important they have been for this book. An exception can clearly be made for two groups of people. The first group includes Elio Berti from UniCredit, Luc Henrard and Ruben Olieslargers from Fortis Group, and Patrick de Fontnouvelle and Victoria Garrity from the Federal Reserve Bank of Boston, who were so incredibly kind to contribute to this book by directly writing some sections, making their experience and competence available directly to the reader. It is hard for me to express completely how much I appreciate their great kindness and support. The second group includes a number of Italian bank managers, risk managers, and supervisors whom I have had the chance to meet repeatedly at conferences of the Association of Italian Financial Risk Managers (AIFIRM) or of the Fondo Interbancario di Tutela dei Depositi (FITD) or even work with in one of the two research risk management projects sponsored by the FITD that I coordinated. It is impossible to list of all them (and I beg their pardon for that), but I must mention at least Fabio Arnaboldi and his team, Pierfrancesco Cocco, Domenico Gammaldi, Renato Maino, Fernando Metelli, Carlo Palego, Sandro Panizza, and Sergio Sorrentino.

This book also benefited substantially from the highly useful suggestions of the two anonymous referees and from the competence and kindness of Karen Maloney from Elsevier, who, together with Dennis McGonagle, supported this project from the beginning, providing me with truly precious advice. I am also indebted to Jay Donahue for his wonderful support in the production phase. It has been a real pleasure to interact with them throughout the writing of this book.

Finally, I must thank all the people who, though they did not contribute directly to the book or my research, are the most important people in my life: my parents and my sister, and my closest friends, who always supported me when needed; and, last in appearance though absolutely first in importance, my wife, Silvia, and our wonderful sons, Alberto and Martino. It is impossible to find the right words to describe what they represent in my life and how much I love them. While many authors dedicate their books to their wives — which may seem unavoidable after they let the authors dedicate so much time (and so many weekends) to a book — dedicating this book to Silvia is far from formal or obvious. She knows quite well how important her support is to me in everything I have been doing, and she knows she is much more important than any book or research achievement I may ever get in my career.

To Silvia,
with all my love

Contributors

Elio Berti is the Head of Capital Allocation within the CFO Department of UniCredito Italiano. He holds an honors degree in economics from the University of Genoa, and since 2001 he has been in charge of capital management functions in Unicredit Holding Company, with the responsibility for planning, allocating, and managing capital to maximize shareholder value creation, for supporting the capital allocation and strategic planning process, and for supporting evaluation and structuring of financial products for the Group Pricing Unit.

Patrick de Fontnouvelle is a vice president in the Supervision, Regulation, and Credit Department at the Federal Reserve Bank of Boston. As head of the department's Quantitative Analysis Unit, he provides analytical support for the supervisory assessment of internal risk modeling and capital allocation at large banking organizations. Patrick received his B.A. in mathematics from Princeton University and his Ph.D. in economics from the University of Wisconsin.

Victoria Garrity is a quantitative analyst at the Federal Reserve Bank of Boston. In this role, Victoria focuses on operational risk measurement, management, and quantification through her involvement in bank examinations and various Basel II–related initiatives (including QIS-4 and the 2004 Loss-Data Collection Exercise). Victoria received her B.A. in mathematics from Ithaca College and her M.A. in economics from Boston University. She is also a CFA charter holder.

Luc Henrard is the Chief Risk Officer of Fortis, and he is a member of the Fortis Bank Management Committee and the Fortis Insurance Management Committees. He is a civil engineer and obtained a Master of Business Administration at the Catholic University of Leuven (KUL). Prior to his current position, he headed the dealing room of the former Generale Bank in Tokyo, was secretary to the ALM Committee, headed the ALM department of Generale Bank, and was a member of the Credit Management Team of Fortis Bank. Luc has spent the last six years at the corporate level developing an internal risk, capital, and value management framework for the entire Fortis organization. This framework is the basis for capital adequacy testing and economic performance assessment. Luc teaches risk management at the Facultés Universitaires Notre Dame de la Paix (Namur) and at the Université Catholique de Louvain (UCL).

Ruben Olieslagers has been active since the 1990s in risk management at Fortis. He has been closely involved in the development of the risk models (e.g., economic capital model) within Fortis. He has represented Fortis Bank in several national and international banking and insurance associations in order to safeguard the interests of financial institutions. Currently he is a Director at Fortis Central Risk Management, responsible for the implementation of risk projects for banking and insurance. He lectures regularly at universities (Belgium, the Netherlands, Germany, Austria, Italy, Switzerland) on financial topics related to risk management and regulation. By training, he is a civil engineer (KUL — Catholic University of Leuven), and he holds a Master's in Finance (Solvay Business School — Belgium) and an MBA (Vlerick — Belgium; Nijenrode — The Netherlands; St. Gallen — Switzerland).

CHAPTER ◆ 1

Value at Risk, Capital Management, and Capital Allocation

Managing risks has always been at the heart of any bank's activity. The existence of financial intermediation is clearly linked with a bank's advantage in evaluating the riskiness of potential borrowers and in building well-diversified portfolios. A bank's ability to survive adverse economic cycles (and phases of high volatility, as far as market risk exposure are concerned) is linked both to the quality of its risk selection and management processes and to its capital endowment. Capital is therefore a key resource for both shareholders and managers who are interested in a bank's ability to survive while offering an attractive return for shareholders. At the same time, capital is important for financial system supervisors who are interested in safeguarding the stability of the system by reducing the risk of bank failures (Berger, Herring, and Szëgo 1995).

While the difference between the perspective of shareholders (who act as principals) and managers (who act as agents) when determining the optimal level of risk and the optimal amount of capital for the bank is common to any firm, the interest of supervisors in controlling the capital adequacy of industry players is typical of the financial sector. All developed countries have in fact witnessed through time, even if with partially different timetables from country to country, an evolution in financial supervision that has gradually favored increased competition in the banking business while strengthening prudential regulation. Capital ratios, in particular, have been considered the best solution to safeguard the soundness of the banking system, despite the increase in competition, and to guarantee a level playing field for banks from different countries. While the Basel I Accord in 1988, which is discussed in Chapter 2, is often considered the first milestone in defining the link between a bank's risk and its capital from the supervisors' point of view, the debate concerning the role of capital as a protection for "unusual" losses from both bankers' and regulators' viewpoint is much older (see as an cxample Watson 1974).

At the same time, the importance of the link between capital and the amount of risk the bank can bear does not derive from supervisors' constraints only but is instead at the heart of the bank's management. For instance, many of the key risk management concepts that are now widely used and that became popular with the public at large beginning in the early 1990s were already in use, perhaps in simpler forms, in some large U.S. banks in the early 1970s. In one of the few publicly available documents, George J. Vojta (1973) from Citigroup stated that one of the functions of bank capital was "to provide protection against unanticipated adversity leading to loss in excess of normal expectations." In the same period, Bankers Trust was developing the concept of risk-adjusted return on capital (RAROC), which is still one of the cornerstones of risk-adjusted performance measurement.

This book deals with risk, capital, and the relationship between the two. Since capital is a costly resource, the issue of jointly determining the optimal amount of risk and capital for the bank (taking into consideration regulatory constraints) is extremely relevant when managing a financial institution. A bank should therefore try to quantify the amount of capital needed to face potential losses deriving from the risks the bank is running and to develop policies and procedures to better manage those risks. *Value at risk* and *capital at risk*, which will be defined shortly, are the typical tools used by most banks for this purpose. The purpose of this chapter is to introduce the value-at-risk concept and its potential applications for capital management and capital allocation. The chapter also aims at clarifying why a bank should be concerned not only with how risks are measured but also with how those measures enter decision-making and performance evaluation processes. Risk measurement on the one hand and the use of risk measures as a management tool on the other hand will be discussed in more detail later in the book.

1.1   An Introduction to Value at Risk

The concept of *value at risk* and its relevance for bank management can easily be introduced through an example. We propose for simplicity a market risk example, even if, from a historical perspective, these measures were originally developed in most banks with reference to credit risk, which is typically the largest single source of risk for a bank. Let us consider a simplified U.S. investment bank that is active in trading three different assets: U.S. equities, British pounds, and U.S. corporate bonds. The bank is structured into three different trading desks (equities, foreign exchange (FX), and bonds) with one trader each that is supervised by a managing director (see Figure 1-1).

The managing director is interested both in preventing the bank from substantially increasing risk and in increasing the value of the bank for its shareholders by producing higher profits. The traditional way to pursue the first aim has always been (apart from direct supervision, which in this simplified case may still be a viable solution) to set notional limits, i.e., limits to the size of the positions each desk may take. For instance, the managing director may allow the equity trader to buy or sell short U.S. equities for a notional amount up to 500,000 U.S. dollars (USD). The FX trader may be allowed to take a long or short position on the GBP/USD exchange rate up to 500,000 USD. And finally the bond trader may be given a position notional limit of 600,000 USD. Since the risk of the bond portfolio will also depend on the sensitivity of the portfolio to changes in interest rates and on the credit quality of the portfolio, the bond trader may be given additional limits, such as a maximum average duration limit for the portfolio or a minimum rating class limit for individual bond issues.

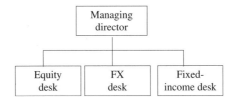

FIGURE 1-1   The structure of the simplified investment bank of the introductory example.

By using notional limits, the managing director would be partially helped in supervising the three trading desks but would still face three major problems. First of all, maintaining the same notional limits would not help him keep a stable maximum level of risk for each desk. The 500,000 USD limit for the equity trader would imply a limited risk in periods of low stock market volatility but a higher level of risk (and potential losses) in periods of high volatility. Just as driving at 40 miles per hour may be too cautious on the highway and too risky when passing in front of an elementary school precisely when all the students are getting out, fixed notional limits do not take into account the variability of external conditions. Incidentally, this may also occasionally force the managing director to ask some of the traders to close or reduce their positions. Unfortunately, this intervention will give a trader who underperformed yearly budget targets a chance to claim that profits would have been greater if a certain trade had not been closed due to the intervention of the managing director.

The second problem is that the managing director has to determine whether traders' limits are consistent with the capital the bank has. Capital is a cushion to cover losses, so the managing director should be concerned with having too little capital (or, equivalently, too high notional limits), which may imply a risk of default for his bank, and with having too much capital (or overly conservative notional limits), which could result in a poor return on equity for shareholders. In fact, there is no link between the limits that have been set and available capital, and there is no tool to assess the potential diversification across the different bets the traders are making on each single market.

Finally, let us assume that at the end of the year the three traders have made an equal profit and start competing for bonus allocation. The FX trader would claim that while obtaining the same profit with the same notional limit, he or she should be awarded a higher bonus than the equity trader, since the GBP/USD exchange rate is less volatile than U.S. equity prices. Similarly, the bond trader would argue that, since bonds are safer than other assets, despite the higher notional limits, the performance of the bond desk was the best one and should hence be rewarded accordingly. The equity trader would argue instead that since notional limits are the only objective measure, they should not be questioned and he or she should therefore be paid at least as much as the FX trader and more than the bond trader. At the end, it is impossible for the managing director to evaluate the risk–return performance of each trader. The problem here is that the measures of exposure behind the three desks are not really comparable: Even if formally they are all in dollars, 500,000 USD invested in equities is not as risky as 500,000 USD invested in a foreign currency.

What could solve the managing director's problems is to express the risk of all positions in terms of how many dollars the shareholder might lose, i.e., as the potential loss of each position. In this case (1) all risks could really be compared on the same ground, thus enabling a clearer perception of the risk–return profile of each business in fair terms, (2) risks could be compared with available capital, and (3) if properly measured, potential losses should be sensitive to the level of volatility in the market. Yet measuring the potential loss requires defining a time horizon and a confidence interval so as to exclude the worst potential loss, which would otherwise coincide again for most positions with the notional amount of the exposure. For instance, the managing director may be willing to consider only 99% of cases, thereby neglecting the losses that might be realized in the worst 1% scenarios. This risk measure is exactly what we define as value at risk (VaR), i.e., the maximum potential loss of a given position or business area or business unit within a given time horizon (e.g., one day, one month, one year) and confidence level (e.g., 99%, 99.97%).

The managing director and the bank as a whole would now face two completely different, even if intertwined, sets of problems. The first one is risk measurement: How should value at risk be calculated? How can risk be measured in a consistent way, especially when it is necessary to consider different kinds of risks (e.g., market, credit, operational, business risk) requiring different methodologies and models? How can those numbers be aggregated at the bank level, taking diversification into account? At the same time, there is a second and equally crucial issue: How should those measures be used in internal decision-making processes? How can a limit system based on value-at-risk measures be built? And which are the consequences of alternative choices? How should a risk-adjusted performance measure be defined? In practice, building a risk management system requires being not only familiar with state-of-the-art risk measurement techniques but also experienced enough to address carefully the organizational issues deriving from the revision of a bank's internal processes.

1.2 Capital Management and Capital Allocation: The Structure of the Book

The simplified example we just developed has introduced the idea that value-at-risk measures may be helpful to the manager in two crucial problems. The first one is *capital management*, which concerns the definition of the optimal capital structure of the bank. The second problem is *capital allocation*, which we define as the set of choices and decision-making processes concerning the optimal allocation of capital across the different business units inside the bank. All decision-making processes leading to capital allocation therefore include, for instance, the definition of risk-adjusted return targets for the different business units and the measurement and evaluation of their ex-post performance. In an ideal world, the risk manager should be able to support in a perfect way top management decisions on both issues. The ideal risk manager should have a homogeneous and sound measure for any kind of risk the bank might take, should be able to aggregate these measures in a single number telling to the CEO how much capital the bank needs in order to support optimal capital management decisions, and should be able to measure perfectly the business units' risk-adjusted returns so as to support the bank's capital allocation decisions.

The real world, however, is strikingly different, and it may be useful to point out why, to identify some of the main problems that are dealt with in the rest of the book. For instance, capital management is complex since the risk manager does not have a perfect measure for all the risks the bank is facing. There are sound methodologies for most, but not all, risk types. And even when these methodologies exist, they cannot always be applied (for the simple reason that they may be too costly to implement). Moreover, since value-at-risk measures for different risks may be heterogeneous and complex to aggregate, deriving a single value-at-risk number for the whole bank is far from easy. And even assuming such a number may have been derived, capital management decisions have to consider many other factors, such as the viewpoint of outsiders (e.g., the rating agencies), who may be cautious in trusting the numbers of aggregated values at risk derived by internal models they are unable to check.

At the same time, capital allocation cannot be considered equal to a simple asset allocation among different asset classes in an equity portfolio. The risk manager may in fact estimate at best with a certain precision past risk-adjusted returns. But future returns can be markedly different and may be estimated only through a deep understanding of the strategic perspectives of each business. Reallocating capital among businesses may imply, whether advertently or not, altering the bank's strategy, and this should not be driven only by measures of past financial performance such as the ones the risk managers may produce. Moreover, measuring risk-adjusted returns for business units and reallocating capital among them (instead of financial assets) has to do with people and is far from being a purely technical exercise. It is linked instead with the internal organization of the bank, with the structure of its incentive systems, and with its culture, so often one cannot look for *the* optimal solution but should rather look for the solution that best fits the bank's current or desired organizational system characteristics.

In summary, while risk measurement may be considered a science, risk management, capital management, and capital allocation remain largely a blend of science, experience, and art. This book starts by discussing in greater detail, in Chapter 2, the problem of capital management, pointing out the different notions of capital that may be relevant for the risk manager and the implications of Basel II and the new accounting standards, IAS/IFRS, for capital management. Chapters 3–6 are devoted to risk measurement and risk integration. They first discuss how market, credit, operational, and business risk can be measured, and then they analyze how a single value-at-risk measure for the bank as a whole may be derived. The rest of the book discusses the use of value-at-risk measures to support the bank's decision-making process and its internal capital allocation and therefore deal with the definition of value-at-risk-based limits for market and credit risk, the definition of risk-adjusted performance measures, and the process of capital allocation and its links with the planning-and-budgeting process.

CHAPTER ◆ 2

What Is "Capital" Management?

Questions such as "How much capital is required to cover potential losses deriving from the risks we are undertaking?," "What is the risk-adjusted return on capital produced by each business unit and by each product?," and "How should capital be allocated within business units?" are crucial for any bank. Yet before discussing them, the word *capital* must be defined. In fact, there are different notions of capital and different capital constraints that the bank should satisfy at the same time.

One well-known distinction is between regulatory capital and economic capital. Required *regulatory capital* is calculated according to regulators' rules and methodologies, defining for each bank a minimum regulatory capital requirement (MRCR). Regulators also clearly identify which components of the bank's balance sheet can be considered to be eligible as capital (i.e., *available* regulatory capital). In contrast, *economic capital* represents an internal estimate of the capital needed to run the business that is developed by the bank itself. This estimate may differ from MRCR since, for instance, the bank may include risks that are not formally subject to regulatory capital or may use different parameters or methodologies. Here we define *required economic capital* as the amount of capital the bank considers necessary for running the business from its point of view, independent of regulatory constraints. Of course, the bank should also be able to compare it with *available* economic capital.

According to the broad definition we have adopted, required economic capital is therefore an internal estimate of the capital the bank needs. In practice, however, the bank has to decide which notion of *capital* it considers relevant. Capital in fact could be identified either with *book capital*, or with the *market value of equity* (i.e., the market value of assets minus the market value or the fair value of liabilities) or with the *market capitalization* of the bank.[1] Intuitively, when internally estimating potential losses with reference to different notions of capital, the relative relevance of different types of risk or of different business units may change.

The chapter starts by analyzing regulatory capital constraints in Sections 2.1 and 2.2; Section 2.3 discusses the alternative notions of bank capital, focusing first on the book value of capital and the main impact of new International Accounting Standards and then on market capitalization and why it should have a greater role as a unit of measure of available and required economic capital.

2.1   Regulatory Capital and the Evolution toward Basel II

Until the 1970s, the choice about the optimal level of bank capitalization was basically an internal decision, since existing minimum capital requirements for banks were largely unrelated to the risks faced by the individual bank. The safety and soundness of the banking system were pursued at the time by controlling the level of competition inside each system (e.g., by imposing constraints on the entrance of new competitors or on branch networks' development for existing ones). The subsequent progressive shift toward more deregulated, competitive, and internationally intertwined financial systems gave prudential regulation a pivotal role. Supervisors agreed on the need to force all internationally active banks to maintain certain minimum adequate capital levels in order to achieve two main objectives. The first one was preserving systemic stability in a context of increasing deregulation and disappearing competitive barriers. The second one was safeguarding a level playing field among banks from different countries, eliminating potential competitive advantages for those banks that were earlier allowed to hold less capital than their competitors. The Basel Committee on Banking Supervision, which had been founded in 1974 by central bank governors of the Group of Ten (G-10) countries, tried to develop a common framework, and this effort led to the Basel I Accord in July 1988. Note that Basel Committee documents are not legally binding for single countries; rather, they represent international guidelines that need to be translated into national regulation, sometimes leaving national supervisors some freedom to define implementation details on certain issues. This is particularly relevant now as far as Basel II is concerned, since the translation into national regulation will differ between the United States and Europe.

2.1.1   The 1988 Basel I Accord and the 1996 Amendment

The 1988 Basel I Capital Accord represented the first key coordinated effort by regulators to define a minimum and partially risk-sensitive level of capital for international banks. The cornerstone of the accord was the *Cooke ratio* (named for its promoter), requiring that the ratio between regulatory capital (RC) and the sum of risk-weighted bank assets be equal to or greater than 8%:

---

1. While it may be claimed that economic capital should be represented by the "true" value of capital, therefore excluding book capital in favor of either market value of equity or market capitalization, our broader definition is consistent with the fact that the term *economic capital* in practice usually refers to any internal estimate of required capital, which sometimes is calculated by implicitly adopting a book capital approach.

$$\frac{\text{RC}}{\sum_{i=1}^{n} A_i \times RW_i} \geq 8\%$$

where A_i is a generic asset and RW_i represents the corresponding risk weight, based on credit risk only. The risk weights for the most important asset classes were 0% for OECD sovereign loans and bonds, 20% for non-OECD sovereign and OECD banks' exposure (as well as for exposures for non-OECD banks with a maturity lower than 1 year), 50% for mortgage loans, and 100% for corporate exposures and non-OECD banks' exposures over 1 year. In the trade-off between sensitivity to real asset risk and simplicity, the 1988 Accord clearly favored the latter. Yet the absence of any distinction within the wide class of corporate exposures in terms of either intrinsic borrower's riskiness or facility seniority or maturity clearly paved the way for regulatory arbitrage. At the same time, the 1988 Accord concentrated on credit risk only, while market risks from the trading book were not considered. Market risks were included later, in the 1996 Amendment to the Capital Accord (see Chapter 3), which set up an MRCR for the trading book. The overall MRCR for the bank became simply equal to the sum of credit and market risk minimum capital requirements, thereby adopting a building-block approach that avoids considering diversification benefits among market and credit risks.

The great innovation in the 1996 Amendment was the possibility for banks to choose between a standard regulatory charge based on a set of fixed coefficients to be applied to the trading book exposures and the adoption of an internal, VaR-based measurement model used also for calculating capital requirements, provided that a number of qualitative and quantitative criteria were met. This was the first move toward greater use of internal risk measurement models, which continued later on with the Basel II Accord.

2.1.2 *The Concept of Regulatory Capital*

The 1988 Basel I Accord, apart from defining the risk weights used to determine the denominator of the Cooke ratio, also defined the concept of regulatory capital (in the numerator). The definition of regulatory capital was then refined in subsequent years (and is still subject to potential future changes as the Basel II Accord implementation proceeds). Broadly speaking, regulatory capital is divided into *core capital* (Tier 1 capital) and *supplementary capital* (divided between Tier 2 and Tier 3 capital). The main components of regulatory capital and the limitations are described in Table 2-1.

The basic distinction between Tier 1 (core) and Tier 2 (supplementary) capital was set out in 1988. Since then, a number of changes have been introduced, the most significant being the introduction of Tier 3 in the 1996 Market Risk Amendment, designed to incorporate market risk into the capital adequacy framework. As far as Tiers 2 and 3 are concerned, potential further constraints on the eligibility of each internal component (e.g., subordinated debt) may be defined by national supervisory authorities. While these national differences can be explained by the need to account for national accounting or prudential rules, it represents an issue for international banking groups that may have to deal with multiple supervisory authorities.

In practice, the ratio of regulatory capital to risk-weighted assets is relevant not just for regulators, since it may also be monitored by rating agencies and by equity analysts. Because any measure of the ratio of *economic* capital at risk versus available capital that can be derived from internal models is, at present, at least, largely unverifiable by outsiders

TABLE 2-1   Components of Regulatory Capital

Regulatory Capital Component	Eligible Components	Main Constraints (further restrictions may be defined at the national level)
Tier 1	• Paid-up ordinary shares and perpetual noncumulative preference shares • Disclosed reserves	• Goodwill has to be deducted from Tier 1
Tier 2	• Undisclosed reserves • Revaluation reserves • General provisions/general loan-loss reserves • Hybrid capital instruments (e.g., cumulative preference shares) • Unsecured subordinated term debt (with original maturity greater than 5 years)	• Total Tier 2 is limited to 100% of Tier 1 (i.e., at least 50% of total capital should be Tier 1 capital) • For latent revaluation reserves deriving from securities evaluated at cost in the balance sheet, only 55% of the difference between market value and historical cost book value may be considered • General provisions and general loan-loss reserves may account for at most 1.25% of weighted risk assets • Subordinated term debt is limited to a maximum of 50% of Tier 1. Moreover, an amortization factor of 20% per year will be applied when maturity falls below 5 years
Tier 3	• Unsecured subordinated debt (with original maturity of at least 2 and less than 5 years)	• Tier 3 can be used only to cover market risk and has to be limited to 250% of Tier 1 used to cover market risks (i.e, at least 28.5% of the MRCR for market risk must be covered by Tier 1 capital)

Source: Basel Committee (2006a).

such as analysts, the only certified information concerning the capital adequacy of a bank is derived from regulatory ratios and in particular from the Tier 1 ratio (i.e., the ratio of Tier 1 capital to risk-weighted assets). As a consequence, risk managers may monitor the ratio bearing in mind both regulators and rating agencies' analysts (and sometimes equity analysts as well). Yet Matten (2000) observes that there is no evidence about a relationship between banks' ratings and their Tier 1 ratio. While this is consistent with the fact that rating agencies consider many other factors in their rating assignment process, it may also be due to rating agencies' lack of trust in Basel I risk-weighted assets. Their attitude may change under more risk-sensitive Basel II capital requirements.

2.2 Overview of the Basel II Capital Accord

The overall structure of the Basel II Capital Accord is based on the so-called *three pillars*. The key idea is that the safety and soundness of the financial system could not be obtained just by imposing on banks some minimum capital requirements (Pillar 1). It must rely also on increased attention and power for the supervisory review process (Pillar 2) and a greater recourse to risk disclosure and hence market discipline (Pillar 3). While most of the debate has so far been concentrated on Pillar 1, supervisory review and market discipline are very important too. We will try to summarize the key elements of the Accord, which are discussed further in Chapters 4 and 5, devoted to credit risk and operational risk, respectively.

2.2.1 Pillar 1: Minimum Capital Requirements — The Main Changes Introduced by Basel II

The main changes to minimum capital requirements introduced by Basel II are the credit risk capital requirements and the introduction of a requirement for operational risk too. The rules on market risk received only minor modifications. Since the requirements for different risks are again simply added, the constraint to be satisfied by the bank is the following:

$$RC \geq MRCR_{credit} + MRCR_{market} + MRCR_{operational}$$

$$= 8\% \cdot \sum_{i=1}^{n} RWA(SF) + MRCR_{market} + MRCR_{operational}$$

where RWA represent the bank's risk-weighted assets, i.e., assets multiplied by the proper risk weight. Note that, at present, credit risk RWA are further increased by a scaling factor (SF) that has been defined by the Basel Committee so as to maintain broadly equal the aggregate level of minimum capital requirements.[2] Alternatively, since $1/8\% = 12.5$,

$$\frac{RC}{\sum_{i=1}^{n} RWA_i(SF) + 12.5 \cdot MRCR_{market} + 12.5 \cdot MRCR_{operational}} \geq 8\%$$

As far as credit risk is concerned, the substantial revision introduced by Basel II implies the ability for the bank to choose among three approaches, thereby modifying the way in which risk weights RW_i are calculated in order to make them more risk sensitive than in Basel I. This of course is achieved at the cost of greater complexity. The first possibility, known as the *standardized approach*, again defines fixed risk weights for all credit exposures, with the main difference being that exposures to the same class of counterparty may receive a different risk weight, depending on the counterparty's external rating issued by agencies such as Moody's and Standard & Poor's (or other external credit assessment institutions recognized by supervisors). Alternatively, banks may move toward the two more sophisticated *internal rating-based (IRB) approaches*, which rely partially or mostly on internal credit risk estimates provided by the bank itself. As a consequence, their adoption is subordinated to a preliminary validation by supervisors that should carefully test the bank's internal data and procedures. In particular, in the IRB approaches, risk weights are expressed for each kind of counterparty as a function of the probability of default (PD) of the borrower, of the loss given default (LGD), i.e., the percentage of the exposure the bank would actually lose if the borrower defaulted and which is influenced by existing guarantees, of exposure at default (EAD), and of the

---

2. Such a scaling factor has currently been set equal to 1.06 (Basel Commitee 2006a, §44), but it is considered only the present best estimate, and its appropriateness will be monitored in the future.

effective maturity (M). In the *foundation IRB (FIRB) approach*, the bank may provide its internal estimates for PD while using fixed parameters set by regulators for LGD, EAD, and M. In the *advanced IRB (AIRB) approach*, instead, all these four key inputs could be produced by the bank, provided that supervisory validation of the internal model has been obtained.

The second main change in minimum capital requirements is the introduction of a capital charge for operational risk, defined as "the risk of loss resulting from inadequate or failed internal processes and systems or from external events" and which "includes legal risk, but excludes strategic and reputational risk" (Basel Committee, 2006a, §644). Even for operational risk, three approaches of different complexity may be adopted. According to the *basic indicator approach*, the capital charge is a fixed percentage of average annual gross return in the last three years. According to the *standardized approach*, the activities of the bank are divided into eight big business lines, and a different percentage of gross income is applied to each business line. Finally, in the *advanced measurement approach*, the capital charge is based on the internal model for operational risk, provided that a number of qualitative and quantitative criteria are met and that regulatory approval has been obtained. In this way, operational risk sort of replicates the opportunity offered for credit risk (and for market risks since 1996) to adopt internal and more sophisticated models, under certain constraints and after supervisory validation, with the expectation that more sophisticated approaches could imply, on average, a lower capital charge than basic ones. This trade-off may be acceptable for regulators since it provides banks an incentive to substantially improve existing risk measurement and management systems.

Box 2-1: Impact of the Basel II Accord on the Level of Minimum Regulatory Capital Requirements

An obvious topic of concern for bankers and regulators throughout the route to the Basel II Accord was related to how the new accord could change overall capital requirements for different banks. The overall ratio has been to give banks the choice to adopt approaches with different levels of sophistication. On average, more advanced approaches should imply a reduction in MRCR and hence an advantage for banks willing to invest more in risk measurement methodologies and processes and data collection. Sophisticated approaches also require initial validating and periodic monitoring by supervisors. Therefore, supervisors may be willing to accept a reduction in MRCR for some banks because this would be counterbalanced by better risk management systems. Since regulators appeared unwilling to accept a reduction in average capital requirements, this would also imply an increase in MRCR for banks maintaining simpler approaches.

Some key figures about the expected effects of the introduction of Basel II can be derived by QIS5, i.e., the fifth Quantitative Impact Study, launched between 2005 and 2006 by the Basel Committee and based on more than 350 banks from 32 countries. Focusing in particular on banks from G-10 countries, the survey included 56 "Group 1" banks (i.e., internationally active and diversified banks with Tier 1 capital in excess of Euro 3 billion) and other 146 "Group 2" G-10 banks. One hundred fifty-four banks belonged to non-G-10 countries. Apart from G-10 banks, a second relevant aggregate was represented by countries participating in the Committee of European Banking Supervisors (CEBS), also including some non-G-10 countries representing current or candidate European Union members, such as Bulgaria, Finland, Greece, Ireland, Norway, Poland, and Portugal.

TABLE 2-2 Impact of the New Basel II Accord on Minimum Regulatory Capital for Credit Risk

	Group	Standardized Approach	Foundation IRB Approach	Advanced IRB Approach	Most Likely Approach
Average change in total minimum required capital relative to Basel I Accord (%)	G-10 Group 1 banks	1.7	−1.3	−7.1	−6.8
	G-10 Group 2 banks	−1.3	−12.3	−26.7	−11.3
	CEBS Group 1 banks	−0.9	−3.2	−8.3	−7.7
	CEBS Group 2 banks	−3.0	−16.6	−26.6	−15.4
Average change in Tier 1 required capital relative to Basel I Accord (%)	G-10 Group 1 banks	1.8	−4.0	−11.0	−10.6
	G-10 Group 2 banks	−1.2	−14.0	−26.2	−12.9
	CEBS Group 1 banks	−0.5	−4.7	−9.5	−8.9
	CEBS Group 2 banks	−2.6	−16.4	−26.1	−15.1

Source: Basel Committee (2006b).

TABLE 2-3 Changes in Minimum Capital Requirements Deriving from Moving to More Advanced Approaches (%)

Group	From Standardized to Foundation IRB Approach	From Foundation IRB to Advanced IRB Approach
G-10 Group 1 banks	−13.3	−5.1
G-10 Group 2 banks	−8.1	−6.6
CEBS Group 1 banks	−13.5	−6.8
CEBS Group 2 banks	−12.4	−6.7

Source: Basel Committee (2006b).

Table 2-2 presents the average change in total minimum required capital and in Tier 1 capital for G-10 and CEBS banks under the three alternative approaches for credit risk and under the approach that each bank declared it would most likely adopt. Note that banks did not generally provide estimates under all the three approaches and that data in Table 2-2 represent averages, while at the individual bank level there were remarkable fluctuations in the individual impact of the adoption of the new Basel II approaches.

Table 2-2 makes clear that the advanced IRB approaches could imply a significantly lower credit risk MRCR. Further evidence is provided by Table 2-3, which, using only data from those banks that reported estimated MRCR under more than one approach, estimates the advantages of moving from a simpler to a more sophisticated approach. Especially larger Group 1 banks declared that they would most likely adopt an advanced IRB approach or perhaps a foundation IRB approach, while smaller banks declared they were oriented mostly to either the standardized or the advanced IRB approach.

As far as the impact of the new requirement for operational risk is concerned, estimates for each of the different possible approaches from different banks were extremely variable. The average contribution of operational risk to total minimum regulatory capital in G-10 banks is reported in Table 2-4.

TABLE 2-4   Contribution of Operational Risk to Total Minimum Regulatory Capital in G-10 Banks (%)

Approach	Group 1 G-10 banks	Group 2 G-10 banks
Basic indicator approach	6.3	8.3
Standardized approach	5.7	7.6
Advanced measurement approach	7.2	n.a.

Source: Basel Committee (2006b).

2.2.2 Pillar 2: Supervisory Review Process

Despite changing MRCR to make it more risk-sensitive, the Basel II Accord clearly states that any bank's ability to survive does not depend only on the amount of capital held to face potential risks, but also on elements such as the quality of risk management systems and procedures, the soundness of its provisioning policy, and its capital management and planning process. Therefore, the second pillar clarifies the role of national supervisory authorities to foster improvements in banks' risk management techniques, setting, if necessary, individual capital requirements higher than Pillar 1 minimums for those banks where risk management procedures and systems appear to be weak. The Basel Committee (2006a, §724 and §§761–778) identifies three areas in particular that might be important from a Pillar 2 viewpoint: risks that are considered by Pillar 1 but perhaps not entirely captured (e.g., a particular concentration risk in the credit risk portfolio); factors that are not taken into account in Pillar 1, such as the interest rate risk in the banking book deriving from the mismatch between the interest rate sensitivity of assets and liabilities; and exogenous factors that may impact the bank's risk profile, such as the business cycle. Basel II states that "increased capital should not be viewed as the only option for addressing increased risks confronting the bank" since improved risk management systems and policies and adequate provisioning systems may also work. Yet the power to force banks with poorer risk management systems to maintain a higher capital base represents a powerful weapon for regulators, even if it raises obvious concerns regarding the coordination and homogeneity of Pillar 2 enforcement among different countries. For this reason, criteria used by regulators in the review of banks' internal risk assessment should be made transparent and publicly available. In any case, Pillar 2 is particularly relevant from the point of view of this book since it stresses the role of processes in bank risk management.

In particular, four key principles of supervisory review are defined (see Basel Committee 2006a, §§725–760):

1. Banks should have a process for assessing their overall capital adequacy in relation to their risk profile and a strategy for maintaining their capital levels.
2. Supervisors should review banks' internal capital adequacy assessments and strategies, taking proper actions if they are unsatisfied with those processes.

3. Supervisors should expect banks to operate above Pillar 1 MRCR and should have the ability to require banks to hold extra capital.
4. Supervisors should look for early intervention to prevent a bank from falling below MRCR and require rapid remedial action if capital is not maintained or restored.

The first principle defines, for instance, the role of board and senior management oversight, the need for a process linking capital to risks, and the need for a comprehensive analysis of all material risks and for reporting and internal control systems. The second principle implies that regulators should question the process and the results (e.g., the composition of capital) of the internal capital adequacy evaluation process run by the bank. The third and fourth principles provide a picture of supervisors' tasks and of their powers under Pillar 2. Note that, for both credit and market risks, supervisory review should evaluate not only "normal" potential losses measurable with VaR, but also the results of stress tests aimed at understanding potential losses under extreme conditions and the way in which those tests have been conducted. This is considered a relevant element in order to assess the overall required capital for the bank.

2.2.3 Pillar 3: Market Discipline

The third pillar aims at strengthening market discipline, i.e., the pressure that financial markets may exert on bank managers so as to promote safe and sound bank management. In particular, Pillar 3 defines a number of disclosure requirements aimed at increasing the transparency of each bank's risk profile and risk policy. Some disclosure requirements are qualitative (e.g., a description of the bank's overall capital adequacy evaluation methodology, definitions used to identify problem loans, and approaches used for loan-loss provisions), while others are quantitative. A few examples of quantitative information the bank must disclose according to Pillar 3 include:

- The total amount of Tier 1, Tier 2, and Tier 3 capital, with details about the composition of Tier 1
- Minimum capital requirements for different risks; for credit risks in particular the bank should specify the capital requirement and the approach (standardized, foundation, or advanced IRB) that has been adopted for each subportfolio
- Total gross exposures divided by major type of risk exposure (e.g., loan, bonds, over-the-counter derivatives), geographic and industry loan portfolio breakdown, data concerning nonperforming loans, allowances and charge-offs divided by major industry and counterparty type

Additional disclosure requirements are defined, depending on the kind of credit risk approach for each portfolio and for market and operational risks. However, Flannery (1998) and Sironi (2001, 2003) have questioned the fact that while banks are forced to bear significant costs to disclose information to the market, disclosure is a necessary but not sufficient condition for effective market discipline, which requires, for instance, the existence of debt holders with no public guarantee, who would really be interested in monitoring the evolution of the risk profile of a bank. This could be achieved by forcing banks to issue subordinated bonds, provided of course they were held by institutional investors with the ability to exploit the benefits of greater disclosure.

2.2.4 The Debate about Basel II Adoption and Implementation

Despite the long process that was necessary to define the final Basel II document, starting from the first consultative paper issued by the Basel Committee in 1999, the debate about Basel II is far from over. In particular, since the document has to be translated into national regulation by those states that will be willing to adopt it, the process is at present markedly different between Europe and the United States. While in Europe the European Parliament rapidly decided to incorporate the Basel II framework into a the Capital Requirement Directive (CRD) to be applied in all member states, the four Federal Banking Agencies (i.e., the Office of the Comptroller of the Currency, the Board of Governors of the Federal Reserve System, the Federal Deposit Insurance Corporation, and the Office of Thrift Supervision) agreed in September 2005 to adopt a slower process, due to concerns about the cost of the adoption of the more complex Basel II framework for smaller banks and the potential competitive consequences in the domestic market between the biggest international banks (applying the Basel II framework) and smaller domestic players. According to the Notice for Proposed Rulemaking issued by the Federal Banking Agencies in September 2006, the advanced approaches for credit and operational risk should be adopted in the United States either by large international banks ("core banks"), which will be obliged to move to Basel II in its most sophisticated version, or by those banks that decide to do so ("opt-in banks"). Banks that decide to adhere to Basel II opportunities will have to adopt the advanced IRB approach for credit risk and the AMA approach for operational risk, while intermediate solutions (e.g., the foundation IRB for credit risk) should not be available according to the current proposal of U.S. supervisors (see Board of Governors of the Federal Reserve Systems 2006). Moreover, restrictive floors defining the maximum reduction in capital requirements for larger U.S. international banks in the Basel II adoption period have been set.

All banks that are neither core nor opt-in banks will remain within the old Basel I framework, even if a parallel effort to develop an alternative and improved revision, labeled "Basel IA," is under way (see Board of Governors of the Federal Reserve Systems 2005). This solution aims to guarantee for large international banks both the potential advantages of the new regime and an improvement in risk management standards. For this reason, they are forced to adhere to advanced approaches only. At the same time, the U.S. federal banking agencies were concerned with implementation costs and potential competitive implications on the domestic market among larger and smaller banks, which may have derived from making the full Basel II framework compulsory for all banks.

Concerns about the competitive impact of Basel II rules on domestic markets are understandable, considering, on the one hand, the costs of Basel II compliance, which are clearly expected to be lower in absolute value but higher as a percentage of total assets, for smaller banks, and, on the other hand, the advantages in terms of capital charges that are expected for those banks moving to advanced approaches for credit and operational risks. Both elements can imply economies of scales for larger banks, which together with a temporary potential capital excess as a consequence of lower expected capital requirements may favor further consolidation in the banking business. Of course, this potential consequence may be considered desirable by some supervisors and undesirable by others, depending also on industry characteristics in the individual country. At the same time, the decisions of the U.S. Federal Banking Agencies as far as Basel II implementation have raised some concerns among bankers for its potential competitive effects among international banks, due to the different timetables and specific constraints in adopting advanced approaches, especially during the transition phase, for U.S.-based and non-U.S.-based international banks.

2.3 Bank Estimates of Required Capital and the Different Notions of Bank Capital

While a bank always has to comply with the constraint of maintaining a sufficient level of regulatory capital, minimum regulatory capital requirements may not coincide perfectly with the internal estimate of the capital needed to run the business, which is usually identified as *economic capital*. Economic capital can differ from regulatory capital for a number of reasons, such as a different treatment of diversification benefits among different businesses and risks and the inclusion of economic capital estimates for risks that have no formal measurement (e.g., business or strategic risks). At the same time, not only may *required* capital be different if we adopt a regulatory or an economic perspective, but *available* capital will differ too. In fact, regulatory capital also comprises components, such as subordinated and hybrid debt, that do not represent a portion of capital in a strict sense. Hence, most banks compare both (i) regulatory requirements with regulatory capital and (ii) internally estimated required economic capital with available economic capital. Economic capital, rather than regulatory capital, is also mainly used for risk-adjusted performance measurement, even if return on regulatory capital may also be reported to top managers as supplementary information.

When defining an internal estimate of economic capital, that is, when trying to measure how much capital the bank should hold to face potential losses over a given time horizon, there are different concepts of bank capital that can be adopted.

The first one is *book value of capital*, which can be defined as the difference between the book value of the bank's assets and that of its liabilities. The second one is *market value of capital*, i.e., the difference between the value of assets and the value of liabilities when both are valued at mark-to-market prices (Saunders 1994). The third one is *market capitalization*, i.e., the value of the bank on the stock market at current market prices. Market capitalization should reflect the complex evaluation the market may make about the market value of the bank's assets and liabilities, the bank's business mix and the perspective of each business the bank is in, its competitive position, and a number of other factors. Since there are different concepts of bank capital, the bank could, at least potentially, measure required capital according to each of these different views. Yet book capital on the one hand and market capitalization on the other are usually the two key measures with which a CEO is concerned. We concentrate mostly on these two.

2.3.1 Book Value of Capital and the Impact of IAS/IFRS

When a bank has to check whether, according to its own measurement methodologies, its capital is adequate to face potential losses, one usual measure of available capital is the book value of capital. In fact, a bank would clearly default if all book value of capital were destroyed. If this view were adopted, then risks should be measured according to the amount of book capital that could be lost due to adverse events or market movements.

The idea that a bank might calculate economic capital (which we defined as the bank's internal estimate of the capital needed to run the business) in terms of book value may seem confusing, since very few would probably agree to consider book value the "true" economic value of a bank. Nevertheless, apart from recalling the broader definition of economic capital we adopted here, it is not uncommon to see banks presenting their available economic capital versus their MRCR and their internal estimate of "economic" capital compared with their book value of equity.

The point we want to make is that when measuring economic capital, that bank could compare either its book value of equity with the amount of book value that can be destroyed under adverse scenarios (i.e., its "book capital at risk") or, similarly, its current market capitalization with its "market capitalization at risk." This may also imply a different measure of risk for different businesses. Failing to capture the difference could imply, for instance, comparing "available" capital, which is typically measured as book value of equity, with a measure of economic capital that has been calculated in an inconsistent way.

Of course, the information conveyed by the book value of equity and its link with the "true" value of the bank also depends on the kind of accounting principles adopted in the individual country. From this point of view, a relevant issue for most European banks has recently been represented by the new International Accounting Standards/ International Financial Reporting Standards (IAS/IFRS) issued by the International Accounting Standards Board (IASB). The IASB is an international organization comprising representatives of nine countries aimed at developing internationally accepted uniform accounting standards, representing an international equivalent of the U.S. FASB (Financial Accounting Standards Board). Principles issued by the IASB are not binding by themselves, but they need to be translated into law by individual countries. The European Union has issued a set of regulations adopting fully (or at least largely) the new principles, which will be mandatory for listed banks (while national rulemakers also have the option to extend it to nonlisted ones).

A detailed discussion of the new accounting principles is beyond the scope of this book, especially since their impact may vary from country to country (depending on preexisting accounting rules, on whether and how the new principles would be translated into legislation, and on how some principles will be applied in practice in certain areas). Yet, with a certain level of simplification, we may point out the main areas that will be affected for those banks that will be subject to the new principles:

1. Hedge and derivative accounting
2. Loan-loss provisions and valuation
3. Insurance businesses in bancassurance groups

Other issues are related to pension plans, leasing contracts, and share-based compensation accounting and to the distinction between goodwill and intangible assets in acquisitions and their consequent amortization treatment.

Hedge and derivatives accounting is affected because principle IAS39 remarkably restricts the number of cases in which derivative positions may be recognized at cost in the bank's financial statement rather than at fair value. This change depends partly on the new and stricter criteria that must be met to classify a derivative position as a hedge for banking book items and partly on the new classification of financial instruments, which are divided into four classes (loans and receivables, held for trading, held to maturity, available for sales), in which assets classified as available for sales, which before IAS/ IFRS would have been evaluated in many countries taking cost into consideration, are now also evaluated at fair value. As a consequence, higher volatility of the bank's financial performance should be expected, and even higher importance should be given to the check of fair value estimates for derivative positions.

The second area (loan-loss provisions and loan valuation) is particularly important from a risk management point of view; this is discussed further in Chapter 4, on credit risk. Anyway, the key issues stem from the following:

1. Loans have to be evaluated at amortized cost (unless the bank decides to evaluate all loans at fair value), implying that the effect of initial costs or fees should be spread over the life of the loan.
2. A reduction in the value of a loan may be made only in case of "impairment," which can be assessed either analytically (by identifying the individual problem loan) or collectively on a group of similar loans; banks should provision (or more precisely, recognize a reduction in loan value) only as a consequence of *incurred* losses, not just expected ones, even if some adjustment may be possible in practice when evaluating collective impairment.
3. When estimating the effects of impairment (and hence making provisions), the bank should consider for non-short-term loans the reduction of future expected cash flow, to be discounted at the original interest rate of the loan.
4. In any case, the bank should disclose to the market the estimated fair value of all loans (even if they are evaluated at amortized cost in the balance sheet).

The main issues here stem from the fact that item 2 implies that generic provisions used to anticipate greater future losses when at the end of a benign economic cycle, and to smooth earnings as well, are ruled out. But this has to be reconciled with regulators' concerns that a bank could maintain adequate provisions to cover expected losses. On the other hand, item 3 implies that in those cases where the borrower is in default, the loss that has to be recognized by the bank as a consequence is not necessarily equal to how regulators or risk managers would define their loss-given-default (LGD) concept (since, for instance, the discounting rate may differ). These issues are discussed in Chapter 4.

Insurance business treatment has not been fully defined so far by the IASB due to the inherent complexity of the topic. While a first relevant principle, named IFRS4, has already been approved, it is still at present unclear when and to what extent the fair value principle should be applied to insurance companies' liabilities, especially for those insurance products implying a nontrivial actuarial risk. This is a potentially relevant issue for some banking groups with significant insurance subsidiaries, even more so for financial conglomerates, also depending on the product mix of the insurance company.

In general, a potential consequence for those countries moving toward IAS/IFRS implementation may therefore be a greater volatility in book values (and hence also indirectly affecting Tier 1 capital), even if the advantage of reducing the gaps in accounting treatment with U.S. generally accepted accounting principles (GAAP) may also be relevant for the indirect effects on Tier 1 capital size and stability.

2.3.2 Market Capitalization and the Double Perspective of Bank Managers

However relevant book value may be, when a manager states that "value creation" is the overall objective of the bank, the crucial concept of "value" is represented by market value rather than book value of equity. Market value of equity, or market capitalization of the firm, is the value of the firm at market prices, and it therefore represents a crucial notion for any bank manager. In practice, however, though this is the notion of capital that is crucially linked to the overall targets of stock price appreciation that managers may define, it is very rarely or never considered as a notion of *available* capital to be compared with economic capital. We argue instead that this should be the case, considering the double perspective the bank should maintain.

In fact, while the supervisor is concerned mainly with preventing a bank from failing to preserve financial system stability, bank managers should be concerned not only with maintaining the bank alive but also with increasing the market value of the bank. As a consequence, even if controlling book capital at risk is crucial for the objective of the bank's survival, which is relevant for both the supervisor and the bank manager, the latter should be able to control *market capitalization at risk* as well. We define market capitalization at risk (MCaR) as the potential reduction in the bank's value that may be produced as a consequence of losses in a given business or part of the bank's portfolio. MCaR will often be very close to book capital at risk, but not always. For instance, if we consider a portfolio of stocks evaluated at fair value in the bank's balance sheet, there is no difference between book CaR and MCaR. Instead, two areas in which there may be substantial difference between book CaR and MCaR are represented by business risk and operational risk. Business risk is defined here as the risk deriving from earnings volatility of fee-based businesses (e.g., advisory, asset management, or payment services). While these businesses may generate only a limited loss in terms of book value (e.g., by producing a negative contribution margin in a given year), the impact of a reduction in profits from these businesses may have a much stronger effect on analysts' evaluations of the target price of the bank stock and hence indirectly on their market capitalization. The same happens with operational risk: Cummins, Lewis, and Wei (2004) have shown that, on average, stock market reactions of banks and insurance companies to announcements of operational losses exceed the size of the announced loss. This can be considered another case in which book capital at risk and market capital at risk differ. The difference between the two measures, especially in the critical case of business risk, is discussed in Chapter 5.

Therefore, comparing separately both book CaR with available book capital and market capitalization at risk with current market capitalization may be useful for the bank. The ratio between MCaR and current market capitalization could give the risk manager an idea about the percentage of the overall value of the bank that could be destroyed over one year in an adverse scenario within a given confidence level. Yet the concept of MCaR we have introduced is even more relevant from the point of view of internal performance measurement and capital allocation decisions. While these topics are discussed more precisely later; in the book, it is useful now to introduce why and how the existence of multiple concepts of capital might affect banks' decision-making processes.

2.3.3 The Impact of Alternative Notions of Capital on Capital Management and Allocation

Capital management is concerned mainly with defining the optimal amount of capital the bank should hold and the optimal regulatory capital mix. Due to the existence of multiple notions of capital and multiple constraints (of both a regulatory and an economic nature), trying to define the optimal amount of capital is at least partly an art. The bank therefore has to control its capital adequacy both in terms of regulatory capital versus minimum regulatory requirement and in terms of available versus required economic capital (which should be measured in terms of book capital at risk and possibly in terms of MCaR as well). Moreover, the potential impact of the evolution of regulatory-based ratios such as the Tier 1 ratios on rating agencies' and equity analysts' evaluation should be controlled. Since multiple constraints have to be met, it is important to reconcile and understand the differences between regulatory and economic required capital. The task is even more complex when applied at the level of the individual legal entity rather than at the banking group level. In fact, while at the group level there may be compensations between legal entities where required regulatory capital is higher than economic capital, differences at the individual level may be more significant, making both capital planning and performance measurement more difficult.

For instance, let us consider a group where minimum regulatory capital and book capital at risk are aligned but where legal entities A and B have a regulatory capital constraint that is respectively higher and lower than book capital at risk. Since MRCR has to be met in any case, A is likely to be overcapitalized relative to its real economic risk (i.e., its available book capital would be much higher than its book capital at risk, so the regulatory target ratio could be met), while the opposite would be true for B. Hence, even if the two units earned the same return on economic capital, the bank's return on (book) equity (ROE) would be higher for B than for A. This could create problems both in evaluating the relative performance of both legal entities (would top management consider only return on economic capital, or would they also consider the biased ROE number in some way?) and in providing a reasonable remuneration for all shareholders if legal entities A and B are not fully owned by the banking group. If this were the case, minority shareholders from A would be in some way subsidizing minority shareholders from B, who are allowed to obtain a higher ROE since the capital excess in A compensates at the group level the capital deficit in B.

As a consequence, the bank will have an incentive to reduce as far as possible the gap between regulatory and economic required capital, even at the legal-entity level. For instance, unit A could either try to reduce its risk-weighted assets (e.g., by securitizing assets) or use to the maximum possible extent Tier 2 capital, so as to reduce the need for core equity in order to meet regulatory requirements. In any case, a perfect proportion between regulatory and economic capital often remains largely an ideal aim.

The discussion concerning units A and B also introduces a second problem. In fact, while problems deriving from multiple measures of "capital" may be an issue for capital management, they matter also (and sometimes more) for risk-adjusted performance measurement and capital allocation. In fact, if capital allocation is aimed at optimizing the risk–return trade-off at the bank level, a distortion in the measurement of risk-adjusted profitability may potentially alter the decisions made by top managers. While capital allocation decisions are not mechanically driven by past business units' performances, past performances may contribute to influencing allocation decisions. Citigroup's 2004 Annual Report states that "Return on risk capital [i.e., economic capital] . . . is used to assess businesses' operating performance and to determine incremental allocation of capital for organic growth" (Citigroup 2005, p. 72).

Consequently, two questions arise: (1) Should performance evaluation be based on regulatory capital, or economic capital, or both? (2) And if economic capital were to be considered, is book capital at risk or market capitalization at risk more suitable to provide a correct measure from a risk-adjusted performance measurement viewpoint?

The first question is relatively simple: As long as regulatory capital is not a binding constraint, i.e., as long as the bank maintains capital in excess of minimum capital requirements, performance measurement and allocation decisions may be based on economic capital only. If instead the bank were forced to hold capital in excess of its economic required capital only to satisfy a regulatory constraint (e.g., because, due to diversification effects that are not recognized in the regulatory framework, economic capital is very low as opposed to regulatory capital), then the cost of extra regulatory capital should be charged to individual business units based on their regulatory capital absorption.

But while most agree that return on economic capital should be the base for risk-adjusted performance measurement, the issue about *which* economic capital should be used is commonly neglected, for the simple reason that book capital at risk and market capitalization at risk are relatively close for market, credit, and operational risk. Yet, as we will see in Chapter 5, the measure may diverge substantially when business risk is considered. Market capitalization at risk should be used as the measure to evaluate performance and could be the driver to define profitability targets for the different business units, since it more properly captures the riskiness of the business from the shareholder's viewpoint. This is why we will spend some time in discussing the differences between BCaR and MCaR for different risks later in the book.

2.4 Summary

When a bank wants to check its capital adequacy, a first key issue is to define *capital*. A first clear distinction is between regulatory capital and economic capital. The former is measured according to the regulators' specifications, which define both what is eligible to be treated as available capital for regulatory purposes and how to calculate required regulatory capital. The latter is based instead on the bank's own risk measurement system and methodology, which may allow the bank to estimate how much capital is needed according to its own internal view and independent of regulators' prescriptions.

Minimum regulatory capital requirements (MRCR) have been remarkably reformed by the new Basel II Accord, which in 2004 led to a radical change aimed at making MRCR more risk sensitive than they were before. The main changes in the Basel II Accord concern credit risk, for which three different approaches (standardized, foundation internal rating based, and advanced internal rating based) have been introduced, and operational risk, for which a new capital requirement has been introduced (which also can be calculated via three different approaches with a different degree of sophistication). In short, moving toward the most advanced approaches to MRCR calculation may require significant investments in risk management technology and datasets for a bank and will be subject to supervisory authorities' validation but should be expected to imply a reduction in the minimum capital requirement. Yet, given that Basel Committee documents are not automatically binding for individual countries, the process of Basel II implementation is proceeding, with remarkable differences between the United States and most other countries. In the United States, large international banks will probably be forced to adopt only the most advanced Basel II approaches; all other banks, which will maintain the option to adopt advanced approaches as well, will likely be allowed to continue to be compliant with the 1988 Basel I Accord or an amended version (Basel IA). In most other countries and remarkably in Europe, instead, the full architecture of the Basel II Accord will be implemented and all banks will have to comply with one of the different available approaches for credit, market, and operational risks.

When considering capital adequacy from the standpoint of economic capital (broadly defined here as an internal estimate of the capital needed to run the business), a second distinction is required, since there are different notions of capital that can be considered by the bank when developing this estimate and, in parallel, assessing available capital to face potential losses. The first one is book value of capital, i.e., the difference between the value of assets and the value of liabilities at book value. The second one is the market value of capital, i.e., the difference between the value of assets and the value of liabilities when they are marked to market. The third one is the market capitalization of the bank, i.e., its value on the stock market. Depending on which view is adopted, not only available capital but also capital at risk (i.e., simply speaking, the capital that can be lost in an unfavorable scenario) may remarkably vary. The need to comply with a set of different constraints is important since it is part of the difficulties in a bank's capital management, while the different risks that different business units may generate, depending on which notion of capital is considered when estimating potential losses, is important for capital allocation issues, which are discussed later in this book.

2.5 Further Reading

The different perspectives in analyzing bank capital are dealt with in detail, even if in a different manner, in Matten (2000). The concept of capital as a hedge against potential losses is already pointed out in Vojta (1973). As far as regulatory capital is concerned, the reader should first refer to documents by the Basel Committee on the Bank of International Settlement on its website. In particular, Basel Committee (2006a) integrates in a single document the 2004 Basel II Accord, the elements of the 1988 Basel I Accord that were not changed, and the 1996 Market Risk Amendment. As far as the implementation process is concerned, in Europe the key document is the Capital Requirement Directive, while the Committee of European Banking Supervisors (CEBS) is actively working to define implementation guidelines (see, for instance, CEBS 2006 guidelines on the supervisory review process). The website of the Federal Reserve Board is at present the best source for information about the developments on "Basel IA" versus Basel II implementation for large international banks.

CHAPTER ◆ 3

Market Risk

Chapter 1 defined value at risk (VaR) as the maximum potential loss that a business unit or a position can generate in a given time horizon within a defined percentage of potential scenarios (the so-called *confidence level*), where extremely adverse scenarios are excluded. In formal terms, if V is the value of a given portfolio, V_0 is its initial value, and $1 - \alpha$ is the desired confidence level (e.g., 99%), then $\mathrm{VaR}_{1-\alpha}$ (i.e., the amount of loss that can be exceeded only in a percentage of potential cases equal to α) is the amount such that

$$\Pr(V - V_0 < -\mathrm{VaR}_{1-\alpha}) = \alpha$$

or alternatively, since $V_0 - V$ represents a loss whenever $V < V_0$,

$$\Pr(V_0 - V > \mathrm{VaR}_{1-\alpha}) = \alpha$$

How can the risk manager estimate VaR in practice? Let us consider VaR for a trader dealing in UK stocks and calculated on a daily horizon at a 99% confidence level. If the trader has invested in a basket of stocks that closely resembles the FTSE100, a simple way would be to consider FTSE100 daily returns in the last 200 business days, sort them in ascending order, and then identify the percentage VaR with the third-lowest return in the sample. If, for instance, the three worst losses were −4.1%, −4.7% and −6.95%, the maximum loss that can be exceeded only in 1% of cases is 4.1%. In fact, according to historical experience, the index (and therefore the trader) may lose more than VaR only in 1% of cases (i.e., two days out of a 200-day sample). This method is known as *historical simulation*, and the risk manager would implicitly be assuming that the distribution of tomorrow's returns could be reasonably approximated by the return distribution of the last 200 days. Of course, it is crucial to decide how many days should be included in the sample. If we use only 100 days, the estimate could be quite consistent with current levels of volatility, but it might represent far too small a sample of possible outcomes. If we include 1000 trading days (i.e., roughly four years), the sample has a better chance of including examples of extreme negative returns with which the risk manager is concerned, but it may not be sensitive enough to changes in the level of volatility in the market. In fact, if there were, for instance, 11 markedly negative returns three years ago, they would continue to determine the 99% VaR estimate even now, since it would be based on the 11th-worst return in the sample.

An alternative solution to avoid this problem is to assume FTSE100 returns to be normally distributed. In this case, the worst daily potential return of the index could be defined based only on the mean and standard deviation (i.e., volatility) of its return distribution. If the risk manager were able to build a measure of expected volatility of FTSE100 returns that is sensitive enough to current market conditions, then the problem he was facing with historical simulations might be solved.

Hence, there are clearly alternative competing methodologies to estimate VaR for a given position. While the literature on this area is large and still burgeoning, we will try to point out here the key methodologies and discuss some of the implementation issues, such as position mapping and back-testing, that play a relevant role in practice. In particular, the critical choices that have to be made when estimating the return distribution of a given position in order to estimate its VaR are mainly four:

1. The choice of the random variables determining the changes in the value of the portfolio
2. The set of assumptions on the return distribution of the predefined random variables
3. How the link between the value of the random variables and the value of the real portfolio is modeled
4. How the desired percentile in the portfolio return distribution is identified

Typically, the main alternative methodologies for market risk measurement are identified with the variance–covariance approach, historical simulation, and Monte Carlo simulation, even if they are mostly concerned with choices 1 and 2 while often remaining open to alternative potential solutions as far as choices 3 and 4 are concerned. Therefore, the overall quality of the market risk measurement system depends not only on which methodology is implemented, but also on how. We discuss these different approaches in Sections 3.1 and 3.2. We then analyze the problem of VaR measurement for options (Section 3.3), introduce the issue of extreme value theory and copulas and the alternative risk measure represented by the expected shortfall (Sections 3.4 and 3.5, respectively) and the issue of model back-testing (Section 3.6). Section 3.7 briefly presents how internal market VaR models can be used to calculate minimum capital requirements. Section 3.8 concludes the chapter by discussing the construction of stress tests as potential alternatives (or complements) to VaR measures in order to control market risks.

3.1   The Variance–Covariance Approach

We discuss first the so-called variance–covariance approach, which is the most well-known approach and which has been first fully explained in detail in J.P. Morgan's (1996) *RiskMetrics^{TM} Technical Document*. Under this approach, VaR for individual positions and portfolios can be easily derived by estimating the variance and covariance (or, alternatively, standard deviations and correlations) of some predefined risk factors' returns and the sensitivity of the portfolio to those risk factors.

3.1.1 A Simplified Example

Let us imagine a trader whose portfolio is represented by a simple long position on stock Alpha for 100,000 USD. The trader knows that the daily volatility of the stock is equal to 2%. Daily volatility is calculated as the standard deviation σ of the daily log return R of a given asset, i.e.,

$$\sigma = \sqrt{\frac{\sum_{i=1}^{n}(R_i - \bar{R})^2}{n-1}}$$

where R_i is the daily log return on day i (i.e., $R_i = \ln S_i - \ln S_{i-1}$, where S is the price of stock Alpha), $\bar{R}$ is the average daily return over the sample period, and n is the number of daily returns in the sample. Note that while this is the most common definition of volatility, we will see later that a different measure of σ is typically used for VaR calculation. If the trader assumes that the return distribution is normal (or Gaussian), then he would be able to derive VaR for his position in a very straightforward manner. The Gaussian distribution is in fact defined by only two parameters (its mean μ and its standard deviation σ), and its distribution function is

$$f(x) = \frac{1}{\sqrt{2\pi}\cdot\sigma}\cdot e^{-\frac{1}{2}\left(\frac{x-\mu}{\sigma}\right)^2}$$

It can easily be shown that the probability of extracting a value in the range $(\mu - k\sigma; \mu + k\sigma)$ centered on the mean μ and whose half-size is a multiple k of the standard deviation depends only on the multiple k. In fact, such probability is equal to

$$\Pr\{\mu - k\sigma < x < \mu + k\sigma\} = \int_{\mu-k\sigma}^{\mu+k\sigma} f(x)dx = \int_{\mu-k\sigma}^{\mu+k\sigma} \frac{1}{\sqrt{2\pi}\cdot\sigma}\cdot e^{-\frac{1}{2}\left(\frac{x-\mu}{\sigma}\right)^2} dx$$

By substituting

$$z = \frac{x-\mu}{\sigma}$$

one can easily obtain

$$\Pr\{\mu - k\sigma < x < \mu + k\sigma\} = \int_{\mu-k\sigma}^{\mu+k\sigma} \frac{1}{\sqrt{2\pi}\cdot\sigma}\cdot e^{-\frac{1}{2}\left(\frac{x-\mu}{\sigma}\right)^2} dx = \int_{-k}^{+k} \frac{1}{\sqrt{2\pi}}\cdot e^{-\frac{1}{2}z^2} dz$$

where it becomes clear that the probability does not depend either on μ or on σ, and can be derived by analyzing the standard normal distribution only.[1] For instance, the

---

1. The standard normal distribution is precisely a normal distribution with $\mu = 0$ and $\sigma = 1$. Any normal distribution can easily be standardized by substituting the original variable, x, with a variable $z = (x - \mu_x)/\sigma_x$.

probability of extracting a value in the range between the mean minus one standard deviation ($\mu - \sigma$) and the mean plus one standard deviation ($\mu + \sigma$) is approximately 68%, irrespective of the values of μ and σ. Since the normal distribution is symmetric, this implies that the remaining 32% is divided into a 16% probability to observe values lower than $\mu - \sigma$ and a 16% probability to observe values greater than $\mu + \sigma$.

This is very useful in order to estimate VaR. Let us imagine that our trader wants to estimate the maximum potential loss in 95% of possible cases. If he assumes the distribution of Alpha's return is normal and he estimates that $\mu = 0.05\%$ and $\sigma = 2\%$ on a daily basis, then the possibility of observing a value smaller than the $\mu - \sigma$, i.e., -1.95%, is 16%. Hence, 1.95% is the maximum potential loss in 84% of cases, or, equivalently, 1.95% is the VaR of the position at an 84% confidence level. If he is concerned with more extreme losses and he identifies risk with the maximum percentage loss he may face in 95% of potential scenarios then he might consider a wider range. For instance, there is a 90% probability of extracting a value in the range ($\mu - 1.645\sigma$; $\mu + 1.645\sigma$) for any normal distribution. Therefore, since for Alpha return distribution $\mu - 1.645\sigma = -3.24\%$ and $\mu + 1.645\sigma = 3.34\%$, there is a 90% probability of extracting a value between -3.24% and $+3.34\%$ and only a 5% probability of facing a return lower than -3.24%. Therefore, 3.24% is the percentage VaR at 95% confidence level for his position on the Alpha stock (see Figure 3-1).

In general, different multiples k can be used, depending on how prudent the trader or the risk manager wants to be when measuring VaR. If one is interested in VaR in $1 - \alpha\%$ of cases, there is for any α a proper value for k; the lower α is, the greater k is and the more conservative is the VaR estimate (see Table 3-1). The proper value for k can easily be derived with the Microsoft Excel function INVNORMST, which gives back the value of x such that the cumulative function of a standardized normal distribution $N(x)$ equals the value specified in the argument of the function. Therefore, k is simply equal to INVNORMST(α); i.e., it is the value such that the probability of extracting values lower than k from a standard normal distribution is equal to α.

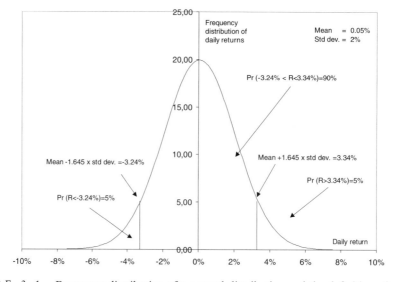

FIGURE 3-1   Frequency distribution of a normal distribution and the definition of confidence intervals.

TABLE 3-1   Some Common Confidence Intervals for the Normal Distribution

k	$Prob(\mu - k\sigma < x < \mu + k\sigma)$	$Prob(|x - \mu| > k\sigma)$	$Prob(x < \mu - k\sigma)$	Corresponding VaR Confidence Level
1	68.27%	31.73%	15.87%	84.13%
1.645	90%	10%	5%	95%
2.326	98%	2%	1%	99%
2.58	99%	1%	0.5%	99.5%

In practice, VaR for markets risks is calculated with the further assumption that the mean return μ be zero. This simplifying and conservative assumption allows one to identify percentage VaR simply as return volatility σ times a given multiple $k_{1-\alpha}$, which is a function of the desired protection level $1 - \alpha$. VaR in dollar terms is simply the product of the market value (MV) of the position times VaR in percentage terms; i.e.,

$$VaR_{1-\alpha} = MV \cdot VaR_{1-\alpha\%} = MV \cdot k_{1-\alpha} \cdot \sigma$$

Therefore, in the simplified example we considered, if the trader had a position on Alpha stocks for a market value of 100,000 USD, his estimated daily VaR at 95% and 99% would have been equal to, respectively,

$$VaR_{95\%} = MV \cdot k_{95\%} \cdot \sigma = 100,000\,USD \cdot 1.645 \cdot 2\% = 3290\,USD$$

$$VaR_{99\%} = MV \cdot k_{99\%} \cdot \sigma = 100,000\,USD \cdot 2.326 \cdot 2\% = 4652\,USD$$

VaR measures clearly vary, depending on the predefined protection level. Typical confidence levels are 99% or greater, e.g., 99.97%. Also, the time horizon matters, since, of course, weekly or monthly return volatility is greater than daily volatility and would produce a higher VaR estimate. We have now introduced the basic idea of the variance–covariance approach, even if with an extremely simplified measure of volatility. We now extend this example to consider how to (1) choose the set of random variables affecting the value of the exposure to be measured, (2) map the real portfolio into a number of stylized positions in order to reduce complexity and computational burdens, (3) calculate VaR for a portfolio, and (4) estimate volatilities and correlations.

3.1.2   The Choice of the Relevant Random Variables

The stock Alpha example we just considered is simple, since the value of the position can clearly be modeled as a function of stock Alpha's returns. But if we had to calculate VaR for a portfolio composed of one 3-yr and one 10-yr Treasury bond, the first choice to be made concerns how to explain changes in values of the two bonds. In general terms, we must choose the random variables that should explain the behavior of the value of our portfolio. The three main alternatives are:

1. The delta normal (or risk factor normal) approach, where the underlying variables are represented by market risk factors (e.g., stock returns, interest rates, exchange rates)

2. The asset normal approach, where underlying variables are represented by returns of a set of benchmark assets (e.g., stock or stock indexes, zero-coupon bonds, exchange rates)
3. The portfolio normal approach, where historical returns of the current portfolio are recalculated and the return of the whole portfolio is considered as the only underlying variable.

In some cases (e.g., a single-position exposure on a single stock or a spot exchange rate) there is in practice no difference among the three. Even in case of security or currency portfolios, the first two approaches in any case do not differ as far as the treatment of a stock index or a currency is concerned, since the currency rate return may be considered both as a risk factor (as in the delta normal approach) and as a benchmark asset return (as in the asset normal approach). Differences may be relevant when considering bonds, where the first approach assumes normal log returns for interest rates, whereas the second assumes normal log returns for a set of zero-coupon bonds with benchmark maturities.

For instance, in the two-bond portfolio we are considering, the risk factor normal approach would consider 3-yr and 10-yr interest rates as risk factors. Then, the reaction of bond returns to changes in rates would be modeled through sensitivity parameters such as their modified duration. Instead, the asset normal approach would transform the two-bond portfolio into a portfolio of equivalent zero-coupon cash flows and then model the bond portfolio as a portfolio of zero-coupon bonds with maturity up to 10 years. Finally, the portfolio approach would reconstruct past returns of the current portfolio and then calculate the return volatility of the historical return series of the portfolio. It is important to point out that the portfolio approach (see Zangari 1997) does not imply considering the series of actual past profit and losses of the trader, because (1) the portfolio may have changed through time, and (2) past P&L may be influenced by intraday trading. Instead, the portfolio approach requires recalculating the theoretical past P&L of the current portfolio. Hence, either a series of risk factor returns (as in the first approach) or a series of benchmark asset returns is required. As a consequence, while it may sometimes be very useful for specific tasks, day-by-day VaR measurement usually adopts one of the other two solutions. The most common is the asset normal approach, which was described by J. P. Morgan's (1996) RiskMetrics™ and subsequently adopted by a number of large banks.

Once the random variables used to model the bank's portfolio return have been selected, all existing exposures must be transformed into positions in the predetermined risk variables. This process is usually called *portfolio mapping*.

3.1.3 Mapping Exposures

In most real banks' trading portfolios, the number of elements influencing portfolio value may often be too large to handle each risk factor individually. In a portfolio of 10 stocks, one could still consider each stock's return as a single risk factor; VaR could then be calculated as a portfolio with 10 risk factors/benchmark assets. As we discuss in the next section, this requires calculating variances and covariances (or, alternatively, standard deviations and correlations) for the risk factors. Since n variables imply n volatilities and $n(n-1)/2$ correlation coefficients to be estimated, with $n = 10$ we would need two standard deviations and 45 correlations. But in a larger portfolio with 100 or 500 stocks, the number of correlations would become, respectively, 4950 and 124,750, making it impossible to consider each stock's return as a single variable. At the same time, even a single 10-yr Treasury bond with semiannual coupons is itself a portfolio of 20 cash flows with different maturities and would require, in theory, considering interest rates or zero-coupon returns on 20 different maturities.

Portfolio mapping is therefore the process through which a real trading portfolio of a bank is transformed and decomposed into a vector of exposures to a certain limited number of random variables (such as stock indexes, exchange rates, interest rates/zero-coupon returns with given benchmark maturities). This process is important, since VaR will then be calculated on the mapped portfolio. Consequently, oversimplifications in the mapping process could result in poor VaR estimates, no matter how sophisticated the methodology for volatility estimation may be. Of course, the overall number of variables to consider is critical, aiming at finding the right balance between making VaR estimates computationally tractable and guaranteeing a fair and reliable representation of the original portfolio. We consider first the case of fixed-income exposures, such as bonds, then equity exposures, and finally simple derivative exposures, such as a forward contract on currencies or a plain-vanilla option.

Let us consider a 10-yr Treasury bond with semiannual coupons. This bond has 20 cash flows that are sensitive to different parts of the term structure. For instance, the first coupon will be sensitive to the 6-month interest rate, while the tenth would react to changes in the 5-yr interest rate and the last one to the 10-yr zero-coupon interest rate. Since a risk manager would clearly like to avoid the strongly simplifying assumption of parallel-only shifts of the term structure, a number of different rates (under the delta normal approach) or benchmark zero-coupon bonds (under the asset normal approach) must be identified. The number of benchmark maturities to consider is an open issue: J.P. Morgan (1996) suggested, for instance, using 14 different maturities (1, 3, and 6 months and 1, 2, 3, 4, 5, 7, 9, 10, 15, 20, and 30 years). According to this choice, 9 of the 20 cash flows of the 10-yr bond would be mapped directly on a benchmark maturity, while the others must be transformed into "equivalent" cash flows with benchmark maturities. For instance, the one-and-a-half-year cash flow should be mapped into two equivalent cash flows with maturities respectively equal to one and two years.

There are two alternative methods to perform that. The first one transforms each original cash flow into two cash flows with the same value and modified duration. Therefore, the market value of any cash flow with generic maturity t that is between the benchmark maturities n and $n + 1$ will be split into two portions with weights α and $1 - \alpha$ such that

$$MD_t = MD_n \cdot \alpha + MD_{n+1} \cdot (1 - \alpha)$$

where MD_t, MD_n, MD_{n+1} represent the modified duration of a cash flow with maturity t, n, and $n + 1$, respectively. This condition is satisfied when

$$\alpha = \frac{MD_{n+1} - MD_t}{MD_{n+1} - MD_n} \qquad \text{and} \qquad 1 - \alpha = \frac{MD_t - MD_n}{MD_{n+1} - MD_n}$$

The second method chooses instead the two weights α and $1 - \alpha$ in such a way that the return volatility of the "portfolio" composed by the two benchmark maturity cash flows equals the return volatility of the original cash flow. Expressing this relationship, for simplicity, in terms of variance rather than in terms of volatility, we have

$$\sigma_t^2 = \alpha^2 \sigma_n^2 + (1 - \alpha)^2 \sigma_{n+1}^2 + 2\alpha(1 - \alpha)\rho_{n,n+1}\sigma_n\sigma_{n+1}$$

where σ_t, σ_n, and σ_{n+1} represent, respectively, the return volatility of the original cash flow and of the new cash flows with maturity n and $n + 1$, while $\rho_{n,n+1}$ is the correlation between n and $n + 1$ benchmark zero-coupon bond returns. The equation has two solutions, but the right one can be selected by imposing the condition $0 \leq \alpha \leq 1$, implying that both the two new cash flows must have the same sign as the original cash flow.

In the case of equity exposures, the reduction in the number of risk factors is usually pursued by modeling each stock's return through some factor model. The simplest is a one-factor model, assuming that in each market the return of a single stock r_i can be modeled as a function of the return of the stock market index r_m and a zero-mean specific component ε_i, according to the equation

$$r_i = \beta_i r_m + \alpha_i + \varepsilon_i$$

where α_i is a constant. In this case, if a bank's portfolio is large enough to diversify specific risk, the specific return components of different stocks would simply offset each other so that they can be neglected. Hence, the return of the portfolio r_p can be written as

$$r_p = \sum_{i=1}^{n} \omega_i r_i = \sum_{i=1}^{n} \omega_i (\beta_i r_m + \alpha_i + \varepsilon_i) = \beta_p r_m + \alpha_p + \sum_{i=1}^{n} \omega_i \varepsilon_i \approx \beta_p r_m + \alpha_p$$

where ω_i represents the weight of each stock in the portfolio, β_p is portfolio beta (equal to the weighted average of the betas of the stock in the portfolio), and α_p is a constant. As a consequence, portfolio volatility and hence portfolio VaR are simply equal to β_p times volatility or VaR of a position in the stock index. In this way for any country/region (or potentially for any sector/industry, if industries are assumed to explain returns better than countries) the stock portfolio can be mapped into an equivalent position in the index, and the whole portfolio is reduced to a number of benchmark assets equal to the number of the stock indexes. The quality of the mapping process will depend on the number and type of stock indexes used to map the equity portfolio. An example is provided in Box 3-1.

Box 3-1: Mapping Equity Positions through Beta: An Example

In order to show how the methodology described so far could work, let us consider the simplified example of a portfolio of 100 GBP invested in three stocks: British Petroleum (50 GBP), Vodafone (30 GBP), and Royal Bank of Scotland (20 GBP). If we consider as the relevant stock index the FTSE100 index, we can calculate β for each of these stocks. Beta for each stock i is in fact equal to

$$\beta_i = \rho_{i,m} \cdot \frac{\sigma_i}{\sigma_m}$$

where $\rho_{i,m}$ is the correlation between stock i and market index returns and σ_i and σ_m are the standard deviations of stock i and market index returns, respectively. Considering, for instance, a 5-year sample of monthly return data from July 2000 to June 2005, we obtain for the three stock the betas reported in Table 3-2. This permits us to map the exposure in each stock into a (hopefully) equivalent position in the index.

TABLE 3-2 Mapping Positions in Three UK Stocks into FTSE100-Equivalent Exposures

	Stock		
	British Petroleum	**Vodafone**	**Royal Bank of Scotland**
Position size	50 GBP	30 GBP	20 GBP
Beta	0.71	1.29	1.27
Equivalent FTSE100 position	35.50 GBP	38.70 GBP	25.40 GBP
Total	99.60 GBP		

The equivalent FTSE100 position is determined by simply multiplying the exposure in each stock by the stock's beta. For instance, since RBS's beta implies that 1 GBP invested in RBS is exposed to systematic risk that is 1.27 times the amount of systematic risk of 1 GBP invested in the index, the equivalent position for RBS is 20 GBP × 1.27 = 25.40 GBP. The 100-GBP portfolio invested in the three stocks is therefore considered equivalent to 99.60 GBP invested in the FTSE100 index.

As a consequence, VaR for this portfolio could be simply calculated as if the portfolio were invested in the index directly. If the daily volatility for the FTSE100 index were equal to 0.930%, then (remembering that the proper multiple $k_{1-\alpha}$ for 99% is 2.326) the 99% daily VaR for the portfolio of the three stocks could be estimated as

$$VaR_{99\%} = MV \cdot k_{99\%} \cdot \sigma = 99.60 \, GBP \cdot 2.326 \cdot 0.930\% = 2.154 \, GBP$$

The example clarifies that mapping has made VaR calculation easier. If we had had 500 stocks from 15 different markets, using this methodology could have simplified the portfolio to 15 positions on different stock markets rather than a much more complex set of 500 different exposures on single stocks. At the same time, mapping has the cost of accepting some simplification. For instance, in this case the three-stock portfolio has been transformed to a portfolio with the same *systematic* risk; but since the portfolio comprises three stocks only, it should be clear that the real portfolio would also have some idiosyncratic (i.e., nonsystematic) risk. Since the mapped portfolio does not take this risk into consideration, the VaR estimate is likely to underestimate the true risk in this case. If instead the portfolio had been much larger (e.g., if it had been made up of 60 different UK stocks, each of which accounted for a small percentage of the portfolio), then assuming specific risk had been diversified would have been more reasonable and the mapped portfolio VaR would have provided a better proxy for the true portfolio VaR.

Alternatively, more sophisticated solutions can be built by using multifactor models of the form

$$r_i = \alpha_i + \beta_{i,1}r_1 + \beta_{i,2}r_2 + \cdots + \beta_{i,n}r_n + \varepsilon_i$$

where $r_1, r_2, \ldots, r_n$ represent returns of the n common factors of the multifactor model and $\beta_{i,1}, \beta_{i,2}, \ldots, \beta_{i,n}$ identify sensitivities of the stock i return to each factor. Again, the number of factors and their ability to explain total portfolio variance is relevant; a specific random component can be added as an extra variable in VaR calculations to model more properly the absolute risk of the portfolio.

For linear derivative positions, mapping implies breaking down exposures into simpler components or building blocks. For instance, a 6-month forward purchase of British pounds against U.S. dollars is equivalent to a spot purchase of British pounds, a 6-month investment in British pounds, and a 6-month borrowing of U.S. dollars and should be treated accordingly for VaR measurement purposes. A fixed to floating interest rate swap, where the bank receives the fixed rate and pays the floating rate, can be decomposed as a long position in a fixed-rate bond and a short position in a floating-rate note, and so on (see, for instance, J.P. Morgan 1996 for examples).

The situation is more critical for nonlinear derivatives, such as options. The simpler solution is to transform them into positions on the underlying asset through a linear approximation based on the option's delta. Delta is the first partial derivative of the option price relative to the price of the underlying asset and is the most important of option sensitivity coefficients (commonly known as option *greeks*). Graphically, delta is equivalent to the slope of the tangent line to the curve expressing the option value as a function of the price of the underlying asset. It is therefore always positive for long call options, whose value increases when the underlying asset price increases, and negative for long put options, for a symmetric argument (see Figures 3-2 and 3-3), and changes as the price of the underlying asset increases or decreases.

Formally, delta can be expressed as $\delta V / \delta S$, where V is the value of the option and S is the spot price of the underlying asset, and it can be used as an approximation of $\Delta V / \Delta S$ when changes in S are small enough. Therefore, if delta $\approx \Delta V / \Delta S$, then $\Delta V \approx$ delta $\times \Delta S$.

Consequently, if the underlying asset price changes by ΔS, the option value will react approximately in proportion to its delta. In practice, by approximating linearly the relationship between the underlying asset price and the option's value, an option on 100 Microsoft stocks with delta 0.40 and 40 Microsoft stocks could be considered as almost equivalent, since both positions would earn or lose approximately 40 if Microsoft stock price increased or decreased by $1. Hence, as a simple solution for mapping purposes an option position could be translated into a position on the underlying asset equal to delta times the notional of the option.

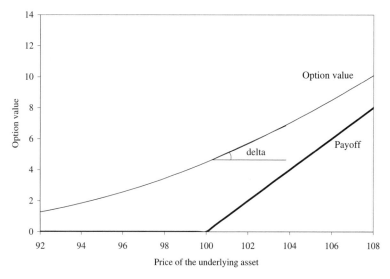

FIGURE 3-2   Value of a European call option as a function of the underlying price and the option's delta (strike price = 100, maturity = 3 months, volatility = 20%).

This methodology is frequently used in the variance–covariance approach, but it is simplistic, since it neglects that (1) the relationship between the underlying asset price and the value of the option is nonlinear (being convex or concave, depending on whether the trader is long or short the option) and (2) the price of the option is also exposed to other risk factors, such as time decay and the level of the expected/implied volatility of the underlying asset's returns. These elements are typically neglected in a simple variance–covariance approach when calculating VaR for nonlinear positions. Alternative and more precise methodologies are discussed in Section 3.3.

It is important to recognize that the mapping process is a crucial phase in VaR calculation. In fact, any sophisticated methodology the risk manager might choose for calculating VaR will not be applied to the bank's *real* portfolio, but to the (hopefully) similar portfolio that was produced after mapping individual positions. Therefore, the precision of VaR estimation will depend both on the choice of VaR methodology (e.g., the choice of a variance–covariance rather than a simulation approach, how volatility has been estimated) and on the quality and care of the mapping process. If model back-testing, which is discussed later, showed that VaR estimates are inaccurate, the risk manager should try to understand whether to change methodology, improve the mapping process, or both.

Moreover, decisions about mapping are often subjective and purpose specific. For instance, a risk manager interested in estimating VaR only at aggregate levels in a bank where the equity trading portfolio is very small relative to other positions may accept measuring the risk of such a portfolio by modeling stock returns through a single-index model. In contrast, for an investment company risk manager concerned with predicting the potential underperformance of an equity fund return from its benchmark such a naive choice would make no sense. But even the same risk manager in the same bank might decide to use a simplified approach such as the one described here for option positions when evaluating overall VaR for the whole bank, if the manager thinks that the risk

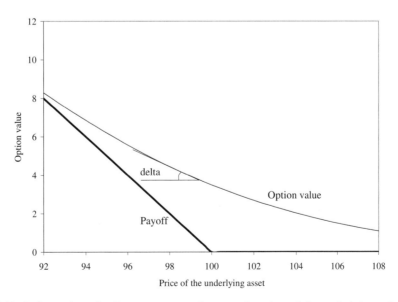

FIGURE 3-3   Value of a European put option as a function of the underlying price and the option's delta (strike price = 100, maturity = 3 months, volatility = 20%).

deriving from that portfolio is negligible, while using a more sophisticated approach in order to set up limits for the option trader.

3.1.4 VaR for a Portfolio

After the portfolio is mapped, VaR should be calculated for a portfolio of mapped exposures. We consider first the asset normal case, in which the risk manager assumes that benchmark asset returns are jointly normally distributed, and we then compare it briefly with the delta normal approach. In the portfolio normal case, in contrast, the problem disappears, since the risk manager would reconstruct the historical series of past returns of the current portfolio, obtaining only a single return series to deal with.

Imagine calculating VaR for a portfolio composed only of (1) a basket of stocks replicating a stock market index and (2) a 5-year zero-coupon bond, whose relative weights are α and $1 - \alpha$, respectively. Portfolio VaR could be written as a multiple $k_{1-\alpha}$ multiplied by the market value of the portfolio, MV_P, times portfolio volatility, σ_P:

$$VaR_P = MV_P \cdot k_{1-\alpha} \cdot \sigma_P$$

where portfolio volatility can be expressed, as usual, in terms of return volatilities σ_A and σ_B of the two assets A and B composing the portfolio and of their linear correlation coefficient $\rho_{A,B}$, i.e.,[2]

$$\sigma_P = \sqrt{\alpha^2 \sigma_A^2 + (1-\alpha)^2 \sigma_B^2 + 2\alpha(1-\alpha)\sigma_A \sigma_B \rho_{A,B}}$$

Substituting this expression into the preceding formula we can easily obtain

$$
\begin{aligned}
VaR_P &= MV_P \cdot k_{1-\alpha} \cdot \sqrt{\alpha^2 \sigma_A^2 + (1-\alpha)^2 \sigma_B^2 + 2\alpha(1-\alpha)\sigma_A \sigma_B \rho_{A,B}} \\
&= \sqrt{(\alpha MV_P k_{1-\alpha} \sigma_A)^2 + [(1-\alpha)MV_P k_{1-\alpha} \sigma_B]^2 + 2[\alpha MV_P k_{1-\alpha} \sigma_A][(1-\alpha)MV_P k_{1-\alpha} \sigma_B]\rho_{A,B}} \\
&= \sqrt{VaR_A^2 + VaR_B^2 + 2VaR_A VaR_B \rho_{A,B}}
\end{aligned}
$$

---

2. In reality, this formula can be applied if portfolio return is equal to a weighted average of the returns of the two assets. This would be true if returns were measured as percentage returns, while it is no longer true if we use log returns, as usually happens for risk measurement purposes (the assumption of normal distribution is in fact referred to log returns and could not be applied to percentage returns). The exact expression for the return of a portfolio of N assets with weights $\omega_1, \omega_2, \ldots, \omega_N$ and log return $r_1, r_2, \ldots, r_N$ is given by

$$r_P = \ln\left(\sum_{i=1}^{N} \omega_i e^{r_i}\right)$$

Nevertheless, for sufficiently small values of r_i (as we would expect in the case of daily returns), the expression can be approximated as

$$r_P \cong \sum_{i=1}^{N} \omega_i r_i$$

enabling us to use the well-known portfolio volatility formula reported in the text. See J. P. Morgan (1996), pp. 48–49.

since $\alpha MV_P = MV_A$ and hence $\alpha MV_P k \sigma_A = VaR_A$ (the same logic holds for B). This expression does not strictly require the distribution to be jointly normal, but it can be applied whenever the multiple of volatility $k_{1-\alpha}$ needed to obtain the desired quantile of the return distribution (i.e., percentage VaR) is the same for both the individual assets and the portfolio as a whole (see Rosenberg and Schuermann 2004).

This formula could be applied also in a delta normal approach, i.e., when the risk manager assumes that risk factors (e.g., stock indexes, interest rates) are normally distributed. In a delta normal approach, the change in the market value of the position is obtained by multiplying the worst-case variation of the risk factor $k\sigma_{rf}$ by the sensitivity δ of the asset to changes in the risk factor. For instance, in a delta normal approach, the risk manager would consider the stock index and 5-year rates (rather than the 5-year zero-coupon bond return) as risk factors. The sensitivity δ of the basket of stocks to the first risk factor would be one, while the sensitivity of zero-coupon bond returns to changes in the 5-year interest rate would be represented by its modified duration. Considering, for example, the bond (position B), VaR_B would be expressed as $MV_B \delta_B k \sigma_{rf} = MV_B k(\delta_B \sigma_{rf})$, where the term in parentheses simply represents the estimated volatility of bond return and is hence equivalent to σ_B, so $VaR_B = MV_B k \sigma_B$. Therefore, the same synthetic formula for portfolio VaR as a function of VaR_A, VaR_B also applies in the delta normal case.

With more than two positions, the portfolio VaR formula would become

$$VaR_P = \sqrt{\sum_{i=1}^{n} VaR_i^2 + \sum_{i=1}^{n}\sum_{j\neq i}^{n} VaR_i VaR_j \rho_{i,j}}$$

or, in matrix form,

$$VaR_P = \sqrt{\overline{V}\cdot C\cdot \overline{V}^T}$$

where $\overline{V}$ and $\overline{V}^T$ represent the individual VaR vector and the transposed VaR vector, respectively, defined as

$$\overline{V} = \begin{bmatrix} VaR_1 \\ VaR_2 \\ \vdots \\ VaR_{n-1} \\ VaR_n \end{bmatrix}; \quad \overline{V}^T = \begin{bmatrix} VaR_1 & VaR_2 & \cdots & VaR_{n-1} & VaR_n \end{bmatrix}$$

and C is the correlation matrix

$$C = \begin{bmatrix} 1 & \rho_{1,2} & \cdots & \rho_{1,n-1} & \rho_{1,n} \\ \rho_{1,2} & 1 & \cdots & \rho_{2,n-1} & \rho_{2,n} \\ \vdots & \vdots & \vdots & \vdots & \vdots \\ \rho_{1,n-1} & \rho_{2,n-1} & \cdots & 1 & \rho_{n-1,n} \\ \rho_{1,n} & \rho_{2,n} & \cdots & \rho_{n-1,n} & 1 \end{bmatrix}$$

Box 3-2: Calculating VaR for a Three-Stock Portfolio

Let us consider again the portfolio of three UK stocks discussed in Box 3-1. If, rather than mapping each position into its FTSE100-equivalent, we wanted to consider each stock's return as a single risk factor, then the formula for portfolio VaR could be applied. The relevant data are reported in Table 3-3.

VaR for the portfolio would be equal to

$$\text{VaR}_P = \sqrt{\sum_{i=1}^{3} \text{VaR}_i^2 + \sum_{i=1}^{3}\sum_{j\neq i} \text{VaR}_i \text{VaR}_j \rho_{i,j}}$$

$$= \sqrt{\text{VaR}_1^2 + \text{VaR}_2^2 + \text{VaR}_3^2 + 2\text{VaR}_1\text{VaR}_2\rho_{1,2} + 2\text{VaR}_1\text{VaR}_3\rho_{1,3} + 2\text{VaR}_2\text{VaR}_3\rho_{2,3}}$$

$$= \text{GBP}\sqrt{\frac{(1.361)^2 + (1.456)^2 + (0.797)^2 + 2\cdot1.361\cdot1.456\cdot0.162}{+2\cdot1.361\cdot0.797\cdot0.335 + 2\cdot1.456\cdot0.797\cdot0.332}}$$

$$= \text{GBP } 2.598$$

TABLE 3-3   Volatility and Correlation Estimates for Calculating Portfolio VaR

	Stock		
	British Petroleum	**Vodafone**	**Royal Bank of Scotland**
Position size	50 GBP	30 GBP	20 GBP
Volatility (σ)	1.170%	2.087%	1.714%
Correlation with British Petroleum	1.000	0.162	0.335
Correlation with Vodafone	0.162	1.000	0.332
Correlation with Royal Bank of Scotland	0.335	0.332	1.000
Stand-alone VaR$_{99\%}$ (position size $\times k_{99\%} \times \sigma$)	1.361 GBP	1.456 GBP	0.797 GBP

Box 3-3: Why Mapping Is Important

Comparing the results obtained in Boxes 3-1 and 3-2 may help us explain why the subtleties of mapping are important. In fact, in Box 3-2 we obtained for the same portfolio a daily VaR estimate equal to GBP 2.598, i.e., 20.6% higher than the GBP 2.154 estimate that was obtained in Box 3-1 for the same portfolio, even if stock and market index volatilities and stock correlations and betas have been estimated based on the same historical sample (for simplicity we used here simple moving average volatility and correlation estimates, even though we describe in the next section why they do not represent the optimal solution).

The reason for this difference, as noted in Box 3-1, is that the mapped portfolio was not considering specific risk, which is instead taken into consideration when considering each stock as a single risk factor as in Box 3-2. While for larger, well-diversified stock portfolios specific risk could be more safely neglected, this is not the case in our simplified example. This case is simple enough that the bias of the mapped portfolio in Box 3-1 could easily be understood and anticipated by many nonspecialists. Yet if we were mapping a portfolio of caps and floors through a delta approximation in order to use a variance–covariance approach, fewer nonspecialists might immediately be able to identify what gets lost during the mapping process (i.e., that first of all we would be transforming a nonlinear position into a linear approximation based on delta, and secondly we would be neglecting that caps and floors also react to changes in their implied volatility and not just to changes in interest rates). Any VaR calculation based on a mapped portfolio would not provide a reasonable estimate for the true portfolio VaR unless the approximation accepted in the mapping process is itself reasonable. This is why it is highly advisable (1) to give substantial attention to key methodological choices concerning mapping, (2) to explain very clearly the key choices and their practical implications to nonspecialists who might need to read and analyze a risk management report, and (3) to back-test VaR estimates carefully (see Section 3.6). At the same time, portfolio VaR makes it clear that mapping is unavoidable, since otherwise the number of correlation pairs to be considered would grow disproportionately if the portfolio had comprised more than the three stocks of our intentionally simplified example.

3.1.5 Estimating Volatility and Correlation: Simple Moving Averages

So far we have assumed that the risk manager knows how to calculate the volatility of returns of any risk factor or benchmark asset. In theory, this relevant input could be estimated either from historical return data (historical volatility) or from option prices (implied volatility; see Section 3.1.7). When estimating volatility from historical data, the simple classical formula for the standard deviation of returns would be

$$\sigma = \sqrt{\frac{\sum_{i=1}^{n}(R_i - \overline{R})^2}{n-1}}$$

where R_i is the daily log return on day i, $\overline{R}$ is the average daily return over the sample period, and n is the number of daily returns in the sample. In practice, the formula would consider each day a rolling window of the last n daily returns.

Nevertheless, using such a simple formula has two shortcomings. First, the average daily return may not represent the true mean of the return distribution. One could therefore identify an equilibrium mean return and substitute it for the average historical return. The typical solution in practice is to assume a zero mean return, which is considered a reasonable approximation of the true average return on a daily basis. Substituting the sample average $\overline{R}$ with any different value also implies producing a higher and more prudent estimate for σ. Please note that while this is the standard on a daily horizon, this is not the case when volatility is estimated on nondaily data: Assuming a stock index has a zero mean *monthly* return may be overconservative, whereas using an equilibrium mean return or at least a risk-free return may be more appropriate.

The second problem with the classical volatility formula relates to the arbitrary choice of the length of the historical sample and the so-called "echo effect." In fact, by increasing the sample size (e.g., using 500 data, i.e., something less than two years of trading days, rather than 250) the risk manager gets a more complete picture of the return distribution and avoids the risk of being too optimistic if, for instance, recent data came from an unusually low-volatility period. At the same time, increasing sample size too much could lead to a very stable volatility estimate that fails to react promptly to new market conditions. Actually, the simple classical formula gives the same relevance to all data in the sample, irrespective of their sequence. Therefore, if the risk manager is using a 250-day rolling window, an abnormal negative return on March 3rd will immediately increase the volatility estimate for March 4th (which is right), but it will then influence in the same way the volatility estimate for the following 249 days, even if no other abnormal return were experienced. Most important, the disappearance of the abnormal data from the sample (occurring 250 days later, when that return would fall out of the 250-day rolling window) would cause the volatility to fall, even if there were no real changes in market conditions. This is the so-called echo effect: By assigning the same weights to all data in the sample, abnormal data markedly influence volatility estimates, once when they enter the sample and then when they exit the sample, producing an undesired "echo" irrespective of true volatility levels in the market. This is why risk managers typically prefer different methods, such as exponentially weighted moving averages.

3.1.6 *Estimating Volatility and Correlation: Exponentially Weighted Moving Averages and GARCH Models*

An easy way to avoid the shortcomings stemming from simple moving averages is to assign a higher weight to more recent data. This is the idea behind exponentially weighted moving averages (EWMAs), which are measured as

$$\sigma_{t,n} = \sqrt{\frac{\lambda^0 r_{t-1}^2 + \lambda^1 r_{t-2}^2 + \cdots + \lambda^{n-2} r_{t-n-1}^2 + \lambda^{n-1} r_{t-n}^2}{\lambda^0 + \lambda^1 + \cdots + \lambda^{n-2} + \lambda^{n-1}}}$$

where volatility at time t based on a sample of n returns is calculated by assigning to the return that occurred i days before the one when the estimate is made a weight equal to λ^{i-1}, with $\lambda < 1$ (note that the formula reports returns squared, since the mean return is assumed to be zero). λ is called the *decay factor*; and since $\lambda < 1$, the older the data, the lower the weight. Higher values for λ imply that the volatility estimate would react more slowly to new information and the effects of past shocks will continue to persist, at least in part, through time. Instead, lower values for λ imply that the volatility estimate is more reactive and has less "memory" about past significant shocks, whose weight rapidly declines as new data enter the sample. The choice of the optimal decay factor is an empirical issue. Many risk managers use $\lambda = 0.94$ for daily and $\lambda = 0.97$ for monthly volatility estimates, since they appeared as the winners in the empirical test presented in J.P. Morgan's (1996) *RiskMetrics^{TM} Technical Document*, albeit using a relatively simple technique.

Since the denominator is a geometric series, it can be substituted by the expression[3]

$$\lambda^0 + \lambda^1 + \cdots + \lambda^{n-2} + \lambda^{n-1} = \sum_{i=0}^{n-1} \lambda^i = \frac{1-\lambda^n}{1-\lambda}$$

3. In fact, it can be shown that

$$\sum_{i=1}^{n} q^i = \frac{1-q^{n+1}}{1-q}$$

which for sufficiently high values of n can be approximated by $1/(1 - \lambda)$. We can therefore write

$$\sigma_{t,n} = \sqrt{\frac{\lambda^0 r_{t-1}^2 + \lambda^1 r_{t-2}^2 + \cdots + \lambda^{n-2} r_{t-n-1}^2 + \lambda^{n-1} r_{t-n}^2}{\lambda^0 + \lambda^1 + \cdots + \lambda^{n-2} + \lambda^{n-1}}} = \sqrt{\frac{1-\lambda}{1-\lambda^n} \sum_{i=1}^{n} \lambda^{i-1} r_{t-i}^2} \cong \sqrt{(1-\lambda) \sum_{i=1}^{n} \lambda^{i-1} r_{t-i}^2}$$

In this way, we can easily show that the EWMA volatility estimate at time $t + 1$ can also be calculated on the basis of the volatility estimate at $t\sigma_t$ and of the last daily return, r_t. In fact, expressing for simplicity the formula in terms of variance rather than standard deviation, we get

$$\sigma_{t+1}^2 = (1-\lambda) \sum_{i=1}^{\infty} \lambda^{i-1} r_{t+1-i}^2 = (1-\lambda) \cdot \lambda^0 r_t^2 + (1-\lambda) \sum_{i=2}^{\infty} \lambda^{i-1} r_{t+1-i}^2$$

$$= (1-\lambda) \cdot 1 \cdot r_t^2 + (1-\lambda) \sum_{j=1}^{\infty} \lambda \cdot \lambda^{j-1} r_{t-j}^2$$

$$= (1-\lambda) r_t^2 + \lambda \left[(1-\lambda) \sum_{j=1}^{\infty} \lambda^{j-1} r_{t-j}^2 \right] = (1-\lambda) r_t^2 + \lambda \sigma_t^2$$

In a similar way the risk manager might easily measure covariances and correlations too. Covariance between the returns of two assets could be estimated through a simple moving average as

$$\text{Cov}(r_1, r_2) = \sigma_{1,2} = \sqrt{\frac{\sum_{i=1}^{n} (r_{1,i} - \bar{r}_1)(r_{2,i} - \bar{r}_2)}{n-1}}$$

But this can be expressed according to EWMA methodology (assuming an infinite sample and zero mean returns) as

$$\text{Cov}(r_1, r_2)_t = (1-\lambda) \sum_{i=1}^{\infty} \lambda^{j-1} r_{1,t-j} r_{2,t-j}$$

which can easily be transformed into

$$\text{Cov}(r_1, r_2)_t = (1 - \lambda) r_{1,t} r_{2,t} + \lambda \text{Cov}(r_1, r_2)_{t-1}$$

It is then easy to calculate the linear correlation coefficient $\rho_{1,2}$, which is given by

$$\rho_{1,2,t} = \frac{\text{Cov}(r_1, r_2)_t}{\sigma_{1,t} \sigma_{2,t}}$$

By assigning a decreasing weight to observations as they become less recent, the exponential weighted moving average (EWMA) method avoids the echo effect of simple average volatility estimates and also makes volatility estimates less sensitive to the choice of sample size. In fact, with a decay factor λ equal to 0.94, if a risk manager doubled the sample size from 250 to 500 trading days (i.e., from almost one year to two years), the aggregated weight of the older 250 days would be as low as 0.00002%.

The observation that market volatility is not constant which underlies EWMA methodology is at the heart of the more general family of GARCH (generalized autoregressive conditional heteroskedasticity) models. EWMA will be shown later to be a particular case of the GARCH model. GARCH models assume that conditional variance of returns is not constant, so asset returns may show alternate periods of higher and lower volatility (*volatility clustering*). The origins of GARCH models can be found in Engle's (1982) ARCH model, which expresses conditional variance at time $t + 1$ (σ_{t+1}^2) as

$$\sigma_{t+1}^2 = \alpha_0 + \alpha_1\varepsilon_t^2 + \alpha_2\varepsilon_{t-1}^2 + \cdots + \alpha_p\varepsilon_{t-p+1}^2$$

where ε_i is the forecasting error (i.e., the difference between the estimate and the realized value[4]) at time i and the α coefficients must be estimated through regression (with $\alpha_0 > 0$ and $\alpha_1, \ldots, \alpha_p \geq 0$). Under this approach, and depending on the values assigned to the α coefficients, significant forecasting errors could result in an increase in estimated volatility. Engle's ARCH model has been generalized by Bollerslev (1986) by also introducing in the conditional-variance equation at time t past estimates of the variance itself at times $t - 1, t - 2, \ldots, t - n$. Therefore, a GARCH (p,q) model is defined by the equation

$$\sigma_{t+1}^2 = \alpha_0 + \alpha_1\varepsilon_t^2 + \alpha_2\varepsilon_{t-1}^2 + \cdots + \alpha_p\varepsilon_{t-p+1}^2 + \beta_1\sigma_t^2 + \beta_2\sigma_{t-1}^2 + \cdots + \beta_q\sigma_{t-q+1}^2$$

with $\alpha_0 > 0$ and $\alpha_1, \ldots, \alpha_p, \beta_1, \ldots, \beta_q \geq 0$. The most well-known version is the GARCH (1,1) model, which considers only one past conditional-variance estimate and one past realized estimation error, so

$$\sigma_{t+1}^2 = \alpha_0 + \alpha_1\varepsilon_t^2 + \beta_1\sigma_t^2 \qquad \alpha_0 > 0, \qquad \alpha_1 \geq 0, \qquad \beta_1 \geq 0$$

If we assume the mean return is equal to zero, we obtain simply

$$\sigma_{t+1}^2 = \alpha_0 + \alpha_1 r_t^2 + \beta_1\sigma_t^2 \qquad \alpha_0 > 0, \qquad \alpha_1 \geq 0, \qquad \beta_1 \geq 0$$

It is quite easy to see that the EWMA RiskMetrics™ model, which can be expressed as

$$\sigma_{t+1}^2 = (1 - \lambda)r_t^2 + \lambda\sigma_t^2$$

can be considered as a particular case of a GARCH model,[5] where $\alpha_0 = 0$ and $\alpha_1 + \beta_1 = 1$. Yet, though EWMA is a particular GARCH case, there are differences from models such as the general case of the GARCH (1,1) as far as volatility estimation over longer time horizons is concerned.

---

4. Therefore, estimating conditional variance also requires estimating a conditional mean, which is usually derived through an autoregressive model AR(1) of the form

$$y_{t+1} = \alpha + \rho y_t + \varepsilon$$

where y_{t+1} and y_t stand for asset returns in time periods $t + 1$ and t respectively, and α and ρ are constants to be estimated through regression, whose error term is represented by ε. See Alexander (2001).

5. GARCH models also comprise more sophisticated variants of the base model, in order to obtain greater adherence to empirical evidence about asset returns, such as the asymmetric GARCH and the exponential GARCH. We do not deal with these extensions for the sake of brevity; the interested reader can refer to Alexander (2001) or Christoffersen (2003).

3.1.7 VaR Estimates and the Relevance of the Time Horizon

While VaR estimates for market risk are usually derived over a daily horizon, it may be often be necessary to estimate potential losses over longer time frames. J.P. Morgan's (1996) RiskMetrics™ document, for instance, suggests adopting a different decay factor λ (0.97 rather than 0.94) to estimate volatility and correlation over a monthly horizon. But it is typically the risk manager's choice to define which solution to adopt when estimating losses over periods such as one or two weeks or, instead, over more than one month. The usual way to solve the problem is to assume that returns were serially uncorrelated, which implies[6] that return volatility over T days can be considered the daily return volatility times the square root of T:

$$\sigma_T = \sigma_{\text{daily}} \cdot \sqrt{T}$$

Most GARCH models allow instead for a more precise term structure of volatility, since a long-run, unconditional average variance is identified and hence expected volatility over a longer time horizon depends partly on current volatility and partly on long-run volatility. In practice, if the volatility estimate for the next day is σ_{t+1} and the long-run unconditional volatility is σ, if $\sigma_{t+1} < \sigma$ then the estimate for volatility over a longer time horizon would be higher than σ_{t+1} times the square root of the number of trading days, since the volatility is assumed to be reverting to its long-term average σ. The opposite would happen if current volatility were higher than long-term volatility (i.e., if $\sigma_{t+1} > \sigma$). Long-run unconditional variance in a GARCH (1,1) model is defined as the expected value of the conditional variance σ_{t+1}^2; i.e.,

$$\sigma^2 = E[\sigma_{t+1}^2] = \alpha_0 + \alpha_1 E[R_t^2] + \beta_1 E[\sigma_t^2] = \alpha_0 + \alpha_1 \sigma^2 + \beta_1 \sigma^2$$

Thus, solving for σ^2, we obtain

$$\sigma^2 = \frac{\alpha_0}{1 - \alpha_1 - \beta_1}$$

Such a value cannot be defined in the RiskMetrics™ EWMA model, which is a particular kind of GARCH (1,1) model where $\alpha_0 = 0$ and $\alpha_1 + \beta_1 = 1$. Therefore, EWMAs are unable to model a time structure of variance of future returns, and in practice current variance is projected forever by simply scaling it for the square root of time. This may lead one to overestimate (underestimate) volatility when current volatility is higher (lower) than long-run unconditional volatility.[7] At the same time,

---

6. Let us define R_T, an asset's log return over T days, which is the sum of daily log returns $R_1, R_2, \ldots, R_n$. If $R_1, R_2, \ldots, R_n$ are independent and identically distributed, the variance for R_T can be written as

$$\sigma_{R_T}^2 = \sigma_{\Sigma R_i}^2 = \sum_{i=1}^{T} \sigma_{R_i}^2 = T \cdot \sigma_{R_i}^2$$

7. The volatility forecast over a horizon of T days for a general GARCH (1,1) model would be equal to

$$\sigma_T = \sqrt{T \cdot \sigma^2 + \sum_{k=1}^{T} (\alpha + \beta)^{k-1} (\sigma_{t+1}^2 - \sigma^2)}$$

Such a value is different from $\sigma_{t+1} \sqrt{T}$, which would be the forecast under the EWMA model. And it is quite easy to see that it produces a higher volatility estimate whenever unconditional volatility σ is higher than current volatility σ_{t+1}, provided $\alpha_1 + \beta_1 < 1$. See Christoffersen (2003) for a discussion of this issue.

using a fixed decay factor is much easier than estimating and continually revising GARCH parameters. This helps to explain the success of the EWMA method in practice.

Another problem when measuring VaR over longer time horizons is that the assumption of zero mean returns, while acceptable over a daily horizon, becomes questionable for long-only portfolios (e.g., bond or equity portfolios where the manager may only buy stocks or bonds without selling them short). In this case, expected losses would be equal to k times the standard deviation of returns over T days minus the expected return over a time horizon of T days. Assumptions about expected return therefore become important, since overestimating expected return would also imply VaR underestimation. A conservative choice that is sometimes preferred is to set expected return equal to the risk-free rate. Of course this problem is nonexistent for a long–short portfolio (e.g., when relative VaR against a benchmark is calculated for an asset manager who is long his real portfolio and short the benchmark), where expected return for long positions can reasonably be assumed to be compensated by expected return on short positions.

3.1.8   Implied Volatilities and Correlations

A theoretical alternative to volatilities and correlations estimated from historical return series is represented by implied volatilities and correlations derived from option prices. Any option price, in fact, requires estimating the return volatility of the underlying asset returns. If the option's payoff depends on a number of different assets, as is the case for basket options and many other exotic options, then return correlations must also be estimated. When (1) the market price of an option, (2) its pricing model, and (3) all other pricing parameters (e.g., the underlying asset price, the strike price, the option's maturity, the risk-free interest rate) are known, it is possible to extract the volatility estimate that is implied in the option's value and hence is defined as *implied volatility*. In theory, implied volatility provides a forward-looking volatility estimate that may incorporate even more information than is contained in historical asset prices. In practice, however, it is difficult to substitute entirely historical volatility and correlation estimates with implied ones. To point out the main problems only, the first is that while market risk measurement is focused mostly on a daily horizon, implied volatilities depend on the maturity of the option, and very short-term options are typically very illiquid. The risk manager should then decide arbitrarily which is the shortest maturity that still has a liquid market, and hence reliable prices, and use implied volatility on such maturity as a proxy for daily volatility. Second, implied volatilities also differ with the strike of the option (creating the so-called volatility smiles or skews); the risk manager should choose whether to consider a weighted average of implied volatilities over different strikes or instead a single specific strike alone as his estimate for future volatility. Third, implied volatilities can be derived for many, but not all, assets or risk factors. Similarly, implied correlations can be derived from exotic option prices only when the market is liquid and there is sufficient agreement on the pricing model to be used. In any case, in practice the risk manager should use a mixture of implied and historical data. Unsurprisingly, therefore, risk managers do not generally use implied volatility or correlation data for daily VaR estimates, while implied data may sometimes be used for a few of the most relevant assets (or risk factors) only as a warning signal to check whether the market might expect shocks in future volatility that historical data are failing to capture.

Box 3-4: Deriving Implied Volatilities from Option Prices

We can clarify how implied volatility can be extracted from equity prices through an example. Let us imagine that a 3-month European call option with strike price equal to 9 USD on the stock Brown Inc. is trading at 1.264 USD. Brown Inc., whose current spot price is 10 USD, will not pay dividends before the option's maturity, and hence we can price the call through the Black–Scholes (1973) formula, according to which the price of the call c is

$$c = SN(d) - e^{-rT} XN(d - \sigma\sqrt{T})$$

where S is the spot price of the underlying asset, r is the risk-free rate, T is the option's time to maturity, $N(x)$ represents the cumulative distribution function of a standard normal calculated in x, σ is the underlying asset expected return volatility, and

$$d = \frac{\ln(S/X) + (r + \frac{1}{2}\sigma^2)T}{\sigma\sqrt{T}}$$

If we assume $r = 4\%$, we can try to find the value of σ that returns a theoretical value of the option equal to its market price (i.e., 1.264 USD); this value is the option's implied volatility. By trial and error, we could first try using two estimates $\sigma_1 = 25\%$ and $\sigma_2 = 35\%$. Since all other parameters ($S = 10$ USD, $X = 9$ USD, $T = 0.25$, $r = 0.04$) are known, by applying the formulas we can see that with $\sigma_1 = 25\%$, we have $d = 1.4129$ and $c_1 = 1.182$, while with $\sigma_2 = 35\%$, we have $d = 1.1806$ and $c = 1.302$. The estimated value of the option grows as the volatility input increases. Hence we can infer that $\sigma_1 = 25\%$ is too low (the corresponding price, $c_1 = 1.182$, is lower than the true market price), while $\sigma_2 = 35\%$ is too high. Through interpolation we can derive a better volatility estimate, σ_3, as

$$\sigma_3 = \sigma_1 + \frac{\sigma_2 - \sigma_1}{c_2 - c_1}(c_{\text{mkt}} - c_1) = 25\% + \frac{35\% - 25\%}{1.302 - 1.182}(1.264 - 1.182) = 31.8\%$$

By using σ_3 we obtain $c_3 = 1.262$, which is very close to the market value. By simply repeating the interpolation, the true value, $\sigma^* = 34\%$, could easily be derived. Since by using $\sigma^* = 34\%$ we obtain exactly $c = 1.264$ USD, 34% is the implied volatility of the 9 USD European call.

3.2 Simulation Approaches: Historical Simulation and Monte Carlo Simulation

The variance–covariance approach, although appealing for its simplicity, is not the only approach that can be used to measure market VaR. Frequently, instead, financial institutions use simulation methods, which can be particularly useful when the relationship between the value of the portfolio and market risk factors is nonlinear and nonmonotonic, as may happen for portfolios containing options. In this case, concentrating on 1.645 or 2.326 standard deviation shocks of the risk factors does not necessarily enable the risk manager to identify the maximum potential loss of the portfolio.

Instead, simulation methods calculate VaR by making certain assumptions on the (joint) distribution of underlying risk factors or benchmark asset returns, extract a sample from the joint distribution, and then revaluate the portfolio of assets, whose VaR should be measured according to each set of risk factors' values. By sorting simulated portfolio values in descending order, it is then possible to identify the desired percentile of the distribution of portfolio values and hence identify VaR. Before considering the different simulation methods, among which the most well-known are historical simulation and Monte Carlo simulation, it may be useful to point out the following.

- Unlike what a few think, simulation methods do not necessarily require portfolio full revaluation (i.e., repricing the portfolio exactly according to the new simulated market risk factors), but often are combined with a partial revaluation; i.e., they revaluate the portfolio through a simplified approach based on partial derivatives. This point is developed when dealing with options' VaR calculation in Section 3.3.
- While these methods are typically explained, in theory, in a one-dimensional setting, i.e., considering an asset exposed to a single risk factor, it is useful to discuss their pros and cons in the realistic case of a portfolio exposed to multiple risk factors. Consequently, evaluating the assumptions not only about marginal distributions and volatilities but also about dependence structure among different risk factors/benchmark assets is relevant.

3.2.1 Historical Simulation

Let us consider a portfolio of assets where w_i identifies the weight of asset i in the portfolio (please note that "assets" could be either individual securities or, more frequently in practice, the benchmark asset exposures obtained through the mapping process). Portfolio return r_P can be calculated as the weighted average of individual asset returns r_i; i.e.,

$$r_P = \sum_{i=1}^{n} w_i r_i$$

Historical simulation (HS) reconstructs a series of the current portfolio's returns by multiplying *current* portfolio weights by past asset returns. The result does not represent the historical return of the portfolio (since weights would have varied in the past), but the return the portfolio would have experienced had asset weights always remained constant. Maximum potential loss at the desired confidence level is then calculated directly by taking the desired percentile of the distribution of portfolio returns. According to the example in this chapter's introduction, if, for instance, the risk manager used a sample of 200 past returns and wanted to estimate 99% VaR, he would associate it to the third-lowest portfolio return in the 200-data sample.

Therefore, the basic assumption behind the HS method is that the joint return distribution of asset returns may be reasonably approximated by the past joint return distribution. As a consequence, the method has some clear advantages and disadvantages. Advantages include (1) its ease of implementation and communication, (2) the absence of explicit assumptions on the joint distribution of benchmark asset/risk factor returns, and (3) the ability to capture the risk of portfolios whose value is nonmonotonic relative to risk factors.

While the third advantage is common to other simulation techniques, as opposed to the variance–covariance approach, and will be discussed further when dealing with options' VaR, the first one is very intuitive. In its simplest form this method does not require estimating huge correlation matrixes or developing GARCH or EWMA estimates to model volatility behavior of the individual risk factor, since basically it assumes the return distribution to be stationary. At the same time, results from this VaR methodology can easily be understood and interpreted by any senior manager, even if he were unfamiliar with volatility-modeling techniques.

The second advantage is equally important but must be carefully understood. HS is not assumption free, since it assumes that the historical joint distribution is a reasonable proxy for the future distribution. Yet HS does not require assuming a joint normal distribution for asset returns, as required by the variance–covariance approach. In the case of single assets, empirical return distributions are usually close to the normal but not exactly normal. In particular, they usually show a higher probability of significantly negative returns than a normal distribution would predict (the left tail of the distribution is hence "fatter" than it should be). By using actual past returns, HS may account for fat tails on the single asset. But, most important, without assuming *joint* normality of asset returns, HS may consider effects such as correlation breakdown in cases of market shocks that cannot be considered in a variance–covariance approach (and that could be difficult and time consuming to model in a Monte Carlo simulation). If, for instance, country A's stock market proved to be relatively insensitive to country B's stock market behavior (i.e., correlation in normal market conditions is low) but also proved to react substantially in those days when stock market B experienced a sharp and sudden fall on days $t–k$ and $t–k'$ (i.e., correlation increases in market crises), the variance–covariance approach would assume the two markets to be jointly normally distributed with an intermediate value of correlation, which clearly fails to capture the nature of the dependence and interaction between the two markets. This more complex, and yet common, dependence structure can be modeled in a more elegant but time-consuming way through copulas, which we briefly discuss later. Yet HS represents a parsimonious way to account for this problem, since returns on days $t–k$ and $t–k'$ for both markets would both be markedly negative and would be jointly used to estimate portfolio returns on those days, thereby reproducing the dependence structure among the two markets.

In addition to these advantages, which make it widely used, HS has clear pitfalls (see, in particular, Pritsker 2001).

1. HS is clearly very sensitive to the choice of the length of the data sample: The longer the sample, the more precise the picture of return distribution but the less sensitive HS becomes to changes in market conditions. Moreover, HS displays an "echo effect" that may be even larger than the one described earlier for calculating simple moving average volatility. If the risk manager uses a 500-data sample (about two years of daily data) and a confidence level of 99%, then HS VaR would be the sixth-worst return in the sample. If there were seven markedly negative returns in the two subsequent months, the HS VaR estimate might remain the same until either a new substantially negative return enters the sample or any of the seven-worst returns drops out of the sample (in the latter case, estimated volatility would then fall substantially about 500 trading days after the shock, independent of market conditions).

2. Available historical series for many assets could be relatively short, making it difficult to estimate VaR at very high confidence levels (such as 99.97%) that, however, are frequently used in practice. While 99% is the confidence level used for calculating market risk capital requirements by those banks that adopt an internal model and is often used for setting VaR limits, higher levels, such as 99.97%, are commonly used to derive aggregated VaR estimates for the bank as a whole.

Unfortunately, it is impossible to use, say, 10,000 past daily portfolio returns (i.e., more than 38 years' worth) to identify VaR with the fourth-lowest return. Hence the desired percentile can be derived either through interpolation or by rescaling 99% VaR by assuming a certain shape for the portfolio distribution (e.g., by multiplying it by 1.47, which is approximately the ratio between the 0.03% and the 1% percentile for a normal distribution expressed in terms of the number of standard deviations). Both solutions have problems, since interpolation results would be very sensitive to the outcomes of just the two closest data points to the desired percentile, potentially generating a significant sampling error. Instead, by assuming a known distribution shape to rescale HS VaR, the advantage of avoiding assumptions on the distribution shape, which is relevant for HS, is almost lost.

3. HS assumes no change in either volatility or correlation through time, by assuming that the distribution is stationary. This is in contrast with empirical evidence that volatility does evolve through time and which is clearly considered, for instance, in a variance–covariance approach with EWMA volatility estimates.

3.2.2 Hybrid Approach

In order to solve at least some of the problems of HS methods, Boudoukh, Richardson, and Whitelaw (1998) proposed to associate to each of the past returns of the current portfolio calculated by HS a weight based on the same logic as EWMA, therefore giving higher weight to recent returns. As for EWMA, the weight assigned to the last return would be equal to $\lambda^0/(1 - \lambda) = 1/(1 - \lambda)$, while the preceding ones would be given an exponential weight of $\lambda^1/(1 - \lambda)$, $\lambda^2/(1 - \lambda)$, and so on. Portfolio returns would then be sorted in descending order, as for the HS method, and the risk manager would calculate accumulated weights of portfolio returns as he moves downward in the ranking of returns. VaR would be identified with the value for which the sum of weights becomes equal to or higher than the desired confidence level (or alternatively, and more precisely, with the interpolated value for which the sum of weights would be exactly equal to the desired confidence level).

By mixing the exponential weighting scheme of the RiskMetrics™ EWMA approach and the actual series of risk factor returns of historical simulation, the hybrid approach tries to combine the advantages of both models. In practice, however, it may blend some disadvantages of both models as well, depending on the value chosen for λ. As λ gets closer to 1, the hybrid approach results get closer and closer to HS (which is a special case with $\lambda = 1$, where all data are equally weighted). As λ diminishes, past shocks become less important and potentially the information about tail events or correlation breakdown may be more rapidly "forgotten" by the model.

3.2.3 Monte Carlo Simulations

While HS assume that historical return distributions could represent future return distributions, Monte Carlo simulations (MCS) require the risk manager to formally model both the marginal distributions of each asset's returns and the dependence structure among returns of different assets. After defining the shape and parameters of the joint distribution of benchmark assets, a random vector of values is extracted from the joint distribution and the portfolio value is revaluated accordingly. In this way, a simulated return distribution of the entire portfolio is derived so as to calculate directly the quantile (e.g., 1%) in order to identify percentage VaR at the desired confidence level.

In practice, MCS effectiveness may depend on a number of different issues.

1. How accurately are marginal (i.e., stand-alone) distributions for each asset modeled? (E.g., is the risk manager assuming a simple normal distribution with constant volatility, or is he fitting a fat-tailed distribution? Which goodness-of-fit tests are adopted to identify the "best" distribution?)
2. How is the dependence structure modeled? (E.g., is the risk manager assuming a joint multivariate distribution modeled through linear correlation or a more complex dependence structure?)
3. Which algorithms are used to generate random numbers?
4. How many simulation runs are used? How does the risk manager check whether results are stable?

While it is beyond the aim of this book to discuss all these topics in details, a few observations on each of them are useful. In fact, when deciding whether or not MCS should be adopted, a risk manager should first carefully consider *which*, and how sophisticated, simulations he could really implement in practice.

Starting from distribution-modeling issues 1 and 2, the risk manager could either assume the joint distribution is multivariate normal or try to fit marginal distribution data to other frequency distributions (e.g., a Student's *t* distribution, which allows for fatter tails than in the normal case, or many others) and then model the dependence structure among marginal distributions in more sophisticated ways (e.g., through copulas; see Section 3.4). If a multivariate normal distribution is used, then MCS would be unable to account for fat-tailed marginal distribution and would share all the limits inherent in the variance–covariance models' assumption that all risk factors or asset returns are jointly normally distributed. In practice, the reason why MCS are often run assuming multivariate normal joint distributions is that this makes both parameter estimation and simulation runs easier and faster than more sophisticated but computationally intensive solutions. Yet this simplification implies that only a part of theoretical MCS advantages are actually obtained.

Rejecting the joint multivariate normal assumption implies the needs to identify which frequency distribution best fits marginal data and to model the interdependence among different asset returns. In the case of fitting marginal data, the risk manager should first question whether a simple set of historical data should be considered (therefore implicitly assuming the return distribution is stationary) or whether historical data should be rescaled in some way to account for the difference between past and current volatility, if it is assumed to be time varying. Then, after the distribution to be fitted has been identified, the risk manager should select the group of candidate frequency distributions to be checked and the kind of test to be applied to select the best fit. While the chi-square goodness-of-fit test is a classical one, in some cases the risk manager may prefer other tests, such as the Anderson–Darling test, that concentrate, in particular, on how the theoretical distribution fits the empirical ones in the tail region, which (in certain cases) may be more relevant for risk management purposes (see Vose 1996). After identifying the optimal marginal distributions and their parameters, the risk manager should move to model the dependence among all the distributions. Obviously, going through this process may be quite time consuming, especially if the risk manager had to revise and check his calibration exercise frequently (let alone on a daily basis).

The third and fourth issues relate instead to how numbers are extracted and how many simulations should be run. The two topics are linked, as is well known since Boyle's (1977) first major contribution on Monte Carlo simulation for option pricing that discussed how variance-reduction techniques could help MCS results converge faster to the true fair value of the option. Unfortunately, the problem for VaR calculation is more complex since (1) it is typically multidimensional, so joint distributions rather than single assets' distributions should be reproduced, and (2) the risk manager is not concerned with the distribution mean only, as in option-pricing applications, but has to capture some extreme percentiles. Consequently, not all techniques that can be used to make the mean value converge faster may work successfully for VaR-oriented simulations. As a general suggestion, techniques that try to represent in a balanced way different quantiles of the distribution should be favored. For instance, stratified sampling or Latin hypercube techniques divide the frequency distribution into n portions with the same probability and extract numbers so as to guarantee that each portion is equally represented in the simulation.

In short, when evaluating MCS pros and cons it is important to consider that MCS are far from being all equal and that they may have substantially different levels of sophistication. Attempting some generalization anyway, among the major advantages we can cite the following.

- Like HS, MCS may solve problems linked to the nonmonotonicity of the relationship between the value of risk factors/benchmark assets and the value of the bank's portfolio (i.e., they identify big losses even when they do not occur as a consequence of extreme market events).
- Unlike HS, MCS may be calculated for any confidence level, provided that a sufficiently high number of simulation runs has been made. They can also enable one to calculate other relevant risk metrics different from VaR, such as the expected shortfall (see Section 3.5).
- If marginal and joint distribution fitting is conducted in a very careful and sophisticated manner, MCS could account for non-normal marginal distributions and for complex dependence structures among asset returns (e.g., joint crashes in different markets).

At the same time, there are shortcomings too.

- Since having a proper fitting of marginal and especially joint distributions is very burdensome, MCS are usually run (at least in the multivariate case) by making relatively simple assumptions about the joint distribution of risk factor/benchmark asset returns. As a consequence, they may fail to represent phenomena such as fat tails for marginal distributions or higher correlation in market crash scenarios (that sometimes may be captured instead by simpler historical simulations).
- MCS are, in general, more computationally intensive than HS, due to the need first to estimate distribution parameters and then to run the simulation.
- The overall effectiveness of an MCS depends on a number of elements (e.g., distribution fitting, random number extraction) that may be difficult to explain to nonspecialists, making overall MCS results harder to communicate and evaluate than HS-based VaR measures.

3.2.4 Filtered Historical Simulations

A variant of MCS and HS that tries to combine features of both is represented by filtered historical simulations (FHS), which was proposed by Hull and White (1998) and Barone-

Adesi, Giannopoulos, and Vosper (1999). The basic idea is to adopt a GARCH-type model of portfolio variance. Taking a series of n past returns, one can estimate the GARCH model with past data and then standardize each past return, $R_{t-\tau}$, based on the estimated standard deviation for the same day; in this way a series of past standardized returns (which do not necessarily follow a normal distribution or any other known distribution) are derived. At the end of the sample, one could obtain the volatility estimate for the next day, σ_{t+1}. Rather than generating a distribution of future returns by assuming a certain return distribution, the risk manager can extract, with replacement, past values of historical standardized returns. In this way the ability to generate as many scenarios as needed and to account for time-varying volatility can be combined while avoiding any formal assumption on return distribution. If the risk manager needs to generate a distribution of returns over a T-day horizon, he could simply build n paths of T daily returns where the same GARCH-type model is used in each of the T days to estimate next-day volatility given the random return of the preceding day.

3.3   Value at Risk for Option Positions

3.3.1   Problems in Option VaR Measurement

Option contracts comprise a wide variety of financial contracts. In the simpler case of a plain-vanilla call (or put) option, the holder pays a fixed premium to the option's writer and then retains the right to buy (or sell) a given amount of the underlying asset at a given price — defined as strike price — in the future, either on a single date (for European options) or on any date before maturity (for American options). Therefore, potential gains and losses for the holder of the option are asymmetric. In fact, maximum loss is equal to the premium paid (plus interest, if the premium is paid up front) if the option is not exercised at or before maturity, while gains are almost unlimited if the underlying price rises (for the call option) or falls (for the put option). The opposite is true for the writer. This asymmetric feature intuitively implies that options' reaction to changes in underlying asset prices would also not be symmetric and is one of the clear sources of problems when estimating options' VaR. More precisely, the three key issues are the following.

1. The relationship between the price of the underlying asset and the value of the option is nonlinear (and may be convex or concave, depending on whether the trader is long or short the option).
2. Moreover, the same relationship may also be nonmonotonic, so extreme losses do not always occur as a consequence of extreme movements of the underlying asset.
3. The price of the option is also exposed to other risk factors, such as time decay and the level of implied volatility.

The first and the third problems are very easy to explain. Let us consider a simple European call option on a non-dividend-paying stock, whose value c can be evaluated through the Black–Scholes–Merton (BSM) formula,

$$c = SN(d) - e^{-rT} X N(d - \sigma\sqrt{T})$$

where S is the spot price of the underlying asset, r is the risk-free rate, T is the option's time to maturity, $N(x)$ represents the cumulative distribution function of a standard normal calculated in x, σ is the underlying asset expected return volatility, and d is

$$d = \frac{\ln(S/X) + (r + \frac{1}{2}\sigma^2)T}{\sigma\sqrt{T}}$$

The value of the option is evidently a function of a number of variables (S, σ, r, T) and hence is exposed to multiple risk factors. And, as is easy to check, it is nonlinear with respect to S (see again Figures 3-2 and 3-3 about the delta approximation for mapping purposes in the variance–covariance framework). The nonmonotonicity problem can instead be explained through an example. Imagine a trader who buys both a call and a put option on Microsoft with a strike price equal to 25 USD (which is also assumed to be the current stock price) and a maturity equal to two weeks. If Microsoft stock either rises or falls, the trader would be able to exercise one of the two options he bought, while the worst possible event for him would be if Microsoft stock remained at the current 25 USD price until maturity. Here, maximum potential losses would not be associated with extreme market movements (so the variance–covariance approach, which considers what happens if the underlying asset price has a 2σ or 2.32σ adverse return, would fail to work properly).

3.3.2 Potential Solutions for Option VaR Measurement

Given the different problems we considered, the chief alternative approaches (see Table 3-2A) can be evaluated, depending on whether and how they address each of these problems. Please note that the nonlinearity issue can be handled in two different ways. The first solution is repricing the option through its appropriate pricing formula; this is known

TABLE 3-2A A Synthesis of the Chief Possible Approaches to Option VaR Measurement

How is option value reaction to risk factor changes calculated? (→nonlinearity)	Which kind(s) of shocks are taken into consideration? (→multiple riskfactors)	How is the relevant percentile identified? (→nonmonotonicity)	
		By linking option position return distribution to a known (cumulative) frequency distribution	By simulation, ordering portfolio values and extracting the desired percentile
Linear approximation (delta only)	Underlying asset price only	Delta-normal RiskMetrics™ — J.P. Morgan (1996)	
Quadratic approximation (delta-gamma)	Underlying asset price only Underlying asset price and implied volatility (and/or time decay and risk-free rate)	Britten-Jones and Schaefer (1999) Zangari (1996)	Delta-gamma HS/MCS Delta-gamma-vega(-theta) HS/MCS Grid MCS (Pritsker 1997)
Full valuation	Underlying asset price only Underlying asset price and implied volatility (and/or time decay and risk-free rate)		Full valuation MCS/HS — underlying price only Full valuation MCS/HS

as *full revaluation*. The second solution (*partial revaluation*) is to approximate the new value of the option through a Taylor expansion using the partial derivatives of the option-pricing formula relative to the different risk factors. The key derivatives — also known as greeks — are relative to the underlying asset price (being delta and gamma, the first and second partial derivatives, respectively), to implied volatility (vega), to the remaining time to maturity (theta). Derivatives of other risk factors can be estimated, depending on the kind of option contract. Risk managers adopting partial revaluation may consider either some or all of these derivatives, depending on how many risk factors they want to include when calculating the options' VaR.

The first, and simpler, solution is represented by the variance–covariance approach, which has already been described and can be conceived of as a way to transform the option portfolio distribution into another well-known distribution (the underlying asset distribution) through a simple linear approximation. Britten-Jones and Schaefer (1999) and Zangari (1996) have proposed alternative ways to obtain a known distribution through more precise approximations. Britten-Jones and Schaefer prove that through a delta-gamma approximation a chi-square return distribution can be obtained, while Zangari (1996) suggests calculating the first four moments of the distribution of the option portfolio value and then matching it to a known distribution with the same four moments. Anyway, in practice the typical alternative to the simplifications of the variance–covariance method is represented by simulation methods. In theory, the first best solution is the one at the bottom right corner of Table 3-2: a full valuation method considering all risk factors (which could be generated either by an HS or by an MCS). In practice, however, full valuation is time consuming and sometimes virtually impossible, especially in the case of exotic options for which no closed pricing formula is available so that option prices themselves are estimated through a Monte Carlo simulation. In this case it is impossible to run an MCS where after extracting the first set of new risk factors another MCS should be run to price the option in the first scenario only. In fact, the number of required simulation runs would grow exponentially. It would then be unavoidable to approximate the changes in the option values through partial derivatives. In the case of a delta-gamma HS or MCS, the changes in option portfolio value ΔV_{pf} are approximated as

$$\Delta V_{pf} \approx \text{delta} \cdot \Delta S + \frac{\text{gamma}}{2} \cdot \Delta S^2$$

where ΔS represents changes in the prices of the underlying asset price that can be generated through either MCS or HS. In order to include more than one risk factor, the Taylor expansion formula for ΔV_{pf} can be extended to consider the impact of changes in implied volatility and time to maturity:

$$\Delta V_{pf} \approx \text{delta} \cdot \Delta S + \frac{\text{gamma}}{2} \cdot \Delta S^2 + \text{vega} \cdot \Delta\sigma + \text{theta} \cdot \Delta t$$

However, using multiple risk factors requires defining how to simulate joint shocks of the underlying asset price and implied volatility (while Δt is clearly fixed). This explains why in this case HS is largely preferred to MCS, since modeling joint changes in S and σ is easy with HS (where they are simply derived from history) but technically challenging with MCS (which would need to define some joint distribution function). This is even clearer for banks with wide portfolios including interest rate options and/or options on a number of different underlying assets, since formally modeling the joint behavior of many benchmark asset returns and many volatilities gets more and more complex.

The only extra problem that some banks with complex portfolios may try to consider is the risk that an option portfolio's partial derivatives may change substantially as a consequence of either price or implied volatility changes or both. Even in the case of a simple delta-gamma approximation, some portfolios may change the sign of gamma if the price of the underlying asset moves.

Consider two weeks before expiration a simple bull spread strategy based on buying a 13 USD call and selling a 13.50 USD call on a stock trading at 13 USD. Figure 3-4 reports the payoff of the bull spread at maturity, the bull spread value today (thick line), and its value after one week (assuming no change in implied volatility). By looking at the two curves expressing the value of the position before maturity it is possible to see that while for $S = 13$ USD the curve is convex (i.e., gamma, the second derivative, is positive), the position becomes concave (i.e., negative gamma) as the price of the underlying moves up to 13.50 USD or more.

In this case a delta-gamma-vega approximation based on conditions at $S = 13$ would model option porftolio values as if the second derivative gamma were positive for any possible value of S and would hence always approximate it with an convex function. Changes in the sign of option greeks, which can occur even with simple portfolios, may be even more substantial with certain kinds of exotic options, in particular with knockout barrier options.

One possible solution suggested by Pritsker (1997) is to adopt a grid Monte Carlo simulation, where the portfolio is fully revaluated and greeks are recalculated in a given set of combinations of underlying asset price and implied volatility levels (see Figure 3-5). Labeling (S_1, σ_1) the couple of values for underlying price and volatility that are randomly extracted in the first simulation run, the method works by calculating the approximated value of the portfolio given (S_1, σ_1) as a weighted average of the values that can be derived through approximation from the closest points in the grid, which are four in the (S_1, σ_1) case and only two in the second run (S_2, σ_2). In this way, provided the points of the grid are carefully chosen, the different values for greeks can be considered in the overall simulation while avoiding the burden of a full valuation.

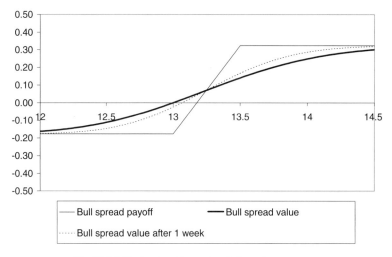

FIGURE 3-4   Example of changing gamma.

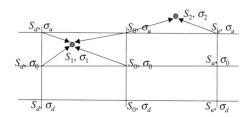

FIGURE 3-5   Example of the grid Monte Carlo methodology.

3.4 Extreme Value Theory and Copulas

When modeling portfolio return distribution, the risk manager should be concerned in particular with extreme events that happen in the left tail of the return distribution. At the same time, when considering a joint return distribution, he may be concerned with the probability that two different markets might crash at the same time, since they can show a higher correlation in strong downside movements than they can in normal conditions. Assuming a simple joint multivariate normal distribution (as is typical in the variance–covariance approach and sometimes in MCS too) may fail to account for both problems. The first problem, i.e., how to model more precisely the extreme tail of a distribution, can be addressed by extreme-value theory, while copulas may help the risk manager in modeling the joint distribution of asset returns in a more flexible way.

3.4.1 Extreme-Value Theory

Extreme-value theory (EVT) is devoted to modeling extreme values of frequency distributions. The crucial idea is that the extreme tail of a large number of distributions can be approximated by the so-called generalized Pareto distribution (GPD). The risk manager could then try to fit real data to the GPD in order better to measure extreme portfolio losses. In order to estimate it, one should first standardize the return series (e.g., through a GARCH model) and then define a certain threshold u identifying the region isolating extreme events. Standardizing returns is necessary not only because asset return variance is in general not constant, but also because most EVT results assume that returns are independent and identically distributed, which would clearly not be true for raw return series. Therefore, one should first standardize returns, then estimate a standardized extreme return at the desired confidence level, and finally rescale it by multiplying them for current portfolio volatility. Defining the threshold is critical, since, on one hand, parameter estimation would be based only on data over the threshold and hence it should not be too high; on the other hand, EVT results apply on the extreme tail only, which implies that u should not be too low. In practice, u is often chosen so that only a small percentage of standardized returns (e.g., 5%) exceed the threshold. The cumulative distribution G of the GPD is a function of return x and parameters ξ and β:

$$G(x;\xi;\beta) = \begin{cases} 1-(1+\xi x/\beta)^{-1/\xi} & \text{if } \xi \neq 0 \\ 1-e^{(-x/\beta)} & \text{if } \xi = 0 \end{cases}$$

with $\beta > 0$ always and $x \geq u$ if $\xi \geq 0$ or $u \leq x \leq u - \beta/\xi$ if $\xi < 0$ (for simplicity, we would assume here that x and u are negative returns, i.e., they are losses rather than returns).

The case that is relevant in finance is that of distributions with fat tails, corresponding to positive values for ξ. If one assumes $\xi > 0$, then VaR estimation using the GPD is quite easy. In fact, VaR in percentage terms can be expressed as the product of estimated return standard deviation σ_t at time t times the quantile of the standardized return distribution for a given confidence level $1 - \alpha$, $F_{1-\alpha}^{-1}$:

$$\mathrm{VaR}_{t,\%} = \sigma_t \cdot F_{1-\alpha}^{-1}$$

It can be shown (see Christoffersen 2003 for a clear and concise demonstration) that the standardized quantile is simply equal to

$$F_{1-a}^{-1} = u \left[\frac{a}{(N_u/N)} \right]^{-\xi}$$

where u is the threshold, α depends on the desired confidence level, N_u/N represents the frequency of data in the sample of size N that exceeds the threshold u, and φ can be estimated simply as

$$\xi = (1/N_u) \sum_{i=1}^{N_u} \ln(y_i/u)$$

where y_i represents each of the N_u observations over the threshold u. In this way it is quite straightforward to use, say, the worst 5% of returns to fit the GPD and then to calculate VaR at a 99% or 99.9% confidence level. We should just remember that the final estimate may be sensitive to both the threshold u and how returns have been standardized before starting the analysis. Failing to account for unstable return variance when standardizing the data may imply a poor GPD fitting no matter how carefully subsequent steps have been made.

3.4.2 Copulas

Let us imagine that a risk manager is measuring the risk of an equity portfolio invested in equal parts in two stocks, A and B. He knows that each of the stocks has a given probability $p_{A,10\%}$ and $p_{B,10\%}$ of losing more than 10% in one day, but he is concerned with estimating the probability $p_{A,10\%\text{-}B,10\%}$ that both stocks may jointly lose more than 10%. Typically, solving this problem requires either simply using historical data or defining a form for the joint distribution function of A and B returns. A simple assumption is to assume that they are jointly normally distributed. But what happens if the risk manager knows this is not the case, e.g., since both A and B returns show fat tails and are better approximated by a fat-tailed distribution such as the Student's-t with a proper number of degrees of freedom? It would be very convenient if it were possible to express the joint probability that A and B have a return lower than -10% as a function C of the two marginal probabilities, in a form such as

$$p_{A,10\%\text{-}B,10\%} = C(p_{A,10\%}, p_{B,10\%})$$

This is the intuition behind copulas. They can be conceived of as functions that express a joint probability distribution as a function of the marginal (i.e., stand-alone individual) distributions. In this way it is possible to disentangle entirely the problem of estimating the best distribution to fit marginal data for, say, stock A or B returns, from the issue of modeling the dependence between stock A and B returns, which can be handled even if the return distributions of A and B are completely different. Sklar's (1959) fundamental theorem states that any joint distribution can be expressed in copula forms, and vice versa, that each copula using marginal probability distributions as arguments underlies a joint distribution. Of course, copula functions should satisfy certain properties. As an example, given a bivariate copula $C(x, y)$ as a function of marginal probabilities x and y of two different events, if the probability of one of the two events were 1, then the copula should be equal to the other argument, since this would represent the probability of the joint event; if either x or y is zero, then $C(x, y)$ should be zero too, since the joint probability of the two events is zero.

Copulas are therefore very important for a risk manager for at least three reasons. First, they can be used to aggregate distributions with very different marginal frequency distributions, so they are a natural candidate to solve problems such as the aggregation of market, credit, operational, and other risks, which are discussed in Chapter 6. Second, in the case of market risk they can be used to model the potential risk of higher correlation in crash phases, which is entirely missed when assuming that returns are jointly normally distributed and that dependence can be measured with the linear correlation coefficient ρ (as in the variance–covariance approach); see in particular Embrechts, McNeil, and Straumann (1999). If two markets are mildly correlated in normal conditions but heavily correlated in crash phases the, "average" ρ estimated by data would fail to give a picture of actual potential losses in distress phases. Instead, the phenomenon of higher correlation in crash phases (which is linked to the statistical concept of *tail correlation*) can be captured by copulas. A third reason to be interested in copulas is that many products whose value depends on joint events (e.g., basket credit derivatives or collateralized debt obligations that are linked to multiple joint defaults of different obligors, multi-asset equity options) are now frequently being priced with copulas. Just checking the fairness of traders' estimated prices therefore requires an understanding of copula techniques.

Unfortunately, defining which is the optimal copula function to describe a joint distribution function, especially in the multivariate case, and estimating its parameters is not an easy and immediate task. The interested reader may refer to Nelsen (1999), Embrechts (2000), and Cherubini, Luciano, and Vecchiato (2004) for a more detailed analysis of the theoretical and empirical issues related to copulas. The only simple comment needed here is that practical applications require a careful analysis of the kind of data that can be used to estimate the optimal copulas and its parameters. In plain words, there may be the risk of being so concentrated on the technical issues of copula estimation and forgetting to check whether the data have been standardized or not to account for time-varying variance, whether the sample size is reasonable, and whether data frequency is suitable for reproducing dependence among returns of assets that may not be traded simultaneously. Again, any error in this phase could impact final copula choice and parameter estimation, with unpredictable results on the final VaR outcome.

3.5 Expected Shortfall and the Problem of VaR Nonsubadditivity

Although VaR considers portfolio returns in extreme regions of the frequency distribution, it has the clear limit that it considers only what the maximum loss that can be exceeded is in only a small percentage α of potential cases, but it says nothing about how large the loss may be in those cases. In other words, while it identifies the maximum potential loss apart from catastrophic losses, it does not measure the potential size of catastrophic losses. The informational content of the left α portion of portfolio returns is therefore destroyed.

Expected shortfall (ES) is a measure that can be used to give the risk manager exactly the information he or she needs concerning the average size of losses in the worst α region of the frequency distribution. If ES is measured with the same α as VaR, it expresses the average size of losses exceeding VaR; i.e., adopting the same notation we used at the beginning of this chapter,

$$ES_{1-a} = E\lfloor V_0 - V | V_0 - V > VaR_{1-a} \rfloor$$

Interest in the ES measure is for both practical and theoretical reasons. The practical argument is that the information about the average loss over the VaR threshold is relevant for the risk manager to understand better the risks the bank is taking and to discriminate among desks that may have a similar VaR but very different potential catastrophic losses. The theoretical reason is that Artzner et al. (1999) have shown that VaR lacks a very desirable property, i.e., subadditivity, which is instead possessed by ES. A generic risk measure g is subadditive if, for any portfolios (or assets) X and Y, $g(X + Y) \leq g(X) + g(Y)$; i.e., the risk of the combination of X and Y is never greater than the sum of the individual risks of X and Y. This is clearly true for VaR if multivariate returns are normally distributed or at least if their joint distribution is elliptic (a particular case of which is the joint normal distribution). In fact, in the multivariate normal case, VaR for a portfolio of two assets as shown in section 3.1.4 is equal to

$$VaR_p = MV_p \cdot k \cdot \sigma_p = \sqrt{VaR_A^2 + VaR_B^2 + 2VaR_A VaR_B \rho_{A,B}} \leq VaR_A + VaR_B$$

Unfortunately, however, VaR is not subadditive in general for any possible joint distribution of asset returns. Artzner et al. (1999) introduced a definition of "coherent" risk measure identifying some requisites an ideal risk measure should satisfy, including subadditivity. Since VaR is not subadditive in general, it is therefore not a coherent risk measure, unlike expected shortfall, which possesses this desirable property. Hence, it has been claimed that expected shortfall should substitute VaR entirely as a risk measure and also replace it in risk-adjusted performance measurement and as a tool for capital allocation.

The perspective we adopt in this book is quite pragmatic. While the lack of subadditivity is a serious conceptual flaw, identifying the cases when departure from elliptic distributions is so strong that VaR becomes nonsubadditive in practice is still an open empirical issue. Moreover, VaR is now so widespread and relatively well understood in practice (and also in some way incorporated in advanced internal models for capital requirement purposes) that it is difficult to imagine substituting it abruptly with expected shortfall. Therefore, we would like to point out (1) that ES should be considered an important complement for VaR, providing extra useful information for the risk manager, and (2) that when calculating VaR for a portfolio, the potential nonsubadditivity problem should be taken into account if the joint distribution is markedly non-normal.

In order to provide extra value, ES should of course be calculated by careful modeling of the extreme left tail of the return distribution. In contrast, if the risk manager assumed a zero-mean normal distribution, ES would be a simple multiple of the standard deviation of returns, exactly like VaR (again see Christoffersen 2003). ES and VaR would then be

BACK-TESTING MARKET RISK MODELS

proportional, and it would be difficult to claim that the value added of controlling both variables is substantial. Instead, the situation would be different if for any portfolio a proper EVT analysis were conducted in order to measure as precisely as possible the left tail of the return distribution.

3.6 Back-Testing Market Risk Models

After building a market risk measurement model, there is a clear need to check its performance. Back-testing is devoted precisely to comparing forecasts from the market risk measurement model with actual portfolio returns. The days in which actual losses exceed VaR are usually called "exceptions." By checking the frequency of exceptions, the quality of the market risk measurement models can be evaluated.

3.6.1 *Which Series Should Be Considered? Actual versus Theoretical Portfolio Returns*

The first relevant issue in back-testing is which portfolio return series should be compared with VaR ex ante estimates. The first candidate is the return series derived from the real trading P&L of the desk whose VaR has been measured. The second candidate is the theoretical portfolio return series by taking portfolio weights at the end of each day t (i.e., the weights based on which VaR for day $t + 1$ had been calculated) and by multiplying them by the vector of day $t + 1$ asset returns. Which of the two should be compared with VaR to back-test the model? The answer is both, since the risk manager could obtain different information from each.

In fact, if the aim is to check whether the volatility forecasts produced by the model are correct and reactive to new information, the theoretical return series is the right choice. Yet also comparing VaR estimates also with the real returns derived from the desk's P&L and carefully understanding the differences between the two return series may be important for the risk manager's ultimate aim, i.e., to control *actual,* rather than theoretical, losses his institution may face. Potential differences between theoretical and real portfolio return series, and hence in the frequency of losses exceeding ex ante VaR estimates, can be explained by many factors, including the following.

- The desks may be involved in substantial intraday trading, so that actual P&L variability may be high even if day closing exposures (and hence VaR) were small.
- Portfolio mapping may have been poorly conducted, so the real portfolio is markedly different from the mapped theoretical portfolio whose VaR is calculated.
- Actual P&L may comprise nontrading profits and commissions, which imply no market risk but shift the return distribution upward, therefore making losses exceeding VaR more unlikely.
- The portfolio may comprise illiquid assets whose bid and ask prices are markedly different from midmarket theoretical prices. Hence, if liquidation risk is not considered by the market risk model, the chances of exceeding VaR are higher in those days in which losing trades are closed and losses are realized. This effect would be absent in the theoretical P&L, which would consider asset returns based on midmarket prices.

Note that while some elements (e.g., intraday trading) may make actual losses exceed VaR more frequently than theoretical losses, others (e.g., inclusion of nontrading profits) may work in the opposite direction. In any case, using both series and trying to understand differences are important in avoiding, for instance, applying a perfect risk measurement technique to a poorly mapped portfolio, in which case back-testing the theoretical return series only would confirm the good quality of the model even if it is unable to predict the bank's actual potential losses. Practices among large banks are quite diverse, at least as far as disclosed data are concerned. For instance, some banks, such as ABN-AMRO, clearly explain that their back-testing exercise is conducted on both series. Others, such as Credit Suisse, state that "profit and loss used for back-testing purposes is a subset of actual trading revenue and includes only the profit and loss effects due to financial market variables" while excluding "items such as fees, commissions, certain provisions, and any trading subsequent to the previous night's positions. It is appropriate to compare this measure with VaR for back-testing purposes, since VaR assesses only the potential change in position value due to overnight movements in financial market variables" (Credit Suisse 2005 Annual Report, p. 79). Finally, banks such as J.P. Morgan Chase test daily VaR against market risk–related revenue that "is defined as the change in value of the mark-to-market trading portfolios plus any trading-related net interest income, brokerage commissions, underwriting fee, or other revenue" (J.P. Morgan Chase 2005 Annual Report, p. 76); a similar definition is also used by Citigroup.

However, examples of back-test results can easily be found in the annual reports of most large banks. For instance, Figure 3-6 presents an example from the Credit Suisse 2005 Annual Report. In this case, even if VaR estimates change as volatility changes, daily losses in 2005 were never higher than estimated VaR. At least in theory, however, a bank should not desire having no exceptions at all, but rather having the "desired" number of exceptions according to the confidence interval that has been chosen, since the absence of exceptions could imply that the risk manager is adopting over, conservative volatility estimates. In some banks, however, the total absence of exceptions in some years is also largely explained by the fact that the mean of the distribution of trading revenues is not equal to zero, as a consequence of the mixture of pure proprietary trading profits

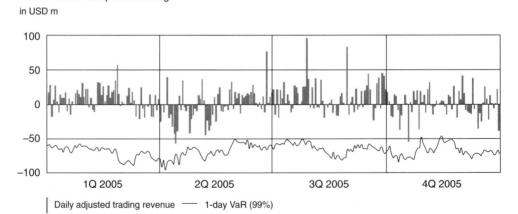

Credit Suisse Group back-testing[a]
in USD m

| Daily adjusted trading revenue   —— 1-day VaR (99%)

[a]Excludes Neue Aagauer Bank and the independent private banks.

FIGURE 3-6   Example of back-testing based on P&L data.
Source: Credit Suisse 2005 Annual Report.

and the intermediation bid–ask spreads earned by large banks in their trading activity. For instance, we can learn from annual report data that at Deutsche Bank the percentage of days reporting a trading profit was 93% in both 2004 and 2005, while for Barclays Capital the percentage was, respectively, 98% and 97%. The mean trading profit was largely positive, and unsurprisingly no exceptions (i.e., daily losses greater than VaR) were reported in either 2004 or 2005.

3.6.2 Back-Testing VaR Forecasts: Unconditional Accuracy and Independence

Back-testing of market risk measurement models can be conducted in different ways, depending on whether one wants to back-test VaR estimates only, ES estimates, or the entire return distribution. Considering the need for synthesis, we will describe VaR back-tests only; the interested reader could refer to Christoffersen (2003, pp. 181–194) for a more detailed analysis of this topic.

In order to test the accuracy of VaR forecasts, one should first check whether the frequency of losses exceeding ex ante estimated VaR (defined here as "exceptions") is equal or close enough to the desired confidence level. In order to check that, it is possible to define a time series $\{I_t\}_{t=1}^{T}$ for each of the T days over which the back-test is run and where I_t is set equal to 1 on any day in which there is an exception and to zero otherwise. If the model were perfect, the sequence of exceptions should be independently distributed, with the same probability of occurrence, equal to α, and the probability of observing T_1 exceptions in a sample of size T according to the binomial distribution is

$$\Pr(T_1; \alpha, T) = \binom{T}{T_1} \alpha^{T_1}(1-\alpha)^{T-T_1}$$

If the model were accurate, the actual frequency of exceptions in the sample ($\pi = T_1/T$) should be equal to α. Therefore, the null hypothesis $\pi = \alpha$ can be tested by calculating the likelihood ratio statistic for unconditional accuracy ($\mathrm{LR_{ua}}$), given by

$$\mathrm{LR_{ua}}(\alpha) = -2\ln\{\alpha^{T_1}(1-\alpha)^{T-T_1}/[\pi^{T_1}(1-\pi)^{T-T_1}]\}$$

which has asymptotically a $\chi^2(1)$ distribution. Intuitively, if $\alpha = \pi$, then $\mathrm{LR_{ua}}$ should be zero. However, this test checks only whether VaR models attain on average the desired percentage of exceptions, but it does not check whether exceptions are serially independent or instead whether they tend to occur in clusters, implying that the model is correct on average but slow to react to new information. If exceptions were clustered, an exception occurring on day t would imply a higher-than-average probability of having an exception on day $t + 1$. We can therefore consider the time series of exceptions $\{I_t\}_{t=1}^{T}$ and test the null hypothesis of serial independence against first-order Markov dependence. The likelihood function in case of first-order dependence would be

$$L_A = (1 - \pi_{01})^{T_{00}} \pi_{01}{}^{T_{01}}(1 - \pi_{11})^{T_{10}} \pi_{11}{}^{T_{11}}$$

where T_{ij} is the number of observations in state j in period $t + 1$ after state i in period t (1 stands for an exception, 0 for a nonexception), π_{01} represents the observed frequency of exceptions preceded by a nonexception, and π_{11} represents the observed frequency of exceptions preceded by another exception. Intuitively, π_{01} and π_{11} should be equal if independence holds. Under the null hypothesis, therefore, the relevant likelihood function is given by $L_0 = (1 - \pi)^{T_{00}+T_{10}}\pi^{T_{01}+T_{11}}$, where π denotes the observed frequency of exceptions. The likelihood ratio statistic for independence of exceptions (LR_{ind}) is

$$LR_{ind}(\alpha) = -2\ln[L_0/L_A]$$

and is asymptotically $\chi^2(1)$ distributed. The two tests can be combined into a test for correct *conditional* accuracy of the model: The likelihood ratio LR_{ca} is obtained by simply adding the two likelihood ratios for unconditional accuracy and independence:

$$LR_{ca}(\alpha) = LR_{ua}(\alpha) + LR_{ind}(\alpha)$$

It follows asymptotically a $\chi^2(2)$ distribution. In order to understand whether the model can be accepted, likelihood ratios should be translated into P-values (which can be defined as the probability of identifying a sample that is even more distant from the null hypotheses, provided the latter is true). Of course, if this probability is low enough, then the risk manager should reject the model as inaccurate. Since the test has a chi-square distribution only asymptotically, P-values can be calculated directly from the cumulative function of the chi-square distribution only when the sample is very large, while in the case of small samples it is better to estimate them through simulation. In practice, the risk manager should extract $n - 1$ random samples of $\{I_t\}_{t=1}^T$ sequences (i.e., sequences with the same size T of the real sample) from the theoretical distribution of exceptions, calculate likelihood ratio statistics for those sampled distributions, and calculate the P-value of the real $\{I_t\}_{t=1}^T$ sequence as the share of simulated LR values that are greater than the LR for the actual series.

3.7 Internal VaR Models and Market Risk Capital Requirements

While so far we have discussed only how VaR for market risk can be measured from the risk manager's viewpoint, we must remember that market risk for the trading book is also subject to minimum regulatory capital requirements (MRCRs), even if, under certain conditions, banks' internal risk measurement models can be validated by supervisors and accepted as a tool to measure MRCRs too. The key reference for MRCRs for market risks is represented by the "Amendment to the Capital Accord to Incorporate Market Risks" issued by the Basel Committee in January 1996 and revised in November 2005 in order also to take into consideration the effects of the Basel II Capital Accord (Basel Committee 2006a). MRCRs apply to interest-rate-related instruments and equities in the trading book and foreign exchange and commodity risk positions throughout the bank. Trading book is defined as all "positions in financial instruments and commodities held either with trading intent or in order to hedge other elements of the trading book. . . . Financial instruments must be either free of any restrictive covenants on their tradability or able to be hedged completely. In addition, positions should be frequently and accurately valued, and the portfolio should be actively managed" (Basel Committee 2006a).

The Market Risk Amendment proposes two alternative ways to calculate MRCRs for market risks. The first one is a standardized approach, according to which capital charges are first calculated separately for interest rate, equity, currency, commodity, and option-related risks and then simply added up in a building-block approach. Capital charges for each kind of risk are based on standard charges for the banks' net exposure: for instance, for interest rate risk, a set of different time bands in terms of either maturity or duration are defined and different percentage charges are applied to net exposures in different time bands, defined at different levels of aggregation, so as to link capital charges with the interest rate exposure mismatch of the trading book of the bank. A charge is also considered in order to cover specific risk, i.e., adverse potential movements in security prices driven by issuer-specific factors (rather than market-wide factors). The standardized approach considers different possible solutions for option treatment, the general principle being that banks with larger option books should adopt more sophisticated standardized MRCR techniques.

The second possible solution is represented instead by the use of an internal market risk measurement model, provided that a number of qualitative and quantitative requirements are satisfied and after an explicit validation of the model by the bank's supervisory authority. In particular, qualitative requirements include standards for management oversight on the use of models and their involvement in the risk control process, the existence of an independent risk control unit responsible for the risk management system, the existence of continuous and rigorous processes for both back-testing and stress testing, and minimum guidelines for identifying key risk factors for risk mapping. Quantitative standards specify that VaR should be calculated on a 10-day horizon, at a 99% confidence level and using a minimum historical sample period of one year. It is allowed simply to rescale 1-day into 10-day VaR through the simple square-root-of-time rule. The 10-day 99% VaR should then be multiplied by a multiplication factor equal to at least 3 and subject to an unconditional accuracy test. In fact, if during each year the days in which losses exceed VaR is markedly higher than expected, the multiplication factor can be raised (Basel Committee 1996). The 1996 Market Risk Amendment has been extremely important since it first allowed banks to adopt internal models to calculate MRCR as an alternative to standardized requirements, introducing the approach that was later further extended by the Basel II Capital Accord and providing to many banks an extra incentive to invest money and effort in developing their market risk management systems.

3.8 Stress Tests

As a complement to VaR and possibly ES measures, a risk manager should conduct regular stress test analyses. A stress test can be defined as a technique to assess the vulnerability of a portfolio or of a financial institution to exceptional but plausible events (Committee on the Global Financial System 2000). Under the definition of stress test, a wide variety of techniques can be considered. If we examine stress tests at the single-portfolio level (rather than at the level of the whole financial institution), we can basically distinguish between univariate sensitivity tests aimed at understanding the impact of a substantial shock on a single variable and scenario analysis based on a set of joint combined shocks of a number of different variables. Of course, scenario analyses might be more relevant for assessing potential extreme events that cannot be captured by market risk models (e.g., cases of correlation breakdown), but their construction is more subjective and requires a lot of judgment and experience. Univariate or multivariate shocks are typically defined either as arbitrary substantial shocks to key risk factors (e.g., a ±200-basis-point shift of the interest rate curve, a high number of standard deviations shock to the stock market) or as significant past shocks whose effect is simulated on the current portfolio (e.g., by simulating the effect of the October 1987 stock market crash or of the 1998 Russian crisis). ES calculations themselves are sometimes considered a stress-testing exercise. Yet while even ES is calculated according to current conditions and assumptions on return distributions that are derived in some way from history, stress tests should also consider events that may fail to be adequately represented by past data already incorporated in market risk models. Berkowitz (2000) usefully points out that the purpose of stress testing should be (1) to simulate shocks that are more likely to occur than the historical database suggests, (2) to simulate shocks that have never occurred (provided, of course, that they are plausible), (3) to simulate shocks reflecting the chance that statistical patterns may break down in some way, (4) to simulate shocks that reflect some structural break that could occur in the future (e.g., a currency moving from fixed to floating exchange rate against another key currency). Berkowitz also suggests integrating potential stress test events into overall risk management analysis by assigning a formal probability to stress events and simulating potential outcomes from a database of events combining risk model–generated scenarios, with probability $1 - \alpha$, and different stress scenarios, each with a probability $\alpha_1, \alpha_2, \ldots, \alpha_n$ adding up to α. Stress scenarios could then be conceived as a tool to complete the historical database with potential events and could be fully integrated into risk analysis. While some banks are trying to use a similar logic in building an operational risk loss database (see Chapter 5), in most banks stress tests are not yet assigned a formal probability of occurrence. Yet they remain a powerful tool for integrating daily VaR analysis, especially if the set of extreme scenarios is well defined and perceived to be unlikely but reasonable by both risk managers and traders. This is a key condition to avoid running stress analysis as a purely theoretical exercise producing outcomes too bad to be true, with no consequences on actual decision making. Note that some banks (a well-known example is Deutsche Bank) claim to be using stress tests rather than VaR in calculating capital at risk for trading business units. Of course, this choice may depend on how VaR is measured: If the bank had a trading book with large option exposures and the VaR measurement system were based on a variance–covariance approach, a stress scenario analysis combining sharp changes in underlying asset prices and implied volatility levels would be much more suitable for identifying real trading risks. However, this practical use of stress test outputs clarifies their potential as a decision-making support, which is not always fully exploited in practice.

3.9   Summary

Different methodologies are available to a risk manager in order to calculate the value at risk (i.e., the maximum potential loss within a given time horizon and confidence level) for trading positions exposed to market risks. One of the most well-known solutions is the variance–covariance approach, which assumes jointly normally distributed returns for either the risk factors or the benchmark assets (e.g., exchange rates, stocks or stock indexes, zero-coupon bonds with benchmark maturities) that can be used to model the behavior of a given real portfolio. The variance–covariance method requires one first to select the key risk factors/benchmark assets and then to map the real portfolio into an equivalent portfolio exposed only to the key risk factors or benchmark assets. This step is conceptually simple but practically very relevant, since it will condition the quality of the final VaR estimate. After one completes the mapping phase, portfolio VaR measurement requires estimating volatilities and correlations of key risk factors or benchmark assets. There are different ways to calculate volatilities, and exponential weighted moving averages or GARCH models, which explicitly recognize that volatility is not constant through time, are usually the favorite solutions. Given volatilities and correlations, portfolio VaR can easily be calculated analytically.

An alternative to the variance–covariance approach is represented by simulation methods. In particular, historical simulations calculate VaR by (1) reconstructing the return distribution of the current portfolio on any of the n past days, based on actual daily historical returns, and then (2) identifying the desired percentile of the portfolio return distribution. VaR would be the difference between the current portfolio value and its value in the extreme percentile. Historical simulations have the merit of not assuming multivariate normal returns, but at the same time they fail to capture time-varying volatility patterns. Monte Carlo simulations require one instead to formally model the joint return distribution of the assets in a portfolio and then to reevaluate the portfolio many times so as to build a return distribution for the portfolio from which the desired percentile (and hence VaR) can be identified. Other simulation methods' variants are represented by the hybrid approach and by filtered historical simulations. A particularly difficult case for market risk measurement is represented by option positions, since their returns typically have a nonlinear and often even nonmonotonic relationship with returns of the underlying asset, and they depend jointly on a number of different risk factors, including their implied volatility. Hence for option positions a risk manager must find the optimal solution balancing computational costs and the precision of VaR estimates. VaR models should be regularly back-tested to check their predictive ability, even if caution is needed in interpreting results, depending on which series of actual returns of the portfolio is compared with ex ante VaR estimates. VaR models can also be used under certain conditions to calculate minimum capital requirements for market risk, according to Basel Committee's 1996 Market Risk Amendment. In any case, VaR measures are not exempt from limits, and the risk manager may wish to complement them either with measures of expected shortfall (i.e., the average loss in the $x\%$ of the worst possible cases) or with stress tests aimed at reproducing the effects of extreme scenarios, including joint extreme shocks in multiple variables, which may not be properly represented in relatively recent past history used to feed the usual market VaR models.

3.10 Further Reading

Many risk management books discuss market risk management in detail. Overall, one book that covers all market risk measurement topics in a very clear and efficient manner is Christoffersen (2003). The variance–covariance approach, historical simulation and Monte Carlo simulation, and stress tests are also discussed extensively in J.P. Morgan's (1996) classic *RiskMetrics^{TM} Technical Document* and Jorion (2002). GARCH model applications for financial risk management can also be analyzed further in Alexander (2001). The reader interested in further exploring Monte Carlo simulations on topics such as alternative goodness-of-fit tests and random number extraction techniques can refer to Vose (1996), Holton (2003), and Glasserman (2003). Option greeks and some alternative methods for calculating options VaR, such as the Cornish–Fisher expansion, can be found in options textbooks such as Hull (2005). The reader interested in developing extreme-value theory and copulas further can refer to Embrechts (2000) and Cherubini, Luciano, and Vecchiato (2004). As far as back-testing is concerned, the reader should refer first to Chapter 8 in Christoffersen (2003), and Berkowitz (2001) suggests a method for back-testing the entire distribution. The latest version of the Market Risk Amendment is in Basel Committee on Banking Supervision (2006a). Interest rate risk measurement for the banking book, which has not been discussed here, is analyzed in books such as Saunders (1994), Bessis (2002) and Sironi and Resti (2007).

CHAPTER ◆ 4

Credit Risk

Credit risk is the single most important risk for a large number of financial institutions. The aim of this chapter is to define credit risk and to analyze how a bank might classify its borrowers, evaluate the expected and unexpected losses that may derive from its credit portfolio, and calculate credit risk VaR. In Section 4.1 we present the difference between expected and unexpected losses. We show that the former are on average unavoidable (hence, they should be treated as a cost of being in the lending business and covered by adequate provisions), while unexpected losses are associated with unfavorable scenarios and should be covered by shareholder capital. In the following sections we will see how those two components can be estimated and managed.

4.1 Defining Credit Risk: Expected and Unexpected Losses

A credit risk management system can consider different sources of losses, depending on the valuation methodology used, which can be based either on a mark-to-market (MTM) approach or on a book-value accounting (BVA) approach. In the MTM approach, the value of a credit risk–sensitive position is the value at which it could be traded on the market if a market for it were available.[1] In principle, this should equate the present value of future cash flows discounted at a rate depending on the riskiness of the exposure. Accordingly, any decrease in this present value due, e.g., to an increase in the risk-adjusted discount rate, will represent a credit loss. Hence, a downgrade of the borrower, leading to

---

1. A secondary market could exist, e.g., for corporate bonds. For most bank loans, however, no such liquid market will be available and a "fair" price will have to be computed by the bank based on a pricing model.

higher credit spreads and to a lower market value of the position, will be considered a source of credit losses.

In the BVA approach, the value of the exposure is identified with its book value, and losses occur only when a reduction in book values has to be acknowledged by the bank. Therefore, downgrades would not typically affect the value of the loan, and credit losses would be driven mostly by the default of the borrower.

The MTM approach is automatically adopted for all assets evaluated at fair value (e.g., marketable bonds). In contrast, for assets evaluated at amortized cost (and notably for commercial loans, which are usually classified as "loans or receivables"), banks can follow either the MTM or the BVA approach.

Although credit risk management covers both expected and unexpected losses (with the former covered by provisions and the latter by bank capital), credit risk in a narrow sense can be defined as the risk arising from an unexpected deterioration in the credit quality of a counterparty (e.g., a bond issuer or bank borrower). This emphasis on *unexpected* events follows from the fact a certain number of defaults in a portfolio is part of the nature of the credit business, can be expected and estimated ex ante, and therefore is not, strictly speaking, a source of risk.[2] Similarly, an insurance company operating in the property and casualty business and selling policies against car accidents knows that a certain number of accidents per year have to be expected. For instance, for a 1 million USD loan portfolio made of 1000 USD loans, all having a 1% one-year probability of default (PD), we should expect that on average 10 out of 1000 borrowers will default (so the amount of defaulted loans would be 10,000 USD, i.e., 1% × 1 million USD). Part of this defaulted exposure may of course be recovered by the bank (e.g., by seizing the assets of the defaulted firm or by selling the defaulted exposure to a third party). The fraction of the exposure that can be recovered is known as the *recovery rate* (RR),[3] while the fraction that is not recovered is known as *loss given default*[4] (LGD); therefore, LGD = 1 − RR. Assuming in our example that the expected recovery rate is 40% (hence LGD is 60%), the expected loss on the portfolio would be 60% of the defaulted exposure, that is, 60% × 1% × 1 million USD = 6000 USD.

If we assume that the value of the portfolio (1,000,000) will stay unchanged until the possible defaults occur (and hence call it exposure at default, or EAD) and that the three components EAD, PD, and LGD are uncorrelated, then we can express expected loss (EL) as

$$EL = EAD \times PD \times LGD = EAD \times PD \times (1 - RR)$$

This simple and intuitive equation holds if and only if the three sources of risk giving rise to losses are uncorrelated. Intuitively, if two of its components (or even all three of them) were correlated, the expected loss would depend as well on those correlations.

2. *Risk* is defined by the *Oxford Thesaurus* as "uncertainty, unpredictability." In this sense, expected losses are not part of risk, since they are predicted by the bank as the "normal" level of losses associated with a credit portfolio.

3. More precisely, the recovery rate (RR) is defined here as the ratio between the value of the credit-sensitive exposure after the default to the exposure at the time of default (EAD).

4. As described in Section 4.6, the Notice for Proposed Rulemaking issued by the U.S. Federal Banking Agencies in September 2006 defines *loss given default* as "an estimate of the economic loss that would be incurred on an exposure, relative to the exposure's EAD, if the exposure were to default within one year *during economic downturn conditions*," while the generic LGD is labeled *expected loss given default* (ELGD). In this chapter, however, we follow the Basel II terminology, in which the generic term *loss given default* is not necessarily linked to a negative phase of the economic cycle (even if the estimate has to be conservative enough for regulatory purposes).

Note that, generally speaking, the expected "exposure at default" could differ from the current exposure, depending on loan characteristics. For instance, when considering a 5000 USD irrevocable loan commitment with a drawn portion currently equal to 1000 USD, we should consider the risk that, at the time of default, the use could have increased to, say, 2000, 3000, or even 5000 USD. This is because, as default approaches, firms typically experience financial trouble and hence increase the drawn portion of the loan commitments available. Therefore, exposure at default could be different from (and typically higher than) current exposure; this is currently referred to as *exposure risk*.[5]

The three components in the expected loss equation represent expected values. However, exposure risk, default risk, and recovery risk imply that actual losses may differ from their expected values. In particular, actual losses could be higher than expected because:

1. The exposure at default for defaulted counterparties are higher than expected.
2. The actual default rate is higher than the ex ante probability of default.
3. The rate of loss given default is higher than expected.
4. A combination of the first three has occurred.

This ex post difference between actual and expected loss is sometimes called *unexpected loss*. Furthermore, from an ex ante perspective, unexpected losses are defined as the difference between the amount of losses associated with some extreme percentile in the probability distribution of future losses and the amount of expected losses. As is shown in Sections 4.9 and 4.10, such a percentile can be estimated by means of a credit risk management model.

From an economic point of view, expected losses are — on average — unavoidable. Accordingly, they should be treated as a cost of being in the lending business and covered by adequate provisions. Conversely, banks should hold capital to face unexpected losses. This principle is also defined in the Basel II Accord, which states that regulatory requirements are defined in terms of unexpected losses, provided that banks prove to have adequate provisioning policies.

Figure 4-1 illustrates the concept. Note that, to keep things more general, percent loss rates are used instead of absolute losses. Given a certain probability distribution, the expected loss (EL, 2.1% of the total portfolio value) can be derived and must be covered by adequate provisions. The figure also reports an estimate of the loss associated with some extreme, unfavorable scenario (8% of portfolio value). The difference between such a loss and the expected loss (5.9%) is equal to the ex ante estimate of the unexpected loss (UL) and represents a measure of value at risk on the portfolio. Since it has to be covered by shareholder capital, we also refer to it as the *capital at risk* on the credit portfolio.

Based on the distinction between EL and UL, we can now identify the steps needed to measure credit risk capital. The first step is how to evaluate the expected loss, estimating PD, LGD, and EAD for each exposure. Regarding PDs, Sections 4.2 and 4.3 discuss agency ratings and quantitative models, such as quantitative credit scoring and structural models; Section 4.4 presents the different approaches to minimum regulatory capital requirements (MRCRs) for credit risk according to the Basel II Accord; Section 4.5 covers internal rating systems. Sections 4.6 and 4.7 are dedicated to LGD and EAD estimation.

---

5. Note that one widely used tool for limiting exposure risk is represented by *loan covenants*. These are clauses that may require the early repayment of the loan if the borrower does not comply with certain limits on financial ratios. This may help banks to terminate loans before companies enter a proper financial crisis and increase drawdowns on loan commitments. For a discussion of different kind of covenants, see Glantz (1994).

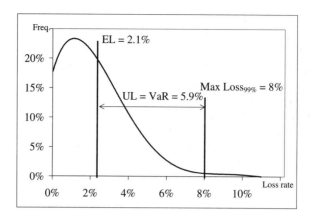

FIGURE 4-1   Expected and unexpected losses.

Before turning to unexpected losses, Section 4.8 discusses the issue of the integration of risk management (including Basel II) and accounting principles. In fact, while risk managers and regulators are widely familiar with the concept of expected loss and clearly recognize the economic need to cover EL with provisions, accounting principles refer to a somewhat different concept: *incurred losses*. This may lead to some misalignments, which may also affect the computation of LGD. Sections 4.9 and 4.10 move from expected to unexpected losses, presenting the main credit portfolio risk models and discussing their advantages and limitations.

4.2   Agency Ratings

Rating agencies represent a valuable source of information on credit risk, since their role is to issue independent credit quality assessments. Rating agencies may produce issuer ratings or issue-specific credit ratings. While the former represent an opinion concerning the obligor's overall capacity to meet its financial obligations, the latter are referred to a specific loan or bond and may reflect the creditworthiness of guarantors and insurers and the quality of any other credit-enhancement agreement specific to the bond or loan (Dinwoodie 2002; de Servigny and Renault 2004). In fact, while ratings are usually requested by issuers (who pay for this service), most agree that the incentive to maintain its reputation for independent judgment is sufficient to prevent a rating agency from becoming too benevolent with rated companies so as to increase its market share.[6] Agency ratings can therefore represent an extremely important source of information for the bank, even if, unfortunately, only a small portion of the borrowers of a typical commercial bank are rated, since while larger firms financing on the bond market have a clear interest in obtaining a rating, this is not the case for the large majority of smaller borrowers. This unavoidable bias in the composition of the universe of rated firms should also be considered when extracting historical data to support credit risk management analyses from rating agencies' data, which still may represent an important resource for many risk managers.

Agency ratings involve assigning issuers to a rating class (see Table 4-1).[7] Rating classes, ranging from AAA (or Aaa) for best issuers to D (default), do not explicitly

---

6. This issue is particularly important after Basel II since, under the so-called standardized approach, credit risk capital requirements are linked to the agency rating of the borrower. However, supervisors will verify an agency's independence before banks are allowed to use its ratings.

7. Short-term ratings are usually expressed according to a scale different from the one in Table 4-1.

TABLE 4-1 Rating Classes: Investment Grade and Speculative Grades

Standard & Poor's	Moody's		Credit quality
AAA	Aaa		Highest
AA	Aa	Investment grade	
A	A		
BBB	Baa		
BB	Ba	Speculative grade	
B	B		
CCC	Caa		Lowest

incorporate any prediction about the probability of default, even if a PD can easily be derived for each of them based on the historical default frequency for issuers in that class. Note that while Table 4-1 compares the rating scales of the two main rating agencies, the grades should not be considered strictly equivalent. The grades in Table 4-1 are also subdivided into "notches" that allow one to distinguish further inside a rating class. For instance, AA is divided into AA+ (best quality), AA and AA− (worst quality).

4.2.1 External Rating Assignment

The rating assignment process takes into consideration both qualitative elements (such as company management and projects, industry perspectives, regulatory outlook) and quantitative elements (financial ratios like leverage, return on capital, free operating cash flow/total debt, for which median or range levels for each rating class may have been defined).

An important feature of agency ratings is that they are assigned with a "through-the-cycle" (TTC) approach. This implies an evaluation of the borrower based on a downside scenario (e.g., the worst phase in the macroeconomic cycle) rather than on current market conditions (as in the so-called "point-in-time," PIT, approach; see Treacy and Carey 2000; de Servigny and Renault 2004). TTC ratings, therefore, tend to be more stable than PIT ratings, so rating migrations (i.e., movements from one rating class to another) are less frequent. Also, historical default rates for each rating class may be more unstable, since in bad years the default rate may increase without companies being moved to a different rating class (as occurs under the PIT approach).

4.2.2 Transition Matrixes and Cumulative and Marginal Default Probabilities

When using agency ratings to assess the riskiness of a credit exposure, transition matrices represent a key tool. A transition matrix reports the distribution of issuers/borrowers based on their initial rating class (on rows) and on their final status (shown in the columns: final rating class, withdrawn rating or default) at the end of a particular time interval (e.g., one year).

Table 4-2 presents an example of a transition matrix. For instance, the third row considers companies A-rated at the beginning of the year and states that 0.05% of them were upgraded to AAA, 1.90% were upgraded to AA, 87.24% remained A-rated, 5.59% were

TABLE 4-2   Standard+ Poor's Average One-Year Transition Rates, 1981–2005 (%)

To From	AAA	AA	A	BBB	BB	B	CCC/C	Default	Withdrawn Rating
AAA	88.20	7.67	0.49	0.09	0.06	0.00	0.00	0.00	3.49
AA	0.58	87.16	7.63	0.58	0.06	0.11	0.02	0.01	3.85
A	0.05	1.90	87.24	5.59	0.42	0.15	0.03	0.04	4.58
BBB	0.02	0.16	3.85	84.13	4.27	0.76	0.17	0.27	6.37
BB	0.03	0.04	0.25	5.26	75.74	7.36	0.90	1.12	9.29
B	0.00	0.05	0.19	0.31	5.52	72.67	4.21	5.38	11.67
CCC/C	0.00	0.00	0.28	0.41	1.24	10.92	47.06	27.02	13.06

Source: Vazza, Aurora, and Schneck (2006).

TABLE 4-3   Standard+ Poor's Average One-Year Transition Rates Adjusted for Withdrawn Ratings, 1981–2005 (%)

To From	AAA	AA	A	BBB	BB	B	CCC/C	Default
AAA	91.42	7.92	0.51	0.09	0.06	0.00	0.00	0.00
AA	0.61	90.68	7.91	0.61	0.05	0.11	0.02	0.01
A	0.05	1.99	91.43	5.86	0.43	0.16	0.03	0.04
BBB	0.02	0.17	4.08	89.94	4.55	0.79	0.18	0.27
BB	0.04	0.05	0.27	5.79	83.61	8.06	0.99	1.20
B	0.00	0.06	0.22	0.35	6.21	82.49	4.76	5.91
CCC/C	0.00	0.00	0.32	0.48	1.45	12.63	54.71	30.41

Source: Vazza, Aurora, and Schneck (2006).

downgraded to BBB, and so on. The withdrawn ratings in the last column may be explained by a number of factors (e.g., the rated company reimbursed all rating debt, did not pay rating fees, or asked the rating agency to withdraw the rating). Since it is difficult to assess the real reasons for rating withdrawals, adjusted transition matrixes (see Table 4-3) are usually defined by simply eliminating withdrawn ratings and proportionally re-scaling transition frequencies upward (see Gupton, Finger, and Bhatia 1997; de Servigny and Renault 2004). The issue of withdrawn ratings is relevant, since Table 4-2 shows that it is a relatively frequent event, especially for speculative-grade issuers. Hence, it may be argued that poorly performing firms anticipating a potential downgrading might be more eager than average to have their rating withdrawn. Anyway, in absence of clear evidence, the simple solution of rescaling transition frequency is the usual one in practice.

As mentioned earlier, while agencies do not explicitly link the rating assignment process to an explicit PD (or PD range) over any horizon, PDs are usually associated with rating classes by observing the historical default rate experience. Since yearly default rates can fluctuate (especially under the TTC approach), one-year PDs are usually calcu-lated as a long-term average of one-year default rates (as in the last column of Table 4-3).[8]

---

8. Default rates can be calculated either as the fraction of defaulted issuers or in dollar-weighted terms (as the value of defaulted issues over the total value of issues outstanding at the beginning of the period). This applies also to CDRs and MDRs, which are covered later in this section.

TABLE 4-4 Average Cumulative Default Rates, 1981–2005 (Adjusted for Withdrawn Rating; Percentages)

	Year									
	1	**2**	**3**	**4**	**5**	**6**	**7**	**8**	**9**	**10**
AAA	0.00	0.00	0.03	0.07	0.11	0.20	0.30	0.47	0.53	0.60
AA	0.01	0.03	0.08	0.16	0.25	0.38	0.54	0.68	0.79	0.92
A	0.04	0.13	0.25	0.42	0.64	0.86	1.11	1.34	1.62	1.90
BBB	0.27	0.81	1.40	2.25	3.11	3.97	4.67	5.35	5.93	6.63
BB	1.20	3.71	6.86	9.94	12.74	15.57	18.02	20.27	22.39	24.04
B	5.91	13.60	20.55	26.23	30.48	34.01	37.23	40.15	42.36	44.75
CCC/C	30.41	40.02	46.13	50.55	56.04	58.53	59.63	60.43	64.38	67.72

Source: Vazza, Aurora, and Schneck (2006).

Tables such as Tables 4-2 and 4-3 are provided with a number of further details by the main rating agencies (e.g., specific transition matrices for sovereign and nonsovereign issuers or for specific geographic regions).

Default frequencies can also be calculated over multiyear horizons. In that case, the probability that a firm in rating class i will default over the whole n-year horizon (that is, in any of the n years) is named *cumulative default probability* (CDP), and — just like one-year PDs — is estimated through the historical default frequency, which is called the *cumulative default rate* (CDR) or *cumulative mortality rate*. CDR can be calculated either as the fraction of issuers that defaulted within year t or, in dollar-weighted terms, as a fraction of the value of issues that defaulted within year t over the value of issues in class i outstanding at the beginning of the sample period. An example of cumulative default rates is given in Table 4-4.

Table 4-4 clearly shows that, while CDRs are always higher for lower-rated issuers, cumulative default rates grow according to a nonlinear pattern. This can be analyzed by observing *marginal default rates* (MDRs). The MDR in year t is defined as

$$_{\text{issuer}}\text{MDR}_i = \frac{\text{number of issuers that defaulted in year } t}{\text{number of issuers that had not defaulted up to the beginning of year } t}$$

MDRs (whose ex ante equivalent are marginal default probabilities, MDPs), introduced by Altman (1989), were originally expressed in dollar-weighted terms rather than in issuer-weighted terms as in the previous formula. MDRs are often used to analyze the long-term default behavior of different rating classes. From Table 4-4 we can observe, for instance, that the MDR for the second year for an A-rated company ($\text{MDR}_{2,A}$) is higher than the 1-year PD. In fact, the share of issuers that defaulted in the second year is 0.09% (0.13% − 0.04%) of the initial population, and hence $\text{MDR}_{2,A}$ is equal to 0.09%/(1 − 0.04%) ≈ 0.09%, which is greater than 0.04%. Instead, for grade CCC/C the MDR in the second year is clearly lower than 30.41% (the default rate for the first year). This is explained by the fact that CCC/C issuers that do not default in the first year have a significant probability of being upgraded (see Table 4-3), hence the average riskiness of survivors may decrease through time. The opposite is true for issuers initially rated A.

One might think that cumulative default probabilities like those shown in Table 4-4 could be computed using migration matrices like the one in Table 4-3. For instance, for an issuer initially rated A, Table 4-3 could give us the probability of migrating in any state (including default) in year 1; the probability of default for year 2 could then be calculated as the sum of the products among the one-year migration probabilities from class A to each class i and the one-year default rate for each class i.[9]

Unfortunately, rating transitions and default rates show some *path dependence*, so, for instance, AA-rated issuers just downgraded to single A are more likely to be downgraded again (to BBB) than those that have had an A rating for several years (see Nickell, Perraudin, and Varotto 2000; Bangia et al. 2002). Also, migration matrices appear to be *dependent on the economic cycle*, so downgrades are more frequent during recessions, even if, in theory, rating agencies' judgments already take stress scenarios into account when assigning a rating.

These two characteristics may be affected by the way rating agencies operate. TTC ratings are more likely to show path dependence and default rates that fluctuate over economic cycles. Instead, PIT ratings (like those used in many banks' internal rating systems) should show, at least in theory, default rates that are less sensitive to economic cycles but migration patterns that are much more sensitive to the cycle (i.e., downgrades during an economic downturn should be much more frequent than for a TTC rating). Therefore, substantial caution should be used when trying to estimate long-term cumulative default probabilities from one-year migration matrixes.

Finally, we should note that cumulative default probabilities (and multiyear migration matrices) can in principle be measured in two different ways. Rating agencies typically start considering all issuers in a given year and record their migrations/defaults in the following n years. Altman (1998) claims that since migration and default rates differ for newly issued and seasoned bonds, pools including both types of issues could give rise to biased estimates. Including only newly issued bonds in the initial population might therefore produce different, and more reliable, migration/default statistics.

4.3 Quantitative Techniques for Stand-Alone Credit Risk Evaluation: Moody's/KMV EDF and External Scoring Systems

Although most banks rely predominantly on internal systems for credit risk estimation, agency ratings are a form of external information that can be used as a benchmark. Other widely known benchmarks are provided by commercial applications of Merton's (1974) model, such as the expected default frequency (EDF) produced by Moody's/KMV, and by scoring models based on publicly available financial data.

4.3.1 Merton's (1974) Model and Moody's/KMV Expected Default Frequency

The first quantitative model we consider has its roots in a paper by Merton (1974), which has subsequently been developed by other authors and then by KMV Corporation, later acquired by Moody's. In order to describe Merton's intuition, let us consider a company

---

9. That is, as the probability to migrate to AAA in the first year times the 1-year default rate of an AAA-rated issuer, plus the probability to migrate to AA in the first year times the 1-year default rate of an AA issuer, plus the the probability to remain A in the first year times the 1-year default rate of an A-rated issuer, and so on.

with a simplified financial structure, where the total value of assets V is financed partly by equity (whose value is E) and partly by debt with face value B, maturity T, and market value F (so $F + E = V$). At time T, two events can occur: If the value of assets V_T exceeds the face value of debt B, the latter will be repaid and the value of equity will be $V_T - B$. If, instead, the value of assets is lower than B, the company will default and the value of equity will be zero, because of the limited-liability principle. Formally, the value of equity at maturity T, E_T, will be given by:

$$E_T = \text{Max } [V_T - B, 0]$$

This is equivalent to the payoff of a *call* option on the company's assets V, with a strike price equal to B. Symmetrically, the position of debt holders can be assimilated to the combination of an investment at the risk-free rate and to the sale of a *put* option on the value of assets; this could also be used to derive a theoretical credit spread to compensate for credit risk (see Box 4-1 below).

Hence, applying the Black–Scholes (1973) formula and using asset value V as the price of the underlying asset and B as the strike price, the current value of shareholders' equity (i.e., the call option) can be computed as

$$E = V \cdot N(d_1) - B \cdot e^{-rT} \cdot N(d_2)$$

where $N(x)$ represents the value in x of the cumulative density function of a standard normal distribution, r is the risk-free rate, and d_1 and d_2 are given by

$$d_1 = \frac{\ln\left(\dfrac{V}{B}\right) + \left(r + \dfrac{\sigma_V^2}{2}\right)T}{\sigma_V \sqrt{T}}; \qquad d_2 = d_1 - \sigma_V \sqrt{T}$$

where σ_V is the volatility of firm asset return.

The Black–Scholes model can be used to compute the probability of default (that is, the probability that at maturity T the value of assets V_T will be less than B, the face value of debt; see Figure 4-2). Namely, if the expected return on the firm's assets is assumed to be r, the Black–Scholes model dictates that the probability of default (probability that $V_T < B$) is equal to $N(-d_2)$.

Box 4-1: Deriving the Theoretical Credit Spread for Risky Bonds in the Merton (1974) Model

If we consider Merton's (1974) firm financing assets with equity and debt with face value B maturing at T, the payoff for equity holders at maturity is $E_T = \text{Max}[V_T - B, 0]$ which is the potentially unlimited payoff of a call option. Debt holders, instead, cannot claim at maturity more than the face value of debt B. Hence, their *payoff* F_T at time T is equal to a maximum of B if the company is not insolvent and otherwise is equal to V_T (which is lower than B if the firm defaults). In fact,

$$F_T = \text{Max}[B, V_T] = B - \text{Max}[B - V_T, 0]$$

where $\text{Max}[B - V_T, 0]$ is exactly the payoff of a put option on the value of the firm's assets with strike B. Intuitively, the difference between the interest rate perceived by debt holders and the risk-free rate is the compensation (i.e., the premium) for the put option they are selling, and that derives from the limited liability feature of equity holders. Hence, since the value of equity is given by

$$E = V \cdot N(d_1) - B \cdot e^{-rT} \cdot N(d_2)$$

and $F = V - E$, it is possible to calculate F. If we express the firm's *leverage* (the ratio of the face value of debt discounted at the risk-free rate, Be^{-rT}, to the value of assets V) as $d = Be^{-rT}/V$, the theoretical market value of debt F is

$$F = V - [V \cdot N(d_1) - B \cdot e^{-rT} \cdot N(d_2)] = B \cdot e^{-rT} \cdot \left[N(d_2) + \frac{V}{B \cdot e^{-rT}} (1 - N(d_1)) \right]$$

$$= B \cdot e^{-rT} \cdot \left[N(d_2) + \frac{1}{d} N(-d_1) \right]$$

This also allows us to identify the theoretical credit spread needed to compensate debt holders for their short put option. Since the debt's market value is F and its face value is B, the continuously compounded rate of return for debt holders is the rate R such that $Fe^{RT} = B$. Accordingly,

$$R = \frac{1}{T} \cdot \ln\left(\frac{B}{F} \right) = -\frac{1}{T} \cdot \ln\left(\frac{F}{B} \right)$$

By replacing F with the foregoing expression, the spread $R - r$ can be derived as

$$R - r = -\frac{1}{T} \cdot \ln\left[N(d_2) + \frac{1}{d} N(-d_1) \right]$$

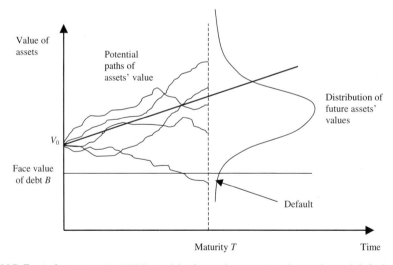

FIGURE 4-2 Merton's (1974) model: alternative assets' value paths and default events.

However, the practical implementation of the Merton model requires us to specify two unobservable parameters: V and σ_v (the volatility of the assets). These parameters can be estimated indirectly based on the value of equity (E) and its volatility (σ_E), two quantities that can easily be observed and recorded, at least for listed companies (if this is not the case, then proxies for E and σ_E must be used). In fact, since E is a call option on the asset value V, both the value of the call and its volatility must be linked to the value and the volatility of the assets. Namely, it can be shown that σ_E is linked to σ_V by the equation

$$\sigma_E = \frac{\partial E}{\partial V} \cdot \frac{V}{E} \sigma_V$$

where $\partial E / \partial V$ is the option's delta. This equation can be combined with the option's value equation,

$$E = V \cdot N(d_1) - B \cdot e^{-rT} \cdot N(d_2)$$

to form a system of two equations and to work out V and σ_v.

This original version of the Merton model has been extended to overcome some shortcomings arising from assuming an oversimplified liabilities structure. Black and Cox (1976) and Geske (1977) considered, respectively, subordinated debt and debt with periodical interest payments; Vasicek (1984) introduced the distinction between short-term and long-term liabilities, which also represents one of the characteristics of Moody's/KMV approach; Crouhy and Galai (1994) analyzed how the presence of warrants might affect equity volatility.

However, the most widely known refinement of the Merton model is the one proposed by KMV Corporation (now Moody's/KMV), to estimate the expected default frequency (EDF), i.e., the PD of individual borrowers, which subsequently evolved into a credit portfolio model for VaR measurement (see Section 4.9).

The Moody's/KMV model differs from the original Merton model in two main features.

1. Liabilities are not assumed to have a single maturity, T, but are divided into short-term and long-term liabilities. The default threshold for assets (*default point*) is no longer set at B (total debt), but now equals short-term liabilities plus half of long-term liabilities.[10]
2. The probability of default is no longer derived from Merton's formula but is based on the following two-step procedure.
   a. The first step is to identify the "distance from default" (DD), which is the difference, expressed in units of σ_V, between the expected value of assets at the future date of valuation (usually one year), $E(V_T)$, and the *default point*, DP.

$$DD = \frac{E(V_T) - DP}{\sigma_V V}$$

---

10. The rationale is that, when measuring one-year PD, even if the assets' value fell below the value of total liabilities, default would not be certain if the maturity of part of the liabilities is long enough to permit the value of assets to increase before the expiry date. Instead, default would be certain if assets fell below the value of short-term debt.

For instance, if $V_0 = 100$, $E(V_T) = 108$, DP $= 64$, and $\sigma_V = 10\%$, then the default distance would be DD $= (108 - 64)/(10\% \times 100) = 4.4$.

b. The second step translates this distance from default into an EDF based on the historical default rate recorded by firms having a similar DD. There is an inverse nonlinear relationship between the distance from default and EDF (see Figure 4-3). For instance, if, in the past, 10 out of 10,000 firms with a DD of approximately 4.4 had defaulted within one year, then a DD of 4.4 could be associated with an expected default frequency of 0.10% (i.e., 10/10,000).

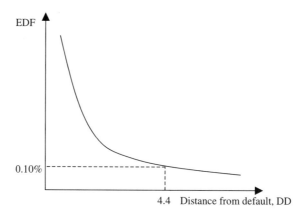

FIGURE 4-3   Relationship between the distance from default and EDF.

Using historical data enables KMV to relax some critical assumptions of "Merton type" models, such as normality and serial independence of asset returns. In fact, if asset value returns are not normally distributed (or serially correlated), then the default probability could not be inferred through a Gaussian distribution. Of course, the quality and size of the database used to infer the link between DD and EDF play an important role.

A remarkable feature of models like Moody's/KMV is that, since they rely on equity prices to infer default probabilities, they are much faster than rating agencies in updating their judgments. In fact, they clearly rate "point in time" rather than "through the cycle." Of course, this could make them overreact in case of sharp stock market crises or make them too optimistic in "bubble" periods.

4.3.2   Credit-Scoring Systems

While Merton-like structural models are used especially (even if not only) in case of listed firms, whose equity values and volatility are easily observable, for smaller or in general nonlisted firms and consumer credit, a widely used alternative is represented by scoring systems, which can be either internally developed by the bank or run by a third party (external scoring systems). In general, the aim of a credit-scoring methodology is to separate firms or individuals with a high PD over a certain time horizon from those with a lower PD. The two most well-known credit-scoring techniques are represented by linear discriminant analysis and logit or probit regressions. A number of other models have been proposed by either researchers or software vendors in the quest to improve the classification ability of the models.

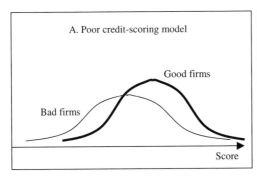
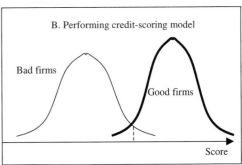

FIGURE 4-4   Graphical illustration of a poor and a performing credit-scoring system.

Linear discriminant analysis was introduced by Fisher (1936) and developed in the 1960s by Beaver (1967) and Altman (1968), whose Z-score substantially contributed to the diffusion of credit-scoring models. The underlying idea can be explained as follows.

Let us consider a population of n firms for which m different variables (e.g., balance sheet ratios) are observable. Some of the n firms are "good," i.e., firms that did not default within a certain period (usually one year) from the time the m variables were observed, while the other, "bad," firms defaulted within the same time frame. Linear discriminant analysis tries to identify a scoring function represented by a linear combination of either all or, more frequently, a selection of the m variables so as to maximize the distance between the mean scores of the two groups (good and bad firms) while minimizing score variance within the same group. This should enable one to classify, with the minimum potential error, a firm as either good or bad, depending on its score. The intuitive idea is expressed in Figure 4-4, comparing two ideal different linear combinations of available variables. On the left-hand side, the weights assigned to the variables produce a score that is unable to clearly discriminate good firms from bad ones; within-group variance is high compared to the difference in the mean. In the second case (Figure 4-4B), the difference among mean scores is higher and within-group variances are smaller.

Obviously, when developing a scoring model, parsimony in selecting the variables is desirable. And there are different stepwise techniques to identify the best combination of a limited number of variables that can maximize the informational content and the discriminatory power of the model. As an example, the famous Altman (1968) Z-score was synthesized in the equation

$$Z_i = 1.2X_{1,i} + 1.4X_{2,i} + 3.3X_{3,i} + 0.6X_{4,i} + 1.0X_{5,i}$$

where $X_1, X_2, \ldots, X_5$ variables for any firm i were represented, respectively, by working capital/total assets, retained earnings/total assets, EBIT/total assets, market value of equity/book value of long-term liabilities, and sales/total assets.

When building a discriminant model, a first issue is represented by the size of the sample and the selection of good versus bad firms. First of all, since average values of financial ratios typically used as discriminant variables can vary, depending on country and industry, different specific subsamples should be defined when possible, i.e., when their size is still sufficiently large. If this is impossible, then some caution may be needed when evaluating results for firms belonging to countries or industries underrepresented in the estimation sample. Second, the definition of default that is adopted has to be consistent. Identifying bad firms as only those that went bankrupt or also as those that were past due more than 90 days according to the definition of default in the Basel II Capital Accord may affect the selection of variables. Obviously, it could be dangerous to use a scoring system based on a certain definition of default to predict PDs according to a different definition. Third, the cutoff score separating firms classified as bad from those classified as good must be carefully established. Apparently, from Figure 4-4B, it could be defined as the point where the two frequency distribution functions intersect.

A more classical solution is to set the cutoff point as the average between the mean scores of good and bad firms' subsamples. Yet, since the consequences of classifying a good firm as bad (e.g., denying a loan and perhaps losing a customer) — usually defined as Type II error — may be different from the consequences of erroneously classifying a bad firm as good (i.e., facing a loan loss due to the firm's default) — that is, a Type I error — the cutoff point should be chosen by taking the cost of errors into consideration.

Often, instead of defining a single cutoff point, two different critical scores are identified. Firms below the first critical level will be classified as bad, those over the second critical level will be classified as good, those with a score between the two cutoff levels will be in a grey area where the scoring model is not considered reliable enough to discriminate between the two groups (and depending on the relevance of the transaction further analysis may be required).

While discriminant analysis can be used simply to facilitate a yes-or-no loan decision, as in the case of consumer credit, a risk manager would also like to translate this into an estimated probability of default (thereby also supporting a classification of counterparties into an internal rating scale). Unfortunately, since a linear combination of different balance sheet ratios is unbounded, it can be difficult to translate it into a PD, which has to range between 0 and 1.

Logit and probit models solve this problem via a transformation of the linear combination of original variables. For instance, the logit model function is defined as

$$F(Z) = \frac{1}{1 + e^Z} = \frac{1}{1 + e^{\alpha + \sum \beta_i X_i}}$$

where Z is therefore a linear combination of variables X with weights $\beta_1, \ldots, \beta_n$ plus a constant α. Yet $F(Z)$ is clearly in the desired range and expresses the PD of a given firm given the value of its financial ratios $X_1, \ldots, X_n$. Since the probability function is logistic, this approach is defined as logit model. The probit model is similar but uses a normal cumulative distribution function rather than a logistic one. The estimation of optimal weights has to be performed in this case through maximum-likelihood techniques.

4.4 Capital Requirements for Credit Risk under Basel II

Having introduced agency ratings, it is now possible to present synthetically the three different approaches to MRCR for credit risk set out in the Basel II Accord. In fact, the standardized approach is precisely a refinement of the Basel I Accord that tries to discriminate better among borrowers with different risks based on their external rating. Foundation internal rating-based (FIRB) and advanced internal rating-based (AIRB) approaches rely instead on bank's internal data, as far as PD only is concerned (in the FIRB approach) or for EAD and LGD as well (in the AIRB approach). It is important to remember that, as noted in Chapter 2, while all the three approaches will be available for banks in the European Union and in all other countries that will adopt the Basel II framework completely, the current proposal by the U.S. Federal Banking Agencies (Board of

Governors of the Federal Reserve System 2006) states that only the IRB approach will be available. More precisely, the approach will be compulsory for large U.S.-based international banks ("core banks"), while it could be adopted on a voluntary basis by other banks. Though the proposal is not yet a final approved document, this crucial peculiarity of the U.S. approach to Basel II implementation must be considered when going through the following discussion. In a few cases, we will point out some relevant differences between the Basel II Accord and the current Federal Agencies' proposal for its implementation in the United States.

4.4.1 Standardized Approach

The standardized approach can be considered an effort to refine the very simple risk weights defined by the 1988 Capital Accord, which differentiated risk weights mainly depending on the nature of the counterparty, with little differentiation in terms of risk class within the same category (the main problem being the 100% weight assigned to any corporate exposure). Under the standardized approach, in contrast, risk weights depend on both the kind of counterparty and the external rating assigned by an external credit-assessment institution (ECAI). An ECAI can be either a rating agency or another institution that has been recognized by national supervisors as a reliable and independent source of rating evaluations (criteria for eligibility are defined in Basel Committee 2006a, §91). Specific rules prevent banks from "cherry-picking" the most favorable assessment for a given counterparty among multiple ECAIs when multiple ratings exist. The risk weights under the standardized approach are given in Table 4-5, using as a reference Standard & Poor's rating classes. Detailed rules are defined to account for credit risk mitigation techniques, such as collateral, third-party guarantees, credit derivatives, or netting agreements (see Basel Committee 2006a, §§109–210).

TABLE 4-5   Risk Weights Under the Basel II Standardized Approach

	AAA to AA−	A+ to A−	BBB+ to BBB−	BB+ to BB−	B+ to B−	Below B−	Unrated	Past due
Sovereigns[a]	0%	20%	50%	100%		150%	100%	100–150%[c]
Banks (Option 1)	20%	50%	100%			150%	100%	
Banks (Option 2)[b]	20%	50%		100%		150%	50%	
Corporates	20%	50%	100%		150%		100%	
Retail	75%							
Claims secured by residential property	35%							100%
Claims secured by commercial real estate	100%[d]							100%–150%[c]

[a] Non-central-government public sector entities can be treated, at national discretion, under one of the two options available for banks.

[b] The choice between option 1 and 2 is left to national supervisors. Under option 2, lower weights can be applied to exposures with an original maturity of three months or less.

[c] The risk weight depends on the level of specific provisions relative to the outstanding amount of the loan; e.g., for nonresidential mortgage loans, the risk weight may be 100% if specific provisions are no less than 20% of the outstanding amount, and — subject to regulatory discretion — may be further reduced to 50% when provisions are at least 50% of the outstanding amount.

[d] A part of the claim may be given a 50% weight under certain conditions.

Retail exposures are given a more favorable weight based on the assumption that they should represent a set of small and very well-diversified exposures. Obviously, precise criteria define whether an exposure can be classified as retail. Table 4-5 clearly shows that one of the main problems in Basel I, i.e., using the same 100% weight for all corporate counterparties, is solved by discriminating risk weights based on borrowers' external ratings. Yet the contribution remains quite limited for those banks whose main customer base is represented by smaller, unrated customers, whose risk weight remains undifferentiated and equal to 100%. For these cases, only more sophisticated internal rating-based approaches might allow for a differentiation in risk weights within this class of counterparties.

4.4.2   *Foundation and Advanced Internal Rating-Based Approaches*

According to IRB approaches, all exposures must be classified into different exposure classes (corporate, sovereign, bank, retail, and equity exposures). For each asset class, the Basel II Accord defines:

1. How key risk components (PD, LGD, EAD, and maturity M) can be derived
2. The risk-weight function that transforms the risk components into the risk weight for each exposure
3. The minimum standards that must be met by a bank applying for the IRB approach

Within the five large exposure classes defined by the accord, different subcategories exist. In particular, within the corporate exposure class, five classes of specialized lending exposures (e.g., project finance) are given a specific treatment, while exposures with small and medium-sized entities (SMEs), i.e., corporate exposures where reported sales for the group to which the firm belongs are below 50 million euros, have a more favorable risk weight deriving from the assumed lower correlation among borrowers. Similarly, risk weights for retail exposures are different among residential mortgage exposures, qualifying revolving retail exposures, and other retail exposures.

For most asset classes, both a foundation and an advanced IRB approach are available. As a general rule, whereas in the former (FIRB) the bank provides its PD estimates while all other risk components are defined by supervisors, in the latter (AIRB) even part or all of the other risk components may be based on the bank's internal data, provided that minimum standards are met. Hence, when building internal rating systems, calibrating PDs associated to each internal rating, and estimating LGD or EAD, banks willing to comply with either FIRB or AIRB should also consider qualitative standards set out by the Basel II Accord. A summary of key requirements is discussed in the next section concerning internal ratings, LGD and EAD.

4.5   Internal Ratings

Internal ratings represent banks' internal and usually undisclosed judgments about the riskiness of a given borrower or exposure. In most cases internal rating scales are bidimensional; i.e., they address separately the PD of the borrower and the LGD of the given facility (which may depend on covenants, third-party guarantees, and similar factors that are independent of the borrower's PD). Internal ratings are typically defined with numerical grades, and the number and granularity of credit grades varies from one bank to another. Larger and/or more sophisticated institutions typically use a higher number of

TABLE 4-6 Example of an Internal Rating System: Internal Rating Grades

Internal Rating Class	1-Year PD	Credit Quality
1	0.03%	
2	0.10%	
3	0.40%	Pass grades — safer loans
4	1.00%	
5	2.50%	
6	5.00%	Pass grades — riskier loans
7	10.00%	
8	25.00%	
9	60.00%	Problem loans
10	100.00%	

different grades, in order to differentiate better among customers for credit risk measurement, pricing, and capital allocation purposes. A hypothetical example assuming 10 internal classes given in Table 4-6.

Before discussing internal rating systems in detail, it may be useful to summarize some of the key qualitative prescriptions from the Basel II Accord for those banks applying for IRB approaches (Table 4-7). While some of them may derive from specific supervisors' needs, most represent best-practice suggestions that would also be relevant for banks that will never consider IRB validation as a target to be achieved. Hence, these may make a useful basis for the discussion of internal rating design issues.

4.5.1 Internal Rating Assignment Process

The way in which internal ratings are assigned may vary not only from one bank to another but within the same bank, depending on the kind of customer segment. Even the Basel II Accord (see Table 4-7) states that banks may decide to run multiple internal rating systems, depending on the customer segment. Typically, loans to companies are evaluated in a more subjective way, and the personal judgment of senior loan analysts plays a major role. At the opposite end of the spectrum, consumer credit is evaluated through credit-scoring systems only. Middle-market and retail borrowers are usually evaluated either based on a detailed analysis of both quantitative and qualitative elements made directly and synthesized in a final judgment by the credit officer or (especially in large banks) by combining in a structured way both quantitative scores calculated by a model (e.g., internal scores based on financial ratios or on the past behavior of the customer with the bank or both) and a qualitative evaluation by the relationship manager. Given the differences that exist among banks and among segments in the same bank in terms of rating procedures, building an effective overall rating system could be a powerful source of competitive advantage.

The sources of information that can be used to define an internal borrower's rating[11] are many and comprise in particular:

1. Financial ratios and cash flow projections derived from the company's accounting statements

---

11. Note that we refer here to a borrower's rating linked to its PD. Recovery and exposure risk estimates (which are also required in order to estimate facility rating) are covered later in this chapter.

TABLE 4-7   Main Requirements for Internal Rating System Design for Banks Applying for Basel II IRB Approaches

Topic	Requirement	Basel II Accord Paragraphs
Rating systems and approaches to rating assignment	• It is possible to use multiple rating systems for different industries/market segments, provided the criteria for assigning a borrower to a rating system are documented and appropriate.	395
	• Ratings should incorporate all available relevant information. Scoring or other quantitative models can be used, but sufficient human oversight is needed to check that all relevant information, even outside the scope of the model, is properly used. Written guidance is needed on how models and human judgment may be combined.	411
Need for bidimensional rating	• The rating systems should consider *separately* the risk of borrower default and transaction-specific factors (e.g., collateral or other guarantees). Hence the rating system should not be based on the overall expected loss of the exposure. For banks using the advanced approach, facility rating must reflect exclusively LGD.	396–399
Granularity of rating grades	• Both borrower- and facility-rating scales should avoid excessive concentration within the same grade. For corporate, sovereign, and bank exposures, a borrower-rating scale must have at least seven different grades for nondefaulted borrowers plus one for defaulted borrowers.	403–407
Rating criteria and processes documentation	• A bank must have specific rating definitions, processes, and criteria for rating assignment. Criteria must be documented and clear enough to allow third parties (e.g., auditors, supervisors) to replicate rating assignments. Rating procedures and responsibilities in rating assignment must be documented as well.	410, 418–421
Rating assignment horizon	• Although the time horizon used in PD estimation is one year, banks are expected to use a longer time horizon in assigning ratings.	414–415
	• A borrower's rating must express the borrower's ability and willingness to perform despite adverse economic conditions.	
Use of internal ratings	• Internal ratings and default loss estimates must play an essential role in the credit approval, risk management, internal capital allocations and corporate governance functions of banks using the IRB approach. It is recognized that the same estimates may not be used for all purposes (e.g., PD and LGD estimates for pricing purposes may differ).	444
Corporate governance and oversight	• All material aspects of rating assignment and estimation processes must be approved by the board and by senior management. Management must ensure on an ongoing basis that the rating system is working properly.	438–440
	• Banks must have independent credit risk control units that are responsible for the design and implementation of internal rating systems, their tests, and their reviews. Internal audit or an equally independent function must review the system at least annually.	441–443
Validation	• Banks must have a robust system in place to validate the accuracy and consistency of rating systems, processes, and the estimation of all risk components.	500–505

Source: Derived from Basel Committee (2006a).

2. Data on the borrower's past behavior (e.g., credit line usage, delays in payment) available either in the bank's credit file (internal behavioral data) or, in some countries, from interbank credit registers pooling data from multiple banks (external behavioral data)
3. External evaluations of the borrower (e.g., third-party scoring models, while agency ratings or Moody's/KMV EDF may be used as a check of the internal rating evaluation)
4. Qualitative assessment on the industry outlook and the firm's specific characteristics (e.g., competitive position, quality of projects, quality of management), which can be made either by a centralized credit function or by the firm's relationship manager.

Clearly, these sources of information should not have the same relevance for different counterparties. For instance, for larger corporations the exposure size may justify a more detailed qualitative analysis than for smaller firms. Specific sectors (e.g., public sector, financial institutions) may also require specific approaches. As a consequence, the art of internal rating design consists in (1) segmenting different borrowers into groups with different internal rating assignment processes and (2) defining for each segment the optimal process for combining all sources of information in the best possible way. At a minimum, the segmentation process should consider the different kinds of exposures defined by the Basel II Accord (corporate, sovereign, bank, retail, qualifying revolving retail exposures), even if corporate exposures are usually further divided into additional subgroups, e.g., large corporate, corporate, and small and medium-sized entities (SMEs). The segmentation process is important since, especially for medium-sized corporate counterparties, different banks may apply different rating processes to evaluate the loan request and to price the loan, and hence the choice of the methodology may have an impact on the bank's pricing policy and market share.

When defining the optimal process for combining all relevant information, the bank should first choose whether all partial elements should immediately be combined into a single rating or whether, and how, intermediate ratings should be created. Let us consider, for instance, the case of an SME for which external ratings are unavailable and the internal rating should be based mostly on financial statements, behavioral data, and the qualitative industry and firm evaluation by the relationship manager. Figure 4-5 illustrates three different ways in which the final borrower rating can be obtained. Please note that here we are still considering a borrower rating only (aimed at classifying the borrower according to its PD), rather than the final rating of the facility, where estimated loss given default should be taken into consideration.

Whereas in case A all different sources of information are combined in a single step to derive a final rating, case B considers an intermediate rating based on all information apart from qualitative judgments. This solution may be used to separate entirely the objective component of the rating evaluation based on unquestionable data (financial ratios and behavioral data) from the human intervention occurring at a later stage. In this way the bank may even try to quantify the value added by qualitative judgments in the overall counterparty classification process. Case C instead considers an intermediate rating that excludes internal behavioral data only. In this case the intermediate rating may be useful because it can allow a consistent metric for evaluating potential new customers versus existing customers asking for new loans, since internal behavioral data are available only for the latter. The choice about whether or not to develop partial intermediate ratings obviously may be segment specific. For instance, the need to control human intervention may be stronger for SMEs, where qualitative evaluation is typically performed by the

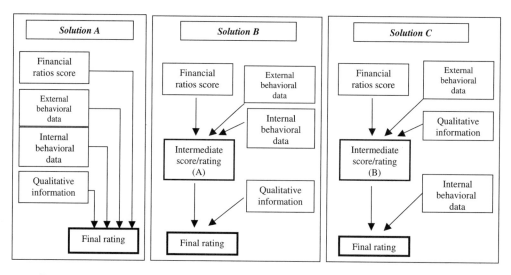

FIGURE 4-5   Alternative ways to derive a final rating: three illustrative examples.

relationship manager, than for large corporate borrowers, whose evaluation relies on independent credit staff (see Treacy and Carey 2000).

A second issue to consider is the technique for aggregating information into the final rating. Considering, for instance, the case of no intermediate ratings (see Figure 4-5A), the final rating may be entirely judgmental or constrained judgmental or even entirely mechanical (see De Laurentis 2005). In the first case, the rater might simply consider all available information and formulate a final judgment. This process may be more frequent in smaller banks, where rating and loan evaluation criteria are largely embedded in the culture and experience of senior credit staff and where the use of statistical techniques is usually lower.

In the second case, the final evaluation may still be judgmental but subject to some constraints. For instance, rating criteria may specify "normal" values for some key financial ratios in each rating grade. One example are the so-called "median values" published by Standard & Poor's, for all rating grades, in its Creditstats reports. Clearly, this does not imply that a firm is assigned to a rating class based on financial ratios alone, even if in a bank adopting a constrained judgmental process it may be stated, for instance, that a borrower whose debt/equity ratio is greater than x should not be assigned in general an internal rating better than y. Another example of constrained judgment could be to evaluate the different areas by translating them into a score, so as to derive the overall rating through a weighted average of scores, using weights defined by the central credit staff.

Finally, the process could even be entirely mechanical and statistically based if qualitative judgments were standardized into a numeric scale and the bank had a large enough internal database of loans to fit a scoring model aimed at assigning optimal weights to financial ratios, internal and external behavioral data, and qualitative evaluations. In similar cases, the bank usually would likely develop partial scores for, say, financial ratios and behavioral data alone and then aggregate statistically the scores on the different information subsets.

A similar choice is also valid when intermediate ratings are produced. For instance, in the case of Figure 4-5B a bank could derive either judgmentally or mechanically an intermediate rating based on objective data and then allow the rater to revise upward or downward the first intermediate rating based on qualitative evaluation.

In practice, the general tendency is to assign a higher relevance to statistical techniques for small borrowers, which do not generate considerable volumes of business, and to assign higher relevance to human judgment as the actual/potential business secured by the borrower becomes bigger. This can be explained by a number of factors.

- Small exposures may not justify the cost for a trained analyst to evaluate the loan.
- Larger borrowers may be too complex to be treated through generic statistical techniques such as scoring models, and they cannot be evaluated through third-party judgements only (e.g., agency ratings, EDF) if the bank wants to anticipate potential deterioration in the borrowers' conditions.
- Larger borrowers may be evaluated more easily by independent credit staff rather than by relationship managers (Treacy and Carey 2000), and it may be easier to check consistency of internal rating assignment due to the relatively lower number of exposures.

Symmetrically, then, especially larger commercial banks with larger portfolios of SMEs as borrowers may use more statistically based techniques, since they possess reasonably large internal databases of firms for which (a) the size of average exposures requires efficiency in the loan evaluation process, (b) a statistical score is required as a rough benchmark, to check whether a few relationship managers might even unconsciously be underestimating the risk of borrowers in their quest to develop new business, and (c) achieving consistent internal ratings throughout the organization could be difficult if the process were based largely on a huge number of decentralized relationship managers. Smaller banks, which lack a sufficiently large internal database, may resort to a mixture of externally provided scores and internal qualitative evaluations, since smaller dimensions may allow them to guarantee a reasonable consistency of rating judgments through a more intense direct supervision by central credit staff on local relationship managers.

In short, the definition of the internal rating assignment process is structurally differentiated among customer segments and banks. For this reason, identifying the proper mix of quantitative techniques and human judgment for all segments is extremely important.

4.5.2 Rating Quantification and the Definition of Default

After having defined internal rating classes as ordinal scales of borrowers with different risk levels, the risk manager should be able to associate with each rating class a given probability of default. This step is relevant internally because banks willing to adopt a Basel II IRB approach must have their methodology validated by their supervisors. The easiest ways to calibrate PDs for internal rating classes is to associate with each rating class the historical default frequency of borrowers in the class. There are at least five critical issues to consider.

1. The bank should understand whether, for each customer segment, internal data are enough to quantify PD based on its own historical experience.
2. If either external or internal data are used, the consistency of default definition implied in historical data must be carefully checked.

3. Sample size for each rating class has to be large enough to reduce sampling error. Small samples can sometimes produce evident problems, such as PD nonmonotonicity (i.e., rating 3 experiencing a higher default rate than rating 4 even if it should be a lower risk class in theory).

4. The length of the historical series available should be long enough to consider a full credit cycle, since PD for each rating class may differ from year to year.

5. In any case, a long period is needed to back-test any estimate, especially if the bank aims at estimating not only 1-year PD but also cumulative PDs and internal rating migration matrixes.

For instance, the Basel II Accord states that for corporate, sovereign, and bank exposures, banks willing to use their own internal PD estimates to calculate MRCR in the IRB approach may use either one or a mixture of (a) internal default experience, (b) external data through a careful mapping of internal data to agency ratings, and (c) a simple average of PD estimates derived from a statistical model. The bank should be able to explain its choices, and the length of the historical observation period must be at least five years for at least one source.

Irrespective of whether the bank uses internal or external data, a crucial issue is the underlying definition of default. According to Basel Committee (2006a, §452),[12] "a default is considered to have occurred . . . when either or both of the two following events have taken place.

- The bank considers that the obligor is unlikely to pay its credit obligation to the banking group in full, without recourse by the bank to actions such as realizing security (if held).
- The obligor is past due more than 90 days on any material obligation to the banking group. Overdrafts will be considered as being past due once the customer has breached an advised limit or been advised of a limit smaller than current outstandings."

While the first item represents an evident condition of default, the second one (relative to borrowers who are "past due") may create problems for PD calibration (and LGD as well, as we discuss later). In fact, historical internal data of many banks did not classify as defaults those delays in payments; as a consequence, recalculation of past PDs according to the Basel definition have been necessary for many banks willing to comply with the IRB approach under Basel II. At the same time, if a bank decides that its internal data are too limited and chooses to map internal ratings to any external source (e.g., agency ratings), it should check how closely the underlying definition of default matches the Basel II definition. The same thing happens if a statistical scoring model is used, since one should check whether "past due" firms that did not go bankrupt were considered "bad" firms when building the estimation sample for the scoring model. Moreover, since in some countries delays in payment were relatively common and did not necessarily lead to default, national supervisors have been allowed to relax the 90-day term to 180 days for retail and public-sector exposures and (only for a transition period of up to 5 years) for corporate exposures as well. Especially in those countries, changes in firms' habits are

---

12. While we refer here to the Basel II definition of default, we must point out that the current U.S. Federal Banking Agencies' proposal adopts a different definition of default, differentiating definitions between wholesale, revolving credit, and retail exposures and identifying, for instance, for retail exposures the critical threshold at 120 days past due. See Board of Governors of the Federal Reserve Systems (2006, pp. 62–65).

likely to occur, which on one hand is going to reduce the percentage of purely "past due" defaults by relatively healthy firms, but on the other hand is going to make calibration on historical data even more complex.

These problems unfortunately make PD calibration back-tests even harder than they would be otherwise. Checking PD estimates for each rating class would in itself require quite a long time, even for 1-year PDs, due to the need to consider at least a full economic cycle. Checking multiyear cumulative PDs or internal rating migration matrixes could require even more. This may be a particular problem when using those data for multiyear-transaction risk-adjusted pricing.

4.5.3 Point-in-Time versus Through-the-Cycle Internal Ratings

The problem of the difference between point-in-time (PIT) and through-the-cycle (TTC) ratings is particularly delicate in internal ratings definition, for at least two reasons, which we now briefly review. First of all, while Basel Committee (2006a) requires banks to adopt a more TTC approach, banks should use internal ratings both for pricing and for capital adequacy purposes. Supervisors' choice is understandable from a systemic view-point as a means to reduce procyclicality, i.e., the possibility of an increase of MRCR in recessions, leading to a reduction in banks' lending in bad times. In fact, PIT ratings would reasonably lead to more downgradings and hence to greater IRB MRCR increases in bad years. Yet, from the point of view of banks' pricing, using TTC ratings calibrated with average long-term PDs may imply relatively stable risk-adjusted prices irrespective of short-term conditions, which may be fine for long-term loans but potentially dangerous for short-term ones. As a consequence, the issue arises of whether different inputs should be used for short-term pricing. Interestingly, when the Basel II Accord states that IRB-compliant banks should prove their rating system is used for a number of decision-making purposes (see Basel Committee 2006a, §444, and Table 4-7), pricing is omitted.

Second, when, as usual in large banks with both wholesale and retail activities, different rating systems are combined for different segments, the risk manager must check the consistency and comparability of the different methods. One critical issue is the point-in-time/through-the-cycle logic. While mainly judgmental rating evaluations, such as those typical of larger and complex companies, may be more long-term, TTC ratings, ratings for small corporate exposures, which are usually driven by a statistical scoring system designed to estimate defaults over 1-year (and often assigning substantial weights to behavioral variables), are clearly PIT ratings, unless qualitative analysis is really able to convert it to a different time horizon. The risk for potential inconsistency across the rating approaches for different customer segments is hence nontrivial.

4.6 Estimating Loss Given Default

Whereas PD has been the crucial issue discussed so far, we now turn to loss given default (LGD) and exposure at default (EAD). In recent years LGD has attracted a growing interest in research, due to the increasing perception of its importance in credit risk management. The key issues to be discussed for LGD are (1) how to define it, (2) how to measure it, (3) which factors affect it, and (4) whether it is correlated with PD. First of all, LGD can be defined in percentage terms as the fraction of the loan that is not recovered in the event of a default. Therefore it is equal to 1 minus the recovery rate (RR).

Unfortunately, this implies that the definition and measurement of LGD depend on the definition of default. This issue has already been covered in the discussion of PD quantification, but it is equally relevant for LGD. Including past-due cases in the definition of default implies a higher PD but a lower LGD, since some obligors who delay payments for more than 90 days may sometimes be relatively sound borrowers that are later able to repay in full (i.e., LGD may be 0%), so it may be wise to model past-due LGD separately from LGD for other defaults (Schuermann 2005).

To avoid misunderstandings, we here define LGD as simply the ratio of the loss incurred on an exposure, relative to the exposure's EAD. This idea is important, since in the U.S. Federal Banking Agencies proposal for Basel II implementation in the United States (Board of Governors of the Federal Reserve Systems 2006) loss given default is defined as "an estimate of the economic loss that would be incurred on an exposure, relative to the exposure's EAD, if the exposure were to default within one year *during economic downturn conditions*" (italics added), while the "generic" LGD is defined as expected loss given default (ELGD). However, here we will follow the common practice in the risk management literature, in which LGD is not necessarily associated with an economic downturn (unless it is explicitly referred to as "downturn LGD").

As far as LGD measurement is concerned, we can distinguish among market LGD, workout LGD, and implied market LGD. *Market LGD* is the ratio of the market value at which defaulted bonds or defaulted loans are traded on the market to their par value. This measure reflects market expectations about discounted future cash flows from recovery, but unfortunately it is available for only a small portion of bank loans. *Workout LGD* is the present value of future cash flows from recovery (also considering negative cash flows for recovery costs). A third (but less common) solution is to derive *implied market LGD* from corporate bond credit spreads.

The problem in practice is that while substantial data are available for bonds' LGD, the same does not apply to bank loans, especially outside the United States. Bank loan recovery rates are generally superior to bond recovery rates (see Figure 4-6), first of all due to the fact that in most countries laws such as the absolute priority rule may favor them in the case of bankruptcy (for a review of main bankruptcy regimes in the United States, the UK, Germany, and France, see, for instance, de Servigny and Renault 2004).

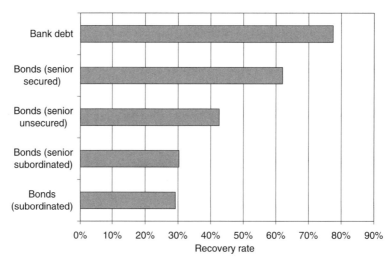

FIGURE 4-6   Recovery rates for bank loans versus bonds (1982–2005, issuer weighted). *Source:* Vazza, Aurora, and Schneck (2006).

Estimates of bank loan recovery rates and hence of LGD are relatively scarce and reveal a remarkable degree of fluctuation. Apart from the data reported in Figure 4-6, older studies, such as Asarnow and Edwards (1995), Carty and Lieberman (1998), and Grossman, Brennan, and Vento (1998), reported average recoveries for bank loans equal to 65.21%, 71.18%, and 82%, respectively. Yet even these average LGD values for large loan samples provide little guidance for the risk manager. Given the limited amount of public data concerning nonsyndicated loans, the need for most commercial banks (and especially those that are more involved in middle-market and retail lending) to develop internal LGD estimates is quite clear. In this case a workout LGD could be derived as 1 minus the present value of future net cashflows NF_i from recovery, divided by exposure at default:

$$\text{Workout LGD} = 1 - \frac{\sum_{i=1}^{t} \frac{NF_i}{(1+i)^t}}{\text{EAD}}$$

where net cash flows should be equal to the difference between recovered amounts and workout expenses. Since values should be discounted, the timing of recovery and the discounting rate matter. The choice of the discounting rate is not easy, since the original loan rate and the risk-free rate do not recognize the risk linked to the defaulted bond, and hence a theoretical risk premium for potential volatility of recovery values must be defined.

Given the difficulties of measuring LGD, the Basel Committee (2006a) has decided that even banks adopting the FIRB approach should use a regulatory estimate for LGD, which has been set at 45%. A partial reduction is possible when collateral is available (see Basel Committee 2006a; Resti and Sironi 2005). Instead, for those banks willing to apply for the AIRB approach and hence also to provide internal LGD estimates for MRCR purposes, supervisors stress that the bank "must estimate an LGD . . . that aims to reflect economic downturn conditions where necessary to capture relevant risks. This LGD cannot be less than the long-run default weighted average loss rate given default" (Basel Committee 2006a, §468).[13] In fact, since supervisors are concerned with potentially higher LGD in recessions for at least some kinds of exposures, the bank is asked to adopt a conservative view and hence use a downturn LGD when needed. The same worry supports the choice to set the inferior limit at the long-run *default*-weighted average. In fact, if in "good" (i.e., low default frequency) years LGD were lower and in "bad" years (i.e., high default frequency) LGD were higher, an equally weighted average across years assigning the same weight to good and bad ones may underestimate the true LGD.

When defining internal LGD estimates for risk measurement purposes or for calculating AIRB capital requirements as well, an analysis of factors influencing LGD is important in order to define, if possible, appropriate subsamples. Quite evidently, LGD depends on the seniority of the claim (as already shown in Figure 4-6). Moreover, the industry of the borrower appears to be relevant too (see, for instance, Altman and Kishore 1996; Acharya, Bharath, and Srinivasan 2003; Vazza, Aurora, and Schneck 2006). For instance,

---

13. Note that also in the U.S. Federal Banking Agencies proposal for rulemaking (Board of Governors of the Federal Reserve Systems 2006) it is clearly stated that the formulas to calculate risk-weighted assets and hence regulatory capital should be based on a downturn LGD (that, as noted earlier, is simply defined as LGD in the Federal Agencies' document) that cannot be less than the "expected LGD" (ELGD). A formula is also proposed to translate the forecast ELGD into a more conservative (downturn) LGD for those banks that will fail to have sufficient data to estimate the latter directly.

TABLE 4-8   Recovery Rates in Expansion Versus Recession Years (Moody's Data, 1970–2003; Percentages)

	Mean	Standard Deviation	25th Percentile	50th Percentile	75th Percentile	Number of Observations
Recessions	32.07	26.86	10.00	25.00	48.50	322
Expansions	41.39	26.98	19.50	36.00	62.50	1703
All	39.91	27.17	18.00	34.50	61.37	2025

Source: Schuermann (2005), based on Moody's 1970–2003 data.

recovery rates for utilities are substantially higher than those for real estate/construction firms. In any case, industries show significant differences in LGD through time, since recoveries are much lower in years in which an industry is in distress (Acharya, Bharath, and Srinivasan 2003; Gupton 2005).

This introduces the crucial issue of whether PD and LGD are linked. In recent years, empirical evidence has shown that PD and LGD are positively correlated, since they both tend to grow in recession years; see Hu and Perraudin (2002), Acharya, Bharath, and Srinivasan (2003), Altman et al. (2005), and the survey by Altman, Resti, and Sironi (2005). A simple picture of the problem is given in Table 4-8, comparing recovery rates (i.e., 1 minus LGD) in recession and expansion years.

Despite the recent literature in favor of the existence of a PD–LGD link, empirical studies are based essentially on market LGD for bonds, and this still leaves some theoretical questions open concerning the correlation between PD and bank loans' workout LGD. For instance, while Acharya, Bharath, and Srinivasan (2003) explain the correlation with industry effects, Altman et al. (2005) find a clear relationship among PD and LGD for bonds but argue that a microeconomic model based on supply and demand of defaulted bonds may explain the link more than a macroeconomic model linking both PD and LGD to the phase of the economic cycle. In other words, lower recoveries (measured by bond prices after default) may be explained because in bad years the higher default rate may imply an excess of supply, and hence a lower market value, of defaulted bonds. If one agrees on the demand-and-supply explanation for the PD–LGD link, it may still be questioned whether expected recovery from nontradable bank loans should be assumed to be as correlated to PD as bonds' recoveries are, or, instead, whether the variability of the loans' LGD should be driven almost exclusively by specific factors (such as the duration of the workout process or the type of underlying assets). Through time, the efforts by larger banks to increase the size and extent of internal databases for LGD quantification will make it possible to give an answer through detailed empirical tests.

The issue of the PD–LGD correlation is critical, since credit portfolio models (discussed later) usually assume LGD to be either fixed or stochastic but independent of PD. While even a stochastic LGD would not substantially change VaR estimates for a portfolio as long as it is independent of the PD, a stochastic and positively correlated LGD would make 99% or 99.97% potential losses become much higher (Altman et al. 2005).

4.7 Estimating Exposure at Default

Exposure at default is defined as "the expected gross exposure of the facility upon default of the obligor" (Basel Committee 2006a). While for certain kinds of loans the amount the bank is lending is fixed and predetermined, the issue of EAD is particularly relevant

TABLE 4-9   Drawn and Undrawn Portions of Loan Commitments as a Function of Initial Rating

Rating Class	Drawn Portion of Loan Commitment	Average of the Normally Undrawn Portion That Is Drawn in Case of Default
AAA	0.1%	69%
AA	1.6%	73%
A	4.6%	71%
BBB	20.0%	65%
BB	46.8%	52%
B	63.7%	48%
CCC	75.0%	44%

Source: Asarnow and Marker (1995).

for loan commitments, since a distressed borrower is likely to use a substantial part of initially undrawn loan commitments before defaulting, unless the bank has the chance to revoke the commitment and is able to anticipate the problem. The problem is more relevant for high-quality borrowers, since they can obtain larger commitments and the difference between the drawn portion in normal conditions and at default may be larger (see Table 4-9).

As a consequence, Basel II forces banks adopting either the standardized or the FIRB approach to translate off-balance sheet items, such as loan commitments, into credit-exposure equivalents by multiplying them by a credit-conversion factor (see Basel Committee 2006a, §§82–87 and §§311–315). Only facilities that are unconditionally cancellable by the bank or are automatically cancelled in case of a deterioration in borrower's credit-worthiness are given a 0% credit-conversion factor. In the AIRB, banks may estimate EAD internally but, again, adopting a conservative approach, especially for exposures where EAD were expected to increase during downturns (Basel Committee 2006a, §475). In fact, both PD and EAD are likely to grow in bad years, and this could make unexpected losses higher than if they were independent. Therefore, even banks that will not apply for the AIRB approach should try to study the potential correlation between the use of the undrawn portion of loan commitments, default rates, and the economic cycle, since this information should enter into the pricing policies for commitments and provide further incentives to continuous credit monitoring. In fact, even in those cases where a credit line can be discretionally revoked and hence would not imply any extra exposure and a specific capital requirement, the undrawn portion of the credit line represents a risk for the bank, unless the bank's credit-monitoring system (based on either a behavioral score or periodic credit review by analysts) proves to be able to anticipate the deterioration of the borrower's financial health.

4.8   Interaction between Basel II and International Accounting Standards

So far we have discussed credit risk management issues from the viewpoint of risk managers and supervisors. But a third perspective has to be considered: accountants' view about credit risk. This topic is particularly relevant now for European banks due to the introduction of new IAS/IFRS accounting principles and the consequent potential concerns for their consistency with supervisors' and risk managers' objectives. We should

TABLE 4-10   Default Versus Impairment

Default (Basel Committee 2006a, §452)	"A default is considered to have occurred with regard to a particular obligor when either or both of the two following events have taken place. • The bank considers that the obligor is unlikely to pay its credit obligations to the banking group in full, without recourse by the bank to actions such as realizing security (if held). • The obligor is past due more than 90 days on any material obligation to the banking group."
Impairment (US FAS 114, §8)	"A loan is impaired when, based on current information and events, it is probable that a creditor will be unable to collect all amounts due according to the contractual terms of the loan agreement. . . . An insignificant delay or insignificant shortfall in amount of payments does not require application of this Statement."
Impairment (IAS 39 as approved by EU Commission Regulation 2086/2084, §59)	"A financial asset or a group of financial assets is impaired and impairment losses are incurred if, and only if, there is objective evidence of impairment as a result of one or more events that occurred after the initial recognition of the asset (a 'loss event') and that loss event (or events) has an impact on the estimated future cash flows . . . that can be reliably estimated. . . . Losses expected as a result of future events, no matter how likely, are not recognized. Objective evidence that a financial asset or a group of financial assets is impaired includes . . . : (a) significant financial difficulty of the issuer or obligor; (b) a breach of contract, such as a default or delinquency in interest or principal payments; (c) the lender, for economic or legal reasons relating to the borrower's financial difficulty, granting to the borrower a concession that the lender would not otherwise consider; (d) it becoming probable that the lender will enter bankruptcy or other financial reorganization; (e) the disappearance of an active market for that financial asset because of financial difficulties or (f) observable data indicating that there is a measurable decrease in the estimated future cash flows from a group of financial assets since the initial recognition of those assets, although the decrease cannot yet be identified with the individual financial asset in the group."

first note that while accounting standards (in particular FAS 5 and 114 in the United States and IAS 39 for IAS/IFRS-oriented countries) are focused on the accounting concept of *impairment*, supervisors are concentrated on *default*. Different definitions are summarized in Table 4-10.[14] While these definitions are similar, they are not identical. At least potentially, in early years of application of IAS/IFRS (whose final version was issued in 2004, while FAS 114 dates back to 1993) there may still be some debate concerning whether a borrower moving "close enough" to default (e.g., by being downgraded in low internal rating classes that are adjacent to default or by being identified as a dangerous borrower by the internal monitoring system, which for smaller borrowers is usually based on a behavioral score only) may be a sufficient condition for impairment or whether impairment on an individual borrower should be considered to have occurred only in case of default.

14. Note that while the Table 4-10 definitions all derive from finally approved documents, the U.S. Federal Banking Agencies' September 2006 proposal for Basel II implementation by large U.S.-based international banks contains another different definition of default (see footnote 11).

Still, the two main topics that should be pointed out when considering differences between accounting and prudential supervision rules (and particularly, at present, between IAS/IFRS and Basel II) concern measuring LGD (or impairment losses) and, most importantly, the issue of provisions for expected losses. As far as LGD measurement is concerned, while the Basel II Accord stresses in general the need for a conservative approach and explains that "for each default asset, the bank must also construct its best estimate of the expected loss on that asset based on current economic circumstances and facility status," accounting principles stress the need to assess value as objectively as possible and state that "if there is objective evidence that an impairment loss . . . has been incurred, the amount of the loss is measured as the difference between the asset's carrying amount and the present value of estimated future cash flows . . . discounted at the financial asset's original effective interest rate (i.e., the effective interest rate computed at initial recognition)" (IAS 39, §63; see also FAS 114, §13 for a similar definition). These definitions potentially imply a different discounting rate (the original effective interest rate for accounting purposes, a current rate taking into consideration the riskiness of a defaulted loan for prudential ones) that should be considered.

The second and perhaps more important issue is related to expected losses and provisions. While Basel II requires the bank to hold sufficient provisions to cover expected losses, IAS39 clearly states that only *incurred* losses matter and "losses expected as a result of future events, no matter how likely, are not recognized." At the same time, reconciliation appears to be possible since IAS 39 allows to recognize impairment losses on a group of financial assets — see point (f) in the third row of Table 4-10 — even if it is impossible to identify the individual asset that is impaired.

If we consider first the requirements defined by the Basel Committee (2006a, §43 and §§374–386), under the IRB approach, general provisions are no longer included in Tier 2 as stated in the 1988 Basel I Accord. Instead, banks using the IRB approach must compare total provisions with expected losses. If provisions exceeded EL, the national supervisor may consider whether to include the difference in Tier 2. If, instead, provisions were insufficient, banks must deduct the difference 50% from Tier 1 and 50% from Tier 2; in other words, insufficient provisions must be covered by capital directly. Since IAS 39 rules out the possibility of making provisions based on expected losses, the risk of forcing banks to cover expected losses with capital would appear to be substantial. Yet, since accounting principles state that all those loans for which individual impairment conditions have not been discovered must still be collectively assessed for impairment (e.g., IAS39, §64), impairment losses for collectively impaired loans may be a substitute for provisions. This is true especially if estimates for collective impairment losses were based mostly on the historical loss experience of the bank (as would happen for expected losses as well). The initial experience with IAS/IFRS implementation has confirmed a tendency to reconcile the two perspectives successfully. The topic has also been addressed in a document by the Basel Committee (2006c), which has expressed an optimistic view about the possibility of developing collective impairment in a way that could comply with the new accounting principles and at the same time satisfy the need to protect against expected losses. Yet there are clearly at least two areas in which there is some unavoidable divergence. The first one is represented by newly originated loans. While from the supervisor's viewpoint the loan implies an expected loss from the loan's inception, accounting principles clearly rule out the possibility of registering impairment losses as a consequence of future events. Hence, the loan must be booked at amortized cost (unless the bank decides to evaluate it at fair value), with no deduction for any expected loss. The second one is the treatment of multiyear loans: While Basel II requires covering expected losses over a one-year horizon, losses on impaired loans should consider the impact on the discounted value of all future cash flows up to the loan's termination, thereby creating a difference between accounting and regulatory evaluations.

Reconciliation between supervisory and accounting treatment of loans and loan losses is likely to become simpler through time as banks and auditors will have a longer experience in IAS/IFRS implementation. Nevertheless the risk manager has to create a consistent database for credit risk management complying with both internal decision-making needs (e.g., loan pricing), Basel II, and accounting requirements. Substantial efforts may then be required to check that end users do not apply data created for one purpose and according to a certain regulation to an entirely different purpose for which the same data may be inadequate.

4.9   Alternative Approaches to Modeling Credit Portfolio Risk

So far we have investigated how rating assignment and quantification can work at the individual counterparty level. While expected-loss analysis can be based on individual loan characteristics, estimating unexpected losses requires understanding the interrelations among different loans. Imagine three ideal banks, A, B, and C, with a 1 million USD loan portfolio each and whose borrowers all have the same EAD (100%), PD (say, 1%), and LGD (50%); hence, expected losses would be identical. Imagine now that bank A's portfolio is represented by one single loan of 1 million USD, bank B's portfolio by 100 loans of 10,000 USD each to borrowers from the same industry and region, and bank C's portfolio by 100 loans of 10,000 USD each to borrowers from different industries and regions. While EL is the same, UL could be maximal for A, lower for B, and even lower for C, due to the different diversification benefits they can achieve at the portfolio level. The key critical point is how to model those benefits; this is the role of credit portfolio models.

Credit portfolio models can be classified mainly according to three different characteristics. The first one is whether they evaluate loans, and hence UL, in terms of mark-to-market value, loss-rate changes, or, at least potentially, in both ways. In fact, since loans are not necessarily marked-to-market in a bank's balance sheet, a risk manager may prefer to consider UL as the difference between worst-case loss rates in bad years and the expected loss rate, rather than as the unexpected reduction in the loan's mark-to-market value. If instead the model has to be applied to corporate bonds in the trading book, or if the bank has decided to evaluate loans in mark-to-market terms, the model should adopt the same view. Due to the different underlying methodology, mark-to-market models always consider both default and migration risk, since both may affect mark-to-market prices, while models following a loss-rate methodology usually consider default risk only (and are therefore usually named *default-mode* models).

The second key characteristic is based on how the interdependence among different borrowers' defaults is modeled. One solution is to adopt a Merton-model approach, where joint defaults should be driven by a joint reduction in asset values (which should be estimated through equity return correlation). The second one is to link default rates for different borrower clusters to macroeconomic factors, which would then become the correlation driver. A third alternative is to assume that, conditional on the bad or good state of the economy, defaults can be considered to be independent. CreditMetrics™ and PortfolioManager™, respectively developed by J.P. Morgan and Moody's/KMV, belong to the first group; CreditPortfolioView, developed by Thomas Wilson in McKinsey, is a macroeconomic-driven model; while CreditRisk+, by Credit Suisse Financial Products, can be considered a champion for the third class (actuarial models).

Finally, models can either be simulation based or analytical, depending on whether VaR must be calculated through a numerical simulation or can be derived directly. All the models we consider here, apart from CreditRisk+, are simulation based. Note that while these models may represent an industry benchmark since they are adopted by a large number of banks, many larger financial institutions have developed internal proprietary models. From this viewpoint, the analysis that follows clearly aims to discuss the key methodological choices that any credit risk model should make, with the help of some classical portfolio models, rather than supporting the choice of a specific model or software vendor against others (such as Standard & Poor's or Kamakura Corporation, to name just two) that have not been presented here.

4.9.1   CreditMetrics^{TM}

The CreditMetrics^{TM} model, developed by J.P. Morgan, aims to evaluate the potential impact of the borrowers' credit quality deterioration on credit portfolio market value, considering both default and migration risk. Specifically, the riskiness of nondefault states is identified by agency rating classes (e.g., Moody's or Standard & Poor's), thereby adopting a discrete classification of possible risk levels. In such a framework, the risk of a single position is identified with the possibility that the borrower may be downgraded or, at worst, may default. For bonds, an unanticipated downgrading should imply an increase in the *credit spread* applied to the downgraded issuer and hence a decrease in market value of already-issued bonds. The same should happen to a loan, provided it were valued at market value. Therefore, if forward credit spreads for any possible future rating class were known, it would be possible to identify the forward value of a loan given any potential rating migration over a certain time horizon (e.g., one year). In nondefault states, the value should be equal to future cash flows discounted on the basis of the proper credit-spread-term structure; in the case of default, the value of the position would be equal to its expected recovery value. In order to evaluate VaR for the single position, it is therefore necessary to know:

- The probability associated with each of the future possible "states" in one year's time (i.e., a one-year migration matrix)
- The credit-spread term structure associated with each rating class one year after the date of evaluation
- The expected recovery rate

The first set of data can be obtained from rating agencies' transition matrixes (see Section 4.2). Instead, the forward credit-spread term structure can be derived from the current credit-spread term structure. For each maturity and rating class, forward zero-coupon rates are derived for each rating classes from zero-coupon spot rates. According to market expectations theory, the expected zero-coupon rate is identified with the forward rate in one year's time for t years ($f_{1,t}$), obtained from one year's and $t + 1$ years' spot zero rates, r_1 and r_{t+1}, from the equation

$$(1 + r_1)(1 + f_{1,t})^t = (1 + r_{t+1})^{t+1}$$

from which we get

$$f_{1,t} = \left[\frac{(1 + r_{t+1})^{t+1}}{1 + r_1} \right]^{1/t} - 1$$

An example of curve of one-year forward zero-coupon rates is shown in Table 4-11.

By combining the transition matrix and the curve of forward zero-coupon rates for each rating class, the distribution of the single position's one-year market values can be obtained (see Table 4-12). For example, the 1-year forward market value of an A-rated 4-year loan ($MV_{t+1,A}$) with a fixed 5% interest rate per year can be calculated as follows, assuming no rating migration:

$$MV_{t+1,A} = 5 + \frac{5}{(1 + 3.72\%)} + \frac{5}{(1 + 4.32\%)^2} + \frac{100 + 5}{(1 + 4.93\%)^3} = 105.30$$

TABLE 4-11   Example of the Curve of Forward Zero-Coupon Rates (One Year from Evaluation Date)

Rating Class	Year 1	Year 2	Year 3	Year 4
AAA	3.60%	4.17%	4.73%	5.12%
AA	3.65%	4.22%	4.78%	5.17%
A	3.72%	4.32%	4.93%	5.32%
BBB	4.10%	4.67%	5.25%	5.63%
BB	5.55%	6.02%	6.78%	7.27%
B	6.05%	7.02%	8.03%	8.52%
CCC	15.05%	15.02%	14.03%	13.52%

Data are referred to Standard & Poor's rating classes.
Source: Gupton, Finger, and Bhatia (1997).

TABLE 4-12   Distribution of the One-Year Bond's Market Value

Rating at Year End	Probability[a]	VM$_{t+1}$ (coupon included)	Adjusted VM	Difference with respect to average price	Adjusted squared differences
AAA	0.09%	105.84	0.10	0.68	0.0004
AA	2.27%	105.70	2.40	0.54	0.0067
A	91.05%	105.30	95.88	0.14	0.0181
BBB	5.52%	104.43	5.76	−0.73	0.0297
BB	0.74%	100.43	0.74	−4.73	0.1656
B	0.26%	97.36	0.25	−7.80	0.1580
CCC	0.01%	83.94	0.01	−21.22	0.0450
Default	0.06%	32.74[b]	0.02	−72.42	3.1467
	Average: 105.16			Std Deviation: 1.89	

[a] Probabilities are derived from a 1-year transition matrix.
[b] Recovery rate is assumed to be equal to 32.74%.
Source: Gupton, Finger, and Bhatia (1997).

where the first term on the right-hand side is the first interest payment and the following terms are the present values of future interest payments and final reimbursement discounted at rating class A forward zero-coupon rates from Table 4-11.

The distribution of market values allows us to compute both the expected value of the loan at one year (i.e., 105.16) and two possible risk measures of the portfolio: the standard deviation of market values at year end and the difference between the average value and any given percentile (e.g., the 99th percentile) of the distribution. While the former is hard to translate into a measure of economic capital, since the distribution is clearly non-normal, the latter could instead represent a possible measure of VaR and of absorbed economic capital, provided it is calculated at the whole-portfolio level. This requires modeling the dependence between different obligors' upgrades or downgrades. Here CreditMetrics™ applies Merton's approach: By assuming that asset values are the drivers of the evolution of a borrower's risk level and that asset value returns are normally distributed, it is possible to identify not only a threshold below which default occurs, but also critical levels whose trespassing implies an upgrade or downgrade (Figure 4-7).

Figure 4-7 reports such thresholds in terms of the standardized distribution of asset returns for a BB-rated company. Default would occur for asset return values below Z_{def}; between the threshold Z_{def} and Z_{ccc}, the firm would have a CCC rating; at the opposite end, in the case of asset returns higher than Z_{AA}, the firm's rating would be upgraded to AAA. Obviously, for an asset return equal to zero the company would maintain its BB rating. In order to reproduce rating transition probabilities, thresholds must be fixed so that the area below the curve and between the two critical thresholds coincides with the probability of migration into the corresponding rating class. For example, if the one-year default probability of a BB-rated firm is equal to 1.06%, the threshold Z_{def} has to be such that

$$\int_{-\infty}^{Z_{def}} f(x)dx = F(Z_{def}) = 1.06\%$$

where $f(x)$ is the function of the density of the standardized normal distribution and $F(x)$ is the corresponding cumulative distribution function. Likewise, if the probability of a

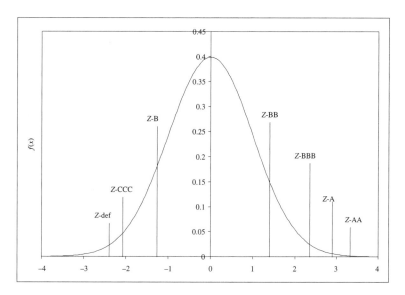

FIGURE 4-7   Critical thresholds for rating migrations for a company with BB initial rating.

downgrading to CCC (which corresponds to the area included between Z_{def} and Z_{ccc}) is 1%, it has to be

$$\int_{Z_{\text{def}}}^{Z_{\text{ccc}}} f(x)dx = F(Z_{\text{CCC}}) - F(Z_{\text{def}}) = 1\%$$

Once the critical thresholds have been defined, rating migrations can be simulated by simply extracting random values from a standard normal distribution and by identifying the correspondent rating. Joint migrations of multiple borrowers can be simulated, too, if their asset return distribution is assumed to be multivariate normal. The tendency of different borrowers to improve or worsen their credit quality at the same time can hence be modeled by properly identifying a measure of asset return correlation.

CreditMetrics^{TM} pragmatically assumes that such a correlation (which is unobservable directly) may be approximated by equity return correlation. Moreover, since directly calculating pairwise correlation coefficients in large loan portfolios would be cumbersome, equity returns for each firm are modeled through a multifactor model based on industry/country indexes (e.g., U.S. consumer staples, Japanese financials) and on a specific return component. For example, returns for two generic A and B stocks might be explained as:

$$r_A = w_{1,A}I_1 + w_{2,A}I_2 + w_{3,A}r'_A$$

$$r_B = w_{1,B}I_3 + w_{2,B}r'_B$$

where I_1, I_2, I_3 represent three industry/country indexes, r'_A, r'_B are the specific components, and coefficients w identify the weight of each component. This breakdown allows one to calculate and update correlation estimates for all firm combinations by calculating statistics for subindexes only. In fact, given $\rho_{I_1,I_3}, \rho_{I_2,I_3}$, if the specific component is assumed to be uncorrelated with industry/country indexes, then the correlation between A and B is given simply by

$$\rho_{A,B} = w_{1,A}w_{1,B}\rho_{I_1,I_3} + w_{2,A}w_{1,B}\rho_{I_2,I_3}$$

Once all pairwise correlations have been determined, portfolio VaR can be obtained through a Monte Carlo simulation. At every simulation run a vector n of correlated random numbers is drawn out of a normal multivariate distribution (where n is equal to the number of firms or homogeneous clusters of firms in the portfolio). Given the critical thresholds for each firm, depending on its initial rating, a joint migration for all borrowers can be obtained, and each loan can be reevaluated, depending on the simulated rating class, so as to obtain a simulated market value for the whole portfolio. For those firms that reach the default state in a given simulation run, it is possible either to consider a fixed LGD or to simulate an independent recovery rate, drawing from a beta distribution. Assuming a fixed LGD or a stochastic but independent LGD is a critical choice, given the empirical evidence in favor of positive PD–LGD correlation discussed in Section 4.6. By running a sufficiently high number of simulations, a full distribution for loan portfolio market value can be obtained, and VaR (and if needed expected shortfall as well) for any desired confidence interval can be calculated. The same simulation can also permit one to derive the marginal VaR for each loan, defined as the increase in the overall VaR obtained by adding the position to the rest of the portfolio, and can also be used to calculate the component VaR of the loan, i.e., its contribution to the overall VaR of the portfolio. Those measures can clearly be useful in either pricing or portfolio management decisions.

4.9.2   Moody's/KMV PortfolioManager^TM

The Moody's/KMV model described in Section 4.3 with reference to EL estimation can be extended to determine UL as well, through an approach that is similar but not identical to the CreditMetrics^TM model. Focusing on differences, whereas in CreditMetrics^TM the borrower's risk level is discretely distributed, since it is measured through agency ratings, in Moody's/KMV model the starting risk level is potentially quantified on the basis of a continuous distribution, measuring borrowers' risk through the individual *expected default frequency* (EDF) (even though, if needed, discrete EDF classes can be built). The second difference is that, unlike CreditMetrics^TM, Moody's/KMV model mainly evaluates exposures at book values, even if extensions to a market value approach are possible.

Still, there also important similarities. For instance, in Moody's/KMV model the relationship among borrowers' creditworthiness is modeled through asset return correlation, which in turn is obtained from equity return correlation. Equity correlation is estimated through a multifactor model similar to the CreditMetrics^TM's model, albeit a bit more complex, that again enables one to derive any pairwise correlation in a simpler and faster way (see Crouhy, Galai, and Mark 2000). Moreover, as with CreditMetrics^TM, through a Monte Carlo simulation of asset returns enough scenarios can be generated to permit the reconstruction of the full portfolio distribution so as to calculate VaR.

The difference here is that, depending on the purpose, both portfolio loss-rate distribution and its market-value distribution can be derived. In the former case, by simulating asset returns for each firm in the portfolio, a new distance from default and hence a new simulated EDF is obtained. From the simulated portfolio loss-rate distribution it is easy to derive the desired worst-case scenario and hence portfolio VaR.

While Moody's/KMV model is typically implemented so as to define portfolio loss rates in a book-value framework, extensions in a market-value framework could be derived in two ways, based either on risk-neutral valuation or on building EDF classes similar to agency rating classes.

The first solution is developed based on the risk-neutral valuation approach to the pricing of contingent claims, which states that the fair value of a claim can be derived as the present value of the expected payoff at maturity in a risk-neutral world. This implies (1) discounting the expected payoff at maturity at the risk-free rate and (2) calculating the expected payoff based on risk-neutral probabilities of the different states of the world rather than on real probabilities. Let us consider a 1-year risky zero-coupon bond, which pays 100 in case of no default and $100(1 - LGD)$ in case of default. If we assume we knew that the risk-neutral default probability is Q, the fair price of the bond could be calculated as

$$P = \frac{1}{1+r}[(1-Q)\cdot 100 + Q\cdot 100\cdot(1-LGD)]$$

where the term in brackets represents the expected payoff at maturity under the risk-neutral probabilities. To understand how risk-neutral default probability is related to real-world default probability, we can consider Merton's (1974) framework, described earlier, according to which default occurs when the value of assets is lower than the face value of debt at debt maturity. In a risk-neutral framework, firm assets' expected return would be set equal to the risk-free rate r (in fact, in a risk-neutral world no investor would ask for extra return on a risky asset) instead of to the real expected return μ, which would be higher than r. Consequently, from option-pricing theory it can be shown that the real and the risk-neutral default probabilities, q and Q would, respectively, be

$$q = N - \left(\frac{\ln\left(\frac{V_0}{B}\right) + \left(\mu - \frac{\sigma^2}{2}\right)T}{\sigma\sqrt{T}} \right) \quad \text{and} \quad Q = N\left(-\frac{\ln\left(\frac{V_0}{B}\right) + \left(r - \frac{\sigma^2}{2}\right)T}{\sigma\sqrt{T}} \right)$$

where N is the cumulative density function of a standard normal distribution, V_0 represents the initial value of assets, B is the face value of debt (i.e, the default threshold), σ is asset return volatility, and T is debt maturity. Since $\mu > r$, the risk-neutral default probability, Q, is higher than the real default probability, q. Even if Moody's/KMV EDF is not derived from a pure application of the Merton model, the risk-neutral solution is similar and hence transforms the EDF into a higher, risk-neutral EDF that can be used for bond-pricing purposes (see Crouhy, Galai, and Mark 2000 for the detailed derivation).

The second possible solution is to define "EDF classes" to be associated to a specific credit-spread term structure, as CreditMetrics™ does for rating classes, and then to estimate the distribution of market values according to migration probabilities in different EDF classes. Note that while "EDF classes" look similar to the *rating* classes utilized by CreditMetrics™, they are different since (a) they are based on a point-in-time measure such as EDF rather than on a through-the-cycle evaluation by analysts, and consequently (b) the probability for a firm to persist in the same EDF class within one year is much lower than for agency ratings (i.e., EDF class migrations are much more frequent). This effect is made clear by comparing probabilities on the diagonal in Table 4-13, an EDF class migration matrix, with the rating agency migration matrix presented earlier (Table 4-2). The process for deriving market values given any possible migration of the loan or bond follows a process similar to CreditMetrics™.

TABLE 4-13   One-Year Transition Matrix Based on Classes of Expected Default Frequency (%)

Rating at the beginning of the year	Rating at Year End							
	1 (AAA)	2 (AA)	3 (A)	4 (BBB)	5 (BB)	6 (B)	7 (CCC)	Default
1 (AAA)	66.26	22.22	7.37	2.45	0.86	0.67	0.14	0.02
2 (AA)	21.66	43.04	25.83	6.56	1.99	0.68	0.20	0.04
3 (A)	2.76	20.34	44.19	22.94	7.42	1.97	0.28	0.10
4 (BBB)	0.30	2.80	22.63	42.54	23.52	6.95	1.00	0.26
5 (BB)	0.08	0.24	3.69	22.93	44.41	24.53	3.41	0.71
6 (B)	0.01	0.05	0.39	3.48	20.47	53.00	20.58	2.01
7 (CCC)	0.00	0.01	0.09	0.26	1.79	17.77	69.94	10.13

Source: Kealhofer, Kwok, and Weng (1998), KMV Corporation.

4.9.3 CreditPortfolioView

Undoubtedly, the economic cycle has an impact on credit risk. And the main objective of the CreditPortfolioView model developed by McKinsey — see Wilson (1997a, b) — is precisely to model this relationship properly. Therefore, whereas in CreditMetrics™ and Moody's/KMV model default dependence is modeled through a Merton-like approach, in CreditPortfolio View macroeconomic variables are the drivers explaining comovements toward either downgrading or default of different borrowers. As with Moody's/ KMV's PortfolioManager™, the model can calculate portfolio value and VaR both at market values and — with a simplified approach — at book values.

The starting assumption is that the default probability p_{jt} of a segment j of customers (e.g., a combination of industry/geographic area/rating class) at time t could be written as

$$p_{jt} = \frac{1}{1 + e^{Y_{jt}}}$$

where Y_{jt} represents the value at time t of a "state of the economy" index for segment j based on macroeconomic factors. Higher values of Y_{jt} indicate better economic conditions for the cluster of borrowers and a smaller default probability (which is clearly bounded between 0 and 1). The index Y_{jt} is modeled as a function of macroeconomic variables X_{j1}, $X_{j2}, \ldots, X_{jn}$; i.e.,

$$Y_{jt} = \beta_{j,0} + \beta_{j,t} X_{j,1,t} + \beta_{j,2} X_{j,2,t} + \beta_{j,3} X_{j,3,t} + v_{j,t}$$

where both the vector of relevant macroeconomic factors X_j and coefficients β are specific for the segment j and must be selected and calibrated based on the past history of default frequency p_j for the segment. In other words, the "state of the economy" index for each segment will be linked to the subset of macroeconomic variables that best explains the variability through time of the historical default rate for the segment. The final term, $v_{j,t}$, is a zero-mean random value with a normal distribution and volatility σ_j and represents the specific risk component for cluster j. Instead, macroeconomic variables represent the common factors that will be used to model the dependence between defaults in different clusters/segments.

In turn, each macroeconomic variable is assumed to follow an autoregressive process AR(2) expressed by

$$X_{j,i,t} = k_{i,0} + k_{i,1} X_{j,i,t-1} + k_{i,2} X_{j,i,t-2} + \varepsilon_{j,i,t}$$

where coefficients k also have to be estimated by regression and ε is the usual zero-mean, standard normal distributed error term.

Once the vectors of parameters β and k have been estimated and given the values of relevant macroeconomic variables at time t, the value of index Y_j (and therefore the PD for segment j) at time $t + 1$ may be simulated by simply drawing the vector of random values

$$E = \begin{pmatrix} v_1 \\ \cdots \\ v_n \\ \varepsilon_1 \\ \\ \varepsilon_m \end{pmatrix} \sim N(0, \Sigma)$$

which identifies random shocks for both the specific risk components for each segment (v) and macroeconomic variables (ε). Such a vector is distributed according to a multivariate normal distribution with mean equal to zero and covariance matrix Σ (which hence defines the volatility of each random variable and pairwise correlation between each couple of variables). By running a sufficient number of random draws, it would be possible to estimate the distribution of portfolio loss rates. In this case the driver for correlation about the loss rate in different clusters would be represented by macroeconomic factors; two clusters would be linked if they either both share one or more macroeconomic factors (e.g., real GDP growth is a relevant factor for both) or are exposed to different factors but these factors are correlated.

At least potentially, the simulated value of p may also be used for more sophisticated analyses, such as to set up a conditioned transition matrix. Intuitively, negative phases of the economic cycle would imply not only an above-average PD, but also higher probabilities of downgradings and lower probabilities of upgradings. Therefore Credit-PortfolioView suggests "deforming" in one direction or the other the long-term unconditional transition matrix, depending on whether the expected PD for the next year is higher or lower than the long-term average. In particular, the critical variable is $\text{SDP}_t/\Phi\text{SDP}$, where SDP_t (speculative default probability) is the default probability for speculative-grade borrowers (which are more sensitive to the economic cycle) in year t, and ΦSDP is the corresponding unconditional default probability. If the ratio is higher than 1 (unfavorable economic cycle), the transition matrix will be modified by increasing probabilities of default and downgrading and by reducing probabilities of upgrading; the opposite would occur if the ratio were below 1. The correction should be more significant for lower rating classes, since their sensitivity to the trend of the economic cycle is higher. If sufficient data were available to properly estimate conditional transition matrixes, this process could allow one not only to calculate the one-year portfolio VaR, but also to simulate multiannual transition processes, by simulating macroeconomic variables over more than one year and consequently derive conditional transition matrixes.

The unquestionable *appeal* of the model is its attempt to model directly the link between the economic cycle and credit risk and to explain correlation among clusters of borrowers (e.g., industry/rating/geographic area clusters) through their sensitivity to common macroeconomic factors, which may help shape portfolio composition strategies. On the other hand, the main disadvantage is the high number of coefficients to be estimated, which can become a problem, especially if limited historical data are available. The level of disaggregation in defining borrowers' clusters also matters in practice, since a more analytical disaggregation and a higher number of clusters may make the relationship with macroeconomic variables more detailed but may imply a higher estimation error in calibrating model parameters.

Finally, while CreditPortfolioView's approach to defining conditional VaR estimates is appealing, efforts have been made to introduce conditional features in models such as CreditMetrics™ as well. Belkin, Suchower, and Forest (1998a, b), after defining the critical thresholds in the CreditMetrics™ approach based on the unconditional transition matrix, have suggested that values for the random standard normal variable driving simulated migrations (or defaults) could be extracted as

$$X = \sqrt{\rho}Z + \sqrt{1-\rho}\varepsilon$$

where Z is a standard normal variable representing the economic cycle, ε is another standard normal variable that defines the specific risk component of the single borrower, and ρ is a parameter to be estimated. The independence of Z and ε ensures that X also has unitary variance while its mean is clearly zero. If Z is considered an indicator of the economic cycle's trend, positive values of Z will increase X and therefore facilitate upgrades; in contrast, negative values of Z (corresponding to an unfavorable economic cycle) will decrease X, thus increasing the probability of downgrading and default events. By adopting such an approach, Belkin, Suchower, and Forest (1998a, b) have retrospectively estimated, on the basis of the real historical transition frequencies for the period 1981–1997, values of Z for each year (also determining a value for the ρ coefficient). This can be considered a first step to accomplish what-if analyses: If the risk manager assumes that the next year is likely to be similar to one of the past years whose values of Z are known, he could simulate portfolio values conditional on Z being equal to the one in the reference year. A subsequent step would be to model a process for Z.

A more sophisticated version of the same approach has been proposed by Kim (1999), which defines Z as a standardized variable given by

$$Z_t = -\frac{\Phi^{-1}(\mathrm{SDP}_t) - \mu_{\Phi^{-1}(\mathrm{SDP}_t)}}{\sigma_{\Phi^{-1}(\mathrm{SDP}_t)}}$$

where SDP_t is the PD of speculative grade borrowers in year t and $\Phi^{-1}(x)$ represents the inverse of the cumulative distribution function of a standard normal distribution, so $\Phi^{-1}(\mathrm{SDP}_t)$ is the value for which the cumulative distribution function is equal to SDP_t. μ and σ represent, respectively, the mean and the standard deviation of such a distribution. Therefore, Z will be positive when the PD of speculative grade borrowers will be lower than its average. Estimating the coefficient ρ should again be derived from empirical data, possibly distinguishing between investment- and speculative-grade rating classes, since the former should, in theory, be less sensitive to the economic cycle.

Kim (1999) argues that the dynamics of $\Phi^{-1}(\mathrm{SDP}_t)$ may be explained through some macroeconomic or financial market factors (similarly to CreditPortfolioView) as

$$\Phi^{-1}(\mathrm{SDP}_t) = \sum_{i=1}^{n} \beta_i X_{i,t-1} + \varepsilon_t$$

where variables X are the relevant explanatory factors and β their coefficients; both should be estimated empirically. Note that unlike in CreditPortfolioView, there would be no differentiation for a "state of the economy" index among clusters, but, rather, a single index Z would be used for every counterparty.

4.9.4 CreditRisk+

When compared to the models described so far, CreditRisk+ differs, since (1) it concentrates on default risk only, without considering migration risk, and (2) it evaluates portfolio VaR in terms of book value only, so that it cannot be used in a market-value framework. While these may be considered limitations of the model, CreditRisk+ has the merit of requiring fewer inputs than other models and of being able to derive portfolio VaR analytically without resorting to computationally intensive Monte Carlo simulations.

The first step is to model the distribution of the number of default events within the portfolio. In the simpler version of the model, this distribution is assumed to be Poissonian, so the probability of having n defaults in a certain cluster or segment of borrowers is given by

$$p(n) = \frac{e^{-\mu} \mu^n}{n!}$$

where μ is the average number of defaults within the cluster (and hence depends on the cluster's PD and the number of borrowers). In order to obtain the distribution of portfolio losses, the portfolio can be divided into a series of homogeneous "loss bands" expressed as multiples of a certain amount. For example, if the bands were calculated for multiples of 10,000 USD, a borrower with a 60,000 USD loan and an expected LGD equal to 70% would create a loss in case of default equal to 42,000 USD and would be assigned to the band of 40,000 USD loss positions (i.e., 42,000 would be rounded off to the nearest multiple of 10,000). By doing so, the implicit assumption is that both exposure and loss given default are fixed. As discussed earlier in this chapter, this may be a significant conceptual simplification, given that part of the difference between EL and UL may derive from actual EAD and LGD differing from expected values, especially considering that they are likely to be positively correlated with default rates. Each band can be characterized by an expected number of defaults, which differs according to the expected PD of borrowers included in the band. Subsequently, a distribution of aggregated portfolio losses can be analytically derived, assuming that that defaults occur independently. While it is not possible for reasons of synthesis to repeat all the analytical passages through which portfolio-loss distribution is reconstructed, the intuition is that the distribution of losses in each band is modeled through its probability-generating function. The assumption of default independence across bands allows us to build the probability-generating function for whole-portfolio losses as the product of probability-generating functions for the different bands. This function can then be reversed into a probability distribution of portfolio losses (see Credit Suisse Financial Products 1997).

A second and more sophisticated version of CreditRisk+ relaxes the assumption that the expected number of defaults in each band is equal to a fixed value μ. By assuming that the default rate X is a random variable with average μ_X and standard deviation σ_X that follows a Gamma distribution, it can be shown that the distribution of the number of defaults in a portfolio would follow a negative binomial distribution. The probability to record n cases of default is therefore equal to

$$p(n) = (1 - p_k)^{\alpha_k} \binom{n + \alpha_k - 1}{n} p_k^n$$

where

$$\alpha = \left(\frac{\mu_X}{\sigma_X} \right)^2, \qquad \beta = \frac{\sigma_X^2}{\mu_X}, \qquad \text{and} \qquad p_k = \frac{\beta_k}{1 + \beta_k}$$

This produces a distribution that, with equal average default rate, is characterized by a more remarkable *skewness* and by the presence of a right tail in the higher distribution. Consequently, the probability associated with the occurrence of extreme losses increases. As in the simpler version of the model, the loss distribution for the entire portfolio can be derived analytically through the aggregation of probability-generating functions for the losses in different bands.

A crucial issue in CreditRisk+ is represented by correlation assumptions. The assumption of independent default is not theoretically desirable, even if it is important in the model to simplify the aggregation of probability-generating functions at portfolio level. Yet, as a consequence, diversification benefits in the model would only derive from an

TABLE 4-14   Conditional Default Independence as a Way to Introduce Dependence

	(1) State of the World 1: Expansion		
	Firm A Does Not Default	Firm A Defaults	Sum
Firm B Does Not Default	98.01%	0.99%	99%
Firm B Defaults	0.99%	0.01%	1%
Sum	99%	1%	

	(2) State of the World (2): Recession		
	Firm A Does Not Default	Firm A Defaults	Sum
Firm B Does Not Default	82.81%	8.19%	91%
Firm B Defaults	8.19%	0.81%	9%
Sum	91%	9%	

	Unconditional Default Probabilities (Assuming (1) and (2) have Same Probability)		
	Firm A Does Not Default	Firm A Defaults	Sum
Firm B Does Not Default	90.41%	4.59%	95%
Firm B Defaults	4.59%	0.41%	5%
Sum	95%	5%	

increase in the number of counterparties, without giving any relevance to industry or geographic diversification. When addressing this criticism, we must first note that assuming a zero *default* correlation is not identical to assume a zero *asset* correlation. Since default is a binary variable (either the borrower defaults or it survives), two borrowers with an asset correlation equal to a given value would typically have a much lower default correlation, and hence assuming a zero default correlation is often not as crude as it may seem at first glance. In any case, this issue is addressed by CreditRisk+ in two ways. The first one, which we have already described, is to make the expected number of defaults for each band a random rather than a fixed value. As a consequence, even if defaults are assumed to be conditionally independent, the effects of bad and good economic cycles (a higher X implying a "bad" year, a lower X a "good" one) are introduced. Since borrowers inside a group experience the same value of X together, defaults are unconditionally correlated. This point may be clarified through an example (Table 4-14).[15]

Conditional on the observed state of the world, defaults for the two firms A and B described in Table 4-14 are independent both in recession and in expansion. In fact, joint default probabilities are simply the product of marginal stand-alone default probabilites (e.g., the probability of joint default in recession, 0.81%, is simply equal to 9% × 9%). Yet, if we build the unconditional default distribution by assuming that recession and expansion have the same 50% probability, the resulting joint distribution (bottom part of Table 4-14, which is obtained as a weighted average of corresponding cells in expansion and recession scenarios) shows that defaults are no longer independent. In fact, the joint default probability (0.41%) is higher than the product of stand-alone default probabilities (i.e., 5% × 5% = 0.25%). Unconditional default correlation is hence positive. Whereas defaults are conditionally independent, the fact that both firms enter recession or expan-

15. I am grateful to my colleague Andrea Resti for suggesting this example.

sion together makes their defaults unconditionally correlated. The same effect occurs when assuming that the same random value of X occurs for all borrowers in the cluster in CreditRisk+ and a conditional independence of defaults given the outcome for X.

In this case, however, the composition of subgroups of borrowers becomes very important. The second refining proposed by CreditRisk+ is therefore to split borrowers by industry. Firms exposed to more than one sector may be handled by dividing their loss in case of *default* into quotas (indicated for firm A with θ_{A1}, θ_{A2}, . . ., θ_{An}) among industries as a function of the firm's exposure (e.g., measured by revenues in each industry). Since different sectors are considered independent, default dependence between firms A and B requires that they share the exposure to some sector. In fact, the correlation between two generic firms A and B is given by

$$\rho_{A,B} = \sqrt{\mu_A \mu_B} \sum_{k=1}^{n} \theta_{Ak} \theta_{Bk} \left(\frac{\sigma_k}{\mu_k} \right)^2$$

where μ_A, μ_B represent the default probability of A and B, θ_{ik} is the share of exposure of firm i in industry k, and μ_k, σ_k represent the average default rate and the relevant volatility for each of n industries. Hence, correlation is zero either (a) if the default rate, as in the first simplified version of the model, is maintained constant ($\sigma_k = 0$) or (b) if the two firms have no sector in common (which would imply $\theta_{Ak}\theta_{Bk} = 0$ for any possible k). This implies that the extension of industry matters: More disaggregation implies lower chances for two firms to share an exposure in the same sector and hence a reduction in portfolio default correlation. At the same time, the solution to split a firm into quotas pertaining to different industries has the conceptual drawback that in practice the firm is treated as if it were a number of different firms, which in theory could default in one industry and survive in others; potentially, concentration risk may not be properly captured.

In contrast with these potential drawbacks, however, CreditRisk+ maintains the advantage of deriving analytically the data required for portfolio VaR calculation, either on a one-year or on a multiyear horizon, with no need for Monte Carlo simulation.

4.10   Comparison of Main Credit Portfolio Models

At the end of the analysis of each model, we can try to summarize their characteristics in comparative terms (Table 4-15) and point out the main pros and cons of each model. In order to perform a critical analysis of the merits and limits of the main models, we must first point out the *trade-off* between precision and sophistication of the model against the difficulty of input estimation. Apart from theoretical merits, the possibility of feeding a model consistently with correct data should be a relevant topic in the final decision. A more sophisticated model may be chosen even if currently available data were relatively poor, provided only that the bank were willing to invest substantial effort in improving input data through time. When considering this trade-off, the two extremes are represented by CreditPortfolio View and CreditRisk+. The first is perhaps one of the most theoretically attractive models, since it builds portfolio correlation effects on macroeconomic variables, which may also provide extra value in managing portfolio composition. However, the risk for estimation error in parameter calibration is much higher, especially if a bank wanted to apply it in a mark-to-market approach using conditional transition matrixes. In fact, while it may be easy to agree that in unfavorable years downgrading and default probabilities should be increased relative to upgrading probability, and vice

TABLE 4-15   Summary of Main Credit Risk Models

	Model			
	CreditMetrics™/ Credit Manager	Moody's/KMV	CreditRisk+	CreditPortfolio View
Type of risk considered	Both migration risk and default risk	Default risk, but adaptable for the migration risk in a market value framework	Only default risk	Both migration risk and default risk
Loan evaluation framework	Mainly at market values	Mainly at book values	At book values	Adaptable to both book and market values
Borrower mapping	By rating class	Individual, based on single borrower EDF	User-defined clusters (rating class/industry)	User-defined clusters (rating class/industry/ geographic area)
Correlation drivers at portfolio level	Asset return correlation estimated through equity return correlation (multifactor model)	Asset return correlation estimated through equity return correlation (multifactor model)	Default rate volatility at cluster level (causing unconditional default dependence) and industry mapping	Macroeconomic variables which jointly impact on default probabilities of different clusters
Drivers of sensitivity to the economic cycle	While exposure mapping is based on through the cycle agency ratings and migration is based on unconditional transition matrixes, a partial effect may be introduced by the credit spread term structure	Individual risk is based on EDF, which is sensitive to equity prices and volatility	No. The rate of *default* is volatile but independent from the economic cycle, unless the expected default rate input is conditioned by the user on the current phase of the cycle	PD are linked to macroeconomic variables, hence their current value may impact PD estimates
Nature of recovery rate	Random	Random	Fixed	Random
Method to obtain portfolio loss distribution	Monte Carlo simulation	Monte Carlo simulation	Analytical, no simulation required	Monte Carlo simulation

versa in favorable years, the optimal size of these increases and decreases is a complex empirical issue that would be hard to back-test in the short run. At the opposite end, in CreditRisk+ required *input* data are reduced to the minimum, and portfolio-loss distribution can be derived without simulations. However, this is obtained at the cost of accepting some simplifications (e.g., assuming a fixed recovery rate, modeling default independence across industries, which in turn makes industry decomposition potentially impact on portfolio VaR).

While the trade-off between refinement and complexity may be one issue to consider in choosing the right approach (either by using an existing model or by trying to develop a proprietary model based to a certain extent on one of these approaches), a second key element is represented by the prevailing customer base of the bank. For instance, investment banks with portfolios exposed mainly to larger, typically rated and listed counterparties may find it easier to adopt CreditMetrics™ or Moody's/KMV PortfolioManager™, while for those commercial banks that are exposed mainly to smaller firms, the interest in models such as CreditRisk+ and CreditPortfolio View increases. On one hand, the latter do not require either rating or EDF (which would be unavailable, or harder to estimate, for a large part of borrowers) to map exposures; on the other hand, the existence of a large enough number of exposures may make it easier for larger banks to estimate parameters even for more sophisticated models such as CreditPortfolio View.

We have presented some of the most well-known models, but a number of banks have developed other, proprietary models based on internal expertise and/or on the support of consulting firms (see Box 4-2). Often these models represent variations, extensions, or adaptations of one of the different approaches described here, and hence in any case they can still represent a useful basis for a proper assessment of the merits and limits of the system in use. In fact, even if budget constraints or input unavailability leads one to choose a portfolio model that is good even if not perfect, clearly understanding the main underlying assumptions and potential limitations is important in order to avoid misunderstanding the model's outcomes and hence making inappropriate decisions.

Box 4-2: Industry Practices Concerning Credit Portfolio Models

Which models do banks actually use? Making general statements on this point is difficult, since the final choice is influenced by a number of elements, including the size of the bank (and hence its available budget for credit portfolio models) and the relative dimension of the segments of its credit portfolio. An investment bank operating in the United States with a larger proportion of rated borrowers is different from a large commercial bank in Germany with a much larger proportion of loans to SMEs. Yet the 2004 survey conducted by Rutter Associates on behalf of the International Association of Credit Portfolio Managers (IACPM), the International Swaps and Derivatives Association (ISDA), and the Risk Management Association (RMA) and involving 44 banks from different countries gives some insights on market practices. Out of 44 banks, 43 indicated that they use a credit risk model to determine economic capital. When asked about their primary credit portfolio model (note that five banks gave multiple answers), 21 banks said they use an internally developed model; Moody's/KMV Portfolio Manager was used by 20 banks, Credit Suisse First Boston's CreditRisk+ and CreditMetrics/Credit Manager by three banks each, while two banks were using other models (Rutter Associates 2006).

While a large number of banks uses proprietary internally developed models, the interaction with vended models is usually significant. In a parallel research project run by IACPM and ISDA with Rutter Associates, 28 banks were involved in an exercise aimed at comparing economic capital results from different credit portfolio risk models. Only 12 of the 28 banks used a vended model directly to determine their economic capital; but among the 16 using an internally developed model, 6 indicated that they obtained their economic capital measure from an internal model that used the outputs produced by one of the vended models, 8 that they used an internal model that was similar to a vended model, and only 2 that they used an internal model that was largely different from the existing chief vended models (IACPM-ISDA 2006).

Box 4-3: How Close Are Results Obtained from Credit Risk Portfolio Models?

Comparing the anatomy of major vendors' credit risk models has been a relevant issue since they first appeared on the market (see, for instance, Koylouglu and Hickman 1998; Crouhy, Galai, and Mark 2000; Gordy 2000). The issue has also been recently addressed in the IACPM-ISDA (2006) Survey just described in Box 4-2 involving 28 different banks, which were asked to run different credit risk models on the same loan portfolio and adopting homogeneous data. The purpose was to check whether models could produce similar results once input data consistence was ensured. The comparison was run between Moody's/KMV Portfolio Manager, J.P. Morgan/RiskMetricsGroup's Credit Manager, and CSFB's CreditRisk+; also, proprietary models close enough to those models were used.

Table 4-16 summarizes the main results in a default-only setting (i.e., considering default risk only and neglecting mark-to-market consequences of downgrades that did not imply a default). Differences in the results between PortfolioManager and the other two models appear to derive mostly from the different treatment of intermediate cash flows and from the different moment in which the evaluation is run. The loans considered in the exercise had quarterly interest payments, and while PortfolioManager assumes that even intermediate payments would be lost, CreditManager and CreditRisk+ assume that intermediate payments would be received and default will affect only the capital payment at a one-year horizon. The difference in coupon treatment is particularly relevant for riskier loans, which were assumed to have higher spreads. Moreover, while CreditManager measures losses at the end of the year, PortfolioManager considers the present value of future losses by discounting them at the risk-free rate. As a consequence, while estimates for economic capital appear to be quite different from each other (Table 4-16, second column), when the effect of these differences is accounted for (third column), differences appear to be minor. Similar results were also obtained when comparing CreditManager and PortfolioManager in a mark-to-market setting (see IACPM-ISDA 2006).

Yet the choice of the model is not irrelevant. In a second step of the IACPM-ISDA empirical analysis it appeared, for instance, that the reaction of the three models to changes in loan portfolio concentration were clearly different. Moreover, estimates concerning individual loan contributions to portfolio risk substantially varied, even if this was due partially to the models and partially to the individual bank's choices and policies. One might argue, therefore, that even with similar parameters and models the dispersion in individual contribution estimates might lead to remarkably different pricing guidelines from bank to bank.

TABLE 4-16   Comparison of Portfolio Manager, Credit Manager, and CreditRisk+ (After Controlling for Input Consistence; Default Risk Only)

Model	Economic Capital at 99.9% (Base Case)	Economic Capital at 99.9% (No Spreads and Risk-Free Rate)
Portfolio Manager and similar models	4419.5	3791.2
Credit Manager and similar models	3816.7	3522.2
CreditRisk+ and similar models	3387.3	3662.0

4.11   Summary

When measuring the impact of credit risk, the bank has to estimate the distribution of potential losses that can be generated by its credit portfolio. The two key concepts are represented by expected losses, i.e., the statistical mean of the loss distribution, and unexpected losses, which can be defined as the amount of losses in some extreme percentile of the loss distribution (e.g., 99%, 99.9%) minus expected losses. Expected losses represent a cost of being in the lending business and hence should be covered by provisions, while capital — assuming an adequate amount of provisions — should be used to cover unexpected losses. The main determinants of the dynamics of the expected and unexpected losses for a given exposure are represented by exposure at default (EAD), probability of default (PD), and the ratio of the loss in the event of default to the exposure at default, i.e., the loss given default (LGD). Agency rating companies support financial institutions and investors in evaluating the riskiness of a borrower by issuing independent judgments on a borrower's credit quality, which are expressed by classifying the borrower in a given rating class. Rating agencies' historical data, such as transition matrixes describing the evolution patterns of borrowers' ratings through time and cumulative and marginal default rates, may represent very important sources of information for a risk manager. Similarly to rating agencies, even if often with different methodologies, banks usually classify borrowers in internal rating classes with different probabilities of default. The assignment of a borrower to a class is a process that usually combines multiple elements, including both quantitative data and qualitative information, which can be aggregated through the human judgment of a credit analyst or a statistical model or a combination of both. The specific solution adopted depends on many factors, including the type of counterparty (the process for a large corporation being entirely different from consumer credit to an individual).

The 2004 Basel II Accord introduces a much greater risk-based differentiation in capital requirements for loans as opposed to Basel I and allows banks (in those countries where the accord has been entirely transformed into national regulation) to choose among a standardized approach (where capital requirements are driven by the type of counterparty and its agency rating), a foundation internal rating-based approach (where capital requirements depend on a formula in which the critical input of the borrower's PD is estimated by the bank), and an advanced internal rating-based approach (in which a bank can also use its own input as far as the loan's EAD, LGD, and maturity are concerned). Both foundation and advanced internal rating-based approaches require prior validation by supervisory authorities of the databases and methodologies used to produce the critical inputs supplied by the individual bank. In the United States the current proposal for the reform of minimum capital requirements, if approved, will force large internationally oriented U.S. banks to adopt the advanced internal rating-based approach and will leave other banks the choice of either doing the same as larger banks or opting for a revised version of Basel I, while the standardized and foundation internal rating-based approaches may not be made available.

The chapter also discusses how LGD can be measured and the issue of the interaction of Basel II and the new international accounting standards, which emphasize the concept of incurred loss as a condition to register a reduction in a loan or loan portfolio value.

After considering the EAD, PD, and LGD of an individual exposure, in order to measure the credit portfolio's unexpected loss, which is equivalent to its value at risk, the bank needs to estimate to which extent defaults or EAD or LGD patterns may be correlated among different borrowers. The calculation of portfolio VaR can be performed through a credit-risk portfolio model. The chapter goes through the four most well-known portfolio models: CreditMetrics[TM], Moody's/KMV PortfolioManager, CSFB's CreditRisk+ and McKinsey's CreditPortfolio View. While these models may differ in terms of the valuation framework adopted (which can evaluate credit exposures at either mark-to-market or book value), on the choice of the correlation driver among different borrowers (which may be represented, for instance, by asset return correlation or by macroeconomic factors), they are all able to produce a VaR estimate and appear to produce relatively similar results when they are fed with consistent data. While many banks use internally developed models rather than one of these vended models, even internal models often either resemble the logic or are partially based on the outputs of one of these four different approaches to credit portfolio modeling.

4.12 Further Reading

Given the burgeoning literature on credit-risk issues, suggesting a selected number of further readings is far from easy. However, the reader interested in agency rating assignment may consider official rating criteria (e.g., Standard & Poor's 2006). Transition matrix properties and problems are further investigated in Altman (1998), Nickell, Perraudin, and Varotto (2000), and Bangia et al. 2002. Empirical applications of Altman's (1989) marginal-mortality-rate approach to commercial bank loans, bonds issued by private placement, and syndicated loans are contained in Asarnow and Edwards (1995), Carey (1998), and Altman and Suggitt (2000), respectively. Quantitative techniques, including credit scoring and the methodologies for their performance evaluation, are discussed in depth in de Servigny and Renault's (2004) book on credit risk, which also discusses the issue of default dependence and its modeling through copulas, which we introduced in Chapter 3 on market risk (see also Chapter 7 in Cherubini, Luciano, and Vecchiato 2004 for copula applications to credit risk).

For full documentation on the Basel II Accord, refer to Basel Committee (2006), which also reports the formulas, deriving from a loan's EAD, PD, LGD, and maturity, the risk-weighted assets to be considered when calculating minimum capital requirements. Readers interested in understanding the risk-weighted asset formulas and their theoretical basis can refer to Basel Committee (2005a) and Gordy (2003).

Internal rating design choices are discussed extensively in Treacy and Carey (2000). Differentiation of internal rating systems for smaller and large borrowers is described in Fritz, Luxenburger, and Miehe (2004); see also Fritz and Hosemann (2000) for an example of development of a behavioral score. Crouhy, Galai, and Mark (2001) offer a clear example of the different steps for a judgmental internal rating assignment process. Aguais et al. (2004) provide an excellent discussion of the different role of point-in-time versus through-the-cycle ratings and how the different kind of ratings can be tested for the best predictive performance over different time horizons. For a detailed review of LGD literature, see Altman, Resti, and Sironi (2005).

A technical but relevant topic is of course represented by the testing and validation of PD, LGD, and EAD estimates. The interested reader can refer to Basel Committee (2005b) and Tasche (2006). For EU countries, a document concerning guidelines on the implementation, validation, and assessment of the internal rating-based approach has also been issued by the Committee of European Banking Supervisors (CEBS 2006). The comparison of loan valuation according to accounting principles and Basel II is discussed in Basel Committee (2006c); interested readers may also check the websites in the accounting section of the list of websites at the end of this book.

As far as credit portfolio risk models are concerned, the main different approaches are reviewed in detail in Crouhy, Galai, and Mark (2000) and Saunders and Allen (2002), while Koyluoglu and Hickman (1998), Gordy (2000), and IACPM-IASD (2006) have empirically tested VaR estimates of different models assuming consistent initial input parameters.

CHAPTER ◆ 5

Operational Risk and Business Risk

While market and credit risks are clearly at the heart of bank activity, operational risk and business risk play an important role as well. Operational risk has gained increasing attention since the mid-1990s not only because of banking crises (e.g., Barings), which were driven mostly by fraud, human error, and missing controls, but also because the Basel Committee made clear since 1999 the intention to introduce a new regulatory capital requirement for operational risk in addition to market and credit risk. The Basel Committee also proposed a regulatory definition of operational risk, whose boundaries often used to vary significantly from bank to bank. Operational risk is defined as "the risk of loss resulting from inadequate or failed internal processes, people and systems or from external events. This definition includes legal risk, but excludes strategic and reputational risk" (Basel Committee 2006a, §644).

Business risk, on the other hand, has not been assigned an MRCR by supervisors, but it is still very important for a bank. Business risk is defined here as the risk of losses deriving from profit volatility for fee-based businesses (such as advisory services in either corporate finance or private banking businesses, asset management, and payment services, among many others). While its impact on book capital may often be limited, its impact on the bank's market capitalization may be much larger. Hence, for business risk the concept of "capital" that is considered (according to the distinctions set out in Chapter 2) is particularly relevant.

This chapter is structured as follows. Section 5.1 summarizes how requirements for operational risk are defined in the Basel II Accord; Sections 5.2–5.4 discuss the practical issues to be tackled when developing an internal risk measure for operational risk. Section 5.5, by Patrick de Fontnouvelle and Victoria Garrity from the Federal Reserve Bank of Boston, presents an interesting case study on recent U.S. banks' progress in operational risk measurement. The chapter then turns to business risk. Sections 5.6 and 5.7 analyze why business risk is important and how it can be quantified through an earnings-at-risk (EaR) measure. Section 5.8 discusses how the EaR measure could be translated in a measure of capital at risk, depending on the kind of "capital" the risk manager is interested in.

5.1 Capital Requirements for Operational Risk Measurement under Basel II

As with credit risk, the Basel II Accord has defined three different approaches to define MRCR for operational risk, which are, in order of increasing complexity and sophistication, the Basic Indicator Approach (BIA), the Standardized Approach (SA), and the Advanced Measurement Approach (AMA). Banks are encouraged to move toward more sophisticated approaches; international or more operational-risk-sensitive banks especially are expected to use something more complex than the BIA. Under certain conditions, a bank may even use different approaches for different parts of its operations, though it would not be allowed, apart from particular exceptions, to revert from a more sophisticated approach to a simpler one, so as to avoid the risk that a bank might cherry pick approaches in an effort to reduce its capital charge.

As we did for credit risk, we must remark that while the Basel II approach has been entirely accepted and translated into binding regulation in most countries and, remarkably, in Europe, according to the September 2006 proposal of the U.S. Federal Banking Agencies (Board of Governors of the Federal Reserve Systems 2006), large U.S.-based international banks will be forced to adopt the advanced measurement approach. As with credit risk, according to the proposal all other banks will have to choose whether to adopt voluntarily the same advanced approach or to remain within the amended version of Basel I (labeled "Basel IA") which is currently under discussion. Any bank forced or willing to adopt the AMA approach will obviously be subject to supervisors' validation and ongoing review.

5.1.1 Basic Indicator Approach (BIA)

According to this simpler solution, the capital charge for operational risk under the BIA (K_{BIA}) should be a percentage α, equal to 15%, of the average of positive gross income GI over the preceding three years. Years with negative gross income should be excluded from the calculation. The formula therefore is

$$K_{BIA} = \left[\sum GI_{1,\ldots,n} \cdot \alpha\right]/n$$

where GI is gross income (i.e., net interest income plus net noninterest income, gross of any provisions and operation expenses), where positive; n is the number of the previous three years in which gross income has been positive. In this case the percentage α has been set by the Basel Committee and is undifferentiated.

5.1.2 Standardized Approach (SA)

Under the standardized approach (SA), the bank is divided into eight business lines, and different percentages β are applied to each business line's gross income (business lines and betas are reported in Table 5-1). The total capital charge K_{SA} is then derived as

TABLE 5-1   Beta Factors Used to Calculate Capital Charges under the Standardized Approach

Business Lines	Beta Factors
Corporate finance / trading and sales / payment and settlement	18%
Commercial banking / agency services	15%
Retail banking / asset management / retail brokerage	12%

$$K_{SA} = \left\{ \sum_{\text{years } 1\text{--}3} \max\left[\sum_{i=1}^{8} GI_i \cdot \beta_i; 0 \right] \right\} \bigg/ n$$

where GI_i is the gross income for business line i, β_i is the corresponding beta factor, and n is the number of years in which the sum of gross income times beta factors is non-negative. In practice, this formula allows for some compensation in the same year within business lines, since a negative gross income in one business line might reduce the overall requirement. Yet, if gross income were so negative in some business lines that the sum of gross income values times their betas were negative, such a year should be excluded both in the numerator (by setting the value equal to zero) and in the denominator (reducing n). Note that national supervisors may also discretionally allow banks to use an Alternative Standardized Approach (ASA), in which retail banking and commercial banking operational risk exposures can be calculated by applying betas to a percentage m of outstanding loans rather than to gross income (see Basel Committee 2006a, §§652–654). The adoption of the SA is subject to some relatively simple qualitative criteria, even if a proper mapping of gross income across the different business lines is important, so that their boundaries are clearly defined. Further requirements are defined for internationally active banks willing to adopt the SA rather than the more sophisticated advanced measurement approach.

5.1.3 Advanced Measurement Approach (AMA)

Under the advanced measurement approach (AMA), the regulatory capital requirement for operational risk will be defined by the estimate generated by the internal operational risk measurement system, provided the bank is compliant with quantitative and qualitative criteria defined by the Basel Committee and that prior supervisory approval had been obtained. Among other qualitative requirements, the bank must have an independent operational risk management function and must clearly integrate the operational risk management system into day-to-day processes (e.g., by using outputs of operational risk measurement processes into risk reporting and capital allocation across business units). Quantitative standards for operational risk loss estimates are quite detailed. In particular they state that (see Basel Committee 2006a, §§667–679):

- The operational risk measure must guarantee soundness standards comparable with credit risk under the IRB approach (i.e., 99.9th percentile over a one-year horizon).
- The regulatory capital requirement should be considered the sum of expected losses (ELs) and unexpected losses (ULs), unless the bank successfully demonstrates that

ELs are already captured in internal business practices and have already been accounted for.[1]

- Risk measures for different operational risk estimates must simply be added when calculating MRCR for operational risk, with no diversification benefit; however, the bank may be allowed to use internally determined correlations by the national supervisor, provided the system for determining correlation is considered sound, is conservative enough to reflect correlation uncertainty in stress periods, and is implemented with integrity.

- Estimates should be derived by a proper combination of (1) internal data, (2) relevant external data, (3) scenario analysis, and (4) factors reflecting the business environment and internal control systems. The optimal combination depends on the kind of operational losses being measured (e.g., intuitively, low-frequency events should not be measured based on limited sets of internal data only).

The Basel II Accord also defines criteria for using each of these four components for operational risk estimates. These include, for instance, guidelines for constructing internal loss databases or for avoiding double counting when considering some operational losses already included in databases for credit risk MRCR (e.g., collateral management failures). The role of external data and scenario analysis based on expert opinion is stressed especially to measure high-severity losses. Factors reflecting the business environment and internal control systems must be considered to make operational risk measurement as forward looking as possible. For instance, the bank should carefully monitor any improvement or deterioration in risk controls or changes in business volumes in certain business lines and adjust operational risk estimates accordingly. Finally, the AMA also allows the bank, under certain strict conditions, to consider the risk-mitigation benefits deriving from insurance against operational risk. In any case the mitigating effect cannot be greater than 20% of the total AMA operational risk requirement (Basel Committee 2006a, §§677–679).

The explicit requirement to integrate different approaches depending on the kind of operational losses being measured makes it quite clear how challenging the task of operational risk measurement may be, especially for rare but high-severity events. Back-testing also would clearly be hard to implement in these cases, whereas it should be applied extensively whenever possible (e.g., for more frequent loss events).

5.2   Objectives of Operational Risk Management

While developing an AMA-compliant operational risk measurement system is a key objective for many large banks, operational risk management clearly matters for any financial institution. Greater product complexity and increased dependence on technology are only two of the main drivers that have justified an increased attention to operational risk. As a consequence, the first aim of the risk manager should be improving operational risk management and control rather than just measuring current operational risk.

---

1. As happened with credit risk as well, there has been some discussion during the development of the final Basel II document about whether operational risk MRCRs should cover both expected and unexpected losses or unexpected losses only. Most banks also appeared to consider operational unexpected losses only in their first loss data collection exercises (see Section 5.5), while they later started considering both expected and unexpected losses.

The first step to make people willing to invest money and effort in internal control systems is to increase managers' awareness of operational risk and its sources and potential consequences. Even for a small bank that adopts a simpler approach for operational risk capital requirements, a clear map of operational risk sources can be extremely useful, since major problems often derive from potential risks that had been entirely neglected.

A second objective is to support top managers' decisions by providing a clearer picture of the real profitability of different businesses. Such a picture would be partial and sometimes misleading if it were based on market and credit risk alone. Existing empirical studies suggest that operational loss severity may differ across business lines, even if they are unable to confirm the statistical significance of these differences due to limited data and the issues deriving from potential reporting bias (de Fontnouvelle et al. 2003; de Fontnouvelle, Rosengren, and Jordan 2004). At a lower hierarchical level, understanding the impact of existing products on operational risk could also help business unit managers create a more careful product pricing strategy (Anders and van der Brink 2004). Finally, operational risk measurement can support decisions concerning risk mitigation through insurance in those cases where it can be used effectively (e.g., losses from external events).

5.3 Quantifying Operational Risk: Building the Data Sources

While the general aim of operational risk management is not primarily to measure operational risk but to reduce and control it by anticipating potential causes of operational events and improving a bank's systems and processes whenever possible and convenient, quantification of operational risk is clearly important. We consider here the case of a bank willing to quantify economic capital for operational risk and also willing to exploit this effort in order to comply with the AMA requirements. As a consequence, the bank may sometimes consider deviating partially from Basel II prescriptions while in any case being able to calculate an operational risk capital that might be compliant with AMA requirements.

The first issue to consider is clearly the construction of the data set to feed quantitative models. As described earlier, the main sets of data that can (and according to Basel II should) be used in conjunction are:

- An internal loss database
- External loss databases
- Scenario analysis
- Factors reflecting the business environment and internal control systems

The first two datasets are objective but backward looking, since they focus only on losses that had already occurred in the bank or elsewhere. The other two are forward looking in nature. The Basel Committee (2006a, §676) stresses that in an AMA framework, "in addition to using loss data, whether actual or scenario-based, a bank's firm-wide risk assessment methodology must capture key business environment and internal control factors that can change its operational risk profile." This is typically performed by defining key risk indicators (KRIs) for each process and business unit, as the consequence of an operational risk–mapping process aimed at identifying and anticipating potential risk sources. Since risk mapping may also represent a relevant starting point for organizing internal loss databases, we discuss this issue first before moving to other data sources.

5.3.1 *Operational Risk Mapping and the Identification of Key Risk Indicators*

Risk mapping is the first step in operational risk measurement, since it first requires identifying all potential risks to which the bank is exposed and then pointing out those on which attention and monitoring should be focused given their current or potential future relevance for the bank. While the risk-mapping process is sometimes identified with the usual classification of operational risks in a simple frequency/severity matrix, what is really needed is to map banks' internal processes in order to understand what could go wrong, where, and why, to set the basis for assessing potential frequency and the severity of potential operational events, and to define a set of indicators that can anticipate problems based on the evolution of the external and internal environments. Careful risk mapping is as important as a first step for operational risk measurement as it is for the audit process, when potential pitfalls have to be identified in advance and properly eliminated or at least monitored. Risk mapping (see Figure 5-1) should start from process mapping and from identifying critical risks in each process phase, linked either to key people, to systems, to interdependencies with external players, or to any other resource involved in the process. Subsequently, potential effects of errors, failures, or improper behavior should be analyzed. This may also lead to identifying priorities in terms of control actions. Of course, special care should be given to high-severity risks, even if they appear unlikely to occur.

Key risk indicators come out as the result of the mapping process and should be used to provide anticipatory signals that can be useful for both operational risk prevention and measurement. In particular, they should provide early warning signals to anticipate the most critical operational events, and they may also be partly derived from the experience of audit departments defining potential risk scores for different business units as a tool for defining priorities in their audit action plan. Scandizzo (2005) notes that ideal KRIs

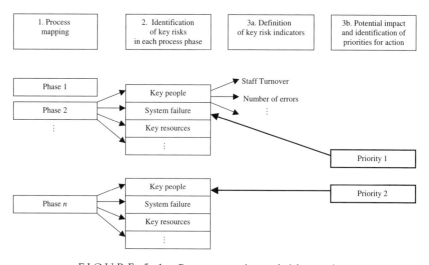

FIGURE 5-1   Process mapping and risk mapping.

should be (1) strongly related to the frequency and/or severity of critical operational risks, (2) nonredundant, (3) as measurable and easy to monitor as possible, and (4) auditable, i.e., subject to easy verification. Examples of KRIs for the trading floor include concentration of business in key staff, abnormal return, P&L volatility or trading patterns, number of deal cancellations, number of new products introduced in the past year, use of system capacity, and number of pricing errors, including those on internal deals. Monitoring similar indicators and providing top managers with continual reporting may help identify trends and forecast potential problems (e.g., insufficient staff or system capacity) before they lead to substantial operational losses. Hence, proper risk mapping and the development of KRIs are important even for those banks that may not try to adopt AMA-based capital requirements in the short term. In fact, those banks may still wish to create a scorecard for operational risk control so as to provide incentives for improving operational risk management even in the absence of sophisticated operational risk measurement methodologies.

5.3.2 Building an Internal Loss Database

While an internal loss database should not be the only data source for operational risk measurement, it should clearly play a major role. In fact, internal data may provide information whose quality is entirely under the bank's control (unlike external databases), can be used as a check for internal self-assessment, and can allow, at least for certain kinds of operational events, to better capture risk trends and the effect of internal risk reduction efforts. As a consequence, the internal loss database should not be conceived as a support to operational risk quantification only, but as a support to the overall risk management strategy of the bank. Yet many decisions must be taken when building such a database (Haubenstock 2004) (Table 5-2):

TABLE 5-2   Key Decisions in Defining an Internal Loss Database

1. Definition of operational risk events	• Basel II definition versus wider definition • Near misses
2. Minimum threshold for operational losses	• Implications of the level of the threshold for quality and collection costs of the internal loss database • Reporting bias • Individual loss versus loss-generating events (treatment of multiple repeated losses)
3. Classification criteria	• Basel II-only versus Basel II and internally driven criteria (e.g., business unit, country)
4. Loss recording	• Direct versus indirect losses • Identification and recording of relevant dates • Treatment of past events with uncertain loss quantification
5. Architecture of the loss collection process	• Division of tasks among business lines, operational risk management, and auditing functions • External data quality verification
6. Internal disclosure policy	• Feedback to business unit leaders • Level of detail for risk committee reports • Data sharing between operational risk management and auditing functions

1. The definition of the operational events that should be captured by the database
2. The minimum threshold of loss to be recorded
3. The classification criteria that should be applied to operational events
4. The way in which loss should be recorded
5. The architecture of the loss collection process
6. The policies concerning operational events' internal disclosure.

As far as the *definition of an operational event* is concerned, the bank should first decide whether to adopt a stricter definition of operational losses or whether also to record other kinds of events that might be relevant for internal operational risk management purposes. One example is represented by credit losses deriving from operational errors (e.g., missing documentation, making it impossible to take advantage of collateral in a case of default, or human error in handling a loan review process, resulting in missing the chance to take appropriate actions to reduce exposure with a borrower that will eventually default). According to Basel Committee 2006a those losses are already taken into consideration under credit risk MRCR, and hence, correctly, they should be excluded from the operational risk loss database to prevent double counting. Yet measuring the frequency and severity of these events may be useful for internal purposes, to understand the relevance of the phenomenon and to support remedial actions.

The second issue is whether also to record the so-called *near misses*, i.e., those events that might have provoked operational losses even if they (luckily) did not. An example of a near miss is a mistake in recording a trading deal that generated an accidental gain instead of a loss. While the severity of such events is clearly zero, their frequency and type may be relevant for providing further data about what could have happened and as useful signals to business line managers who should take these events as a relevant warning signal. Cases of operational error implying faulty profit allocation across business units (e.g., due to an incorrect internal deal transcription, which did not affect overall bank profit) could be placed in this category. A bank may therefore adopt a broader definition of operational event than Basel II suggests, while it should still use a subset of data only when estimating AMA-compliant operational risk capital.

The *threshold over which losses should be recorded* (with the potential exception of near misses) is a particularly critical choice for risk quantification. Intuitively, if the threshold were too high, only a relatively limited number of medium- to high-impact events would be recorded, providing a weaker base for estimating the frequency and severity of *all* operational events. A lower threshold allows one to model operational risk severity and frequency better but also implies higher collection costs. Moreover, lower thresholds require greater effort to enforce the rules of the loss collection process at the bankwide level. In fact, larger operational losses cannot clearly be either hidden or forgotten. Yet, as the threshold decreases, the risk of incomplete reporting of operational loss in some business units increases, and great care is required to avoid alterations of data quality (with the likely effect of underestimating frequency and overestimating average severity of losses).

Another problem is whether the threshold should be applied to the individual loss or to the event generating the loss, since there are cases in which a single event may generate small but repeated losses (e.g., the fraudulent behavior of an employee, implying repeated small appropriations, or trading-room front-office problems in the evaluation of a financial instrument, resulting in repeated pricing errors in different deals). Considering the events, generating multiple losses would be useful, but data-collection costs and difficulties would increase. Yet, even in the Barings cases, operational losses were not determined by a single loss in a single day; rather, they were the result of mounting losses deriving from a behavior that had been repeated through time. Even if, hopefully on a lower scale, this might happen in many other cases (e.g., minor software malfunctions, lack of due care in transaction processing in the back office), measuring these repeated losses might help keep management attention high, even on these apparently minor sources of operational risk.

Loss classification criteria are apparently strictly dictated by the Basel Committee (2006a, §673), which requires one to map events based on both (a) the eight main business lines defined in Table 5-1 and (b) seven categories of events (execution, delivery, and process management; clients, products, and business services; system failures; internal fraud and illegal activity; external fraud and illegal activity; employment practices and workplace safety; damage to physical assets). Yet, while at a minimum the database should be consistent with this classification, the risk manager may be willing either to add categories (if, for instance, the operational event definition is also larger) or to add further classification criteria (e.g., the business unit and the country where the operational loss was generated). Business unit or country specifications may be relevant not only to support a back-test of operational risk mapping and self-assessment evaluations conducted at the business unit level or to provide elements for a better allocation of operational risk capital at the individual unit level. Moreover, they might allow for subsequent rescaling of loss size if needed. In fact, the same operational event may sometimes generate completely different operational losses in different countries or business units (see Frachot, Moudoulaud, and Roncalli 2004), as a consequence, for instance, of different volumes of activity or different sizes of the average transaction. Failing to provide adequate documentation to an investor might result in different losses in the case of a small retail investor versus a big private banking customer; the same would be true for loans related to different borrower segments.

This also introduces the issue of *how losses should be recorded*. Potential decisions to be taken concern (1) whether to extend loss recording to indirect losses of a reputational nature, which are excluded from the Basel II definition of operational risk but may be important for internal analysis and risk-reduction strategies; (2) the definition of the date to be associated with operational events; and (3) the treatment of events that occurred but whose impact is still hard to quantify (e.g., because they engendered court litigation). As far as indirect losses are concerned, it would in any case be necessary to record them separately from direct ones, in order to preserve the AMA compliance of the subset of data used for operational MRCR calculation. Event dates may be an issue, since any operational event can have an initial date, a termination date, the date of its detection, the date of its recording, and the date in which quantification of consequences becomes possible. Clearly, these do not necessarily coincide (Haubenstock 2004).

Yet proper data recording is important if the bank wishes to provide high-quality internal data to support internal estimates of correlation of operational event frequency across different categories or business lines. These estimates clearly require a precise allocation of operational events to individual periods. As a consequence, many may prefer to record the event in the database within a reasonably short time following detection and termination, even if perfect quantification is still not possible, leaving to a later stage the revision of the severity associated with the event when it becomes effective and certain.

The *event-collection process* must also be defined, by assigning proper responsibilities for the detection, collection, quantification, and data quality control of any event. These responsibilities should be divided among business units, the operational risk management function, and the audit function. While making business units actively participate in the process helps them understand why the process is useful for themselves, even apart from risk measurement purposes, leaving them the first move in event detection could result in reporting bias. Hence, external data-quality verification by independent functions is required (Haubenstock 2004).

The final point is related to *operational event disclosure policies within the bank*. Even if keeping operational events as confidential as possible facilitates the event-collection process, periodic feedback must be given to business unit leaders to help them perceive both the potential impact of operational events on their business and the benefits they can derive from more careful monitoring of operational risk events. At the same time, the aggregate picture should be disclosed to the audit department to exploit synergies between this function and the operational risks management team. While reported events may support the definition of auditing priorities, outcomes from auditing reports on individual business units may help identify potentially critical processes that have failed to be captured in the initial risk-mapping exercise or help identify problems in collection and reporting of operational loss data in some business units of the bank.

5.3.3 *External Loss Databases*

Available external loss databases may comprise either consortium databases, in which a group of banks agrees to share data about operational losses over a certain threshold, or databases based on publicly reported losses that have appeared in the news. In the first case, the consortium should make decisions similar to the ones for internal loss databases, even if the definition of operational events is evidently unlikely to differ from Basel II requirements. Moreover, the threshold is likely to be higher than most of the thresholds used for internal data, since (a) banks may try to preserve as far as possible data that might be considered confidential, and (b) the main reason to integrate with external data an internal loss database may be the need to estimate better the severity of low-frequency, high-impact events rather than those of frequent but low-impact events. The higher threshold and the potential reporting bias linked to the unwillingness of some participants to disclose smaller losses fully may create problems when such a database is integrated with internal loss data (see Section 5.4.2). In particular, incomplete reporting of lower-severity losses may lead one to overestimate average loss severity.

Similar problems may also clearly occur for external databases based on publicly available information (de Fontnouvelle et al. 2003), since many are the elements — such as the location of the company, the type of loss and the business line involved, and the existence or absence of legal proceedings — that affect the chances that the loss is reported first by the company and then by the news and finally captured by the loss database. If either of these steps were missing, then the loss would not be recorded in an external database based on public information, and this is especially likely to occur for relatively smaller losses. Moreover, de Fontnouvelle et al. (2003) compared two well-known databases based on public information, noting that while data on U.S. banks appeared to be quite similar, greater divergence existed for non-U.S. loss data.

It could also be questioned whether data deriving from sometimes significantly different institutions should be rescaled to account for these differences. Yet the complexity of required adjustments and the absence of clear empirical evidence about the materiality of the problem may suggest that one maintain original data (Frachot, Moudoulaud, and Roncalli 2004). In any case, in an ideal world external databases should be used as a complement to internal data rather than as the only source of information. In fact, they are unable both to provide detailed information critical for operational risk management to business unit leaders and to adapt operational risk estimates to changes in the internal control environment.

5.3.4 *Scenario Analysis*

While internal and external loss databases are focused on what has already happened, scenario analysis should contribute by suggesting what might happen, even if it never happened before. Hence, its purpose should be not only to supplement existing internal data when estimating the impact of potentially rare but high-impact events, but also to represent a continual exercise to anticipate potential new risks that might derive from changes in the external environment as well as from internal changes, such as the launch of new products, new procedures or business practices, and internal reorganization. The need for such scenarios could emerge from a periodic or ad hoc revision of the initial operational risk mapping process or as a consequence of warning signals provided by the key risk indicators chosen for a given business unit.

In order to support risk quantification, scenarios must also be associated with probability and severity estimates of the events that are taken into consideration. More specifically, Anders and van der Brink (2004) identify different conceptual steps for scenario modeling. The first one is *scenario generation*, which consists of associating scenario classes with different event types or key resources with organizational units and identifying those scenarios that might be relevant for each unit.

Subsequently, *scenario assessment* defines the potential frequency and severity of losses for each scenario, based on either historical experience, when available and reliable, or expert opinions. The third step is then the *data quality check*, to ensure, for instance, that expert opinions are approved by independent experts or members of the audit function and that the overall frequency and severity estimates appear to be reasonable given past loss experience. *Parameter calibration* is then required in order to translate qualitative frequency and severity estimates into distribution parameters allowing a Monte Carlo *simulation* to take place, which represents the subsequent step. Finally, the simulation *model output* is produced and analyzed; some sensitivity analysis on the results should also be required. In practice, however, scenarios can be used to integrate internal data rather than fully substitute it. This topic is discussed in the next section.

5.4 Quantifying Operational Risk: From Loss Frequency and Severity to Operational Risk Capital

Given available data sources, the process of estimating operational risk capital requires a number of logically linked steps. Hence we will discuss, in order, (1) modeling severity of operational losses based on internal data only, (2) the effects of extending the database to external data or scenarios, (3) modeling loss frequency, (4) estimating correlation and dependence of loss frequency and severity, and (5) the derivation, through a Monte Carlo simulation, of the operational risk capital estimate.

To begin, however, we should clearly set out the definition of operational risk capital, since according to Frachot, Moudoulaud, and Roncalli (2004) different definitions are sometimes used in practice. Operational risk would be identified by some with (1) the sum of expected and unexpected operational losses, by others as (2) unexpected operational loss only, and by still others as (3) unexpected operational loss considering only losses over a certain threshold (typically, the same threshold over which operational losses are recorded). While the difference between the first and the second definition may lie in the deep confidence a bank may have in convincing regulators that expected operational losses have already been accounted for, e.g., through proper provisions, the third definition would clearly lead to a lower estimate of operational risk capital that would be dependent on the threshold: The higher the threshold, the lower the estimated frequency of losses and hence (despite their higher average severity) the lower the estimated risk capital. From here on we adopt the first definition, even if, of course, the deduction of expected losses (which may be derived from the same Monte Carlo simulation used for the measurement of operational risk capital) may be allowed in an AMA approach under certain conditions (see Basel Committee 2006a, §669).

5.4.1 Modeling Severity Based on Internal Loss Data

Let us assume initially that the bank is willing to estimate parameters based on internal data only. In this case the first logical step would be severity estimation. In practice the issue is how to derive the loss severity distribution given the empirical severity distribution (conditional on losses being greater than the threshold) from the internal loss database. In this case the main choices concern which frequency distributions should be tested for goodness of fit against the empirical distribution and which test should be used or, alternatively, whether the test should be concentrated on properly fitting the "core" of the loss distribution rather than its extreme tail only.

For instance, de Fontnouvelle, Rosengren, and Jordan (2004) tested nine alternative distributions — the exponential, Weibull, gamma, log-normal, log-gamma, Pareto, Burr, log-logistic, and generalized pareto distribution (GPD) — with data from each of six major banks. Data included operational losses of over 10,000 euros during 2001. The first four distributions have lighter tails than the remaining five, and only the log-normal distribution among the light-tailed ones appears to fit the data almost as brilliantly as the five heavy-tailed distributions. Since their analysis is conducted at the bank and business-line levels, none of the distributions appear to fit well the full range of available data over all business lines.

As an alternative, risk managers might consider concentrating on the tail of the distribution in order to check whether it could be modeled through a generalized Pareto distribution, which was discussed in Chapter 3, whose distribution G is given by

$$G(x; \xi; \beta) = \begin{cases} 1 - (1 + \xi x/\beta)^{-1/\xi} & \text{if } \xi \neq 0 \\ 1 - e^{(-x/\beta)} & \text{if } \xi = 0 \end{cases}$$

where x represents operational losses with β always greater than zero and $x \geq u$ if $\xi \geq 0$ or $u \leq x \leq u - \beta/\xi$ if $\xi < 0$. The GPD is a natural candidate for fitting extreme loss values, even if the estimation of the parameter ξ is critical. Note that typically only the case in which $\xi \geq 0$ and x can assume any value over the threshold u is considered for operational risk. As a consequence, some prefer an alternative formulation in which the independent variable represents losses exceeding the threshold (i.e., $x - u$) rather than losses (Moscadelli 2004). However, even in this alternative formulation the parameters ξ and β would remain the same. The shape parameter ξ is particularly important since the kth moment of the distribution is infinite if $k \geq 1/\xi$. In practice, for $0.5 \leq \xi < 1$ the distribution has finite mean but infinite variance; while for $\xi \geq 1$, even the mean would be infinite (with clearly unacceptable results in terms of expected losses and operational risk capital measurement). We have already seen in Chapter 3 that ξ is typically estimated through the so-called Hill estimator by setting

$$\xi = (1/N_u)\sum_{i=1}^{N_u} \ln(y_i/u)$$

where y_i represents each of the N_u observations over the threshold u; i.e., ξ is set equal to the average of the log of the ratio of extreme losses to the threshold. de Fontnouvelle, Rosengren, and Jordan (2004) note that by using this estimator, operational expected loss and required capital estimates would come out unreasonably large, and they suggest adopting a technique proposed by Huisman et al. (2001) to enhance the estimates provided by the Hill estimator and to reduce its dependence on the threshold. According to this technique, the Hill estimator $\gamma(k)$ should be estimated repeatedly, each time using a different number of values $k = 1, 2, \ldots, K$ exceeding the threshold (and hence with different thresholds). Since according to Huisman et al. (2001) the bias in the Hill estimator is linearly related to k, they suggest running the regression

$$\gamma(k) = \beta_0 + \beta_1 k + \varepsilon(k)$$

and considering β_0 the bias-corrected estimate for ξ. By applying this technique, de Fontnouvelle, Rosengren, and Jordan (2004) obtained parameters that no longer imply infinite (i.e., with $\xi \geq 1$) or disproportionately large operational risk capital estimates. Intuitively, if a distribution such as the GPD is used to estimate data from the tail only, then when simulating severity of losses, a combination of different distributions should be used; i.e., the risk manager should first simulate the severity of a loss through the empirical distribution or through the distribution used to fit full data and, if the simulated loss exceeds the threshold over which the GPD has been estimated, the risk manager should replace that loss with a simulated loss extracted from the GPD.

5.4.2   Integrating Internal Severity Data with External Data and Scenario Analysis

While internal data clearly represent a fundamental component for both operational risk management and its measurement, available internal evidence for extreme operational losses might be insufficient. Given the relevance that estimates concerning the severity of operational losses may have in estimating information on operational risk capital, it would then be necessary to complement internal data with other sources. The first natural candidates for this purpose would be external loss databases, gathering either consortium or publicly reported operational losses for many different banks. However, these databases suffer from a reporting bias, since even if they should formally comprise all losses over a certain threshold (usually much higher than the threshold used in internal loss data-collection exercises), only part of such losses are actually captured. Since the probability that a loss will be reported is higher the higher the loss size, such databases typically overstate the average severity of losses and might lead one to substantially overestimate operational risk capital. The possible solution is to assume that external losses are reported only over an unobservable truncation point, which can be estimated through a maximum-likelihood technique proposed in Baud, Frachot, and Roncalli (2002) and applied, for instance, in de Fontnouvelle et al. (2003). This allows one to reconstruct the unconditional loss distribution from the sample distribution, which is in reality a distribution conditional on the loss's being reported. In general, in fact, if $f(x)$ is the true distribution of losses, then the reported sample distribution based on a truncation point H is identified by $f(x|H)$ and is equal to

$$f(x|H) = \mathbf{1}\{x \geq H\} \cdot \frac{f(x)}{\int_{H}^{+\infty} f(y)dy} = \mathbf{1}\{x \geq H\} \cdot \frac{f(x)}{1 - F(H)}$$

where $\mathbf{1}\{x \geq H\}$ is a function equal to 1 if $x \geq H$ and to zero otherwise and $F(H)$ is the cumulative distribution function of severity calculated in H (Frachot, Moudoulaud, and Roncalli 2004). A correction for the reporting bias of external databases has been applied in de Fontnouvelle et al. (2003) on a data set composed of only external databases (OpVantage and OpRisk), resulting in a dramatic reduction of extreme percentiles of operational losses (the 99th percentile in their test changed from $300 million with raw data to $20 million after correcting for the reporting bias).

A possible alternative to integrating internal data is represented by scenario analysis. In this case, the risk manager may have to integrate internal data and scenario-generated potential outcomes. When scenarios are quantified in a clear manner, they can be integrated with internal data in the distribution that the risk manager has to fit. This can also be performed when scenarios have alternative formulations. For instance, if the scenario says that a loss equal to or higher than x occurs every n years, then the duration between losses equal to x or higher can be calculated given the distributions of loss frequency and loss severity and expressed as a function of distribution parameters. By using a sufficiently high number of scenarios, distribution parameters can be derived directly. Potentially, even complex functions derived as a weighted sum of both internal data and scenario goodness-of-fit measures can be obtained and used as a criterion to define parameters for a loss distribution function integrating internal and scenario data (Frachot, Moudoulaud, and Roncalli 2004).

5.4.3 Estimating Operational Loss Frequency

The subsequent step is represented by estimating the distribution of operational loss frequency. If internal or external data are used and potentially integrated, the issue of thresholds and truncation points in the databases are relevant. Intuitively, in fact, the higher the threshold a bank sets, the lower the frequency of an operational event. Given the severity distribution parameters, it is possible to rescale frequency so as to infer the number of operational losses below the minimum reporting threshold (Frachot, Moudoulaud, and Roncalli 2004). If, for instance, the frequency of losses is assumed to follow a Poisson distribution with parameter λ (which also represents the distribution mean) and $F(x)$ is the cumulative distribution function for loss severity, then the true (unconditional) λ is linked to the database sample λ (i.e., the value from the distribution conditional on losses higher than the threshold H) by the relationship

$$\lambda = \frac{\lambda_{\text{sample}}}{\text{Prob}\{\text{Loss} \geq H\}} = \frac{\lambda_{\text{sample}}}{1 - F(H)}$$

Apart from the correction for reporting bias, frequency estimation requires defining potential candidate distributions and testing their ability with a time series of loss events during different years (this is often a problem, given the limited length of most historical data series). In any case, the frequency distribution is frequently assumed to follow a

Poisson process that is often used in actuarial estimates. A potential alternative candidate is the negative binomial frequency distribution function, which implies a higher variability in the number of loss events from year to year. The effects of using a negative binomial rather than a Poisson distribution to model loss frequency vary, however, depending on how severity is modeled. For instance, in their thorough empirical test on data from six large international banks, de Fontnouvelle, Rosengren, and Jordan (2004) note that the impact of the change is relevant when severity is assumed to be log-normally distributed while it is not material when severity is modeled through a GPD.

The need to construct a reliable database through time to better calibrate frequency distribution explains why the level of the threshold and the ability to properly register the timing of the events generating losses are both important. The threshold level is important because, while the existence of a threshold implies the need to correct for reporting bias, lower thresholds would clearly imply a higher frequency of directly recorded data and would then provide a more reliable data set for operational risk measurement. The way in which the timing of losses is recorded is relevant because, if loss data were linked only to the date when the loss was recorded or when the loss became certain (rather than with the date when the generating event took place), the frequency of losses across different subperiods might be partially altered. This in turn may make it more difficult for the bank to build consistent empirical estimates for frequency correlation across different business lines. As a consequence, it would be more difficult to persuade regulators to take into consideration imperfect correlations among operational loss events when calculating the overall operational risk capital requirement.

5.4.4 Estimating Correlation or Dependence among Operational Events

When estimating operational risk capital, a crucial issue is represented by the assumptions about the correlation (or, more generally speaking, dependence) between operational losses in different business lines. Quantitative requirements for the AMA state that "risk measures for different operational risk estimates must be added for purposes of calculating the minimum regulatory capital requirement. However, the bank may be permitted to use internally determined correlations . . . provided it can demonstrate to the satisfaction of the national supervisor that its systems for determining correlations are sound and implemented with integrity and take into account the uncertainty surrounding any such correlation estimates" (Basel Committee 2006a, §669). Providing supervisors with convincing data concerning the existence of an imperfect correlation among operational losses in different business lines could therefore result in significant advantages for banks adopting the AMA. This issue is also important for those banks that will not adopt (or not immediately adopt) an AMA but are measuring operational risk capital for internal purposes.

The correlation among operational risks in different businesses can derive either from a link between loss frequencies across different business lines or from a link among loss severities. Yet, while there may be a few extreme events (e.g., linked to events such as the attacks of September 11 and natural catastrophes) that imply joint and severe losses in multiple business lines, apart from these cases, assuming dependence in severity across business lines may be hard to justify given that actuarial models typically assumed severity independence even within the same business line.

Frachot, Moudoulaud, and Roncalli (2004) and Frachot, Roncalli, and Salomon (2005) discuss this issue and show that assuming severity independence across business lines implies that, even if frequencies were perfectly correlated, it could be possible to define an upper boundary for operational loss correlations that appears to be very low, especially for high-loss businesses. In fact, in those businesses the primary driver for operational risk capital is the variability in loss severity, and hence severity independence would largely dominate dependence in loss frequencies. Of course, if the risk manager wanted to model some form of dependence across different business lines, a relevant issue would also be represented by the technique to be adopted for this purpose. Considering the limitations of linear correlation coefficients, copulas could be extremely useful for modeling dependence for both loss frequency (see, for instance, Chapelle et al. 2004) and severity.

5.4.5 Deriving Operational Risk Capital Estimates through Simulation

After choosing and calibrating distributions for loss frequency and severity, expected and unexpected operational losses can be estimated through a Monte Carlo simulation. For each simulation run it would be necessary to draw from the loss frequency distribution a random number n of operational losses and then to extract randomly n values from the loss severity distribution. The simulated operational loss in the first simulation run would simply be equal to the sum of n losses. By repeating this process a sufficiently large number of times, the operational loss distribution can be obtained, and hence expected and unexpected losses can be calculated.

Of course, since the bank may also be interested in determining the potential sensitivity of simulation results to distribution parameters, one could perform either some simple what-if analysis or a more sophisticated effort to build confidence intervals for operational risk capital by taking into consideration the distribution of parameter estimators (see, for instance, Frachot, Moudoulaud, and Roncalli 2004).

This framework, which could also allow banks to apply for AMA operational risk capital measurement, enables banks to evaluate the direct impact of operational losses. Recalling the distinction between Book Capital at Risk (BCaR) and Market Capitalization at Risk (MCaR) presented in Chapter 2, we can see that the approach described so far is consistent with the former view, while considering the impact of market capitalization would require us to study the market reaction to the announcement of operational losses. Works by Cummins, Lewis, and Wei (2004) and Perry and de Fontnouvelle (2005) suggest that market reaction may be larger than the operational loss. The larger value disruption may be interpreted as reputational risk, especially when the operational loss is generated by an external event such as fraud. In any case, the initial evidence about the fact that operational losses may sometimes imply an even larger reduction in the bank's value implies that if a market-capitalization-at-risk approach were adopted, the potential impact of operational risk would be even greater.

5.4.6 Is Risk Measurement the Final Step?

While estimating operational risk capital is a very hard task for the risk manager, after the simulation has been performed the process should not be considered complete. Deciding how to disclose data and how to set up a continuous process to gradually improve operational risk management is as important as defining an adequate estimate of operational risk capital. In parallel with the effort to develop better and longer loss-data series to improve estimate quality, substantial care should be devoted to monitoring and improving the risk-mapping process, to increasing business unit managers' involvement in the operational risk control process, and to promoting risk reduction or risk mitigation when needed. As a consequence, incentives should be provided to report losses correctly rather than to hide them. This is why it may be dangerous immediately to link estimates of operational risk capital and the evaluation of business unit managers' performance. Rather, business unit managers may also be evaluated based on an operational risk scorecard, considering elements such as key risk indicators, the quality of risk mapping, and business unit involvement in the process of preventing operational risk.

5.5 Case Study: U.S. Bank Progress on Measuring Operational Risk, *by Patrick de Fontnouvelle and Victoria Garrity (Supervision, Regulation, and Credit Department, Federal Reserve Bank of Boston*[2]*)*

This section provides an overview of U.S. bank progress in implementing the Advanced Measurement Approach (AMA) for operational risk. Our observations are drawn from the operational risk portion of the Fourth Quantitative Impact Study (QIS-4). QIS-4 was an exercise conducted by U.S. federal banking regulators in the latter half of 2004 to assess the potential impact of Basel II's credit and operational risk capital requirements on the U.S. banking industry.[3] The exercise requested data only on Basel II's advanced approaches (the advanced internal ratings–based approach for credit risk and the AMA for operational risk) since these are the only approaches proposed to be implemented in the United States. QIS-4 consisted of quantitative data and a detailed questionnaire to provide additional qualitative information. The operational risk portion of QIS-4 requested estimates of firmwide operational risk exposure as well as descriptions of the methodologies underlying these estimates. It is important to note that QIS-4 was conducted on a best-efforts basis on the part of participating institutions, using limited data and without the benefit of fully articulated final rules for U.S. implementation.

First we review the extent to which banks used each of the four AMA data elements (internal data, external data, scenario analysis, and business environment and internal control factors (BEICFs)) and consider how banks combined these elements within their AMA frameworks. We then discuss the range of practice regarding three particular aspects of AMA frameworks: offsets for expected operational losses (EOLs), assumptions for dependence, and adjustments for insurance benefits. We conclude with a comparison of QIS-4 exposure estimates across banks and consider the extent to which variation in certain assumptions (EOL offsets, dependence assumptions, BEICFs, and insurance) affect estimated exposure.

---

2. The views expressed in this section are those of the authors and do not necessarily reflect those of the Federal Reserve Bank of Boston or the Federal Reserve Board.

3. The overall findings from QIS-4 were released on February 24, 2006, by U.S. banking regulators. The data reported in QIS-4 reflect capital methodologies at the time of the exercise. Because U.S. banks are continuing to develop their AMA frameworks, QIS-4 results may not reflect current practices.

In the past several years, U.S. banks have made progress in measuring their exposure to operational risk. For QIS-4, 24 banks provided estimates of operational risk exposure, and 14 reported that their estimates were derived using a framework broadly resembling an AMA. The remainder of this section focuses on the 14 QIS-4 banks, which we refer to as AMA banks, and the range of practice among these institutions. The reader should be mindful that our discussion is based on the results of QIS-4, which was initiated in late 2004, and it is likely that capital methodologies at U.S. banks have progressed further since that time.

From a quantification perspective, all of the AMA banks used a loss distribution approach to estimate operational risk exposure. While a few incorporated all four data elements into their quantification system, the others were still working toward this goal. Most AMA banks have developed internal loss databases and used these data as a direct input into their quantification system. Internal data were also used indirectly to inform scenario analysis. Most AMA banks employed external loss data, but used it in several different ways. One use was as a direct input into the quantification system, particularly for units of measure where there wasn't sufficient internal loss data. Another was as an indirect input, where external data were considered via their effect on another element (e.g., to inform scenario analysis).

Most AMA banks have established tools to assess BEICFs, such as risk and control self-assessments and scorecards, although only some incorporated the results into their QIS-4 operational risk exposure estimates. The most common use of BEICF results was as a qualitative adjustment in allocating capital to business lines, while some banks factored BEICFs into scenario analysis. Incorporating BEICFs has been somewhat challenging as banks determine how to aggregate the detailed information in the tools to obtain qualitative adjustments to operational risk exposure estimates. Of the four data elements, scenario analysis was the least developed, with less than half of the AMA banks using this element as an input to their QIS-4 operational risk exposure estimate. Given that time has passed since QIS-4, more banks may now be incorporating scenarios.

Given the different developmental stages of the four data elements at the AMA banks and the inherent flexibility of the AMA, it is not surprising that there is a range of practice across these banks in the weight placed on each element in the quantification process. Some relied primarily on internal data and used external data and scenario analysis only where internal data were insufficient. Some used internal data to estimate loss frequency and the body of the severity distribution, while relying on external data and/or scenario analysis for the tail of the severity distribution. Other banks, including some with limited internal data, relied primarily on scenario analysis, using the other elements as inputs to the scenario generation process.

Next, we consider the range of practice regarding three particular aspects of bank AMA frameworks: treatment of EOL, assumptions for dependence, and offsets for insurance. Methodologies around each of these areas varied across AMA banks, with efforts to quantify dependence and insurance offsets in the developmental stages at some institutions. Although some institutions have previously expressed the opinion that capital be for unexpected losses only, most AMA banks reported capital as the sum of EOL and unexpected operational loss (UOL) for QIS-4.[4]

---

4. The opinion that capital be held for UOL only was made evident in a benchmarking exercise that was conducted during 2004. Findings from the benchmarking exercise are contained in a presentation entitled "Results of the AMA Benchmarking Exercise," which was given on May 19, 2005, at the Implementing an AMA for Operational Risk conference hosted by the Federal Reserve Bank of Boston. Presentations from this conference are available at: http://www.bos.frb.org/bankinfo/conevent/oprisk2005/index.htm.

TABLE 5-3   AMA Exposure Estimates as a Percentage of Total Assets and Gross Income

	AMA Exposure Divided by Total Assets	AMA Exposure Divided by Gross Income
Unadjusted AMA Exposure Estimate		
Cross-firm median	0.43%	11.04%
Interquartile range	(0.37–0.53%)	(8.41–12.67%)
AMA Exposure Estimate Adjusted to Include EL and Exclude Insurance and Qualitative Adjustments		
Cross-firm median	0.53%	12.81%
Interquartile range	(0.37–0.65%)	(9.64–15.23%)
AMA Exposure Estimate Adjusted to Include EL and Exclude Insurance, Qualitative, and Dependence Assumptions		
Cross-firm median	0.43%	9.46%
Interquartile range	(0.37–0.70%)	(7.41–14.22%)

In QIS-4 about half of the AMA banks assumed no statistical dependence (i.e., zero correlation) across business lines and event types. Some made this zero-dependence assumption explicitly, while others made it implicitly by estimating one loss distribution at the firmwide level. The other half assumed some degree of dependence across business lines and event types. While some analytical work is being done on measuring the level of dependence across units of measure, it is in the early developmental stages. AMA banks derived dependence assumptions from methodologies based primarily on judgment rather than statistical analysis.

About half of the AMA banks in QIS-4 incorporated an adjustment to reflect a reduction in operational risk exposure from insurance coverage. However, most did so as an expost adjustment to the exposure estimate, rather than by embedding the impact into the quantification process. The size of the insurance benefit for U.S. banks is not clear, given the early stage of modeling in this area for many institutions.

We conclude with a brief analysis of the operational risk exposure estimates reported in QIS-4. To compare the operational risk exposure estimates across AMA banks, we scale these estimates by total assets and gross income. The top panel of Table 5-3 reports results for exposure estimates unadjusted for any methodological differences across banks. As shown, the median ratio of unadjusted AMA estimates to total assets is 0.43%, indicating that the average AMA bank's estimated operational risk exposure was 0.43% of its total assets. The reported interquartile range indicates that half of the AMA banks' operational risk exposure estimates fell between 0.37% and 0.53% of total assets. Similarly, the median ratio of estimated exposure to gross income is 11.04%, with half of the banks reporting a value between 8.41% and 12.67%. A comparison of these gross income ratios with the 15% Alpha specified in the Basel II framework's basic indicator approach and the Basel II range of Betas (12–18%) for the standardized approach suggests that the majority of AMA banks have lower gross income percentages under the AMA than under the two simpler approaches.

The second and third panels remove the effects of certain assumptions from unadjusted AMA exposure to improve comparability across banks. The second panel adjusts exposure estimates to include EOL and exclude the benefits of insurance and BEICF adjustments. These adjustments have a measurable impact on estimated exposure, in that excluding them raises the median ratio of exposure to gross income from 11.04% to 12.81%. The third panel presents AMA exposure estimates that are further adjusted to remove the impact of assumptions for dependence across business lines and event types.[5] Removing these dependence assumptions results in a decline in the median gross income ratio from 12.81% in the second panel to 9.46% in the third panel.

In summary, recent regulatory exercises have shown that U.S. banks have made progress in measuring their exposure to operational risk. In QIS-4, 14 banks provided exposure estimates based on an AMA-like framework. The operational risk exposure estimates generally fell in the range of 8%–12% of gross income, or a bit below estimates using a basic indicator or standardized approach. Significant variation in AMA frameworks continues to exist, with some framework components (e.g., dependence assumptions) having a measurable impact on exposure estimates.

5.6 The Role of Measures of Business Risk and Earnings at Risk

Whereas market, credit, and operational risks are usually given greater attention because they are also associated with a specific minimum capital requirement, business risk also deserves to be carefully considered. Business risk is defined here as the risk of losses deriving from earnings volatility for fee-based businesses, such as asset management, brokerage, corporate finance advisory, and payment services. This concept can also be applied to businesses that may apparently be linked to market risks (e.g., sales departments for structured products) but do not directly undertake market risks and are remunerated and evaluated mostly based on the business volume they generate. Businesses such as asset management and advisory do not usually imply a direct market or credit risk for the bank, even if they imply operational risk. Apart from events that may cause operational risk losses, however, these businesses usually generate an important but unstable contribution to a bank's P&L. Please note that business risk should be identified not with the volatility of revenues, but with profit volatility. As a consequence, business risk should not depend only on how volatile a business unit's volumes and revenues may be, but also — for instance — on its ability to adapt its cost base to changes in business volumes.

It is important to note that business risk has a minor impact if the only concern is to avoid the short-term default of a bank (which may explain why regulators did not introduce any formal requirement for business risk). Intuitively, the book capital that may be destroyed by a fee-based business unit in a single year can hardly threaten the bank's survival in the short term. Instead, business risk's relevance is much higher if the bank wanted to measure the potential impact of different businesses on the market capitalization that could be destroyed under adverse scenarios. Hence, from the point of view of market capitalization at risk, which was introduced in Chapter 2, business risk may be crucial.

According to a top-down analysis over a sample of U.S. banks and to a survey of 11 large international banks, Kuritzkes (2002) estimates that business risk may account for around 55–60% of nonfinancial risk, while the other 35–40% would be linked to event-driven operational risk. Figure 5-2 provides some data about the weight of business risk over total risk capital and the ratio between estimated risk capital for business risk and operational risk in some of the relatively few major international banks that disclose their business risk estimates. Despite the variations in the estimates from bank to bank, the

---

5. Because some banks included dependence assumptions while others did not, we use a zero-correlation assumption across business lines and event types for all AMA banks in this panel This is done purely to achieve comparability and should not be interpreted as an indication that we believe there is no dependence across business lines and event types.

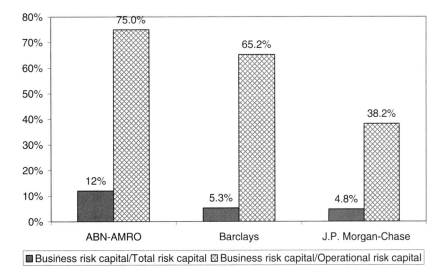

FIGURE 5-2   The relevance of business risk over total risk capital and relative to operational risk in three large international banks.
Source: 2005 Annual Reports.

fact that business risk accounts for as much as 38–75% of operational risk (which has been given remarkable attention by most banks) is extraordinary, especially if we consider the lack of a clear industry consensus about how business risk should be measured.

The lack of consensus becomes quite apparent if we simply go through the annual reports of many large international banks, which often say explicitly that business risk (or other concepts that may be linked to it, such as strategic risk or expense risk) is a source of risk for the bank but may sometimes fail to provide an exact definition. Unsurprisingly, even risk measurement methodologies may substantially vary. Table 5-4 provides some excerpts from J.P. Morgan-Chase and Credit Suisse 2005 Annual Reports, which dare to state clearly how business risk (or the similar concept of expense risk, in the Credit Suisse case) is defined and to provide some sense of how this risk is measured, even if there are clear differences in their approaches. The Credit Suisse Annual Report also mentions explicitly that while this risk has remarkable importance, there is no industry consensus about how it should be quantified.

Given the relevance of business risk on one hand and the difficulties in extrapolating a best practice from public information on the other hand, we would like to try to describe how a value-at-risk (or, equivalently, a capital-at-risk) measure for business risk could be derived, according to the definition of business risk we adopt here. The basic alternatives are the following:

1. Measure the capital of a sample of mono-business competitors and set capital at risk for the fee-generating business unit equal to some average of that sample (*benchmark capital*).
2. Identify business risk economic capital with *earnings at risk* (EaR), e.g., a certain multiple of the volatility of earnings of the fee-generating business unit.
3. Calculate earnings at risk as in case (b) as an intermediate step, and then translate it into a different measure of capital at risk.

We must note that when measuring business risk, the risk manager may be interested in either a "book capital at risk" (BCaR) or a "market capitalization at risk" (MCaR)

TABLE 5-4   Defining and Measuring Business Risk: J.P. Morgan-Chase and Credit Suisse

Bank (Risk Label)	Definition
J.P. Morgan-Chase (business risk)	"The risk associated with volatility in the firm's earnings due to factors not captured by other parts of its economic capital framework. Such volatility can arise from ineffective design or execution of business strategies, volatile economic or financial market activity, changing client expectations and demands, and restructuring to adjust to changes in the competitive environment. For business risk, capital is allocated to each business based on historical revenue volatility and measures of fixed and variable expenses." (J.P. Morgan-Chase Annual Report 2005, p. 57)
Credit Suisse (expense risk)	"Financial organizations do not simply represent warehouses of financial assets but also act as originators and distributors of financial services. . . . Although there is widespread recognition that the risk and return characteristics of non-warehouse businesses have profound implications on the need for economic capital and the capacity to bear risks, no industry consensus has emerged as to how exactly alter the asset-based economic capital calculations (for example, based on value-at-risk type calculations) to reflect the non-warehouse businesses. Given the lack of consensus, . . . the Group's expense risk economic risk capital estimates are designed to measure the potential difference between expenses and revenues in a severe market event . . . using conservative assumptions regarding the earnings capacity and the ability to reduce the cost base in a crisis situation." (Credit Suisse Annual Report 2005, p. 74)

measure, according to the two alternative notions of capital discussed in Chapter 2. As a consequence, while benchmark capital measures can be built in either terms, depending on whether the book capital or the market capitalization of monobusiness peers is considered, the second and third solutions do not really represent alternatives but, rather, help provide answers to different questions, i.e., determine the BCaR rather than the MCaR impact of business risk.

We would focus in particular on creating business risk measures based on internal earnings data, rather than by using benchmark capital measures. In fact, while benchmark capital is conceptually simple and fast, its practical application raises a number of problems. First of all, it may not be possible to identify purely mono-business competitors. A clear example is represented by retail payment services (apart from credit cards). Second, even if mono-business competitors existed, their capital may cover not only business but also operational risk, and hence the risk manager should be able — even as an outsider — to distinguish among the two in order to avoid a double counting of operational risks. Third, since the size and the nationality of mono-business competitors may differ, their book capital may be influenced by minimum regulatory requirements that may be binding for a mono-business competitor, while this would not happen if the same activity were conducted within a diversified group. Fourth, when measuring benchmark capital in terms of market capitalization, nonlisted mono-business peers would be excluded from the sample, further reducing its size, and averages across different stock markets might become unstable due to differences in the stock market cycle in different countries.

Therefore, even if simplistic benchmark capital estimates or similar judgmental estimates are frequently used, trying to measure business risk through internal data may be worth the effort. Since determining an earnings-at-risk measure is a prerequisite for both BCaR and MCaR estimates, we discuss first how such a measure can be derived and then its possible translation into a capital-at-risk measure.

MEASURING BUSINESS RISK IN PRACTICE

5.7 Measuring Business Risk in Practice: Defining a Measure of Earnings at Risk

In general terms, earnings at risk (EaR) can be identified with the losses generated by a given business unit under the maximum adverse variation in its earnings within a given time horizon and confidence interval. For instance, for the asset management business, one could try to build a distribution of the earnings produced by the fund management company and identify EaR at a 99% confidence level as the one one-hundredth quantile of the earnings distribution. The first thorough discussion of the EaR concept for business risk is contained in Matten (2000). Matten identifies EaR as a multiple of the standard deviation of earnings of a given business unit. Let us assume, for instance, the hypothetical revenue volatility model of a business unit presented in Table 5-5.

If we assume revenues have a standard deviation equal to 1000 around their expected value of 5000, variable costs are 10% of revenues, and taxes 40% of net profit before taxes, then the table allows us to transform revenue scenarios into corresponding scenarios for net profit before taxes and net profit. Of course, absolute differences between a +1/−1 standard deviation scenario decrease as we move from revenues to net profit, as a consequence of variable costs and taxes. Earnings at risk could hence be identified with a given multiple of earnings volatility. Matten (2000) suggests that this measure does not represent capital allocated to fee-based businesses, which should be considered equal, instead, to earnings at risk divided by the risk-free rate. In practice, capital at risk for business risk should be identified with the amount of capital that should be invested at the risk-free rate to compensate for the earnings that could be missed in an adverse scenario.

The link between EaR measures and economic capital for business risk are discussed in the next section, but it is useful to discuss in greater detail the issues involued in deriving an estimate of earnings volatility:

1. The choice of the starting point (revenues rather than earnings directly) for EaR calculation and the consequent role of fixed and variable cost estimates
2. The availability and size of the desired time series
3. The problems in rescaling of data series
4. The choice to include or exclude expected earnings

First of all, earnings volatility can be modeled either directly or by modeling revenues so as to derive a net profit distribution from revenue distribution. In the second case,

TABLE 5-5   Example of Earnings Volatility Model for Business Unit Alpha

	−2σ	−1σ	Mean	+1σ	+2σ
Revenues	3000	4000	5000	6000	7000
Fixed costs	(2500)	(2500)	(2500)	(2500)	(2500)
Variable costs	(300)	(400)	(500)	(600)	(700)
Net profit before taxes	*200*	*1100*	*2000*	*2900*	*3800*
Taxes	(80)	(440)	(800)	(1160)	(1520)
Net profit	*120*	*660*	*1200*	*1740*	*2280*

Source: Adapted, with modifications, from Matten (2000).

TABLE 5-6   Role of Fixed and Variable Cost Mix in Earnings Volatility

	Business Unit Alpha				Business Unit Beta			
	−1σ	Mean	+1σ	Std Dev.	−1σ	Mean	+1σ	Std Dev.
Revenues	4000	5000	6000	1000	4000	5000	6000	1000
Fixed costs	(2500)	(2500)	(2500)		(1500)	(1500)	(1500)	
Variable costs	(400)	(500)	(600)		(1200)	(1500)	(1800)	
Net profit before taxes	*1100*	*2000*	*2900*	**900**	1300	2000	2700	**700**
Taxes	(440)	(800)	(1160)		(520)	(800)	(1080)	
Net profit	*660*	*1200*	*1740*	**540**	780	1200	1620	**420**

assumptions about the mix of fixed and variable costs are relevant; business units with a different cost structure would have a different earnings volatility even if revenue volatility were the same. Table 5-6 compares business unit Alpha, already depicted in Table 5-5, with a second one (Beta), with lower fixed costs and higher variable costs. While expected net profit in the base scenario is the same and revenue volatility is identical, the standard deviation of net profits for business unit Beta is only 420 versus 540 for Alpha.

In practice, the risk manager may be tempted to use revenue volatility as a proxy for earnings volatility, since a revenue historical series may be more easily available and more reliable (e.g., because cost data allocation through different months or quarters may not be as precise as revenue allocation). While deriving an earnings series from revenues may sometimes be the right choice, care is needed to ensure that the cost structure of the business and the potential cost variability are adequately reproduced. Failing to model properly which costs are directly linked to revenues or failing to account for the variability of the cost structure itself may result in improper estimates of earnings volatility. For instance, variable costs such as bonuses may play a significant role in certain businesses, but they do not usually depend on revenues in a linear manner.

A second set of problems is linked to the characteristics of the time series used of either earnings or revenues. In some cases, the desired series may barely be available, for instance, due to business units' merging or restructuring, unless the accounting information system is flexible enough to reconstruct a theoretical time series for "new" business units. Moreover, data series have to be cleaned of the effects of adverse events that are linked to other risks (market, credit, operational) that are measured separately. Otherwise an event such as an operational loss would affect risk calculations twice, first by being included in the operational risk database and second through its impact on earnings and earnings volatility. The size and data frequency of the data series are also relevant. If the past historical period is too long, the measure may depend on old data that may no longer be representative of the volatility of the business unit.

If, in contrast, one decides to consider a relatively short time interval, than two other shortcomings emerge. The first is that with a shorter historical sample and hence with fewer data, it is very difficult to estimate the exact shape of the distribution of earnings empirically. Hence, the identification of the desired distribution percentile used to derive an EaR measure cannot be based on sound grounds (and many may end up assuming that the earnings distribution of any business unit is — magically — normally distributed). The second shortcoming is that in order to avoid having too few data points, a bank would frequently use monthly earnings data. Yet, using monthly data can lead to an incorrect estimate of earnings volatility if there is serial positive autocorrelation in earnings changes or if the way in which accounting earnings are calculated tends to alter in some way the volatility of the "real" results of the business units.[6] Since it is not always possible to scale monthly return volatility into annual volatility in a simple manner, the annual earnings-at-risk figure may be derived by numerically simulating a series of monthly shocks, and autocorrelation — provided it exists — in monthly returns could simply be taken into account through the same simulation procedure.

A third problem relates to the potential need to rescale earnings series and/or transform them into some sort of "returns." First of all, if the size of the business unit has substantially changed through time, higher or lower earnings in certain periods may reflect a structural size change rather than earnings volatility. Of course, it is not easy to separate structural size changes (which would suggest either using some sort of returns or rescaling the earning series) from business volume volatility, which is a clear component of business risk. For instance, a change in assets under management in the asset management business due to higher market share should not require rescaling, while a merge with a smaller asset management company would. If a clear measure of size or exposure is identified, an earning series may be transformed into a series of returns by dividing earnings by the "exposure" measure.

A fourth issue is whether to identify earnings at risk with the deviation from expected earnings or only with actual losses. Imagine, for instance, that for business unit Alpha expected earnings were equal to 50 and the maximum adverse reduction in earnings at a 99% confidence level were equal to 120. Should earnings at risk then be 120 (the maximum potential reduction in earnings) or just 70 (the actual loss in the worst-case scenario)? Using actual losses has the disadvantage that the measure may become very sensitive to changes in the cost allocation: A bank that allocates a higher share of its indirect costs to final business units would measure — everything else being equal — higher potential actual losses for each business unit than an identical bank that allocates only direct costs. This may affect the relative evaluation of different business units. Moreover, expected earnings estimates would likely be based on history, and since businesses with good past performances would hence be attributed a relatively lower risk, their ex ante risk-adjusted profitability is likely to be overstated.

5.8   From Earnings at Risk to Capital at Risk

Once an EaR measure has been obtained, it should be understood how it may be linked with the economic capital required by the business unit. Matten (2000) observes that using the EaR measure as an estimate for capital at risk would imply a disproportionately high RAROC (risk-adjusted return on capital)[7] to fee-based business units. He therefore suggests translating EaR into capital at risk by dividing EaR by the risk-free rate:

$$CaR = \frac{EaR}{r}$$

where r is the risk-free rate. Capital at risk should in fact be identified, according to Matten, with the amount of capital that should be invested at the risk-free rate in order

---

6. This phenomenon may not depend on a precise will to influence financial results, but it may simply derive from the way in which costs are attributed (e.g., being equally split in each month even if they are partially variable).

7. We define RAROC here in general terms as a ratio between a measure of earnings of a given business unit (or business area or even transaction) and the capital at risk associated with it.

to cover losses (or missed earnings) from business risk (CaR × r = EaR), and this would produce reasonable results in risk-adjusted performance measurement. While Matten's method has the merit of simplicity, it is clear that the amount of capital obtained is not capital that is lost forever (as would happen, for instance, for a market risk CaR in the case of an adverse move of the markets) but only an amount of capital for which the investor faces an opportunity cost. Moreover, it fails to capture the strong difference there may be between book capital at risk and market capitalization at risk for fee-based businesses.

If we consider, for instance, how much book capital can be destroyed by an asset management division in bad years, we should be concerned only with potential negative accounting profits that the division may produce in those years in which revenues may be insufficient to cover costs. If EaR is intended as the worst potential deviation from expected earnings, BCaR can be identified either with EaR directly or with EaR minus a conservative measure of expected profits. This measure should not be used for risk-adjusted performance measurement purposes, but only to assess the short-term risk of default. Since a bank typically has a substantial level of general fixed costs, the risk manager might, for instance, identify the overall business risk measure as the joint EaR of all fee-generating businesses minus a conservative measure of expected earnings plus all general costs. In fact, accounting losses would occur whenever the sum of the contribution margins generated by the business units proved to be unable to cover them. In any case, the contribution of fee-based businesses to accounting losses should in general be quite limited.

In contrast, the impact that either losses or missed earnings may have on the market capitalization of the bank might be sometimes substantial. The contribution of some fee-based businesses to a bank's profit is often carefully considered by bank equity analysts, since, unlike profits from pure trading, they may represent a continuing profit for the bank rather than one-time gains from a brilliant speculative trade. As a consequence, we propose here some alternative ways to translate EaR into an MCaR measure (i.e., to measure the impact on the economic value of the bank of a loss equal to EaR) by adopting an equity analyst's point of view. In practice, we should consider how the reduction in earnings would affect the target price and therefore the theoretical economic value of the bank. There are obviously different possible solutions, depending on the criteria the analyst is assumed to follow.

For instance, let us assume the analyst simply evaluates the value of the equity stake in the bank through a multiple, such as the price/earnings ratio (P/E). Then the adverse change in the market capitalization of the bank (i.e., the change of economic capital in the worst-case scenario, ΔEC_{wcs}) that would derive from an unpredicted reduction in earnings would be

$$\text{MCaR}_x = \Delta EC_{\text{wcs},x} = \left[\frac{P}{E}\right]_x^* \Delta \text{Earnings}_{\text{wcs}} = \left[\frac{P}{E}\right]_x^* \text{EaR}$$

where the term

$$\left[\frac{P}{E}\right]_x^*$$

is the fair price/earnings ratio attributed to business unit x (in fact, profits from different divisions may be valued by analysts with different multiples).

A similar logic could be followed if analysts were assumed to adopt a dividend-discount model. In the simple case of a constant-growth dividend-discount model, defining k_e as the discount rate, g as the estimated dividends' perpetual growth rate, and D as the next dividend per share, the price P of the share should be

$$P = \frac{D}{k_e - g}$$

so expressing the dividend D as earnings per share times the payout ratio, p, and multiplying both terms by the number of outstanding shares, the market capitalization EC is

$$\text{EC} = \frac{p \cdot \text{Earnings}}{k_e - g}$$

If investors used this approach to estimate the economic value of the bank, then market capitalization at risk would be[8]

$$\text{MCaR}_x = \Delta \text{EC}_{\text{wcs},x} = \frac{p \cdot \Delta \text{Earnings}_{\text{wcs},x}}{k_e - g} = \frac{p}{k_e - g} \cdot \text{EaR}_x$$

This MCaR estimate could be considered too conservative, since it implicitly assumes that the unexpected reduction in earnings represented by EaR would last forever. At the same time, some may consider it to be too mild, since reductions in earnings are sometimes combined with a downward revision of the growth expectations for certain areas of business. Thus, at least for certain business units, a cautious risk manager may also consider the potential adverse variation of g.

Translating EaR into MCaR and adopting the analyst's view can also lead, under certain simplifying assumptions, to a solution that is quite close to Matten's (2000) proposal. Let us assume the analyst evaluates the total value of the bank as the sum of discounted cash flows, so the value of the bank V is

$$V = \sum_{t=1}^{\infty} \frac{F_t}{(1+i)^t}$$

where i is the proper discount rate. Since a change in V would affect directly the shareholders' wealth, MCaR is equal to ΔV. If we assume also (a) that a reduction in earnings equal to EaR_x in business unit x would imply an equal reduction in cash flows and (b) that this reduction is perpetual, then labeling V_0 the value before the shock in earnings and V_{wcs} the postshock value, capital at risk is

$$\text{MCaR}_x = V_0 - V_{\text{wcs}} = \sum_{t=1}^{\infty} \frac{F_t}{(1+i)^t} - \left(\sum_{t=1}^{\infty} \frac{F_t - \text{EaR}_x}{(1+i)^t} \right)$$

$$= \sum_{t=1}^{\infty} \frac{\text{EaR}_x}{(1+i)^t} = \text{EaR}_x \cdot \sum_{t=1}^{\infty} \frac{1}{(1+i)^t} = \frac{\text{EaR}_x}{i}$$

8. Note that if one accepts the assumptions of the constant-growth dividend-discount model, then the term $p/(k_e - g)$ is the theoretical value of the P/E ratio, so this equation would be equivalent to the previous one, based on the $[P/E]^*$ multiple.

This solution is close to the one suggested by Matten (2000), but it has a completely different derivation and uses the discount rate i rather than the risk-free rate (and therefore produces a lower equivalent capital at risk, since $i > r$). Matten's proposal could hence be considered too pessimistic since it implies that capital at risk is even higher than the loss in economic value that the bank would face if the loss of cash flows were *perpetual*. Of course, if we assume equal changes in cash flows and earnings and that a loss equal to EaR would last for n years only (rather than being perpetual), than the estimated MCaR would reduce to

$$\mathrm{CaR} = V_0 - V_{\mathrm{wcs}} = \sum_{t=1}^{\infty} \frac{F_t}{(1+i)^t} - \left(\sum_{t=1}^{n} \frac{F_t - \mathrm{EaR}}{(1+i)^t} + \sum_{t=n+1}^{\infty} \frac{F_t}{(1+i)^t} \right)$$

$$= \sum_{t=1}^{n} \frac{F_t}{(1+i)^t} - \sum_{t=1}^{n} \frac{F_t - \mathrm{EaR}}{(1+i)^t} = \sum_{t=1}^{n} \frac{\mathrm{EaR}}{(1+i)^t} = \mathrm{EaR} \cdot \frac{1 - 1/(1+i)^n}{i}$$

While the solutions proposed here are a bit more complex than Matten's method, they have the advantage of modeling explicitly the link between EaR and market capitalization and also allow us to differentiate the impact among different business units or divisions considering the proper valuation methodology and, if necessary, the proper multiple or discount factor. If these methods are used, it is important to consider EaR as the maximum potential deviation from *expected* earnings (including, therefore, missed gains) rather than only as the direct potential loss, since this would be more consistent with analysts' views. Given that all MCaR measures end up, one way or other, being a multiple of estimated EaR, the precision with which earnings at risk can be estimated remains important.

5.9 Summary

Operational and business risks represent important components of the overall risks of a bank. The former can be defined, according to the Basel Committee definition, as "the risk of loss resulting from inadequate or failed internal processes, people, and systems or from external events." Business risk, in contrast, identifies the risk of losses deriving from profit volatility for fee-based businesses (e.g., advisory services and asset management).

The Basel II Accord has introduced a capital requirement for operational risks defining three alternative approaches of increasing complexity: the Basic Indicator Approach, the Standardized Approach, and the Advanced Measurement Approach. The last is essentially based on the bank's internal operational risk measurement system but requires prior supervisory validation. Developing an operational risk measurement system requires going through a number of steps, starting from a preliminary risk mapping and the acquisition of different data sources about operational events. Ideally, sources should best combine internal-loss experience with external databases, scenario analysis, and a monitoring of factors reflecting the evolution of the business environment and internal control systems, even if the QIS-4 study in the United States still reported that in 2004 the level of development of some of these components was still limited in many banks. Based on these data, the bank can derive a distribution for the frequency and severity of loss events and derive an aggregated operational risk capital estimate. Reaching this final step requires addressing different technical issues, including the integration of the internal-loss database with external databases and scenario analysis, and the assumptions about the dependence among operational events.

Business risk, in contrast, is not associated with any regulatory capital requirement, nor has it received an agreed-upon definition. And yet, with some differences, it is considered a relevant component by many large international banks. We have shown that its impact can be measured first through earnings volatility. Its corresponding capital at risk may be substantially different, depending on whether we want to consider business risk's usually limited impact on book capital or the typically much larger impact on market capitalization. In fact, an underperformance in fee-based businesses may intuitively imply a reduction in the bank's stock market capitalization which is much larger than missed earnings.

5.10 Further Reading

An example of an operational risk management framework is offered in J.P. Morgan (2004). Risk mapping and the development of key risk indicators are discussed in Scandizzo (2005), while Haas and Kaiser (2004) and especially Haubenstock (2004) analyze in detail the issues concerning internal loss databases. Reconciliation between external and internal data and the reporting-bias issue are discussed in Baud, Frachot, and Roncalli (2002), de Fontnouvelle et al. (2003), and Frachot, Moudoulaud, and Rocalli (2004). Anders and van der Brink (2004) suggest how scenario analysis can be performed. Empirical studies by de Fontnouvelle et al. (2003), de Fontnouvelle, Rosengren, and Jordan (2004), and Moscadelli (2004) provide evidence about the possibility of calculating operational risk capital by modeling loss frequency and severity distributions and discuss many of the problems any risk manager would face in applying internal operational risk models. As far as the background on extreme-value theory relevant for operational risk management is concerned, see Embrechts, Klüppelberg, and Mikosch (1997). Giudici (2004), Kühn and Neu (2004), and Leippold and Vanini (2005) propose interesting alternative approaches to operational risk measurement that, for brevity, we could not present in this chapter. Finally, business risk measurement has been discussed mainly in Matten (2000), while a top-down estimate of its relevance on overall nonfinancial risks for the bank is contained in Kuritzkes (2002).

CHAPTER ◆ 6

Risk Capital Aggregation

So far we have discussed how different risk types, such as market, credit, operational, and business risks, can be measured. Yet in order to support top-management decisions concerning capital management and capital allocation, an integrated picture of risks is needed. The challenge of risk aggregation, i.e., the development of quantitative risk measures, such as an aggregated estimate of economic capital, incorporating multiple types or sources of risk (see Joint Forum 2003) across different business units, is therefore particularly important.

Risk aggregation and the size of diversification benefits that might result from being exposed to different risks in different businesses are relevant both from a regulatory and from the individual bank's point of view, even if we focus mainly on the bank's perspective. The debate about the extent of diversification benefits that can be achieved by running different activities in the financial sector has been a topic of discussion in the past during the debate concerning whether restrictions on U.S. bank activity should be abolished by adopting a universal banking approach as in European countries (see Saunders and Walter 1993). In this context, a number of empirical studies were conducted in order to understand whether "nonbank" activities could reduce overall risk for bank holding companies (for a survey, see Brewer, Fortier, and Pavel 1988). At present, the regulatory debate is related to whether and how diversification benefits among businesses or risks can and should be taken into account in setting minimum capital requirements (see Kuritzkes, Schuermann, and Weiner 2001, 2002; Joint Forum 2003).

However, apart from minimum regulatory capital requirements, understanding how risk could be aggregated and, consequently, the size of diversification benefits is extremely important from the point of view of bank decision making in an economic capital perspective. Risk aggregation is important for capital management, since it can enable the risk manager to give top managers a measure of the overall capital needed to run the bank from an internal, economic capital perspective. Moreover, it is important for capital allo-cation, since understanding diversification benefits even among risks can help top manag-ers quantify the contribution to risk diversification that is offered by the main divisions within the bank.

Yet in order to be able consistently to support decisions about the optimal capital level of the bank, the risk manager should live in an ideal bank in which (1) all risks are being measured, (2) all of them are measured in a consistent and homogeneous way, (3) a clear, best-practice methodology exists for estimating aggregate economic capital from indi-vidual risks' economic capital measures. Unfortunately, none of these assumptions is entirely true. In fact, not all the risks are consistently being measured in all banks. Risks such as operational risk and in particular business risk are sometimes evaluated in a simplified manner. Second, risk measures for different risks are typically not homoge-neous and need to be harmonized (see Section 6.1). Moreover, at present there are no clear best practices to aggregate different risk measures into a single number. Problems concerning alternative methodologies and parameter estimation are discussed in Sections 6.2–6.5.

Before discussing how an integrated economic capital measure could be derived, we must review the nonsubadditivity problem introduced in Section 3.5: Given two exposures or portfolios X and Y, it is unfortunately not always true that VaR$(X + Y) \leq$ VaR$(X) +$ VaR(Y). As a consequence, it must be not taken for granted that when multiple risks or business units are considered together, overall capital at risk should be less than the sum of stand-alone CaR figures. This problem has also fostered the development of a literature on capital allocation based on "coherent" measures of risk, such as the expected shortfall, satisfying, among others, the subadditivity condition. In practice, however, banks still always identify economic capital with the aggregated value at risk of the bank as a whole, and hence their efforts in developing an integrated risk measure are entirely concentrated on aggregating VaR or CaR measures. There are different potential explanations for that, ranging from the greater difficulties of ES measurement whenever there are problems with data availability (think about operational and business risk) to the fact that the Basel II architecture links internal-model-based capital requirements to a VaR framework. Moreover, while it is possible to provide examples of particular situations in which VaR is not subadditive (e.g., Artzner et al. 1999), there is no conclusive evidence that the problem is material when aggregating VaR measures at a bankwide level across business units or risk types. As a consequence, even if we do not neglect the conceptual importance of remembering the potential problem of VaR nonsubadditivity and the relevance of the stream of literature that has tried theoretically to suggest alternative measures for capital allocation, we pragmatically focus here on aggregation of value at risk only.

6.1 The Need for Harmonization: Time Horizon, Confidence Level, and the Notion of Capital

The different VaR measures determined for individual risks are not naturally homoge-neous. The two main issues that are usually pointed out (see Joint Forum 2003) relate to the time horizon, which is usually daily for market risk VaR estimates and yearly for other risks, and the confidence interval, since while 99% is the usual standard for market risk, the bank is usually willing to estimate potential losses at a higher confidence level (for instance, banks willing to achieve an AA target rating, whose historical 1-year PD is 0.03%, would claim to use a 99.97% confidence level so as to cover losses in all scenarios except the worst 0.03%). While these effects are well known, the third issue related to the different concepts of "capital" underlying the measures of capital at risk is typically neglected.

As far as time horizon harmonization is concerned, the common solution is to adopt a one-year horizon for all risks. Therefore, market risk capital must be scaled, usually by multiplying it by the square root of the number of trading days during the year, transposing to capital at risk the solution that is often adopted with asset return volatility under the assumption of serial independence of asset returns (see Section 3.1.7). This solution may be used if the risk manager wants to translate a given point-in-time VaR measure (say, capital at risk for market risk on December 31) based on a daily horizon into an equivalent yearly measure, whereas it is improper if the risk manager wanted to assess ex post the annual equivalent of a string of daily VaR values, to compare, for instance, the capital at risk absorbed by trading versus lending business units in order to compare their risk-adjusted performance. (This topic is discussed in the next chapters.) Note that problems might also derive from the fact that some credit risk exposures may be undertaken through assets that are inside the trading book (e.g., as credit derivatives) and whose risk is measured for regulatory purposes over a 10-day horizon, when internal models for market risk are adopted, or through assets that might enter the credit risk portfolio in the banking book and whose risk would be measured over a one-year horizon. Apart from regulatory concerns in defining clear rules for trading book eligibility (see Basel Committee 2006a), the way in which these assets are mapped and the time horizon reconciled if necessary in an economic capital perspective may be a relevant issue.

The harmonization of the confidence interval is a bit more complex, even if, again, simplifying assumptions are usually adopted to overcome the obstacle. Let us consider the case of the typical AA-rated bank aiming at a 99.97% confidence level. While credit risk VaR is often calculated by simulation and hence estimating the 99.97% confidence level directly is not a problem, market risk VaR is often calculated through a 99% historical simulation. In fact, for large banks with significant option-trading books, HS allow one to simulate (by replaying past history) joint changes in asset returns and implied volatilities that would be much harder to model according to other approaches. Unfortunately, with HS the size of the historical sample is important, and it is clearly impossible to estimate directly a 99.97% confidence level (unless the risk manager decided to consider the last 10,000 returns, i.e., almost a 40-year sample). In practice, the desired confidence level is usually obtained either by interpolation or by fitting a continuous return distribution to the simulated discrete return distribution obtained by HS or by rescaling 99% VaR to 99.97% *as if* the portfolio return distribution were normal. All these solutions have shortcomings. The first solution, for instance, can produce unstable results (since they would generally depend only on the values of the two worst returns in the sample). The second solution is better, but the risk manager should choose carefully whether to fit data to the entire distribution or to the tail only below a given arbitrary threshold. The third solution is the easiest one, since it does not imply any additional work, such as tail distribution fitting, but it is based on a brave assumption (normality of portfolio returns) that could easily be questioned, especially for portfolios that include options.

Moreover, since different business units would have different mixtures of different risks that, in turn, have different shapes of return distributions, the choice of the confidence level is not neutral with respect to the relative capital-at-risk absorption of different business units (see Hall 2002). Therefore it could influence not only the absolute level of reported RAROC for a unit, but also its relative ranking within the organization. This is why, on one hand, defining the confidence interval in an objective manner (e.g., linking it to the target rating the bank is willing to maintain) is very important and, on the other hand, a certain amount of discussion about the rescaling methodology might emerge (from a purely pragmatic point of view, rescaling from 99% to 99.97% as if the distribution were normal has at least the advantage that it does not change the relative ranking of market-risk-sensitive business units).

Yet a third relevant problem, which is usually neglected, is whether VaR measures for different risks are measuring losses with reference to the same concept of capital. Market risk VaR is measured in mark-to-market terms and hence also potentially identifies the reduction in market capitalization subsequent to adverse market changes; book capital at risk would be the same too, provided that all assets are evaluated at fair value. In the case of credit risk, in contrast, credit portfolio models may value loans either at book value or in mark-to-market terms. For both operational and business risk, different numbers might be obtained, depending on whether the focus is on the one-year accounting loss that operational and business risk can generate or on the market capitalization impact of those losses.

This potential lack of consistency between capital-at-risk measures could be solved differently, depending on the objective. If the goal is to measure risk-adjusted performance (RAP) measures to support capital allocation consistently, then the market cap value of capital is likely to be the correct solution, since it is the most consistent with the shareholder's view of the bank.

If the purpose is to support decisions about the bank's optimal capital structure policy, then in theory two different aggregated measures (based on BCaR and MCaR, respectively) could be created and compared with actual book capital and market capitalization as measures of available capital. In practice, however, the main emphasis would be attributed to book capital at risk.

This approach clearly differs from the common practice of assuming that all — albeit different — measures of capital at risk have to be compared against a single measure of available capital. Clearly, it may be costly to maintain different measures of capital at risk according to different criteria and to explain the differences to senior management members who have to make key decisions. Yet recalling this difference — which is stronger for some risks, such as business risk, than for others — is relevant, since the choice of either a BCaR or an MCaR approach may impact on the relative share of the bank's capital allocated to different businesses and then on how return targets for those businesses should be assigned (see Chapter 9). Note that from now on we use CaR rather than VaR to remind us that aggregation should be based on measures of capital at risk calculated or harmonized over a yearly horizon, at the same confidence level, and after harmonizing to the maximum possible extent the concept of capital behind each risk measure. In this way CaR values could differ from VaR values used for day to day risk monitoring and control.

6.2 Risk Aggregation Techniques

After harmonizing capital-at-risk measures as much as possible, aggregating those measures into a single number for the whole institution requires tackling three different issues: (1) identifying the components that have to be aggregated, (2) identifying the aggregation technique or algorithm to be used, and (3) calibrating the parameters (e.g., correlation coefficients) needed to derive the single risk measure. We approach these issues in this sequence. As a necessary premise, risk aggregation represents a very important area, but it is still not as developed as individual risk modeling.

In 2003, the Basel Committee on Banking Supervision, the International Organization of Securities Commissions, and the International Association of Insurance Supervisors published the results of a survey of 31 financial institutions in 12 different countries devoted to understanding the key trends in risk aggregation and integration (Joint Forum 2003). The research concluded that risk aggregation appeared to be "still in early stages of evolution," clearly describing the problems that were faced by those institutions trying to develop an aggregated measure and the lack of data available to estimate correlations (let alone more complex dependence structures) among different risk types. Even though some improvement has certainly occurred since that survey, most of the conceptual difficulties remain. Therefore, in this section we discuss alternative solutions, even if we know that simplified methodologies are likely to be used in most cases due to the lack of adequate data. In contrast, Section 6.3 discusses how empirical correlation estimates could be derived.

6.2.1 Choosing the Components to Be Aggregated: Business Units versus Risk Types

Assuming that a banking group is composed of a number of legal entities or business units, each of which is often exposed to different risks (even if there is usually a main risk for each business unit), the first choice is whether business units or risk types should be the starting point for risk aggregation (Joint Forum 2003).

Aggregating across business units has the advantage of a clear link between the individual divisions' CaR measures and the overall capital requirement of the bank. Moreover, correlation coefficients can be estimated through the series of the P&Ls of the business units. At the same time, there are two clear disadvantages. First, since a single business unit is typically exposed to multiple risks, the need to define or assume a correlation coefficient across risks is not avoided when calculating stand-alone CaR for the individual business unit. Second, if the same kind of risk is common to two or more business units, this method could fail to capture the compensations between exposure in different business units (imagine the case in which business unit A is exposed to the risk of rising interest rates while B has an opposite risk profile). Opposite exposures can in fact be netted correctly only if there is first a groupwide risk mapping and then an aggregation among risk types. Yet aggregating groupwide risk-factor exposures becomes more difficult in the case of a financial conglomerate, and accordingly the Joint Forum survey notes that conglomerates often aggregate exposures among all the banking divisions of the group but exclude insurance divisions.

In theory, therefore, an aggregation across risk types should be preferred, at least when the main purpose is to derive the best possible measure of the total capital at risk at the groupwide level. Yet risk aggregation across business units is necessary to provide top managers with some idea of the diversification benefits deriving from the existing portfolio of business units the bank is composed of, and hence the problem of estimating correlation coefficients across business units cannot be avoided.

6.2.2 Alternative Risk Aggregation Methodologies

When choosing the methodology through which different risk type or business unit CaR measures could be aggregated, we should try to manage the trade-off between methodological soundness and ease of estimation, especially as far as parameter calibration is concerned. The simpler solution would be to apply the formula for portfolio risk that we introduced for the variance–covariance approach:

$$\text{CaR}_p = \sqrt{\sum_{i=1}^{n}\text{CaR}_i^2 + \sum_{i=1}^{n}\sum_{j\neq i}^{n}\text{CaR}_i\text{CaR}_j\rho_{ij}}$$

While in the variance–covariance approach this formula derives from the assumption of multivariate normal asset returns, it can be applied whenever the desired α-quantile of the standardized return distribution of the portfolio as a whole and of its components is the same. As Rosenberg and Schuermann (2004) clearly describe, the portfolio CaR of the bank in percentage terms can be written as

$$\text{CaR}_{p,\%}(\alpha) = \mu_p + \sigma_p F_p^{-1}(\alpha)$$

where $F_p^{-1}(\alpha)$ is the α-quantile of the standardized return distribution. The variance of portfolio return can be written as

$$\sigma_p^2 = \sum_{i=1}^{n} w_i^2\sigma_i^2 + \sum_{i=1}^{n}\sum_{j\neq i}^{n} w_i w_j \sigma_i \sigma_j \rho_{ij}$$

where w_i, w_j represent the weights of the portions of the portfolios that are being aggregated, σ_i, σ_j are the standard deviation of their returns, and ρ is the correlation coefficient between returns on assets i and j. Therefore, by merging these equations, we get

$$\text{CaR}_{p,\%}(\alpha) = \mu_p + F_p^{-1}(\alpha)\sqrt{\sum_{i=1}^{n} w_i^2\sigma_i^2 + \sum_{i=1}^{n}\sum_{j\neq i}^{n} w_i w_j \sigma_i \sigma_j \rho_{ij}}$$

$$= \mu_p + \sqrt{\sum_{i=1}^{n} w_i^2\sigma_i^2[F_p^{-1}(\alpha)]^2 + \sum_{i=1}^{n}\sum_{j\neq i}^{n} w_i w_j \sigma_i \sigma_j \rho_{ij}[F_p^{-1}(\alpha)]^2}$$

If the quantiles of standardized returns of each portion of the portfolio $F_x^{-1}(\alpha)$, $F_y^{-1}(\alpha)$, $F_z^{-1}(\alpha)$ are assumed to be identical to the quantiles of the portfolio returns, then $F_p^{-1}(\alpha)$ could be substituted with the appropriate quantile, and portfolio CaR can be expressed as a function of individual percentage capital at risk for each component ($\text{CaR}_{i,\%}$, $\text{CaR}_{j,\%}$) so that

$$\text{CaR}_{p,\%}(\alpha) = \mu_p + \sqrt{\sum_{i=1}^{n} w_i^2\sigma_i^2[F_p^{-1}(\alpha)]^2 + \sum_{i=1}^{n}\sum_{j\neq i}^{n} w_i w_j \sigma_i \sigma_j \rho_{ij}[F_p^{-1}(\alpha)]^2}$$

$$= \mu_p + \sqrt{\sum_{i=1}^{n} w_i^2\sigma_i^2[F_i^{-1}(\alpha)]^2 + \sum_{i=1}^{n}\sum_{j\neq i}^{n} w_i w_j \sigma_i \sigma_j F_i^{-1}(\alpha)F_j^{-1}(\alpha)\rho_{ij}}$$

$$= \mu_p + \sqrt{\sum_{i=1}^{n} w_i^2[\text{CaR}_{i,\%}-\mu_i]^2 + \sum_{i=1}^{n}\sum_{j\neq i}^{n} w_i w_j [\text{CaR}_{i,\%}-\mu_i][\text{CaR}_{j,\%}-\mu_j]\rho_{ij}}$$

If we further simplify the formula by neglecting the expected-return terms (both for prudential purposes and considering their difficult estimation) so as to set all μ terms equal to zero and, by expressing CaR in absolute rather than percentage terms, multiply-ing both terms for the value of the whole portfolio V, than the same formula becomes simply

$$CaR_p = \sqrt{\sum_{i=1}^{n} CaR_i^2 + \sum_{i=1}^{n} \sum_{j \neq i} CaR_i CaR_j \rho_{ij}}$$

Rosenberg and Schuermann (2004) refer to this formula as the Normal CaR or hybrid CaR formula, depending on whether stand-alone CaR values are calculated assuming normality or not. The formula relies on a critical assumption concerning the relationship between individual distribution quantiles and portfolio quantiles, which is satisfied in the case of elliptic distributions (a particular case of which is a joint normal distribution). If this assumption is not satisfied, then alternative techniques are necessary.

The first alternative solution would be to use copulas to model the dependence across risks and then, as a consequence, to resort to a Monte Carlo simulation to derive the bank portfolio return distribution and obtain the desired percentile. Copulas would be highly desirable here since they can be much more flexible, and risk aggregation requires merging distributions that may be significantly different. Unfortunately, since there are many different possible copula functions, it is complex to identify the optimal one, and the risk manager generally lacks the amount of data that would be needed to support the choice with clear empirical evidence. In fact, identifying the copula function that can best model the dependence structure of two or more stock indexes' returns is a relatively simple problem that can be solved by analyzing many years of daily data. When instead the problem is the aggregation among business units or risk types, it is virtually impos-sible to have time series of returns/earnings long enough to conduct a similar analysis.

Consequently, the choice of a particular copula function might become partially sub-jective. This could be a major problem if the aggregated capital-at-risk measure is expected to enter into the bank's decision processes. For instance, if business units were evaluated on a risk-adjusted performance measure based on diversified capital at risk, then the aggregation technique could influence the allocation of diversification benefits among different business units, and the risk manager might find it hard to defend a subjective choice against the critiques of those division managers that feel they are damaged by the specific copula function that has been chosen (at least until a clear "best-practice" solution emerges in the industry). Rosenberg and Schuermann (2004) have empirically tested the impact of different copula functions by comparing a Gaussian copula with Student's t copulas with 5 and 10 degrees of freedom. They found out that while other elements (e.g., the relative weight of market, credit, and operational risk and the correlation between operational risk and other risks) have a greater impact on the aggregate risk estimate, the choice of the copula also has a relevant effect. For instance, the difference in aggregated CaR produced by using a normal rather than a Student's-$t(5)$ copula is around 11%.

A second possible alternative solution is the multifactor approach proposed by Alex-ander and Pezier (2003), who suggested building a multifactor model for the profit-and-loss distributions $P_1, P_2, \ldots, P_n$ of each business unit, so

$$P_i = \alpha_i + \beta_{i,1} x_1 + \beta_{i,2} x_2 + \cdots + \beta_{i,n} x_n + \varepsilon_i$$

where α_i is the expected P&L, $\beta_1, \beta_2, \ldots, \beta_n$ are the sensitivities of the P&L of business unit i to changes in the risk factors represented by $x_1, x_2, \ldots, x_n$, and ε_i is the residual that is not explained by the risk factors. By modeling P through this linear regression, the variance of aggregate P&L can easily be computed. Yet identifying the scaling factor that can transform the standard deviation into an economic capital estimate requires simulation. Alexander and Pezier (2003) also discuss the possibility of considering a normal mixture distribution for risk factors and of using tail correlations rather than the usual correlations to model the dependence among risk factors. A more complex situation would be the case of nonlinear relationships between the P&L and the factors.

From a practical standpoint, the solution they proposed might be particularly appealing if a risk manager could derive a stable scaling factor to translate the standard deviation of the aggregate P&L of the bank into an economic capital measure. In this case, simulation would be used just once (or very infrequently) to derive the scaling factor, and then the standard deviation of the aggregate P&L could be derived in closed form from the multifactor model by knowing the β vector, the covariance matrix of risk factors, and the covariance matrix of residual terms. One might still question whether (and how long) the mix of businesses and especially of P&L exposures for each business could be considered stable enough to maintain the same scaling factor.

In practice, however, we suggest a fourth solution, a simple variant of Alexander and Pezier's proposal. We would label this solution a "mixed multifactor approach" (Saita 2004). In fact, for most banks, credit risk accounts for a huge part of overall risk. As a consequence, in order to estimate aggregate capital at risk, a correct estimation of stand-alone credit risk economic capital is necessary, and the precision in measuring it should not be sacrificed in order to adopt a simplified model that makes it easier to model correlations. As Kuritzkes, Schuermann, and Weiner (2002) clearly point out, when the overall risk is dominated by a single type of risk, diversification benefits get smaller. Therefore, the overall CaR may be more sensitive to errors in modeling the single major risk than to errors in estimating correlation coefficients.

In this case one could first use the already-existing credit portfolio risk model in order to estimate credit risk economic capital. In default-mode models used by commercial banks, this estimate is often derived through a simulation that models the relationship between credit risk losses and some factors representing the state of the economy. It would therefore be possible to extract a value of portfolio losses conditional on a vector of values of the n common factors used for the portfolio model. A multifactor technique à la Alexander and Pezier could then be used for the other risks to estimate the linkage between the P&Ls of the remaining components of the bank portfolio and a set of m factors. This set would comprise the n factors used for the credit risk model and a further set of $m - n$ factors that might be relevant only to the other kinds of risk. Then for each of the k scenarios simulated by the credit portfolio risk model — which uses a specific vector of n factors and produces a specific credit P&L — it would be possible, given the dependence structure between risk factors, to extract a correlated vector of the remaining $n - m$ factors (and of the residual terms ε_i for each business unit) so as to derive a simulated P&L for all the remaining business units/risk portfolios into which the bank's overall portfolio has been divided.[1] The logic of the approach is shown in Figure 6-1.

This simulation approach is computationally intensive, but it may have advantages when credit risk is particularly significant (as typically happens). More specifically, this approach:

1. Of course, for all the other parts of the bank's portfolio, the choice of whether to use a simplified multifactor model or a more sophisticated model (consider, for instance, the case of market risk) will depend on an analysis of the relative relevance of the risk at an aggregate level and the cost of developing or using a more sophisticated model. The key requisite is to use a simulation approach across all risks and to condition the $m - n$ values of the remaining common risk factors on the n values of the factors extracted for the credit risk portfolio model.

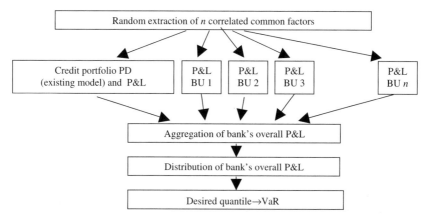

FIGURE 6-1   The mixed multifactor approach.

1. May use the existing credit portfolio risk model, with its typical nonlinear relation-
    ships between factors and portfolio losses, rather than an approximation (hence,
    there is also no need to estimate betas for credit risk). This is important given that
    credit risk typically accounts for the largest share of a bank's capital at risk.
2. Derives capital at risk simply as the desired percentile of the distribution of the
    aggregate P&L of the bank, obtained by simply adding up business unit P&Ls in
    the same scenario.
3. Since it reconstructs the full distribution of P&L values, may also enable one to
    estimate (provided the number of simulations is high enough) other risk measures,
    such as the expected shortfall, which can complement the capital-at-risk measure
    in more sophisticated approaches.

A relatively similar approach has also been proposed by Dimakos and Aas (2003) and
implemented at Den Norske Bank. Even in this case, market and operational risk are
estimated conditional on credit risk, but the authors suggest — as a simplifying assumption
— modeling the dependence on credit risk only through the relationship with the frequency of defaults, instead of through macro factors (including interest rates), to which
simulated defaults are typically linked in a credit risk VaR simulation. In a subsequent
paper, Dimakos, Aas, and Øksendal (2005) extended the kinds of risks and used a set of
common factors for market, credit, and insurance risk and then aggregated operational
and business risk through copulas (using, in this second step, dependence parameters
based on expert judgment).

All the aggregation techniques we have considered have in fact to face the relevant
problem of parameters estimation. Before evaluating the relative merits of alternative
methods, we should therefore discuss this issue in more detail.

6.3 Estimating Parameters for Risk Aggregation

When choosing the aggregation methodology, one major constraint is represented by the
need to feed any methodology with adequate parameters. Even in the simplest formula
based on the normal or hybrid VaR method, a matrix of linear correlation coefficients
among risks would be needed. Unfortunately, it is hard to be confident on correlation
estimates, due to the lack of data and to the potential differences between correlation in

detail or extreme scenarios vis-à-vis normal market conditions (see Carey and Stulz 2005). In order to estimate correlation coefficients, four main solutions may be adopted:

1. Defining correlation coefficients in a judgmental way
2. Deriving historical correlation coefficients from publicly available stock return series of listed financial institutions
3. Deriving historical correlation coefficients from internal earnings series of different business units
4. Deriving correlation coefficients between risks through a simulation of existing internal risk measurement models

According to Joint Forum (2003), the first solution is already used by some institutions, which determine coefficients judgmentally. Coefficients may be entirely determined either in a judgmental way, through a subjective evaluation made by top managers, or by resorting to coefficients used in one of the few existing papers on the subject (Kuritzkes, Schuermann, and Weiner 2001; Ward and Lee 2002) or, in part, by blending empirical coefficients with judgmental ones (Joint Forum 2003). A judgmental evaluation requires substantial care since many potential experienced "judges" are represented by business unit managers whose results might be affected by the final correlation estimates, and this of course might alter the outcomes of an internal panel on "perceived" correlation.

The second alternative solution consists in observing stock return correlations of stand-alone, mono-business (or mono-risk) financial institutions. If they existed, the task would be easy, but it is very difficult in practice to find — for all the possible divisions of a real bank — competitors that can be considered specialized enough (as already noted in Chapter 5 regarding benchmark capital measures of business risk).

The typical solution is therefore the third one, i.e., estimating correlation between earnings' time series of different business units, as suggested in Matten (2000). Nevertheless, there are at least four problems in using this method.

- Historical correlation coefficients may simply be impossible to derive when business units have recently been restructured (e.g., due to a merger) so that the historical time series of returns is either nonexistent or far too short.
- Available time series are typically series of earnings, not returns, and translating them into return series may in some cases be partially arbitrary since it requires a measure of "exposure" to the risk.[2]
- They are typically based on business unit P&Ls, so — if individual CaR estimates were based on risk type — business unit correlation coefficients would only provide a proxy for the required correlation, since it would be necessary to associate a risk type to the business unit where the single risk is predominant.
- If (in order to increase available data despite short time series) they are calculated on infra-annual and especially on monthly data, there are good reasons to expect that historical correlation coefficients can provide a downward-biased estimate of the "true" correlation, due to the existence of serial cross-autocorrelation in returns.

While the first and the second problem are quite simple and usually well recognized by risk managers, the third one deserves an explanation. Simply speaking, when a monthly

---

2. Again, see Chapter 5. Note that if the exposure of different business units were considered fixed, then correlation among returns and earnings would be the same, since both earnings' series would just be scaled by a constant. If, instead, exposure were variable, then the choice of the exposure measure becomes much more relevant.

TABLE 6-1 Example of the Problem of Earnings Cross-Autocorrelation

	Monthly Earnings		Quarterly Earnings	
	X	Y	X	Y
1	**10**	−200	120	−205
2	**−30**	5		
3	140	**−10**		
4	−70	55	100	25
5	−60	35		
6	230	−65		
7	200	85	430	470
8	140	215		
9	90	170		
10	80	115	490	370
11	260	85		
12	150	170		
13	60	205	100	360
14	40	105		
15	0	50		
16	190	20	390	340
17	260	95		
18	−60	225		
19	−60	100	−50	45
20	70	−60		
21	−60	5		
22	130	5	300	180
23	150	35		
24	20	140		
Correlation	$\rho_{monthly} = 0.001$		$\rho_{quarterly} = 0.675$	

series of P&Ls of the different divisions is used to estimate earnings correlations, if the earnings of business unit X in month t are correlated not only with the earnings of business unit Y in month t, but also to its earnings on month $t + 1$, $t + 2$, and so on, then the correlation estimate may prove to be wrong. We first show (see Table 6-1) a purely theoretical example of the effects of serial cross-autocorrelation between earnings series, and then we explain why this effect is likely to occur in practice.

Let us consider business units X and Y, whose monthly earnings are reported in Table 6-1. According to those data, the correlation ρ between monthly earnings is close to zero. Yet it can easily be seen that from the third month onward, the earnings of Y are simply equal to the average of the earnings of X in the two months before (see, for instance, the boldface numbers in Table 6-1). In practice, an event that has direct and immediate influence on X's earnings in month t is assumed to impact Y's earnings partly in month $t + 1$ and partly in month $t + 2$ (and therefore there is serial cross-autocorrelation). Unsurprisingly, then, correlation based on quarterly data is markedly higher than correlation based on monthly data (0.675 rather than 0.001). Please note that while the example is related to earnings series for sake of simplicity, the same result would occur with returns if the size of exposure in X and Y were constant through the sample period (in fact, returns for both units would be equal to earnings divided by a constant, and the correlation would be unaffected by such scaling).

Therefore, earnings serial cross-autocorrelation may make correlations calculated on short-period data completely misleading, since those data fail to capture the interdependence between the two business units/areas. Why, then, should we suspect the existence of earnings serial cross-autocorrelation? There are at least two reasons. First, cross-autocorrelation may derive from the different accounting practices used for the profit centers inside the bank. A rise in interest rates might represent bad news both for the Treasury bond trader and for the head of the asset and liability management strategies of the banking book (e.g., because there is a negative maturity gap so that interest-sensitive liabilities are greater than interest-sensitive assets). Yet, while an adverse rate move would immediately impact the bond portfolio, which is marked to market, it would influence the profit of the banking book only gradually, through a reduction of the net interest margin in the following months.

Second, earnings cross-autocorrelation may derive from structurally different reactions of businesses to the same event. Consider the impact of a sharp stock market drop. In an equity trading division with a long position in the equity market, this may produce immediate losses, which are promptly recognized in the profit and loss of the business unit. The same event may have instead diluted but prolonged effects on areas such as the investment banking division (since firms' potential equity offerings may be rescheduled or suppressed) and the asset management division (due to the reduction of asset under management and, consequently, management fees and to the indirect effect of the switches that might take place from equity to bond mutual funds, reducing the average level of fees for the asset manager). In both cases, the effects of the stock market fall in month t may be material even several months later.

Hence, since there are reasons to suppose that earnings serial cross-autocorrelation may be frequent, in practice the risk manager has to choose whether to estimate correlation coefficients between different business units' earnings using a larger but less reliable sample of monthly data or instead aggregate earnings over longer time intervals, accepting the calculation of correlation coefficients with fewer earnings data points, unless a convincing way to filter out this cross-serial autocorrelation effect from earnings series is identified. This is why banks willing to be able first of all to measure business risk and second to assess internal correlation coefficients empirically should try to take advantage of existing management information systems and invest their efforts in building reliable earnings data series. As in the case of operational risk, the patient construction of an internal database may allow, after some years, to estimate parameters directly from empirical data or, at least, to use available empirical data to test and possibly refine subjective assumptions.

A fourth possible solution could then be to derive correlation coefficients by simulating scenarios using existing internal-risk models (e.g., the credit portfolio risk model and the market risk model). Since they often define potential losses as a function of a set of different factors (e.g., market factors for the market risk model, macroeconomic or other common factors for the credit risk portfolio model), it would be possible to produce a joint simulation of the different risk models (of course, under a consistent set of values of the key factors) and then to derive correlation coefficients from the simulated scenarios. Yet, adopting this solution to derive linear correlation coefficients for simplified models, such as the normal or hybrid VaR, has two clear shortcomings. First of all, risk models are available only for some of the risk types or business units. Second, if they existed and it were possible to run a joint simulation, then a mixed multifactor approach would be much better to aggregate CaR then using the simplified normal/hybrid VaR equation.

The problems we have discussed so far in estimating linear correlation coefficients also apply to parameter calibration for copula functions, where a longer series would be even more desirable. In practice, historical data would fail to provide an adequate data set, so model-generated scenarios would appear at present to be the only possible solution. But, again, they are not available for all risk types, and, moreover, once scenarios are generated, losses could be aggregated directly. Yet copula functions can be used when clearly non-normal distributions have to be aggregated and correlation parameters are derived through expert estimates. They can also be used in the mixed multifactor approach to model the dependence among common factors when running the simulation, even if this would increase the computational burden.

In the multifactor approach à la Alexander and Pezier (2003) and in the mixed multi-factor approach, the dependence structure among different business units is instead driven by (1) the existence of common factors that impact individual P&Ls and (2) the dependence structure among common factors. Therefore it is important to identify correctly the common factors and their relationship with the P&L of each business unit. In the "pure" multifactor approach this aim could be attained either through historical earnings data or through an existing risk model, whenever available (e.g., for business units exposed mainly to credit or market risk). This is also true for the mixed multifactor approach, even if there is no need to develop estimates, at least for credit risk and for those business units that are exposed mainly to credit risk, since the credit portfolio risk model would be used as it is. The problems deriving from the absence of long-enough earnings data series and from the likely presence of cross-autocorrelation in earnings data when they are measured on short intervals still apply, and these may affect the estimate of P&L sensitivities to common risk factors (with only the partial remedy that in a mixed multifactor approach credit risk capital would not be affected).

In any case, a critical issue for both approaches is the choice of the number of factors and the way in which residual risk is modeled. In fact, since aggregated CaR is determined by simulation, it could be desirable to be parsimonious in the choice of common risk factors (a clear example is market risk, where the market risk model may be based on a wider set of factors, which it may be wise to reduce before running a firmwide simulation). The lower the number of common risk factors, the faster the simulation but at the same time the greater the importance of how residual risk is defined.

In theory, if there were a large number of business units with a reasonably similar size and if residual components were uncorrelated, then the residual components could be assumed to be irrelevant due to diversification. In practice, however, some divisions typically account for a substantial part of the overall risk; and if the number of common factors is limited, then the residual components are unlikely to be completely independent. In this case, modeling the variance and dependence structure of these components (at least for larger business units) would be important.

The dependence structure of common factors is also important. Assuming joint normality and simulating correlated risk factors through a simple Cholesky decomposition would be the easier path to follow, but this assumption may not be the best one for all risk factors. In this case, more sophisticated techniques (and even copulas, applied to risk factors instead of to earnings distribution directly) may be desirable, provided that data series related to selected risk factors are sufficient to support the estimation of their parameters.

Box 6-1: Examples of Linear Correlation Coefficient Estimates from Existing Studies and Their Implication on Aggregated Risk Capital

Some of the relatively few empirical exercises on risk aggregation also report correlation coefficients among major risks. Yet these coefficients may often vary substantially. As an example, Table 6-2 compares correlation coefficients used in Kuritzkes, Schuermann, and Weiner (2001), Ward and Lee (2002), and Dimakos and Aas (2003). Note that Ward and Lee (2002) also consider many other risks, including P&C and life insurance risks, while we concentrate here on market, credit, and operational risks.

In order to give some sense of the difference that using these different estimates can imply, we use as an example data from the 2005 Citigroup Annual Report, which describes economic capital for credit, market, operational, and insurance risk and provides an estimate of diversification benefits (see Table 6-3).

By using Citigroup's 2005 data on individual risks and the correlation matrixes in Table 6-1 (and assuming that the simplified normal CaR/hybrid CaR formula can be used), we could obtain different values for total capital after diversification and different consequent estimates of diversification benefits (see Table 6-4). Table 6-4 clearly shows that given the remarkable differences between the more conservative assumptions used in Kuritzkes, Schuermann, and Weiner (2001) and the more optimistic ones formulated by Ward and Lee (2002), estimated economic capital could also vary substantially. Incidentally, the Citigroup estimate is even higher than the highest one in Table 6-4, even if no disclosure is provided about whether this or a more refined aggregation methodology is used. Differ-

TABLE 6-2   Linear Correlation Coefficients among Credit, Market, and Operational Risks in Three Different Studies

Risks	Kuritzkes, Schuermann, and Weiner (2001)	Ward and Lee (2002)	Dimakos and Aas (2003)
Credit risk–market risk	0.80	0.20	0.30
Credit risk–operational risk	0.40	0.20	0.44
Market risk–operational risk	0.40	0.20	0.13

TABLE 6-3   Risk Aggregation and Diversification Benefits: Citigroup Estimates (2003–2005, Billions of Dollars)

Component	2003	2004	2005
Credit risk	28.7	33.2	36.1
Market risk	16.8	16.0	13.5
Operational risk	6.1	8.1	8.1
Insurance risk	0.3	0.2	0.2
Sum	51.9	57.5	57.9
(Diversification benefits)	(5.2)	(5.3)	(4.7)
Total after diversification	46.7	52.2	53.2
Diversification benefits as a % of the sum of individual risk components	10.0%	9.2%	8.1%

Source: Citigroup 2005 Annual Report and subsequent elaborations.

ences in the second and fourth column of Table 6-4 may be striking if we consider that in this case credit risk accounted for more than 60% of the sum of all risks. Of course, correlations might have played an even greater role if the business mix had been more balanced with a greater relevance of market and operational risks as opposed to credit risk.

TABLE 6-4   Effect of Different Correlation Inputs on Total Economic Capital Estimates (Assuming Economic Capital for Individual Risks Equal to Citigroup 2005 Data)

Correlation Input Source	Total Estimated Economic Capital	Estimated Diversification Benefits	Diversification Benefits as a % of the Sum of Individual Risk Components
Kuritzkes, Schuermann, and Weiner (2001)	51.6	6.3	10.9%
Ward and Lee (2002)	43.8	14.1	24.4%
Dimakos and Aas (2003)	46.2	11.7	20.2%

Correlation for insurance risk has been assumed equal to 0.4. In any case, this choice is almost irrelevant to the results, given that insurance risk is negligible in relative terms.

6.4   Case Study: Capital Aggregation within Fortis (by Luc Henrard, Chief Risk Officer, Fortis, and Ruben Olieslagers, Director, Central Risk Management, Fortis)

Fortis is a large, complex financial conglomerate that faces a wide range of risks across its various banking and insurance activities. Risk management is a core part of Fortis business and has an impact on all areas of management. To ensure that these risks are measured, monitored, and managed properly at all times, Fortis has implemented a solid framework for internal control and risk management. Hence, by the mid-1990s Fortis had developed and implemented risk management frameworks for Asset and Liability Management (ALM), market risk, and credit risk.

Since its inception in 1989, Fortis has undergone explosive growth, both organically and through acquisitions. Its banking operations have been strengthened by several takeovers. Therefore, given the different origins of the banking and insurance pool entities, they developed very different approaches and terminology for risk assessment, and as a result these risks were only measured separately.

Given the organizational complexity of Fortis, it was difficult to identify the main risk areas, and given the inconsistencies in the risk measurement methodologies, an adequate comparison of the risks taken was not possible. In 2000, the Executive Committee therefore decided to launch the Fortis Capital Adequacy Project (ForCAP), with the aim of developing a groupwide and consistent risk measurement framework in order to determine the capital adequacy and to allow the Executive Committee and the Board to understand the general distribution of economic capital consumption across risk types and activities. An integrated approach allows one to maximize the group advantages of scale and diversification (e.g., hedging net ALM positions and optimizing reinsurance group level) and to maximize knowledge sharing within Fortis entities.

In a first stage, ForCAP was not meant to replace any other risk metric developed by either the bank or the insurance pool. Rather, it aimed at developing an additional risk metric to improve Fortis' risk management capabilities and to support stakeholder discussions (e.g., rating agencies, analysts, investors, regulators). The project was organized in two phases: first, top-down measurement, and in a second stage bottom-up. The aim of the top-down phase was to arrive, within very tight deadlines, at robust relative results using a pragmatic approach based on the available risk measures from local risk management departments in the operating entities. Where necessary, some benchmarks and assumptions have been made to fill possible gaps while paying attention to keeping consistency as high as possible. In the second phase, bottom-up refinements have been constantly implemented to replace existing benchmarks and to increase the granularity of the calculations.

Fortis has been very active within the field of risk management, and there is a strong commitment to risk and control awareness. Continuous efforts have been made to refine and improve the economic capital risk framework, to complete the integration of risk discipline into the business decision processes, and to embed consistent risk measurement and management tools at all levels in the organization. Therefore, a variety of applications have been installed:

1. Reserve and capital adequacy calculation (available versus required capital from different points of view: regulatory, rating agencies, economic capital)
2. Limit setting (concentration limits)
3. Portfolio optimization
4. Relationship performance measurement (clients, relationship managers)
5. Risk-based pricing (price should reflect risk in a consistent way)
6. Transfer pricing (distinction between interest rate/commercial performance)

Within Fortis, each business is responsible for managing its own risks and ensuring that it has excellent risk management in place, covering the full risk taxonomy. The Chief Risk Officer is supported by a central team of risk specialists and develops, in collaboration with the businesses, methodologies, policies, and limits for approval by the appropriate risk committees. Cascading Risk Committees monitor risks, approve methodologies, policies, and limits, and make key risk recommendations to the Executive Committee and the Board. The double full reporting line between business risk management and the business CEO on one side and central risk management on the other guarantees that the principles of transparency, compliance, independence, and representation in different risk committees are reinforced.

In response to the continuous changes in the world of risk management and to accomplish the regulatory requirements, the Fortis risk framework and organization have been modified significantly over time. The risk management structure is more and more integrated and centralized to ensure consistency in methodologies and policies throughout the whole organization (banking and insurance).

The capital aggregation approach of Fortis encompasses four main aspects:

1. Definition of the risk taxonomy
2. Metric for measuring risk: accounting- and value-based metrics
3. Calibration: confidence level and time horizon
4. Aggregation of capital requirements

As far as the definition of a risk taxonomy is concerned, many different ways of classifying risk are possible, and no single taxonomy is inherently better than another. Within

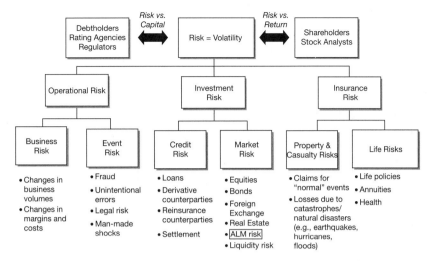

FIGURE 6-2   Risk taxonomy at Fortis.

TABLE 6-5   Different Risk Measurement Approaches Used in Banking and Insurance

	Banking	**Insurance**
Terminology	• Expected loss • Rating master scale • VaR • Economic capital • RAROC	• Claims • Mortality tables • Embedded value • Reserves/solvency/risk-based capital • Different performance measures
Focus	• Expected and unexpected losses • One year • Asset risks	• Prudent estimates • Multiyear • Liability risks
Historical weaknesses	• Oversimplified modeling • Customer behavior	• Insufficient use of modern finance theory • Little use of transfer pricing (ALM)

Fortis, the risk taxonomy has been designed to ensure that all risks are adequately captured according to the relative importance of the different risk types (see Figure 6-2).

The second step is the definition of the risk metric, where the main alternatives are accounting-based metrics (e.g., GAAP, IFRS) and value-based metrics (such as economic/fair value). External communication is in general executed, through accounting metrics, toward regulators and rating agencies. But since ForCAP has been developed to define a common risk measure, risk has been defined in terms of adverse changes in economic or fair value and is hence independent of accounting principles. However, accounting measures are gradually moving toward a greater use of the "economic value" type of approaches (see Basel II, Solvency II, IFRS).

A critical issue in Fortis' case was the difference between traditional approaches to risk in the banking and insurance businesses (see Table 6-5), which derive from the differences in the dominant risk type.

The third step is represented by calibration and harmonization of the value-at-risk measures within a confidence interval of 99.97% and over a horizon of one year[3] so as

---

3. Different time horizons are used within banking and insurance. The one-year horizon is a compromise between conventions in the banking pool (relatively short term) and the insurance pool (relatively long term). This horizon is also consistent with the capital budgeting process and in line with market standards.

to provide a consistent and comparable measure of economic capital across all risk types. All economic capital measurements within Fortis are calibrated to this confidence interval, reflecting the risk appetite of the Board (AA-rated financial institution).

As far as the final step is concerned (risk aggregation), after estimating the economic capital separately for each type of risk per business, the total economic capital is calculated at the business level, at the banking and insurance level, and for Fortis as a whole. Since it is extremely unlikely that all risk events will take place at the same time, an allowance is made for diversification benefits when combining the individual risks. This results in a total economic capital at the group level that is significantly lower than it would be if the individual risks were simply added together.

The aggregation of different risks across business lines can take place at different levels (see Kuritzkes, Schuermann, and Weiner 2001): single risk factor within a business line (level I), across risk factors within a single business line (level II), and across business lines (level III). Typically, the diversification effects are the largest within a single risk factor (level I), decrease at the business line level (level II), and are the smallest across business lines.

The present main options for aggregating risks across risk types and business lines are summation of the stand-alone economic capital figures (a simple approach but overly conservative), variance–covariance (relatively standard, easy and more accurate than summation), simulation (potentially more accurate but rather time consuming and with the danger of false accuracy), and copulas (current topic of research but difficult to parameterize and to build joint distributions).

The selection of an appropriate approach is a trade-off between complexity, efficiency, and data availability (historical series of revenue). Within Fortis, it was decided in the first stage to use the var–covar approach for aggregating the economic capital across risk types for the different businesses. Most leading financial conglomerates that have implemented groupwide risk frameworks have typically adopted this kind of approach.

A relatively crude and conservative matrix has been designed to provide a reasonable approximation for the correlations of risks across businesses. The estimation of correlation effects, and hence diversification benefits, is difficult, due to the lack of data and the fact that correlations tend to be unstable in crises.

Several assumptions are possible for quantifying these correlation effects across risk types. In the first stage, Fortis opted for a rather pragmatic approach. To assume a 100% correlation between all risks is very conservative. Within Fortis, the correlation between the financial risks (credit risk, ALM, trading) has been assumed close to 100%, because in times of high volatilities (i.e., high confidence intervals), the systematic risk factors move financial risks in the same direction.

The correlation of the other risk types with business risk is assumed to be lower but not neglectable, because in financial crises, business volumes and the ability to cover expenses have typically fallen. Liability risks are assumed to be minimally correlated with the other risk types because there is no reason to believe at times of high credit losses that claims and mortality rates should also rise sharply.

A few notes on Fortis' approach may be useful.

- The conceptually simple correlation matrix becomes quite large when implemented in a complex organization like Fortis, characterized by a lot of risk types and businesses. If Fortis considered seven risk types and 27 businesses, there would be 189 clusters of stand-alone economic capital and a 189×189 correlation matrix. Changes in the structure of businesses within Fortis would require a change in the setup of the correlation matrix.

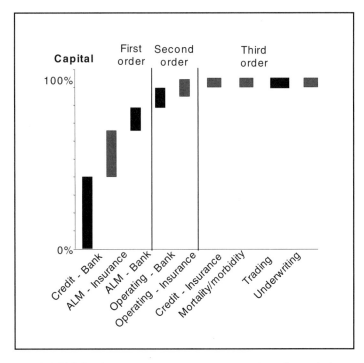

FIGURE 6-3   Relative capital consumption (illustrative).

- The integration of the risk capitals via a correlation matrix computation is assumed to take place in one step, beginning from a stand-alone situation per risk type and per business to a fully diversified total.
- The var–covar approach uses only first- and second-order information and ignores information of higher order.
- In addition to the more general diversification, Fortis benefits from a netting effect across bank and insurance interest-rate risk, due to the fundamental differences between their balance sheets.

In recent years, the major efforts within Fortis have been dedicated to the improvement of the granularity of the calculations (at the obligor and/or transaction levels) and the individual parameters for measuring, among others, credit risk and operational risk (implementation of Basel II). For example, in the computation of credit economic capital, the key parameter, labeled the "Capital Multiplier," i.e., the multiplier to be applied to the standard deviation of the loss rate distribution in order to obtain economic capital, was based on a benchmark that has been assessed and refined by a methodology developed by the Actuarial Research Group of the University of Leuven (Dhaene et al. 2003). Also, when calculating the (stand-alone) economic capital for a risk type within a business (see Figure 6-3), more specialized and advanced models and correlation approaches are in use (e.g., default correlation matrix calculated with internal data and asset correlations based on KMV data). Additional research has also been done to analyze the sensitivity of the correlations between the different risk types to the total economic capital.

In our view, current regulatory requirements for banking (Basel II) and insurance (Solvency I) do not adequately recognize diversification benefits, while it is well known that the industry risk diversification may be substantial. Therefore, Fortis has actively been participating in the Chief Risk Officer Forum (which comprises risk officers of major European insurance companies and financial conglomerates), the Comité Européen des Assurances (CEA), and the Groupe Consultatif, so as to contribute to the design of a framework for incorporating diversification in the solvency assessment of insurers (Solvency II and possibly Basel III).

In the years to come, Fortis will continue to fine-tune the models, to make risk and governance structures work in practice, and to improve the consistency of risk/return performance measures (for example, reconciliation between RAROC, European embedded-value, and fair-value measures).

6.5 A Synthetic Comparison of Alternative Risk Aggregation Techniques

Evaluating the different methodologies for risk integration requires considering both the theoretical properties of the methodology and the practical issues that arise when trying to estimate its parameters. Another relevant objective is the ability to produce a measure of "diversified" capital at risk (i.e., capital at risk after accounting for diversification benefits at the firmwide level) for individual business units. The issue of diversified CaR is discussed in Chapter 7, but it is intuitive that some of the aggregation techniques (e.g., the simpler normal or hybrid CaR) may make it easier to assess the relative contribution to diversification benefits of individual business units than more complex solutions, such as risk aggregation through copulas.

Therefore, there are a number of different criteria that should be considered when evaluating a risk integration methodology. Some of them are objective and structural; others are still objective but may become less important through time (e.g., the ability to reduce sampling errors or model risk due to the absence of adequate time series of earnings). Still others are subjective, since they depend on the purposes for which the risk manager will use the aggregation technique. For instance, attributes such as transparency, fairness and the ability to produce diversified CaR measures may have a relevance that varies substantially, depending on whether the risk aggregation exercise is intended to support only top management's decisions on capital structure or also to guide the internal capital allocation process. This also means that choices of different techniques made by different banks might find a rationale in the different breadth of purposes to be pursued.

The advantages and disadvantages of the four methods that have been discussed are presented in Table 6-6. Calibration problems are stressed, since in practice the difficulty of feeding the risk aggregation technique with reasonable numbers may be a major obstacle in its adoption. This is particularly true when the same numbers will also be used to evaluate individual units. On one hand more stakeholders may be willing to question the procedure used to derive those numbers. On the other hand, if individual risk measures are used to drive or to support decisions on the business mix and the internal allocation of resources, then estimation errors may be a more serious problem. Caution is therefore required when bringing the aggregation technique and its formula from the R&D laboratory to the plants, and — at least in the early stages of development — a risk manager might decide not to use the technique to evaluate diversification effects inside the bank and their attribution to business units.

Therefore, Table 6-6 suggests that while in theory copulas clearly represent the right answer to the otherwise-complex problem of aggregating the different distributions of

TABLE 6-6   Comparison of the Different Risk Aggregation Techniques

Methodology	Advantages (calibration issues in *italic*)	Disadvantages (calibration issues in *italic*)
Classic square root formula (normal CaR or hybrid CaR)	• Simple, intuitive, and easy to explain to nonexperts • Aggregated capital at risk can be derived analytically from individual CaR figures and correlation coefficients • Diversified CaR figures for individual business units are easy to calculate • *Parameter estimation is technically simpler (even if subject, as in all other cases, to data problems)*	• Theoretically incorrect when the standardized quantiles of the portfolio distribution are not identical to portfolio standardized quantiles. • *Correlations are often estimated through historical earnings' series. Yet, the lack of long series of earnings data may lead one to use short-term (e.g., monthly) earnings, which might imply underestimated correlations if earnings are serially cross-autocorrelated.*
Aggregation through copulas	• Very flexible, since it is not necessary to assume a particular joint distribution of returns/earnings for all risks/business units. • The choice of the right kind of copula function can enable one to model dependence (and also tail dependence) correctly while maintaining the original distribution of returns/earnings for the single risk/business unit	• The method is more complex and harder to explain to nonexperts. • If also used for allocation to individual business units, diversified CaR figures might be sensitive to the choice of the copula function and its parameters, increasing political resistance. • It may be more difficult to develop consistent diversified CaR measures for individual units. • *The choice of the optimal copula function and its parameters requires significantly long series of earnings data, which are missing in most banks. Shorter series may lead to higher subjectivity of the choice of the copula function and its parameter and more calibration risk.*
Multifactor approach à la Alexander and Pezier (2003)	• Intuitive approach that forces one to understand better the common factors behind different business units. • If CaR is assumed to be a fixed multiple of portfolio standard deviation, then aggregated CaR can be derived analytically. • Interesting solution to model correlation among fee-based business units exposed mainly to business risk and between those units and the rest of the bank. • The method can be consistent with different levels of complexity in modeling risk factor returns and their relationship with P&Ls.	• If normality of portfolio returns is not assumed, the right multiple has to be estimated (and periodically re-estimated) through simulation. • The method is also likely to simplify the relationships between factors and business unit P&L for those business units that already possess a more sophisticated model. This can affect overall results, especially for those business units exposed to credit risk. • *The number and type of risk factors must be carefully selected; a specific risk component is also required, especially for larger business units.* • *Estimating factor sensitivities is exposed to problems, due to lack of long time series (as for other alternative methods).* • *The dependence structure between different risk factors may be critical.*
Mixed multifactor approach	• The precision of the credit risk portfolio model, which often accounts for a relevant share of overall CaR, is completely preserved. • Aggregation occurs through simulation in each simulated scenario and is therefore extremely straightforward and easy to explain to nonexperts. • It is possible to derive diversified and undiversified measures of CaR as a by-product of the simulation. • *Factor sensitivities must be estimated only for those business units that are not exposed to market and credit risk, which are already captured by existing models.*	• Computationally intensive • *The number and type of risk factors must be carefully selected; a specific risk component is also required, especially in the case of large business units that are not mainly exposed to credit risk.* • *Estimating factor sensitivities is exposed to problems due to lack of long time series (even if this problem applies only to a subset of business units, which may not be the larger ones).* • *The dependence structure between different risk factors may be critical.*

potential outcomes that are produced by different risk models (e.g., credit, market, operational, business risk models), their practical application has to face remarkable problems as far as calibration is concerned. Further research on the topic is surely warranted, but at the same time it would not be easy for copulas to substitute the simpler normal/hybrid CaR approach that is still largely used in practice despite its limitations. The pure and the mixed multifactor approaches represent interesting compromises between theoretical soundness and the need to feed a model with reasonable data. By modeling business unit P&L versus common factors, moreover, some extra useful information could be obtained by decision makers. The methodology might also be easier to explain to top managers than a copula function, and this may help make the methodology accepted and successful.

Yet the issue of data availability is important in any case, so the problem of time series is stressed frequently in Table 6-6. Note also that when a sophisticated technique is fed with a very short series of historical data (e.g., monthly earnings of certain business units), model parameters may change substantially from one year to another, simply because of the increase in the size of the historical sample. It would then be problematic to provide top managers with a report that could contain major changes in overall and individual CaR values, even in the absence of similar changes in business unit activity. Consequently, it may be advisable to test how the results of different methods change when new data are added, especially if the sample is not totally reliable. In general, as Pezier (2003) points out, it is important to make clear to all of the potential users that single CaR numbers are estimates and often very uncertain ones. Yet a potential suggestion when designing aggregated risk capital reports for senior managers would be to provide a range of values rather than a single and apparently precise number. Knowing that aggregated capital is not equal, say, to 1823.27, but rather is somewhere in the range between 1780 and 1870 (or perhaps between 1700 and 1950) may be a better support for decision makers, without giving a false sense of certainty, which might be dangerous. Moreover, making the range explicit may also convince senior managers to make the bank invest more money and effort in improving its risk aggregation techniques if the importance to achieve better and sounder measures were perceived.

6.6   Summary

After measuring market, credit, operational, and business risk, a bank still has to derive an aggregated capital measure in order both to support capital management decisions and to better understand the size of diversification benefits arising from its business mix. The starting point is to harmonize the different risk measures for each risk in terms of time horizon, confidence level, and their underlying notion of capital. There are different aggregation methodologies that can be used and that should be selected taking into consideration its conceptual soundness, its computational complexity, and the actual possibility of consistently estimating the parameters that the aggregation methodology requires. While adopting the usual portfolio VaR formula applied by the variance–covariance approach in a context of multivariate normally distributed returns is the easiest and perhaps currently most common solution, alternative and more refined solutions should be considered, such as copulas, the multifactor approach, and the mixed multifactor approach proposed here. Even in the simpler solutions, however, estimating proper parameters to model the dependence among different risks is far from easy. We pointed out in the chapter potential risks deriving from using short series of monthly earnings data without considering their potential impact on correlation estimates. The chapter has also presented the experience of the Fortis Group, large diversified group active in both the banking and the insurance business, in developing an aggregated VaR measure.

6.7 Further Reading

The best introduction to the challenges of risk aggregation and the simplifications that are often adopted in practice is Joint Forum (2003). The document also discusses the issue of whether regulators should consider diversification benefits in setting minimum capital requirements; on this problem, see also Kuritzkes, Schuermann, and Weiner (2001, 2002). The Joint Forum survey also clarifies that most financial institutions are currently mainly concerned in aggregating economic capital based on the value-at-risk concept, despite criticism about the potential VaR nonsubadditivity raised by Artzner et al. (1999).

Risk aggregation issues have also been widely discussed in the actuarial literature with reference to insurance companies or financial conglomerates. See Wang (2002), Ward and Lee (2002), Venter (2003), and Society of Actuaries (2004). With particular reference to the Fortis case study presented in this chapter, the methodological background can be further investigated in Dhaene et al. (2003), Dhaene, Vanduffel, and Tang (2004), Henrard and Olieslagers (2004), and Goovaerts, Van den Borre, and Laeven (2005). As far as the aggregation methods are concerned, the multifactor approach is developed in Alexander and Pezier (2003), while the mixed multifactor variant was first proposed in Saita (2004). Dimakos, Aas, and Øksendal (2005) also provide a very interesting concrete application to Den Norske Bank, while Rosenberg and Schuermann (2004) not only provide an excellent discussion of theoretical problems in risk aggregation, but also develop a very interesting test based on public data about the relevance of different elements in determining diversification benefits and their relative impact on overall estimated aggregated capital. A very interesting effort to estimate diversification benefits through earning series is developed in Kuritzkes and Schuermann (2006).

CHAPTER • 7

Value at Risk and Risk Control for Market and Credit Risk

So far we have focused mostly on value-at-risk measurement, first considering the individual risk types and then aggregating different risk types into a single VaR estimate (or into a range of possible values). Yet, from a practical point of view, VaR relevance depends substantially on whether and how it helps improve decision-making processes. It is therefore necessary to understand how VaR measures can be used and integrated into organizational processes, such as the definition of pricing guidelines or risk limits and performance measurement and incentive compensation. Given the differences among banks in terms of characteristics, business mix, organizational structure, style of management, and culture, in this field it would be wrong to look for *the* best choice to be made, as if a one-size-fits-all approach could be adopted. Organizational processes that take into consideration VaR-based measures should instead fit with the individual characteristics of the single organization, and therefore the contribution of these final chapters would be to discuss critically the pros and cons of different alternative solutions so as to support choices of the individual institutions.

When considering which processes can be supported by VaR measures, we can broadly identify three other areas (apart from pure risk measurement) that might be relevant: risk control, risk-adjusted performance measurement, and capital allocation (Figure 7-1).

In particular, value at risk can be measured not only to measure risk once risk has already been taken, but also to set up ex ante limits that can ensure that risks do not exceed the maximum risk capacity the bank is willing to accept and that risks being undertaken are properly priced (risk control). Note that by defining VaR limits for individual business units and hence accepting a certain potential loss, the bank is already implicitly allocating capital. As a further step, the bank can use VaR in order to evaluate

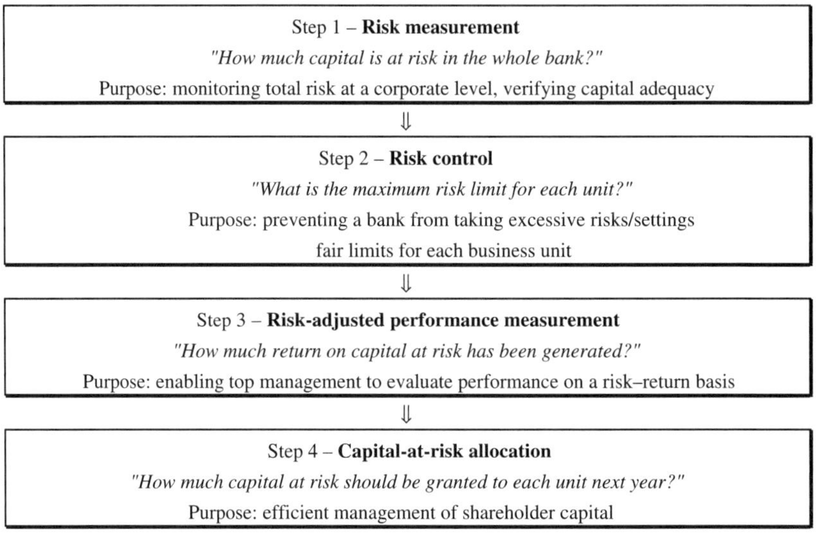

Step 1 – **Risk measurement**

"How much capital is at risk in the whole bank?"

Purpose: monitoring total risk at a corporate level, verifying capital adequacy

⇓

Step 2 – **Risk control**

"What is the maximum risk limit for each unit?"

Purpose: preventing a bank from taking excessive risks/settings

fair limits for each business unit

⇓

Step 3 – **Risk-adjusted performance measurement**

"How much return on capital at risk has been generated?"

Purpose: enabling top management to evaluate performance on a risk–return basis

⇓

Step 4 – **Capital-at-risk allocation**

"How much capital at risk should be granted to each unit next year?"

Purpose: efficient management of shareholder capital

FIGURE 7-1   The four main processes of a risk management system.

the performance of different businesses not only in terms of pure profits, but by comparing profits with the risk that has been undertaken or potentially with the capital that has been allocated to those businesses (risk-adjusted performance measurement). Finally, since capital is a scarce resource whose use should be optimized, the bank should develop a continuous process to reallocate capital toward those businesses that can produce a higher return in risk-adjusted terms (capital-at-risk allocation).

Moving from pure VaR measurement to the allocation of capital at risk among business units implies coping not only with technical risk measurement problems, but with organizational issues as well, since it implies defining or modifying internal processes and procedures and the performance evaluation system and more generally having an impact on the mechanisms through which the organizational behavior of different business units is coordinated. Moreover, the way in which risk-adjusted performance measures are designed can affect top managers' perceptions and judgments about the past performance of different businesses and might impact the bank's overall strategy. The design of the capital allocation process (e.g., the choice between a centralized and a decentralized, participative process or the choice between an episodic, ad hoc process and a repeated process incorporated into the annual planning and budgeting process) also has a potentially relevant effect on strategy formation.

With this premise in mind, this chapter deals with the first set of problems linked to using VaR measures in order to define risk limits for market risk and to set pricing guidelines for credit risk. Chapter 8 is devoted to risk-adjusted performance measurement, while Chapter 9 deals with the capital allocation process and its potential integration with the planning and budgeting process. In this chapter we discuss how the risk measurement tools developed in previous chapters could be used to define VaR-based limits for market risk, first considering risk control for traders (Sections 7.1–7.3). Section 7.4 is devoted to the analysis of the incremental contribution of new deals to VaR and to the decomposition of overall VaR among exposures. The concepts of incremental VaR, component VaR, and

VaR delta are described. Section 7.5 concludes the chapter by analyzing autonomy and pricing limits for credit risk.

7.1 Defining VaR-Based Limits for Market Risk: Identifying Risk-Taking Centers

When defining a risk policy for business units in the trading business, which would be exposed mainly to either market risks (e.g., in the case of equity trading) or the credit risk of traded financial instruments (e.g., corporate bonds, credit derivatives), the first topic to be considered is identifying which units should be given a limit. This in turn requires (1) defining the highest level in the hierarchy of business units and desks to which VaR limits should be set and (2) checking whether the boundaries between the tasks of different units allow one to define VaR limits efficiently by reducing risk overlaps as much as possible.

The first problem is related, for instance, to whether VaR limits should be set only up to the equity trading business unit or also to the level of the main desks composing the unit (e.g., cash, futures, plain-vanilla options, exotic option trading) or even to the level of the individual trader. A more detailed disaggregation of VaR limits might help if VaR is considered an efficient way to set operational risk limits for the single entity (i.e., business unit, desk, or individual trader) and if the bank is willing to measure the performances based not only on expost utilized VaR, but also on the amount of capital assigned to the unit, which depends precisely on its VaR limit. As we see later on, this may also be used to create incentives to use more intensively the allocated capital for each entity, i.e., to reduce the percentage of idle, unutilized capital. In theory, then, a more pervasive attribution of VaR limits would be desirable.

At the same time, there may be reasons to keep VaR limits at a higher hierarchical level. One case is when VaR limits may control only partially the real risk of the exposures of a desk. A bank adapting a variance–covariance approach could hardly use it to control the day-to-day risk of its equity option desk. Of course, a more sophisticated VaR model could be more helpful, but a bank with a small option desk may still consider that investing in a better VaR model is not worth the extra cost and effort. In this case, VaR limits should be set at a higher level and the desk should simply be given limits based only on option greeks such as delta and vega (i.e., sensitivities to changes in the underlying asset price and implied volatility). These simpler limits are also widely used in more sophisticated banks, since they help in capturing the risk profile of the option portfolio, even on an intraday basis, when VaR measurement with a more sophisticated model could be too difficult.

More generally, it is useful to recall that VaR is usually calculated based on the trader's portfolio after the mapping process has been performed. A poorly mapped portfolio in which some of the real risks "disappear" during the mapping phase (e.g., an option position that is transformed into a linear equivalent through a delta-only approximation, an undiversified stock portfolio whose VaR is approximated as beta times the stock index VaR) can hardly be controlled through VaR limits. Failing to model existing risks properly could be considered one of the sources of operational risk in the trading business, but a careful check of existing limitations is important when defining a VaR limit system (see also Box 7-1).

Box 7-1: Clarifying VaR Measurement Limitations: Deutsche Bank's Example

Complex portfolios and finite risk manager budgets can make unavoidable accepting a few reasonable compromises between measurement cost and precision. Yet it is important to make the limitations of existing systems clear to all potential users and to define risk control limits accordingly, so as to avoid overconfidence in numbers or misinterpretations of risk measurement outcomes. An interesting example is offered by Deutsche Bank, which, in its 2005 Annual Report (pp. 65–66) clearly states, "Although we believe that our proprietary market risk models are of a high standard, we are committed to their ongoing development and allocate substantial resources to reviewing and improving them. . . . Our value-at-risk analyses should also be viewed in the context of the limitations of the methodology we use and are therefore not maximum amounts that we can lose on our market risk positions." Deutsche Bank points out, for instance, that "we calculate value at risk at the close of the business on each trading day. We do not subject intra-day exposures to intra-day value-at-risk calculations" and that "the way sensitivities are represented in our value-at-risk models may only be exact for small changes in market parameters." Note that this point makes clear the unavoidable limitations deriving from mapping option positions through partial derivatives such as delta, gamma, vega, and theta while being unable to revaluate the portfolio fully (as often happens in the case of exposures in different kinds of complex exotic derivatives). Therefore, Deutsche Bank concludes, "we acknowledge the limitations in the value-at-risk methodology by supplementing the value-at-risk limits with other position and sensitivity limit structures, as well as with stress testing, both on individual portfolios and on a consolidated basis."

The second issue is represented by a check of the existing organizational structure of risk-taking centers to assess whether there might be pitfalls in VaR limit assignment or management, especially due to significant risk overlap among different business units. Let us imagine, for instance, the ideal situation of a bank with an organizational structure like the one presented in Figure 7-2. In this case, equity trading and equity derivatives trading are separated into two different business units. For example, imagine business unit 1 is the national legal entity of the group in Spain, which maintains responsibility for equity trading on Spanish stocks, while derivatives trading is centralized in the London trading room, i.e., business unit 2. In such a situation, there is, at least potentially, the risk that the Spanish legal entity and the London desk may take opposite positions on the Spanish market (e.g., the Madrid desk is long equities while the London desk is shorting futures on the Spanish stock market). This would imply an inefficient use of capital, since while the two positions are taken into account when considering stand-alone VaR limits of the two units (and hence those positions prevent the desks from making other deals), the aggregate exposure (and also the aggregate return produced) is close to zero. A careful design of the architecture of risk-taking centers, including all equity trading within the same unit, would help reduce the risk of inefficient use of capital. In any case, some risk overlap sometimes has to be accepted among different organizational units (which may even compete on the same market).

Note that although Bankers Trust, one of the U.S. investment banks pioneering the use of value at risk and RAROC, claimed in the early 1990s to apply a rigid, "one risk, one owner" principle by concentrating all risks of a certain kind into a single desk, apply-

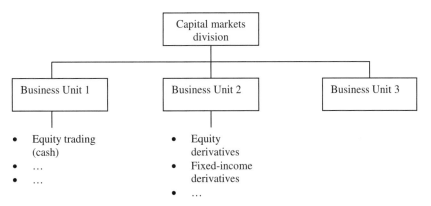

FIGURE 7-2   Problem of risk overlap: An example.

ing the principle in practice could be difficult to implement completely. For instance, a currency trader making a 3-month forward purchase of British pounds against U.S. dollars would assume a position on 3-month interest rates in the United States and in the UK, which may be offset by opposite positions at the money market desk. In theory the bank might force the currency trader to transfer interest rate risks to the money market desk (therefore enforcing the "one risk, one owner" principle), but it might also simply accept this partial risk overlap, as long as it is not considered material and its potential costs are lower than those necessary to define a strict risk specialization policy.

7.2   Managing VaR Limits for Market Risk: The Links between Daily VaR and Annual Potential Losses

When defining limits for market risk, one of the main problems is how to reconcile limits that are typically expressed in terms of daily VaR with the acceptable loss that the bank might consider acceptable over a longer horizon, usually one year. In fact, while the definition of the maximum acceptable loss (i.e., the capital at risk that the bank is willing to accept) has to be defined for harmonization purposes over a one-year horizon, an annual VaR limit would be difficult for the trading desks to handle.

Of course, a possible solution is to set no link at all between the two values. For instance, for those banks, such as Deutsche Bank, that clearly state they use stress-test scenarios to allocate capital to market risk divisions and use separate daily VaR limits only for the purpose of day-to-day risk management, the two values might even be entirely separate if stress scenarios are based on a longer time horizon. Yet, even for those banks the problem of reconciling daily VaR values with annual capital at risk might remain relevant as far as ex post performance measurement is concerned. In fact, the bank needs, for instance, to compare the risk–return profile of a trading/capital markets division and measured daily VaR with the corresponding information for other divisions (e.g., commercial banking) exposed mainly to credit risk whose VaR is calculated over a yearly horizon. Moreover, an equivalent yearly measure of daily VaR limits can also be used to assess how prudent stress scenarios look when compared to VaR assessed in "normal" market conditions.

To discuss this problem, we start for simplicity from the ex post case, i.e., from understanding how at the end of the year, given n daily VaR values, a single equivalent ex post yearly VaR can be derived for performance evaluation purposes. This, of course, would also be relevant for risk-adjusted performance measurement, which is discussed in Chapter 8. Then we consider the ex ante problem, i.e., how to define ex ante daily VaR limits given a maximum yearly acceptable loss. Finally, we consider how this solution might be extended if VaR limits were linked to actual cumulated losses.

7.2.1 Translating Actual Daily VaR Values into an Equivalent Ex Post Yearly VaR

Let us consider the case of a bank willing to aggregate 256 or 260 daily VaR values of a desk during a given year in order to calculate an equivalent yearly VaR that could be compared with the one-year VaR for the credit risk portfolio. Two apparently easy solutions would be to:

- Calculate, each day, an annual VaR (i.e., VaR assuming an annual shock in market risk factors) and then take an average of those values, or
- Calculate the average daily VaR, and then rescale it in some way into a yearly equivalent.

The first solution is clearly hard to implement (especially for banks using historical simulations) and highly questionable for those portfolios that either mature before one year or contain nonlinear positions such as options (especially if they are "negative gamma," i.e., if nonlinearity plays against the trader). In fact, the relevance of the gamma effect grows exponentially with the size of the shock in the underlying market factor. In the example in Table 7-1, for instance, both in the delta-gamma approximation and in the full-valuation case, the impact of curvature effect is from seven to nine times larger when passing from a one-day to a one-year horizon. But since the gamma effect here represents the amount of money the trader would lose due to a price shock, provided he is unable to change his delta while the shock occurs, assuming a yearly shock and no intervention by

TABLE 7-1   Relevance of Negative Gamma on VaR Estimation for Long Holding Periods

Holding period (days)	1	22	256
Price shock	2.18	10.23	34.90
Delta-gamma approximation			
Delta effect	1.16	5.42	18.49
Gamma effect	0.06	1.39	16.15
Delta-gamma 99% VaR	1.22	6.81	34.64
Gamma effect as a % of VaR	5.2%	20.4%	46.6%
Full valuation			
Delta effect	1.16	5.42	18.49
Higher-order-moment effect	0.06	1.28	10.58
Full valuation 99% VaR	1.22	6.70	29.07
Gamma effect as a % of VaR	5.1%	19.1%	36.4%

Short can option with $S = 100$, $t = 1$ year, $r = 5\%$, $q = 0$, strike price = 105.13, volatility = 15%.

TABLE 7-2 Limitations of Average Daily VaR (Hypothetical Daily VaR Values for Three Traders)

Trader	Day										Average daily VaR
	1	2	3	4	5	6	7	8	9	10	
A	10	10	10	10	10	10	10	10	10	10	10
B	8	5	12	15	6	14	12	8	13	7	10
C	0	0	0	0	100	0	0	0	0	0	10

the trader throughout the year would clearly be unrealistic and would lead to a substantial risk overstatement.

The second solution, which is much more frequent in practice, is represented by considering the average daily VaR, $\overline{\text{VaR}_d}$, and then rescaling it by the square root of the number of trading days. So, for instance, in a year with 260 trading days, the equivalent yearly VaR would be

$$\text{Year} - \text{equivalent VaR} = \overline{\text{VaR}_d} \cdot \sqrt{260}$$

The analogy with the relationship between yearly and daily return volatilities σ_y and σ_d when returns are serially independent, i.e., $\sigma_y = \sigma_d \cdot \sqrt{\text{no. of trading days}}$, is evident. In this case, the method is simple and creates no problems with nonlinear positions. But at the same time it has no formal justification and fails to consider exposure peaks, which instead may be a problem from the risk manager's viewpoint.

Let us consider an ideal extreme case of three traders with the sequence of daily VaR values reported in Table 7-2. While the three traders have different exposure peaks, the average daily VaR is the same. This implies that their equivalent yearly VaR (if calculated according to the frequent practice of averaging VaR and then rescaling it with the square root of the number of trading days) would yield the same one-year equivalent, even if trader C is clearly much riskier from the bank's point of view than trader A.

Yet there is a third and sounder alternative that can be proposed. One-year cumulated profit and loss (P&L) can be considered a random variable Y that is the sum of n independent daily P&Ls $(X_1, X_2, \ldots, X_n)$. As a consequence, the variance of yearly P&L, σ_Y^2, can easily be derived from the variance of daily P&Ls:

$$\sigma_Y^2 = \sum_{i=1}^{n} \sigma_{X_i}^2 + 2\sum_{i=1}^{n}\sum_{j \neq i} \sigma_{X_i} \sigma_{X_j} \rho_{i,j}$$

where $\rho_{i,j}$ represents correlation coefficients between the P&Ls on different days. If they can be considered independent, then the equation simplifies to

$$\sigma_Y = \sqrt{\sum_{i=1}^{n} \sigma_{X_i}^2}$$

Now, assuming that value at risk can be considered the volatility of daily profit and loss multiplied by a value k needed to achieve the desired confidence level according to a bank's risk aversion, the value at risk on a n-day horizon ($\text{VaR}_{\alpha,n}$) is related to daily VaR by the formula (Saita 1999)

TABLE 7-3   Exposure Peaks and Equivalent VaR Measures over Nondaily Horizons

| Trader | Day | | | | | | | | | | Average daily VaR | $\sqrt{\sum_{i=1}^{10} VaR_{\alpha,1}^2}$ |
	1	2	3	4	5	6	7	8	9	10		
A	10	10	10	10	10	10	10	10	10	10	10	31.62
B	8	5	12	15	6	14	12	8	13	7	10	33.41
C	0	0	0	0	100	0	0	0	0	0	10	100.00

$$VaR_{\alpha,n} = k \cdot \sigma_Y = k \cdot \sqrt{\sum_{i=1}^{n} \sigma_{X_i}^2} = \sqrt{\sum_{i=1}^{n} k^2 \sigma_{X_i}^2} = \sqrt{\sum_{i=1}^{n} VaR_{\alpha,1}^2}$$

under the assumption that the same multiplier k applies both to the yearly cumulated P&L distribution and to daily ones. In any case, when compared to the average daily VaR method, this solution has two advantages. First, rather than assuming serial independence of *market* returns, it requires only that there be no serial independence for the *trader's* returns, which is much easier to achieve. Consider, for instance, a trader who is allowed to take both long and short positions and whose portfolio can be liquidated in one day. Even if there were positive serial correlation in daily market returns, the trader's returns would not necessarily be affected, since, for instance, after a negative shock the trader will have the chance to get out of the market by liquidating the portfolio or by inverting the direction of his or her exposure. In any case, just extending the formula to account for first-order autocorrelation between returns on two consecutive days would be extremely easy.

Second, this solution properly takes exposure peaks into consideration. In fact, if we applied this methodology to the three traders in Table 7-2 (considering, for simplicity, an equivalent 10-day VaR rather than an equivalent yearly VaR), this method would be able to discriminate the growing risk that the bank runs when moving from trader A to trader C, due to the exposure-peak problem (see Table 7-3). While the increase in trader B's equivalent 10-year VaR is still moderate (+5.6%), the issue may still be important when comparing ex post the profitability of desks with different VaR fluctuation patterns over time. A real-life example is also reported in Box 7-2.

Box 7-2: Daily VaR Fluctuations and Their Implications for Equivalent Ex Post Yearly VaR: An Example Based on Real Data

In order to try applying the two different ways of calculating equivalent ex post yearly equivalent VaR to real data, we can consider the data reported in Table 7-4, based on Credit Suisse and Deutsche Bank disclosures on the maximum and minimum daily VaR values for some trading desks, according to the banks' 2005 annual reports. While maximum and minimum values alone do not allow us to understand the true distribution of daily VaR values, we simply arbitrarily assumed a uniform distribution of daily VaR values throughout the year. According to this assumption we also derived an average VaR value for the year (which obviously is close but not identical to the true average daily VaR reported by Deutsche Bank). By using either the average daily VaR rescaled by the square root of 260 or the square root of the sum of squared daily VaR values we obtain

TABLE 7-4   Example of The Relevance of Daily VaR Fluctuations Based on Deutsche Bank Data

Bank	Desk/ Type of Risk	Reported Daily VaR Values (1-day, 99% confidence level)		Average (assuming uniform distribution)	Yearly VaR 1: $\overline{\text{VaR}_{1\,day}} \cdot \sqrt{260}$	Yearly VaR 2: $\sqrt{\sum_{i=1}^{260} \text{VaR}_{1\,day}^2}$	Difference (%)
		Minimum	Maximum				
Deutsche Bank	Interest rate	41.9	61.6	51.75	834.44	839.51	0.6%
	Equity	22.9	43.1	33.00	532.11	540.42	1.6%
	FX	5.5	18.2	11.85	191.08	200.08	4.7%
	Commodity	3.5	11.3	7.40	119.32	124.76	4.6%
Credit Suisse	Interest rate	35.9	77.9	56.90	917.48	938.24	2.3%
	Equity	23.4	62.6	43.00	693.35	717.14	3.4%
	FX	6	30	18.00	290.24	311.15	7.2%
	Commodity	0.8	15.5	8.15	131.41	148.28	12.8%

equivalent yearly VaR values whose differences range from 0.6% to 12.8%. Of course, the value of the difference at each desk would depend not only on the extent of the fluctuations between the minimum and maximum exposures, but also on the real distribution of daily VaR values during the year, since in practice this it may be more or less dispersed than the uniform distribution considered here for simplicity and in the absence of internal information.

Source: Credit Suisse and Deutsche Bank 2005 annual reports (first three columns) and subsequent elaborations.

7.2.2 Translating Yearly Ex Ante Acceptable Loss into an Equivalent Daily VaR

The link between ex post daily VaR and the equivalent annual potential loss could also be used to derive a simplified rule of thumb to link annual maximum potential loss, defined typically at the beginning of the year, and the daily VaR limit. In fact, the equation could be rewritten by substituting ex post VaR values with the ex ante VaR limits on a yearly and a daily basis (respectively, VL_Y and VL_D):

$$\sqrt{\sum_{i=1}^{n} \text{VL}_{D,i}^2} = \text{VL}_Y$$

The difference from the previous case is that while ex post there are *n* known variables (past VaR values for *n* trading days) and just one unknown term, the situation here is the opposite, since only VL_Y is known. Yet by assuming for simplicity that the limit can remain the same on every single day (independent from actual losses or profits during the first part of the year or from other exogenous events), the equation would simplify to

$$\mathrm{VL}_D \sqrt{n} = \mathrm{VL}_Y$$

where n identifies the number of trading days per year (e.g., 256). Therefore (Saita 1999b; Härtl and Johanning 2005),

$$\mathrm{VL}_D = \frac{\mathrm{VL}_Y}{\sqrt{n}}$$

In this way, for instance, a maximum yearly potential loss of 1600 would be translated into a daily VaR limit of 100, or $1000/\sqrt{256}$. This rough solution can be considered only an approximation, and those banks that separate capital allocation based on stress tests from actual limit management based on VaR limits may prefer to set VaR limits based on past experience only or starting from the actual VaR of the portfolio plus some safety margin. Yet this solution may be useful for checking whether daily VaR limits are too small when compared to the yearly capital at risk assigned to trading desks (i.e., a daily limit of 40 with an annual maximum potential loss equal to 1000, or 25 times the daily limit, may be too low). To conclude when daily limits are too high is not so simple, for one can assume, in case of actual losses, that the bank would have time to reduce the size of existing VaR limits. This introduces us to the next topic, i.e., the relationship between VaR limits and actual cumulated losses.

7.2.3   The Case of Variable VaR Limits and the Role of Cumulated Losses

The solution proposed so far assumed that a trader who has been given a VaR limit would maintain the same limit even if he experienced relevant actual losses. Of course, this may be unrealistic, and one could think about establishing a formal relationship between past cumulated performance and VaR limits for the trader.

Before discussing how this could happen, we should remark that even for a bank implementing a sophisticated VaR limit system, it may be useful to maintain stop-loss limits on individual trades or cumulative loss limits for traders. In fact, their purpose is different from VaR limits. Stop-loss limits on individual trades may force the trader to close the position after a certain loss has occurred, even if the trader may be psychologically reluctant to admit having been wrong. Cumulative loss limits may instead capture, for instance, a sequence of small but prolonged losses that grow smoothly through time (and which would not be captured by daily VaR limits).

Therefore, stop-loss limits on individual trades and cumulated-loss limits on single desks can be maintained in combination with VaR limits. Interestingly, cumulative-loss limits could also be merged in some way with VaR limits. A simple and effective way to do so is to set a variable VaR limit that is reduced in the case of losses. Consider a trader who has been assigned a VaR limit equal to 100 at the beginning of the period and who experiences the sequence of gains and losses reported in Table 7-5. According to this methodology, VaR limits are reduced in the case of actual losses, and therefore the limit would be reduced in the first few days, since cumulated losses are negative. Yet, after gains in days 3 and 4, the limit will be set back to 100 at the end of day 4 and will still remain 100 at the end of day 5 (despite the small loss), since cumulated P&L is still positive. We could define this VaR limit as a *variable* VaR limit, while we use the term *constant* VaR limit to define the case in which the VaR limit is unaffected by actual losses.

TABLE 7-5   Example of a Variable VaR Limit

Day	Initial VaR limit	Daily P&L	Cumulated P&L	VaR Limit for the Next Day
1	100	(10)	(10)	90
2	90	(5)	(15)	85
3	85	12	(3)	97
4	97	5	2	100
5	100	(1)	1	100

Apparently, a bank can simply set a variable VaR limit for the trader equal to the maximum potential loss the bank would accept for the entire year. In this way, the relationship between the maximum yearly potential loss and maximum daily VaR would be simple and clear. Yet this solution should be rejected for two reasons. First, it might lead to unacceptable exposure peaks (in one day the trader could put at risk the amount the bank might accept losing in an entire year). Second, a variable VaR limit would force the trader to stop trading in the extreme case when his cumulated losses reached his or her total initial limit, and hence it would be wise to maintain an extra amount of capital so as to be able to give the trader a second chance, even in the case of significant losses at the beginning of the period. A possible solution, then, is to assign to the trader a VaR limit that is reestablished each month (or each quarter) independent of the previous months performance. What happens in this case to equivalent yearly VaR limits? Even if the variable VaR limit is compared every day with the trader's actual daily VaR, if the limit is reset each month from the bank's viewpoint the limit now represents the maximum potential loss on a *monthly* basis.

Therefore if monthly losses cannot exceed this limit, the yearly equivalent could again be determined by assuming independence among consecutive P&Ls in different periods. The only difference is that the length of each period is now equal to one month, and therefore the maximum loss on a monthly basis (VL_M) can be translated into a yearly equivalent by the formula

$$VL_Y = VL_M \sqrt{12}$$

Again, this should only be considered a pragmatic rule of thumb for determining how much larger the limit should be — keeping the equivalent yearly maximum loss fixed — if the limit is structured as a variable VaR limit that can be reduced in case of losses rather than as a constant VaR limit. Of course, all banks unwilling to merge VaR limits with cumulated-loss control could simply use the two limits by keeping them separated. We would only like to remark that since cumulated-loss controls play a different role than constant VaR limits, cancelling them when introducing even a refined VaR measurement system with constant limits could imply losing useful information.

7.3   Managing VaR-Based Trading Limits

Even after they have been set, VaR limits can be managed in different ways. Apart from the distinction between variable and constant limits that we just discussed, a second relevant distinction is between flexible and inflexible limits. A limit is *flexible* when the

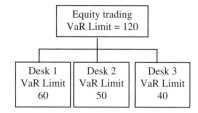

FIGURE 7-3   Example of trading limits in an equity trading business unit.

trader is allowed to exceed it, provided authorization has been received either from some-body at a higher hierarchical level in the trading room or from the risk manager or from both (depending on the authorization procedure the bank has defined). A limit is *inflexible* when it can never be exceeded. In practice, trading divisions can adopt either of these two different methodologies. It is useful to focus on their relative advantages and disadvantages.

When VaR limits are considered flexible, the maximum individual loss assigned to each trader is a tool for forcing the trader to ask for a senior officer's permission (thereby checking the underlying trading idea) when he or she wants to assume risks above a certain threshold. The limit therefore does not necessarily represent the actual maximum amount of VaR for the individual trader. The procedure for authorization is important to ensure the integrity of the limit system, and it should clearly define:

- The maximum extra VaR that is allowed
- How long the trader may remain over the limit
- Who is allowed to grant authorization

Consider a simple structure such as the one depicted in Figure 7-3, where we consider an equity trading business unit comprising three different desks. Both the trading units and the desks have been given a VaR limit; the limit for the business unit as a whole would be lower than the sum of the desks' limits, since correlation among desk returns is lower than 1. Yet, since correlations can be unstable, the business unit limit should be calculated by adopting a prudent estimate for intradesk correlations. In such a structure, the authorization procedure could specify, for instance, that:

- When VaR is exceeded at the desk level by no more than $x\%$ of the limit (e.g., 10%), and the limit is not exceeded at the business unit level, the head of the equity trading business unit has the power to authorize the event. In any case, the event must be reported to the risk management function.
- When instead either the VaR exceeds the limit by more than 10% or exceeding the limit at desk level implies that even the business unit would exceed its limit, then authorization should be granted by the risk control function or by a risk manage-ment committee.

The distinction between the roles of the business unit manager and the risk control or risk management function is important, in addition to defining reasonable VaR limits. In fact, authorizations should be infrequent. The key advantage of flexible limits is that they reduce the chance of rejecting good profit opportunities as a consequence of a rigid VaR limit system. If inflexible limits were enforced, such opportunities would be lost were they to occur when the trader is already close to the VaR limit.

While flexible limits have merits, they have disadvantages as well. First, flexible limits are time consuming and therefore costly, especially considering the amount of senior managers' time that might be devoted to authorizing transactions. Second, if traders were allowed to exceed limits too easily or too frequently, limits would no longer represent a real constraint on their risk-taking attitude. Third, performance evaluation becomes a bit more difficult. A problem of fairness arises whenever traders operating at certain desks are authorized to trespass limits more easily than others. This is not uncommon when the senior manager responsible for such authorizations has substantial personal experience in certain products/risks only and, as a consequence, feels more comfortable relaxing limits related to those risks. Moreover, if risk-adjusted performances are calculated against allocated capital (i.e., the total limit received at the beginning of the year) instead of utilized capital (i.e., the actual amount of risk undertaken by the trader throughout the year), then if the initial limit is frequently exceeded, it would no longer represent a reasonable measure of allocated capital (see Chapter 8 for a discussion of the choice between allocated and utilized capital).

Of course, even inflexible limits have some pitfalls. While the advantage is that performance evaluation is easier and less questionable, traders may be worried about exceeding limits and hence they are likely to maintain a much lower ratio between actual VaR and the maximum limit. Hence their usage rate of the available limit, i.e., of available capital, would be lower, reducing the performances for shareholders. Moreover, inflexible limits are not necessarily fairer than flexible ones. If the head of the business unit is responsible for defining individual desk limits, desks whose strategies are more familiar to the business unit manager might still be favored, all else being equal.

In practice, the choice between a flexible and an inflexible interpretation of VaR limits should be linked, on one hand, to whether the bank has opted for variable or constant limits (i.e., to whether or not VaR limits are reduced in the case of losses) and, on the other hand, to the prevailing style of management. The choice for variable or constant limits matters, since banks with variable VaR limits tend to allow higher VaR limits. Consider, for instance, a bank granting the trader a variable VaR limit equal to the amount the bank would accept losing in one month. Such a bank is likely to register a lower ratio of average utilized capital to the total VaR limit (i.e., the trader should usually have a daily VaR well below the maximum monthly potential loss) and a more rigid interpretation of VaR limits. If limits were flexible, the trader would in fact potentially be allowed to lose in a single day the full amount of money the bank can accept losing in a month. Instead, when VaR limits are constant and remain unchanged in the case of losses, the VaR limit is likely to be lower, the ratio of utilized capital should be higher, and the need for exceptions increases. Therefore, a bank with constant VaR limits should be expected to have a more flexible attitude toward the limits.

The management style has an important influence, too. The more flexible the limits, the higher the reliance on coordination mechanisms based on direct supervision by senior managers. Hence, the performance evaluation of the desk can be affected by the exogenous authorization decisions of the business unit manager. And vice versa, inflexible limits imply a lower interdependence with the business unit manager, so the picture that a risk-adjusted performance measure can provide about the trader's performance is much cleaner.

However, it is difficult to imagine no intervention at all by the business unit manager at the desks he or she is supervising. If this were the case, the manager would lose any control over the overall exposure and may be unable to optimize the portfolio of exposures.

Consider, for instance, the head of a U.S. bank currency-trading business unit supervising (for simplicity) only three individuals, who are responsible for currency trading in

British pounds, Japanese yen, and Mexican pesos, respectively. Business unit VaR will depend on individual VaR values for the three positions and on correlations among the three currencies. Usually, a bank would like the senior manager, who is responsible for the portfolio as a whole, to manage the unit's overall portfolio of exposures actively. If the manager considers the risk–return profile of the business unit, he might make decisions that are in the interest of the unit even if they are not in the interest of the individual trader. For instance, if currency returns were all positively correlated and two traders had long positions on their currencies, a short position held by the third one might act as a hedge (we discuss in the next section how this effect could be measured through VaRDelta). Hence, the business unit manager would be more willing to allow the third trader to exceed his or her VaR limit if the position is a short one than in the opposite case. The discretional power of the senior manager, which is desirable for the bank since it helps achieve an optimization of exposures (see also Litterman 1997a, b), implies unavoidably that the trader's performance may be partly influenced by the senior manager's decisions. Of course, this is not going to be a problem as long as the role of senior manager does not become too invasive (e.g., by forcing the trader to close positions the senior manager does not like). If this were the case, then the trader's evaluation should assign more weight to qualitative elements than to the simple observation of the trader's ex post risk–return track record. In short, VaR limit policies may be defined in many different ways, provided there is a fit between how limits have been set and managed and how traders' performance are evaluated ex post.

7.4 Identifying Risk Contributions and Internal Hedges: VaRDelta, Component VaR, and Incremental VaR

So far we have considered limits from the point of view of a stand-alone business unit. In practice, however, diversification matters, since the correlation among the exposures of different business units can significantly affect portfolio VaR for the trading and capital markets divisions. Apart from those particular and reasonably infrequent cases in which VaR may prove to be subadditive (Artzner et al. 1999) even for market risks, portfolio VaR would be lower than the sum of individual, stand-alone VaRs for the business units comprising a certain division.

Let us consider, for instance, the example presented in Table 7-6 and Figure 7-4. The trading division of Omikron Bank is composed of three business units, whose individual VaR is equal to 50, 40, and 30, respectively (so the sum of individual VaRs would be 120), have an overall aggregated VaR equal to 90 thanks to diversification effects. Hence the problem here is whether VaR limits should be set in terms of their stand-alone (i.e., undiversified) VaR or in terms of of a lower measure of "diversified" VaR that takes into account the diversification benefits within the three business units (and not only, as is obvious, those inside each business unit).

The problem is remarkable, given that in practice the relevance of diversification benefits among different market risks can be substantial (see, for instance, Table 7-7). Therefore we should first discuss how VaR measures that take into consideration diversification benefits and correlations among the different exposures in the trading division can be considered, introducing the concepts of VaRDelta, component VaR, and incremental VaR, which are also considered in Chapter 8 when discussing ex post risk-adjusted performance measurement.

TABLE 7-6   Example: VaR Calculation for the Three Business Units of Omikron Bank

	Business Unit 1: Fixed-Income Trading	Business Unit 2: Foreign Exchange Trading	Business Unit 3: Equity Trading
Exposure (e.g., USD/1000)	1000	500	300
Return volatility × k*	5%	8%	10%
Value at Risk	50	40	30
Correlation with BU 1	1	0.28	0.46
Correlation with BU 2	0.28	1	0.25
Correlation with BU 3	0.46	0.25	1
Trading division VaR	$\mathrm{VaR}_{pf} = \sqrt{\sum_{i=1}^{3}\sum_{j=1}^{3} \mathrm{VaR}_i \mathrm{VaR}_j \rho_{ij}} = 90$		

Daily volatility is scaled by the multiplier needed to obtain the desired confidence level.

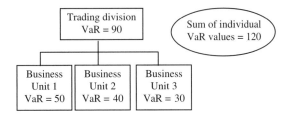

FIGURE 7-4   Diversification benefits across business units.

TABLE 7-7   Relevance of Diversification Effects Among Market Risks in Four Large International Banks (Average daily VaR values, January–December 2005)

Risk Type	Bank			
	Barclays (GBP million)	Credit Suisse (CHF million)	Deutsche Bank (EUR million)	J.P. Morgan-Chase (USD million)
Interest rate	25.3	60.5	52.8	67.0
Credit spread	23.0			
Foreign exchange	2.8	13.4	10.3	23.0
Equities	5.9	40.7	33.3	34.0
Commodities	6.8	6.5	7.0	21.0
Sum	63.8	121.1	103.4	145.0
Diversification effects	(31.9)	(54.9)	(37.5)	(59.0)
Total daily VaR	31.9	66.2	65.9	86.0
Diversification effects/ sum of stand-alone daily VaR values	50.0%	45.3%	36.3%	40.7%

Source: 2005 annual reports.

In theory, the easiest way to calculate a diversified VaR measure would simply be to split diversification benefits proportionately over the different business units (splitting method). In the Omikron Bank example, since overall VaR is equal to 90, which is 75% of the sum of undiversified VaR values (which amounts to 120), diversified VaR according to the splitting method for each business unit would be set equal to 75% of undiversified VaR. For instance, diversified VaR for business unit 1 (fixed-income trading) would be set equal to $75\% \times 50 = 37.50$. Similarly, diversified VaR would be equal to 30 and 22.50, respectively, for business units 2 and 3. However, such a method would fail entirely to consider the different roles of the businesses in producing diversification benefits within the bank. Intuitively, for instance, one should expect that business unit 2, which has a lower stand-alone VaR and lower correlations with the other businesses than business unit 1, should be attributed a greater share of diversification benefits.

Understanding the interaction between different exposures is relevant when managing limits in the trading division and as a way to assess the impact of further trades that might increase or decrease exposures. Developing measures able to capture either the impact on the VaR of the portfolio of new trades or the contribution to overall portfolio risk of existing exposures is therefore extremely important. Thus we now consider a general portfolio with exposures $X_1, X_2, \ldots, X_n$ to different risk factors. Though we build numerical examples on the Omikron Bank case assuming, for simplicity, the existence of only three risk factors each of which belongs to a single business unit, our analysis could easily be applied to a portfolio of $X_1, X_2, \ldots, X_n$ exposures (as the result of risk factor mapping described in Chapter 3) even within the same trading desk.

To introduce the necessary notation, let $X_1, X_2, \ldots, X_n$ be the dollar exposures to n different benchmark assets (as in the classic Riskmetrics™ framework) in the generic portfolio whose overall VaR is VaR_p. Therefore, any new trade involving multiple risks (e.g., a forward currency sale involving both currency and interest rate risk) must therefore first be decomposed into a set of benchmark asset exposures. Assuming that returns are jointly normally distributed, let us define σ_{ij} as the covariance between daily returns of benchmark assets, and let $\sigma_{kij} = k^2\sigma_{ij}$ be the daily return covariance after scaling for the multiplier k needed to attain the desired confidence level (e.g., 2.32 for 99% VaR).

Portfolio VaR can be calculated according to the variance–covariance method:

$$\text{VaR}_p = \sqrt{\sum_i \sum_j X_i X_j\, k^2 \sigma_{ij}} = \sqrt{\sum_i \sum_j X_i X_j\, \sigma_{kij}}$$

If the trader or the risk manager wanted to understand the impact of a potential substantial change in the portfolio, i.e., a change in the vector of exposures from $X_1, X_2, \ldots, X_n$ to $X_1', X_2', \ldots, X_n'$, the only way would be to calculate the change between the old portfolio VaR, VaR_p, and the new value, $\text{VaR}_{p'}$. This difference can be named *incremental* VaR (*I*VaR; see Carroll et al. 2001; Hallerbach 2002):[1]

$$\text{IVaR} = \text{VaR}_{p'} - \text{VaR}_p = \sqrt{\sum_i \sum_j X_i' X_j'\sigma_{kij}} - \sqrt{\sum_i \sum_j X_i X_j\, \sigma_{kij}}$$

---

1. When applied to different business areas or business units, this measure has sometimes been called marginal VaR (see, for instance, Merton and Perold 1993; Saita 1999). Since the term *marginal VaR* has been used in a different way by other authors (e.g., Carroll et al. 2001; Hallerbach 2002), we would use the term *incremental VaR* to avoid potential misunderstandings.

Note that incremental VaR will not necessarily be positive if new positions are added, since, depending on their correlation with the existing portfolio, the new trades might act as a hedge. However, it may be useful to measure the reaction of portfolio VaR to small changes in the exposures derived from extra trades. This could be performed by deriving portfolio VaR (VaR_p) relative to each of the exposures $X_1, X_2, \ldots, X_n$; the derivative, named VaRDelta, was proposed by Garman (1996, 1997) for evaluating the impact on portfolio VaR of new trades when exposure changes are small relative to the existing portfolio. VaRDelta for the exposure in each benchmark asset i is therefore

$$\text{VaRDelta}_i = \frac{\partial \text{VaR}_p}{\partial X_i} = \sum_j X_j \, \sigma_{kij} \cdot \left(\sum_i \sum_j X_i X_j \, \sigma_{kij} \right)^{-\frac{1}{2}} = \frac{\sum_j X_j \, \sigma_{kij}}{\text{VaR}_p}$$

As an example, let us calculate VaRDelta for the fixed-income exposure in Omikron Bank's business unit 1. From scaled return volatilities and correlations reported in Table 7-6 we can easily derive σ_{kij}, which for simplicity are reported together with exposures in Table 7-8. For instance, σ_{k12} is obtained as $k\sigma_1 \times k\sigma_2 \times \rho_{1,2} = 5\% \times 8\% \times 0.28 = 0.00112$. Remembering that $\text{VaR}_p = 90$, we can calculate VaRDelta for the fixed-income exposure as

$$\text{VaRDelta}_1 = \frac{\sum_j X_j \, \sigma_{k1j}}{\text{VaR}_p} = \frac{1000 \cdot 0.0025 + 500 \cdot 0.00112 + 300 \cdot 0.0023}{90} = 4.17\%$$

VaRDelta describes the impact on VaR of an increase of one dollar of benchmark asset exposure. For instance, if the fixed-income exposure were increased from 1000 to 1010, the expected new VaR for the portfolio would be

$$\text{VaR}_{p'} \approx \text{VaR}_p + \text{VaRDelta}_i \cdot \Delta X_i = 90 + 4.17\% \cdot 10 = 90.417$$

In practice, VaRDelta offers a first-order Taylor approximation of the impact of exposure changes on VaR. Since individual trades can often imply exposures to multiple risk assets, the change in VaR should often be estimated by multiplying the vector of VaRDelta values relative to any benchmark exposure by the vector of exposure changes implied by

TABLE 7-8   Omikron Bank Example: Exposures and Scaled Covariances as Inputs for Calculating VaRDelta

	Business Unit 1: Fixed-Income Trading	Business Unit 2: Foreign-Exchange Trading	Business Unit 3: Equity Trading
Exposure (e.g., USD/1000)	1000	500	300
Scaled covariance (σ_{k1j}) with BU 1	0.0025	0.00112	0.0023
Scaled covariance (σ_{k2j}) with BU 2	0.00112	0.0064	0.002
Scaled covariance (σ_{k3j}) with BU 3	0.0023	0.002	0.01
VaRDelta	4.17%	5.47%	7.00%

TABLE 7-9   The Performance of VaRDelta Approximation for Different Exposure Changes

	Fixed Income	Foreign Exchange	Equity	Estimated VaR$_{p'}$ (VaRDelta approx.)	Estimated IVaR (VaRDelta approx.)	Actual VaR$_{p'}$	Actual IVaR
Initial exposure	1000	500	300			90	
Case 1 (smaller change)	1010	500	300	90.4167	0.4167	90.4171	0.4171
Case 2 (larger change)	1300	450	400	106.7667	16.7667	107.4402	17.4402

TABLE 7-10   Calculation of Component VaR

		Fixed Income	Foreign Exchange	Equity	Total
[1]	Exposures	1000	500	300	
[2]	VaRDelta	4.17%	5.47%	7.00%	
[3]	Component VaR ([1] × [2])	41.67	27.33	21.00	90
[4]	Undiversified VaR	50	40	30	
[5]	CVaR/undiversified VaR ([3]/[4])	83.3%	68.3%	70.0%	

any new trade. Of course, like any first-order Taylor expansion, VaRDelta would only offer an approximation of the real incremental VaR if the increase of exposure is substantial. In this case, calculating incremental VaR as the difference between the new and old portfolio VaR remains necessary if the estimate has to be accurate. This idea is expressed in Table 7-9, where the effects of a small change and a larger change in exposures are compared. Whereas in the former case VaRDelta works almost perfectly, in the latter it provides only a good approximation of incremental VaR.

VaRDelta can also be particularly useful for calculating component VaR (CVaR), i.e., the contribution of the individual business unit or benchmark asset exposure to portfolio VaR. By definition, the sum of component VaRs should then be equal to portfolio VaR, i.e.,

$$\sum_{i=1}^{n} \text{CVaR}_i = \text{VaR}_p$$

The aim of component VaR is hence to provide a measure of diversified VaRs whose sum adds up to total portfolio VaR while taking into consideration the correlation of each exposure with the rest of the portfolio. The component VaR that can be attributed to a single benchmark exposure X_i is given simply by

$$\text{CVaR}_i = X_i \cdot \text{VaRDelta}_i$$

Again, we provide a numerical example based on the Omikron Bank case (Table 7-10). The total CVaR is 90, i.e., the value of portfolio VaR. Different from the splitting method, however, the ratio of component VaR to undiversified VaR is not equal for all positions, and, as we should have expected, is lower for business unit 2, which has lower correlations against the other two positions.

The fact that the sum of component VaRs should be equal to portfolio VaR can easily be checked by remembering the expression for VaRDelta. In fact,

$$\sum_{i=1}^{n} CVaR_i = \sum_{i=1}^{n} X_i \cdot VaRDelta_i = \sum_{i=1}^{n} X_i \cdot \frac{\sum_j X_j \sigma_{kij}}{VaR_p} = \frac{\sum_i \sum_j X_i X_j \sigma_{kij}}{VaR_p} = VaR_p$$

Note that while we have considered here a simplified case in which each position or business unit implies one benchmark asset exposure only, it is trivial to extend the concept to the realistic case in which each of m trades in the portfolio is represented by a vector of benchmark asset exposures $\mathbf{x}_z = \{X_{1z}, X_{2z}, \ldots, X_{nz}\}$, so given $z = 1, 2, \ldots, m$, the portfolio exposure in each benchmark asset i is simply the sum of exposures to benchmark asset i for the m different trades (i.e., $X_i = \sum_{z=1}^{m} X_{iz}$).

Component VaR for each trade z could then be calculated (Garman 1996, 1997) as the product of the vector of VaRDeltas for each benchmark exposure for the vector of exposures:

$$CVaR_z = \sum_{i=1}^{n} X_{iz} \cdot VaRDelta_{iz}$$

Component VaR can also be relevant to identify positions that are natural hedges inside the portfolio, since they contribute to reducing portfolio VaR. Those positions will have a negative component VaR, deriving from the negative correlation with the overall bank portfolio (see also Litterman 1997a, b). An example is provided in Table 7-11, where assuming that trade B has a negative correlation with the remaining two exposures, its CVaR turns out to be negative.

TABLE 7-11 Identifying Internal Hedges: Example of Negative CVaR

	Trade		
	A	B	C
Exposure (e.g., USD/1000)	1000	300	300
Return volatility × $k*$	0.06	0.05	0.08
Value at risk	60	15	24
Portfolio VaR	65.466		
VaRDelta	5.69%	−2.52%	5.39%
Component VaR	56.86	−7.56	16.17

Box 7-3: Variant for the Calculation of Component CVaR

A question that can be raised by looking at the example is what happens when the three business units are not represented by three trading desks, since, for instance, component VaR would be much harder to calculate. In fact, the alternative formulas

$$\text{CVaR}_i = X_i \cdot \text{VaRDelta}_i = X_i \cdot \frac{\sum_j X_j \sigma_{kij}}{\text{VaR}_p}$$

may seem hard to implement for nontrading positions (or business units). We now want to show how to rearrange it in a more convenient way. In order to do that, we assume that $\text{VaR}_i = X_i k \sigma$ (the VaR of a position should be equal to the size of the position times a multiple k of the volatility σ_i), with k being the same multiplier for the single position and the portfolio as a whole. In fact, in this case we have

$$\text{CVaR}_i = X_i \cdot \frac{\sum_j X_j \sigma_{kij}}{\text{VaR}_p} = X_i \cdot \frac{\sum_j X_j k^2 \sigma_{ij}}{\text{VaR}_p} = k X_i \cdot \frac{\sum_j X_j k \sigma_i \sigma_j \rho_{ij}}{\text{VaR}_p} = k X_i \sigma_i \cdot \sum_j \frac{X_j k \sigma_j}{\text{VaR}_p} \rho_{ij}$$

$$= \text{VaR}_i \cdot \sum_j \frac{\text{VaR}_j}{\text{VaR}_p} \rho_{ij}$$

That is, the component VaR of exposure i is equal to its stand-alone, undiversified VaR times a weighted sum of the correlation of business i with all other exposures. For instance, component VaR of the equity desk in Table 7-10 could be calculated in this way as

$$\text{CVaR}_{\text{equity}} = \text{VaR}_{\text{equity}} \cdot \sum_{j=1}^{3} \frac{\text{VaR}_j}{\text{VaR}_p} \rho_{ij} = 30 \cdot \left(\frac{50}{90} \cdot 0.46 + \frac{40}{90} \cdot 0.25 + \frac{30}{90} \cdot 1.00 \right) = 21.00$$

Remember from Chapter 6 that the assumption we made to derive this expression is the same one needed to apply the formula

$$\text{VaR}_p = \sqrt{\sum_{i=1}^{n} \text{VaR}_i^2 + \sum_{i=1}^{n} \sum_{j \neq i} \text{VaR}_i \text{VaR}_j \rho_{ij}}$$

in order to aggregate risk capital. Since we know that banks often use this simplified formula to estimate correlation among businesses using VaR values that are not necessarily derived assuming multivariate normally distributed returns, we could say that whenever (1) this aggregation formula can be applied and at the same time (2) individual VaR values and correlation coefficients are known, these two formulas can easily derive both portfolio VaR and the contribution of each component to portfolio VaR.

7.5 Managing Risk and Pricing Limits for Credit Risk

Risk management tools linked to VaR measurement can be used to support risk policies and procedures for credit risk control processes too. While for market risks VaR can be used, especially to set maximum limits for the trading desks, in the case of credit risk, potential applications include:

- The definition of the autonomy limits for lending decisions (at the individual loan level)
- The definition of pricing limits (i.e., minimum required profitability for loans) as a necessary condition to have a loan approved

We briefly explain how these limits can work and — since their implementation can be extremely different depending on the type of bank and of counterparty — we then analyze their potential application in two extreme cases: the case of a loan to a large corporation by a large wholesale-oriented investment bank and the case of a small loan to an SME by a smaller, retail-oriented commercial bank.

7.5.1 Setting Loan Autonomy Limits: From Notional Size to Expected Loss

Any bank has credit approval policies defining who is entitled to approve a loan. When defining these policies, the usual problem is how to divide those loans that could be authorized at lower hierarchical levels from those requiring approval by senior managers, by credit committees, or even by the board. Traditionally, the notional size of the loan has been the main driver for defining the approval process for a loan. For instance, internal lending procedures may have stated that any loan with size up to x could be approved by a senior credit officer, while loans with size between x and y should require approval by the central credit committee, and those over y should be approved by the board. Of course, any bank could define a number of different intermediate steps in any way it considers convenient to promote efficiency as well as credit control. However, the development of internal rating systems and credit portfolio models suggests that autonomy limits could be defined in terms of either expected loss or value at risk rather than in terms of notional size.

Defining autonomy limits in terms of expected loss is easier, and it is possible whenever there is an internal rating-based system associating expected loss rates to rating classes (i.e., even if the bank had not yet developed a credit portfolio risk model reliable enough to set autonomy limits based on VaR). Since expected loss (EL) can be obtained as a product of the exposure at default (EAD) times probability of default (PD) times loss given default (LGD), determining a maximum EL limit implies that the maximum size of the loan that can be approved by a given decision maker is no longer a constant, but depends (inversely) on the loan's PD and LGD:

$$\max \text{EL} = \max \text{exposure} \times \text{PD} \times \text{LGD} \Rightarrow \max \text{exposure} = \frac{\max \text{EL}}{\text{PD} \times \text{LGD}}$$

Hence, loans with a higher internal rating (i.e., lower PD) or more guarantees (and therefore lower LGD) can be approved at lower hierarchical levels. At the same time, loans to riskier customers and with lower guarantees might be checked at a higher hierarchical level, different from what would happen with size autonomy limits, even if their size is relatively smaller.

Alternatively, autonomy limits could be based on VaR, which better captures the real contribution of a loan to the risk of the loan portfolio. Intuitively, this would lead to different limits, since expected loss and value at risk are not linearly related. A small unsecured loan and a larger and partially guaranteed loan to two different borrowers with the same rating and PD may imply the same expected loss but a remarkably different value at risk. Moreover, while EL depends on the individual loan only, VaR should depend on the characteristics of both the loan and the preexisting portfolio composition. Hence, using VaR is in practice more complex, since VaR calculation for an individual loan would require either rerunning the credit portfolio model simulation engine or calculating the sensitivity of credit VaR to discrete increases in loan exposures in certain segments and using these sensitivities to measure the loan's impact on the portfolio. This is why a bank must pragmatically check whether setting autonomy limits based on VaR rather than EL only would be worth the effort, and it also explains why expected loss–based autonomy limits are frequently used in practice.

7.5.2   Setting Loan-Pricing Limits

Apart from setting a loan authorization procedure based on loan risk rather than on its size, a bank could also use EL and credit VaR to check that loans are properly priced. Let us assume the bank measures its profitability through risk-adjusted return on capital (RAROC), i.e., the ratio of profit divided by the value at risk (or capital at risk) of a certain position. Let us consider a 1-year bullet loan for which the bank will receive an interest rate equal to i, which will be funded at an internal transfer rate ITR, and let PD and LGD be the associated probability of default and percentage loss given default, respectively. The expected profit on the loan at the end of the year (assuming, for simplicity, no operating costs) is

$$\text{Expected profit} = 100(1 + i)(1 - \text{PD}) + 100(1 - \text{LGD})\text{PD} - 100(1 + \text{ITR})$$

where the first term on the right-hand side of the equation is the payoff in case of survival of the borrower, the second term is the payoff in case of default, and the third term is the amount that should be returned to the Treasury department, which provided funding for the loan. The bank can impose expected RAROC (i.e., expected profit divided by VaR) equal to the RAROC target RAROC*. This implies the condition

$$\frac{100(1+i)(1-\text{PD})+100(1-\text{LGD})\text{PD}-100(1+\text{ITR})}{\text{VaR}} = \text{RAROC*}$$

which can be solved for i to determine the minimum interest rate that is compliant with the RAROC target. A few passes lead to

$$i = \frac{\text{ITR} + \text{PD} \cdot \text{LGD} + \text{VaR} \cdot \text{RAROC*}}{1 - \text{PD}}$$

which explains, in this simplified setting, the different components that the interest rate should comprise. First, and obviously, the interest rate charged by the bank should cover the funding rate ITR. Second, it should cover the expected loss (expressed here in percentage terms and hence equal to PD times LGD). Third, it must properly remunerate shareholders for the capital they are providing to cover potential unexpected losses. The division by 1 − PD derives from the fact that the interest rate is assumed to be received only in the case of nondefault.

While there are different possible variations of this simplified formula, what matters here is the sense of how an ex ante risk-adjusted fair interest rate could be derived. As a consequence, a bank may decide to set up limits in terms of pricing limits as well as autonomy limits. This could imply, for instance, either completely refusing to approve loans that are priced below the risk-adjusted interest rate or asking a business unit to bear the cost of the insufficient profitability of the loan, or requiring a stricter authorization process. Some of these alternatives can be better discussed by considering the two extreme examples of a large borrower in an investment bank and a small borrower in a retail-oriented commercial bank.

7.5.3 Case 1: Large Borrower Applying for a Loan from an Investment Bank

Let us first consider the case of a large borrower asking an investment bank for a loan. In this case, the relationship manager may propose a loan for an existing customer that is attractive for the services he might acquire from the investment bank. If the loan is large, even if the rating is good, the loan proposal should be reviewed at a higher hierarchical level. What is interesting here is how pricing limits could be applied.

In fact, considering the size of the borrower and the competition among banks in offering to the borrower other fee-based services, the firm may be able to obtain in the market a loan rate that is lower than the risk-adjusted rate. Therefore, pricing limits should ensure that the transaction is productive for the bank. Rather than preventing the loan from being made, risk-adjusted pricing guidelines allow one to define an internal deal between the lending division (that is asked to earn less than the risk-adjusted rate) and those divisions that benefit indirectly from reinforcing the customer relationship with the borrower. Let us assume the borrower is particularly important for the trading and capital markets division, which expects to sell derivatives to the firm for risk management purposes. If it is impossible for the bank to make the borrower accept the risk-adjusted rate on the loan, and if the relationship manager supports the loan since the overall relationship is assumed to be profitable, then the trading and capital markets divisions will have to subsidize the lending division explicitly. The payment is often set equal to the difference between the fair value the loan would have had at risk-adjusted rates and the actual fair value of the underpriced loan being granted. Note that objectively determining the fair loan rate and hence the amount to be transferred from one business unit to another is easier in this case, since the large borrower would likely be a listed firm for which an external rating or an EDF or both are available.

The problem of dealing with loans whose rate of return is lower than the risk-adjusted rate is important, given that cross-subsidizations in a bank are often unavoidable and very frequent. This is why checking the risk-adjusted profitability not only of individual business units, which may be specialized on individual products, but of the customer relationship with major counterparties as well is important. Measuring RAROC for a major customer is often complex, especially when multiyear transactions are involved. A multiyear loan granted today to a company at a rate below the risk-adjusted rate might be viewed as an investment that should be justified in part by the future business the bank will have with the company, and hence both its current and future profitability may be hard to measure. Nevertheless, the development of more sophisticated risk-adjusted pricing techniques and improvements in customer profitability measurement can provide a bank manager with better tools to make the right decisions in the bank's best interest.

Interestingly, in the ISDA-IACPM-RMA 2004 survey on credit portfolio management practices (Rutter Associates 2006) only 12 of the 44 interviewed banks of different sizes said that when a transaction is proposed whose rate of return is below the risk-adjusted rate, the consequence is that either "the business sponsor pays the portfolio manager directly" or "the business sponsor creates an internal IOU." In most of the cases (25 out of 44) respondents simply said that "the business sponsor decides," apparently suggesting that no formal internal transfer pricing rules existed.

7.5.4 Case 2: SME Applying for a Loan from a Smaller, Retail-Oriented Bank

Let us now consider an SME asking a retail commercial bank for a smaller loan. In this case, autonomy limits based on expected loss can be used to assess which authorization level is required to have the loan approved. Given the smaller loan size, the loan approval process is unlikely to involve senior credit committees. Depending on the organizational structure of the bank and its procedures, in some cases the loan might even be approved by the branch manager directly. Defining authorization levels here requires finding a balance between obtaining proper risk control and safeguarding cost efficiency, given that the loan portfolio for this retail-oriented bank may be composed of a very large number of smaller loans.

Similar to the large borrower considered previously, pricing equations can be used to identify the suggested risk-adjusted loan rate, even if the contribution of the loan to portfolio VaR can be estimated in some simplified way (e.g., linking it to loan PD and LGD). Potentially, since for any internal rating class the bank will have identified an upper, mean, and lower PD, it would be possible to define either a single suggested rate (based on mean values) or a suggested pricing range based on upper and lower PD. Imagine, for instance, a given internal rating class whose mean, lower and upper PD, and VaR values are as reported in Table 7-12 (we assume here that VaR values were derived in a simplified manner). It would then be simple to derive mean, lower, and upper values for the loan risk-adjusted rate through the simplified formula in Section 7.5.2.

In the case of a smaller loan, the explicit subsidy that was described for the case of the large corporation is almost impossible, also considering the much larger information asymmetries between the lending division and other divisions of the bank in the case of a smaller unrated borrower. In this case the bank may decide, for instance, that failure to

TABLE 7-12   Identifying Pricing Guidelines Based on Internal Rating Class PD Ranges

	Mean	Lower Bound	Upper Bound
PD	0.10%	0.05%	0.20%
VaR	1%	0.50%	2%
Loan risk-adjusted rate	3.153%	3.077%	3.307%

Assumptions: ITR = 3%, LGD = 50%, target RAROC = 10%.

comply with the suggested risk-adjusted rate (or rate range) may not be an obstacle for granting a loan provided that (1) a formal authorization is required, even if autonomy limits were satisfied and (2) the proponent is able to provide at least qualitative evidence that the overall relationship would be profitable for the bank.

In any case, the critical element when handling limits for credit risk for smaller borrowers derives from the incentive problems that might emerge whenever the individual who is subject to the limits participates in the rating assignment process. Let us consider a relationship manager acting as the loan proponent for a small loan to an SME, in a bank in which the internal rating system is also based on his or her qualitative judgments (e.g., by defining an overall score also based on a standardized qualitative questionnaire filled out by the relationship manager). In such a case, defining autonomy limits and pricing limits for the relationship manager may provide a strong incentive to game the system. In fact, by providing overoptimistic qualitative information, the relationship manager may improve the final rating, thereby lowering both the hierarchical level required for loan approval and the requested risk-adjusted rate. Moreover, if ex post performances were based on risk-adjusted returns, even ex post returns would be upward biased. As a consequence, emphasis on risk-adjusted autonomy and pricing limits must be placed with caution in these cases, unless the bank is certain that gaming behaviors could be either avoided or detected. The risk manager should be certain that proper audit controls, a deep-rooted credit culture, and ethics would suffice to avoid the potentially counterproductive effects of autonomy and pricing limits for loans to smaller borrowers, whenever there are informational asymmetries not only between the bank and the borrower, but also between the credit department and the relationship manager who owns qualitative information about the small borrower.

7.6 Summary

One of the typical uses of value-at-risk measures is supporting risk control, in particular by assigning value-at-risk limits to traders and risk-adjusted pricing policies to credit officers. However, using VaR for risk control purposes requires taking into account both technical risk measurement and organizational issues, since, for instance, the way in which responsibilities among trading desks are divided may affect the efficiency of risk capital use by traders. As far as trading limits are concerned, relevant topics dealt with in the chapter range from the link between daily VaR and their annualized equivalent and between the yearly maximum acceptable loss and the daily limit, the importance of controlling cumulated losses and how they can be linked with VaR limits, and the choice between a rigid and a flexible interpretation of VaR limits.

However, it is also extremely important how to account for diversification benefits so as to identify different desks' risk contributions and potential internal hedges. From this viewpoint the concepts of incremental VaR, VarDelta, and component VaR presented in this chapter are particularly relevant. Incremental VaR is the change in VaR of a portfolio after adding/eliminating a new position or a set of positions. VaRDelta for a given benchmark asset (e.g., a currency rate, a stock index) is the derivative of portfolio VaR relative to the exposure in that asset, and it enables the bank to easily understand the approximate portfolio effect of increasing/decreasing the exposure on a given risk factor/benchmark asset. Component VaR is the contribution of each exposure to portfolio VaR, and it can be derived from VaRDelta. Since the sum of all component VaR values of the positions of a portfolio equals portfolio VaR, component VaR enables us to identify internal hedges, i.e., position with a negative component VaR that helps to reduce portfolio risk. This can obviously support dynamic management of trading limits by the head of the trading units or decisions by a market risk management committee about authorizations for temporarily exceeding limits.

In the case of credit risk, the use of VaR to support risk control is different, but it can also be very important. First of all, autonomy limits defining at which hierarchical level a credit can finally be approved can be defined in terms of VaR or (more frequently) of the expected loss of the loan rather than in terms of its size, as typically happened in the past. Second, risk policies can define a risk-adjusted pricing target that can be proposed to the relationship manager as the benchmark to price a new loan given the riskiness of the borrower. Of course, the application of risk-adjusted pricing guidelines needs to be tailored, based on the organizational structure of the bank and the characteristics of the counterparty, as we discussed by comparing two benchmark cases: a loan from an investment bank to a large borrower and a loan from a smaller, commercial bank to an SME.

7.7   Further Reading

VaR limits have sometimes been blamed for potentially forcing traders to liquidate positions after increases in market volatility, thereby self-inducing further volatility. This argument has been critically discussed in Persaud (2000) and Jorion (2002). The issue of how to harmonize VaR limits for the time horizon of one day, given the maximum acceptable loss, has been discussed in Saita (1999b) and Härtl and Johanning (2005); both papers also discuss the linkage with cumulative losses. The concepts of VaRDelta, incremental VaR, and component VaR are described in Garman (1996, 1997). Litterman (1997a, b) explains how component VaR can be used to identify natural hedges and to optimize the portfolio of exposures of the bank. Carroll et al. (2001) discuss how component VaR can be measured when risk measures are based on scenarios, while Hallerbach (2002) considers the case of the absence of joint normality. The issue of defining VaR limits with ex ante uncertain correlations and exposure directions has been discussed by Strassberger (2004). Hallerbach (2004) extends the analysis of portfolio optimization discussed by Litterman (1997a, b) for market risks to the credit risk portfolio. Finally, risk-adjusted pricing for loans is discussed in Matten (2000) and Bessis (2002).

CHAPTER · 8

Risk-Adjusted Performance Measurement

A risk-adjusted performance (RAP) measure is a profitability measure that jointly takes into consideration the margin or profit produced by a business and its capital at risk (CaR). As noted in Chapter 6, we use CaR to refer to a one-year equivalent (if translation from subannual to annual data is necessary) of the VaR measures we discussed earlier in the book.

Perhaps the most well-known RAP measure is RAROC (risk-adjusted return on capital), which can generally be defined as the ratio between the profit and CaR for a given business area/unit. Another frequently used performance measure is Economic Value Added, EVA® (originally developed by Stern Stewart and Co.), which is defined for banks as profit minus the cost of equity capital times capital at risk, i.e.,

$$RAROC = \frac{\text{Profit}}{\text{CaR}}$$

$$EVA = \text{Profit} - \text{cost of equity capital} \times \text{CaR}$$

Many banks use either of these measures or variants of these measures. While some have developed different acronyms, in most cases the underlying measures are only slight modifications either of the return-on-capital idea underlying the basic RAROC or of the concept of the value added over the cost of risk capital implied in EVA. In this chapter, we first clarify the two main reasons why a RAP measure may be calculated (Section 8.1). We then discuss the issues concerning the measure of profit and the difference between capital investment and allocation (Sections 8.2 and 8.3). The choice of the capital-at-risk measure to be used for RAP calculation is addressed in Sections 8.4 and 8.5. Section 8.6 critically compares RAROC and EVA measures. Section 8.7 considers a few extensions and variations of classic RAP measures, and Section 8.8 discusses the links between RAP and the evaluation of managerial performance.

8.1 Business Areas, Business Units, and the Double Role of Risk-Adjusted Performance Measures

Why can RAP be measured? Let us consider equity trading. Equity trading can be conceived of both as a business area, i.e., a portion of the bank representing a relatively homogeneous combination of activities whose results can be measured, and as a business unit, i.e., an organizational unit that is typically in charge of a business area. The bank may need to measure the risk-adjusted performance of equity trading for two different reasons:

1. To understand whether equity trading has been a profitable business for the bank
2. To understand whether equity traders, or the head of the equity trading unit, have achieved their targets (which has potential consequences for their bonuses).

In practice, when considering equity trading as a business area, the purpose is to *support top-management decisions*. While decisions are clearly never mechanically based on past performances, inadequate profitability could lead to managerial actions, to a reduction in allocated risk capital, or even to a dismissal of the business area, while excellent profitability might suggest trying to increase exposure in the area.

When the RAP measure is instead referred to equity trading as a business unit, it can also be used to evaluate the performance of the organizational unit and its components. Whenever a RAP target is a part of the set of objectives assigned to a given business unit in a management-by-objectives (MBO) framework, its main role is to *serve as a target aimed at coordinating the behaviors* of different players inside the bank. An MBO framework, which Mintzberg (1979) would define as "output standardization," could be considered an alternative way to coordinate behaviors relative to other organizational mechanisms (e.g., direct supervision), which may be less efficient in complex organizations.

This distinction is relevant since, depending on the purpose pursued, the requisites of the "best" RAP measure may differ. Hence, the "best" RAP measure can sometimes differ, depending on the aim, even if we apparently want to measure the RAP for the same entity (e.g., equity trading). In fact, while a measure aimed at supporting top managers' decisions should be precise and reliable, a measure that is used as an MBO target that influences business managers' behaviors should essentially be evaluated based on its ability to produce the desired behaviors. Hence, such a measure should be as fair as possible, i.e., should not depend too much on elements beyond the managers' control. If the result depended mainly on external events or on pure fate, the measure would fail to motivate business managers to increase their efforts so as to improve the unit's performance. The fact that the "best" RAP measure can differ will become clearer when later in the chapter we discuss a few practical examples, such as the choice between building RAP measures based on utilized CaR or on allocated CaR, on "diversified" CaR or on "undiversified" CaR.

8.2 Checking the Measure of Profit

When developing risk-adjusted performance measures, the main emphasis is typically on the capital-at-risk component. However, the measure of profit is equally important. Transfer prices, cost allocation, and the difference between capital allocation and investment are some of the main issues deserving attention.

8.2.1 Transfer Prices

The profit of a business unit is often influenced by the prices of internal deals with other business units of the bank. A classic example is represented by commercial and retail banking divisions funding their loans by internally borrowing money from the treasury department at a proper internal transfer rate. Whether the internal transfer rate is set at either bid, ask, or mid-market rates clearly affects the profit allocation among these profit centers. Moreover, there are cases (e.g., transactions without a specified maturity, such as checking account deposits) in which the definition of transfer rates is nontrivial.

Transfer prices are also relevant for trading desks, especially if it is suggested that they concentrate only on their main risk while hedging other risks internally. Imagine a foreign exchange trader entering a 3-month forward transaction on euros against British pounds: The value of the trader's position is sensitive to changes in the 3-month euro area and UK interest rates. If the trader were invited to hedge these interest rate exposures with the money market desk, the rates of these internal deals would affect the currency desk's final profit. As in any classic transfer price problem (see, for instance, Eccles 1983), the bank has to decide whether the trader should be given the option to hedge with another investment bank or should instead be forced to hedge internally. The former solution would grant the trader the opportunity to transfer risk at the best available conditions, which implies that any internal deal has been made at a rate the trader considered fair. At the same time, with this solution the bank increases its exposure to counterparty risk that could be avoided in case of internal hedges. This is why the solution to force hedging internally is often preferred, even if it might raise tough internal discussions about the fairness of the internal-deal pricing system. This issue is particularly important for banks willing to adopt a rigid risk specialization policy similar to the Bankers Trust's "one risk, one owner" principle discussed in Chapter 7.

Transfer prices are required for credit risk as well. An example was in Section 7.5.3, discussing how explicit subsidies between different divisions of an investment bank might be needed when the relationship manager asks the lending division to offer a loan to an overall potentially profitable customer at rate below the risk-adjusted rate. Another example is represented by the sale of derivatives (especially long-dated interest rate derivatives) to small and medium nonfinancial companies for risk management purposes. These over-the-counter derivative positions imply counterparty risk for the bank, and credit officers have to define a credit line for derivative transactions for those borrowers. Intuitively, then, some of the profit of the transaction should be allocated to the business unit bearing credit risk. A particularly obvious case occurs when the counterparty has a rating below AA. Since market rates for swap on information providers' screens typically assume an AA-rated counterparty, an A-rated firm entering into a plain-vanilla swap where the firm receives the floating rate and pays the fixed rate would pay slightly more than the market swap rate; the extra payment is a compensation for credit risk. If this were not recognized, then all the profit (including this credit-risk-driven extra component) would be allocated to the trading and sales division, while counterparty credit risk would be included in the CaR of the lending division. The solution is to define a charge for the credit risk of the transaction serving as a transfer price between the trading and sales division and the lending division (of course, the existence of collateral and netting agreements would also matter when pricing this risk). While these considerations are obvious for large investment banks, they are not as obvious for smaller retail banks selling derivatives for risk management purposes to their smaller and perhaps unrated customers. In this case, checking the correct allocation of profits and capital at risk between the lending business unit and the derivative sales business unit is important, to avoid overstating the profitability of the derivatives business.

8.2.2 Cost Attribution and Its Impact on RAP Measures

A second relevant issue is related to which costs are considered when calculating RAROC or more generally RAP measures. In theory, all business units' profits should take into account at least all direct specific costs. While this typically happens in most cases, in some banks — especially in the trading and capital markets divisions — the issue of specific costs is sometimes neglected, and the "profit" considered for RAP calculation is simply made up by realized and unrealized capital gains and losses, without deducting the specific costs of the desk. While this is the profit the risk manager is usually concerned with for different purposes (e.g., for back-testing), forgetting specific costs may be a problem when calculating RAP measures. In fact, failing to consider specific costs (e.g., the fixed salaries of the different traders, the software and infrastructure required for managing their portfolios, and potentially their bonuses) could result in a faulty picture about the relative profitability of different businesses.

A simplified ideal example of this problem is presented in Table 8-1, which compares two trading desks where the former (Treasury bond trading) is a lower-margin business with lower specific costs (e.g., traders with lower fixed salaries and simpler hardware and software requirements), while the latter (exotic option trading) has opposite characteristics. While comparing only trading profits with CaR would suggest that the exotic option desks produce higher margins, when taking into consideration specific costs the picture might be reversed.

Obviously, even shared costs could be attributed to each business unit, based on proper cost drivers. While some banks might prefer to attribute a portion of shared costs, this could make the RAP measure less transparent and partially influenced by factors beyond the power of business unit managers. For instance, if business volumes of different units are used as the driver to allocate shared costs, a reduction of the business volume of one business unit might result (all else being equal) in an increase in the share of fixed costs being allocated to other units and hence to lower profits. While deducting shared fixed costs through some proper driver provides useful information to top managers, this measure could be unfair if it were used to evaluate business unit managers. Hence this provides an example of how different RAP measures can be linked to different purposes.[1]

TABLE 8-1   Role of Specific Costs in Relative Profitability Rankings

		Treasury Bond Trading	Exotic Option Trading
(1)	Trading profit	200	300
(2)	Traders' salaries and bonuses	70	120
(3)	Dedicated hardware/software	30	90
(4)	Profit net of specific costs	100	90
(5)	Capital at risk	1000	1200
(6)	RAROC based on trading profit [(1)/(5)]	20.0%	25.0%
(7)	RAROC based on net profit [(4)/(5)]	10.0%	7.5%

1. Note that while the allocation of shared costs may be questioned, few objections can be raised against considering specific costs, as in the Table 8-1 example, since specific costs are clearly linked to an individual business unit alone.

8.3 Capital Investment versus Capital Allocation

Before discussing the choice among alternative CaR measures for RAP measurement, we must clarify the difference between capital investment and capital allocation (see Matten 2000). Let us consider a branch making a 100,000 USD 5-year fixed-rate loan whose CaR is equal to 4000 USD. The loan must be entirely funded at a 5-year fixed internal transfer rate by the treasury department. In fact, if instead the loan were assumed to be financed 4% by equity capital and 96% by the treasury department at the 5-year internal transfer rate, the result of the lending division would be affected by changes in interest rates during the life of the loan. But if (correctly) the loan is considered funded entirely at the 5-year internal transfer rate, then the 4000 USD equity capital the loan requires is not *invested* in the loan, but is only *ideally allocated* as a cover for potential unexpected losses the loan might generate.

The distinction between capital investment and capital allocation has a relevant consequence: If capital at risk is ideally allocated to only a business unit, it could also be "physically" safely invested somewhere else (e.g., in a risk-free asset). Thus, part of the target return on equity capital may be produced by capital investment, while the remaining part should be produced by capital allocation. Assuming the target return k_e on equity capital were 15% and capital could be invested at the risk-free rate $r_f = 3\%$, then the return required on allocated capital in order to obtain the target overall return should be equal to $k_e - r_f = 12\%$.

While the assumption to invest equity capital at the risk-free rate is the simplest solution, a potential alternative is to assume transfering equity capital to the treasury department in order to fund assets together with the bank's liabilities. In this case, a proper internal transfer rate for equity (ITR_e) and a precise maturity should be defined. For instance, the one-year Libor rate at the beginning of the year could be assumed to be the transfer rate; note that the maturity might also matter when defining asset and liability management policies for the treasury department. In theory, the maturity could be either a one-year rate or a long-term rate; the choice should be made according to how the return target for the bank has been set. If the target is defined as the long-term (short-term) risk-free rate plus an equity premium, than equity capital should be assumed to be either safely invested or transferred to the treasury department over the same long (short) horizon.

As a consequence, when evaluating the risk-adjusted profitability of different business units, the target level for business unit RAROC (assuming it should be the same for all units, a topic that is critically discussed in Chapter 9) should be equal to $k_e - r_f$ rather than to k_e only. In fact, a business unit having a RAROC equal to $k_e - r_f$ implies that by adding up return on capital investment the overall profitability target would be met. Similarly, when calculating EVA the cost of capital should be equal to $k_e - r_f$ rather than to k_e only.

8.4 Choosing the Measure of Capital at Risk: Allocated Capital versus Utilized Capital

Whenever a business unit is given a VaR/CaR limit as discussed in Chapter 7, there are two potential CaR measures that could be used in ex post RAP measurement. The first one is *utilized* CaR, i.e., the actual, ex post CaR measuring the overall risk accepted by the business unit during the year. The second one is the CaR limit, representing the amount of risk that *could have been* accepted and, most important, the amount of capital

TABLE 8-2   Hypothetical Example of RAP Based on Allocated versus Utilized CaR

	Business Unit A	Business Unit B
Profit	80	120
Allocated CaR	640	1000
Utilized CaR	500	600
Utilized CaR/allocated CaR	78.125%	60%
RAROC (allocated CaR)	12.5%	12.0%
RAROC (utilized CaR)	16.0%	20.0%
EVA (allocated CaR, cost of capital = 12.5%)	0.0	−5.0
EVA (utilized CaR, cost of capital = 12.5%)	17.5	45.0

that has been *allocated* to the business. Since allocated CaR is usually higher than utilized CaR (unless CaR limits are flexible and frequently exceeded), RAP measures based on allocated CaR are usually lower. If we define as CaR "usage rate" the ratio of utilized CaR to allocated CaR, this also implies that the choice of either allocated or utilized CaR could change profitability rankings for business units with a different CaR usage rate (see Table 8-2). In Table 8-2, business unit A has a higher usage rate and while its relative performance is lower if based on utilized capital, it is higher if allocated capital is considered. For business unit B, in particular, EVA may change from positive to negative, depending on whether the cost of capital is charged on utilized capital only (i.e., EVA = $120 - 12.5 \times 600 = 45$) or on all allocated capital (EVA = $120 - 12.5 \times 1000 = -5$).

How can the "right" RAP measure be identified? As anticipated in Section 8.1, we should distinguish whether the aim is to provide top managers with a measure of historical profitability to support their decisions or instead to define a target for business unit managers in order to coordinate their behaviors.

When the purpose is to support top-management evaluation of business profitability, relative profitability should be evaluated based on utilized capital. In fact, if top managers want to understand the risk–return profile of certain businesses, they should compare return with the actual risk that has been taken (i.e., utilized CaR) without also considering the risk that could have been taken but was not (i.e., the difference between allocated and utilized CaR). The intrinsic risk–return profile of a business area depends on actual profit compared to actual absorbed capital at risk. Whether actual utilized CaR was less than allocated CaR is a decision of the organizational unit in charge of the business, which should not affect this evaluation.

Yet, as a second step, a comparison between profitability based on allocated versus utilized capital and an analysis of CaR "usage rate" patterns may be useful to top managers too. In fact, it could help explain whether a low CaR usage rate is depressing a business unit's performance, hence suggesting a change in capital allocation or a more aggressive growth strategy of business volumes.

Let us now consider the second potential objective, i.e., assigning a fair risk-adjusted target to organizational units. In this case the choice is more complex, because there would be arguments in favor of using allocated CaR as well. One key argument is that allocated capital represents the capital that was received by shareholders. Shareholders would clearly be unhappy if return on utilized CaR were high but return on total capital were low due to a low usage rate (i.e., to large amounts of unutilized capital). Hence, by setting target returns based on allocated capital, business units would have an incentive to exploit fully the capital they receive.

We have noted, however, that when a return target measure is defined, the key criteria should be to build a fair measure that could provide incentives to managers, since an unfair measure would not motivate managers to maximize their efforts to improve the business unit's performance. Hence, the choice between allocated and utilized CaR should depend largely on whether or not allocated capital is influenced by business unit decisions. Let us consider the two extremes of the spectrum.

In a completely centralized, top-down allocation process, business units would have no influence on allocated capital and should not be responsible for potential excesses; hence, they should be evaluated on utilized CaR only. If the performance based on allocated CaR were too low, this would provide an incentive to headquarters' top managers — who would be responsible for allocating too much capital — to promote a better capital allocation or even a reduction of the bank's capital base (e.g., through a buyback) if needed.

Let us consider now an opposite capital allocation model, based on a decentralized internal market for capital, where business units might ask their corporate headquarters for any amount of risk capital they want (provided they agree to accept a given RAROC target). Their ability to ask for any amount of capital would not be unrealistic if we assumed that the bank has a good profitability track record and can convince shareholders to subscribe new equity as long as it can credibly promise them attractive returns. If business units were really able to obtain any amount of capital they wanted, than these amounts should be "paid" in full; i.e., they should be evaluated based on allocated CaR. If this were not the case, they would have an incentive to require a disproportionately high amount of CaR during the planning process while then trying to maximize returns on a much smaller portion of capital, hence frustrating corporate headquarters' and shareholders' expectations.

However, in most banks the capital allocation process is designed as a negotiation process, which is in between the two extremes of a top-down centralized process and decentralized internal markets (Saita 1999a; see also the UniCredit case study in Chapter 9). In this case two intermediate solutions can be adopted. The first one is to evaluate RAP measures based on utilized CaR while setting a penalty for unutilized CaR (i.e., the difference between allocated and utilized CaR). For instance, RAROC could take the form

$$RAROC = \frac{Profit - pc \times (Allocated\ CaR - Utilized\ CaR)}{Utilized\ CaR}$$

where pc is the penalty charge on unutilized CaR. Similarly, EVA would be

$$EVA = Profit - (k_e - r_f) \times Utilized\ CaR - pc \times (Allocated\ CaR - Utilized\ CaR)$$

In this case, different penalty charges could be determined, depending on how centralized or decentralized the allocation process is, or (more reasonably) on the nature of the business. For instance, those businesses where increasing and decreasing the exposure is easier (e.g., trading on exchange traded derivatives) should be charged a higher penalty, as opposed to other businesses, such as lending, where exposures are easier to take on but more difficult to be reduced. In fact, in the second case, the business unit should consider more cautiously investments that may increase capital requirements, and hence a lower penalty for leaving capital unutilized should be set.

The second possible solution is to measure RAP based on both allocated CaR and utilized CaR and to use both measures jointly in a balanced scorecard approach to business unit manager evaluation. This solution can be desirable in all cases in which managers would not like to evaluate performance based on a single measure. This can make performance evaluation more complex and subjective but at the same time more articulated and complete. If (1) a balanced scorecard is used and (2) business units have a partial influence on the capital at risk they receive, then introducing both RAP measures into the balanced scorecard is the easiest solution.

What happens, then, in practice? Frequently only measures based on utilized capital are calculated, used as targets for business unit managers and presented to top managers. While this may be a precise choice (e.g., due to a fully centralized allocation process), there are alternative explanations:

- VaR limits could be set only at higher hierarchical levels, and hence only at these levels can RAP on allocated CaR be measured.
- When the bank first started measuring performances based on (lower) utilized CaR, business unit managers became reluctant to be evaluated based on allocated CaR also, since RAP measures based on allocated CaR would generally appear to be lower.

Yet, as we noted, either including return on allocated CaR in the manager's scorecard or controlling capital usage rate is important in those cases where units might influence the amount of capital they receive, since it reduces the risk that poor capital-at-risk usage rate will depress the performance offered to shareholders.

8.5 Choosing the Measure of Capital at Risk: Diversified Capital versus Undiversified Capital

Since business areas and units in a banking group often offer diversification benefits to the group, overall CaR is usually strictly lower than the sum of individual, stand-alone CaR values for each business unit (see, for instance, Table 8-3).[2] Consequently, any business unit or business area could be evaluated based either on stand-alone (undiversified) CaR or on a measure of diversified CaR taking into account diversification benefits. The bank should then choose (1) whether RAP measures should consider an undiversified or a diversified CaR and, in the latter case, (2) which measure of diversified CaR should be used. We therefore first compare the different measures of diversified CaR that could be utilized by incorporating the concepts of incremental VaR and component VaR introduced in Chapter 7, and we then discuss when diversified rather than undiversified CaR measures should be used in RAP measurement.

8.5.1 Comparison of Alternative Diversified CaR Measures

We saw in Chapter 7 that there are different ways to calculate a measure of diversified CaR: the splitting method, the incremental CaR method, and the component CaR method. The three methodologies can be summarized as follows.

---

2. Note that this happens despite the potential nonsubadditivity problem raised by Artzner et al. (1999). VaR critics can probably argue that this may derive from the fact that some banks still use a simplified framework for risk capital aggregation (such as the classic normal CaR/hybrid CaR formula presented in Chapter 6), which still makes it impossible for the nonsubadditivity problem to emerge.

TABLE 8-3   Diversification Benefits at the Group Level: Credit Suisse Example (CHF million)

	Economic Risk Capital, Credit Suisse			Economic Risk Capital, Credit Suisse Group, including Winterthur		
	2005	2004	2003	2005	2004	2003
Interest rate, credit spread, and foreign exchange	2,443	1,879	1,572	4,566	4,224	4,045
Equity investment	2,529	1,743	1,841	4,082	2,937	2,397
Swiss and retail lending	2,215	2,239	2,375	2,301	2,329	2,475
International lending	3,059	2,151	2,240	3,093	2,188	2,416
Emerging markets	1,443	1,562	1,699	1,965	2,016	1,952
Real estate and structured assets	2,967	2,263	1,849	3,715	2,920	2,473
Insurance underwriting	0	0	0	811	801	695
Simple sum	14,656	11,837	11,576	20,533	17,415	16,453
Diversification benefits	(4,215)	(3,435)	(3,178)	(6,651)	(5,568)	(5,053)
Total economic risk capital	10,441	8,402	8,398	13,882	11,847	11,400

Source: Credit Suisse 2005 Annual Report.

1. The splitting method evenly splits diversification benefits among different entities; i.e., diversified CaR is set equal to undiversified CaR multiplied by the ratio between actual portfolio CaR and the sum of individual CaR values.
2. Incremental CaR is the difference between portfolio CaR before and after a change in exposures. Hence, incremental CaR for a business is equal to the difference between portfolio CaR and portfolio CaR if that business disappeared or were sold out. This measure is also known as marginal CaR (see, for instance, Merton and Perold 1993).
3. Component CaR is equal to the part of portfolio VaR that can be attributed to a given exposure (or business) by taking into account the correlation with the other businesses/exposures.

We discuss them using our earlier Omikron Bank example, whose basic data are reported in Table 8-4. While the example considers business units in the trading division, it could be extended to any group of business units or divisions within the bank, provided the measures of diversified capital can be calculated (the issue of dealing with joint distributions markedly different from the joint multivariate normal is discussed in Hallerbach 2002).

We can now apply all these methodologies to the three trading units and compare the results (see Table 8-5). As far as the splitting method is concerned, since the sum of stand-alone CaR values is 120 and portfolio CaR is equal to 90 (i.e., 75% of 120), every stand-alone CaR is simply multiplied by a 75% factor. In order to calculate incremental CaR relative to the business unit as a whole, it is necessary to compare portfolio CaR (i.e., 90) with the combined CaR of two units if the third one were excluded. For instance, since the aggregated CaR of business units 1 and 2 alone would be equal to 72.25, marginal CaR for business unit 3 would be $90 - 72.25 = 17.75$. Component CaR is calculated according to the steps discussed in Chapter 7.

While the splitting method clearly fails to provide a convincing technique for attributing diversification benefits to business areas/units according to their real contribution in

TABLE 8-4 Omikron Bank Example: Key Data for the Three Business Units

	Business Unit 1: Fixed-income Trading	Business Unit 2: Foreign Exchange Trading	Business Unit 3: Equity Trading
Undiversified capital at risk	50	40	30
Correlation with BU 1	1	0.28	0.46
Correlation with BU 2	0.28	1	0.25
Correlation with BU 3	0.46	0.25	1
Trading division CaR	$\text{CaR}_p = \sqrt{\sum_{i=1}^{3}\sum_{j=1}^{3}\text{CaR}_i\text{CaR}_j\rho_{ij}} = 90$		

In contrast to Chapter 7, where data were considered to be based on daily volatility, here we assume that values represent equivalent yearly CaR values.

TABLE 8-5 Comparison among Alternative Measures of Diversified CaR

	Business Unit 1: Fixed-Income Trading		Business Unit 2: Foreign Exchange Trading		Business Unit 3: Equity Trading	
	Absolute Value	% of Undiversified CaR	Absolute Value	% of Undiversified CaR	Absolute Value	% of Undiversified CaR
Undiversified CaR	50		40		30	
Diversified CaR (splitting)	37.5	75%	30	75%	22.5	75%
Incremental/marginal CaR	34.32	68.6%	20.86	52.2%	17.75	59.2%
Component CaR	41.67	83.3%	27.33	68.3%	21.00	70%

generating those benefits, incremental and component CaR do take it into consideration. Unsurprisingly, for instance, business unit 2 enjoys the greatest reduction when moving from undiversified to either incremental or component CaR. This is consistent with the facts that correlations with the remaining two business are lowest and that its size is not remarkably higher than the size of other business units.

The fact that size matters too (since an increase in size could imply a higher concentration risk in the same exposure) is illustrated by Table 8-6, which reports diversified CaR figures and the ratio between diversified and undiversified CaR, assuming the size (and hence undiversified CaR) for business unit 2 doubled from 40 to 80. While correlations remain the same and remain lowest for business unit 2, due to larger size, diversification benefits for the unit are lower. This is evident from the ratio of diversified CaR to undiversified CaR being highest for business unit 2 both for incremental CaR and component CaR, while they were the lowest in Table 8-5, where business unit 2 stand-alone CaR was assumed to be much smaller.

A second, small consideration concerns the fact that with the incremental VaR method the sum of incremental (or marginal) CaR values does equal the total portfolio CaR. In both Tables 8-5 and 8-6 the total incremental CaRs are much lower than 90 and 120.92, respectively, unlike component CaR, which is clearly able to allocate portfolio CaR entirely to the different components. This should be noted because if business units were asked to remunerate incremental CaR only and the division's target RAROC were 15%, then business units should be assigned a higher target RAROC, since some of the portfolio

TABLE 8-6   Role of Relative Size in Determining Diversified CaR

	Business Unit 1: Fixed-Income Trading		Business Unit 2: Foreign Exchange Trading		Business Unit 3: Equity Trading	
	Absolute Value	% of Undiversified CaR	Absolute Value	% of Undiversified CaR	Absolute Value	% of Undiversified CaR
Undiversified CaR	50		80		30	
Diversified CaR (splitting)	37.79	75.6%	60.46	75.6%	22.67	75.6%
Incremental/marginal CaR	28.72	57.4%	51.78	64.7%	15.37	51.2%
Component CaR	35.65	71.3%	67.16	83.9%	18.11	60.4%

Diversified CaR values assume a 100% increase in stand-alone risk for business unit 2; portfolio CaR = 120.92.

CaR would not be allocated to any unit. Intuitively, then, incremental CaR may not be the best measure for driving target definition for business units.

8.5.2 Criteria for Choosing between Diversified and Undiversified CaR

After analyzing the alternative diversified CaR measures, we must address the issue of whether and when undiversified CaR or diversified CaR should be used for RAP measures. Let us consider first the purpose of providing profitability measures to support top managers' decisions. In this case, diversification should matter, and the right measure could be incremental CaR or component CaR, depending on the type of decision they have to make. We will see later, however, that measures based on undiversified CaR may be useful to top managers too.

Incremental CaR may be relevant if top managers want to understand how much capital could be saved if the bank exited from a certain business area. Moreover, it can also be used to assess the effects of increased business volume and risk in a certain area (if the change in exposure were small enough, estimates of incremental CaR could also be derived through the VaRDelta concept presented in Chapter 7). If, instead, top managers want to evaluate the contribution of different businesses to the overall bank risk, then component CaR is the right diversified measure.

When considering, instead, the purpose of assigning business unit managers a target to coordinate their behaviors, we should realize that a measure that was largely dependent on elements beyond their control could hardly motivate business unit managers. Since correlations among businesses should in general be assumed to be exogenous, fairness would suggest adopting undiversified CaR. The shortcoming in this case could be that the bank might have to use two different measures based on either diversified or undiversified CaR, depending on the purpose.

This problem obviously has a different importance depending also on whether or not correlation parameters among business units and their relative sizes are stable. If they were highly unstable, then evaluating business unit managers based on diversified CaR could be frustrating: A manager obtaining the same performance based on undiversified CaR might in different years be assigned a completely different risk-adjusted performance measure based on diversified CaR, depending only on correlation fluctuations through

TABLE 8-7   Impact of Increasing Size on RAP Measures Based on Diversified CaR

	Business Unit 1: Fixed-Income Trading	Business Unit 2: Foreign Exchange Trading	Business Unit 3: Equity Trading
Year 1			
Profit	5	4	3
Undiversified CaR	50	40	30
Component CaR	41.67	27.33	21
Risk-adjusted return on undiversified CaR	10.0%	10.0%	10.0%
Risk-adjusted return on component CaR	12.0%	14.6%	14.3%
Year 2			
Profit	5	8	3
Undiversified CaR	50	80	30
Component CaR	35.65	67.16	18.11
Risk-adjusted return on undiversified CaR	10.0%	10.0%	10.0%
Risk-adjusted return on component CaR	14.0%	11.9%	16.6%

Assumption: Fixed 10% RAROC on undiversified CaR.

time. If, on the contrary, correlations and businesses' stand-alone CaR figures were both stable through time, then the noise in evaluating managers' performances based on diversified CaR would be limited. The relevance of size should not be neglected, since the fact that a business unit whose stand-alone CaR gets larger may have lower diversification benefits could influence RAP measures when these are based on diversified CaR measures.

The example in Table 8-7 may help explain the problem. Let us imagine that the three business units earn the same 10% return on undiversified CaR for two consecutive years (i.e., all managers are equally clever in both years). The only difference between years 1 and 2 is that business unit 2 doubles its size, and, as a consequence, according to the numbers shown earlier in Tables 8-5 and 8-6, its component CaR increases remarkably. If we calculated the effects on risk-adjusted return based on component CaR, this implies that RAROC would fall from 14.6% to 11.9% for business unit 2, while it would rise for both business units 1 and 3. This has nothing to do with how each business unit manager has performed in managing his or her own risks, nor has it to do with correlations, which are unchanged. Instead, it is linked only to the growth of the size of business unit 2.

The example also suggests that while top managers should care about diversification and then use diversified CaR measures, mainly, providing them profitability measures based on undiversified CaR could also help us understand the time series of profitability measures for certain business units. In fact, data based on undiversified CaR could be used, for instance, to understand whether the declining risk-adjusted profitability in a given business derives from bad management or deteriorating competitive positioning for the bank in that area or, instead, simply from adverse changes in correlations or even from the growth of business volume of the business unit, which may reduce diversification benefits and hence generate a lower return on diversified CaR.

8.6 Choosing the Risk-Adjusted Performance Measure: EVA vs. RAROC

After defining the measures of profit and CaR, the final step to calculate a RAP measure is the choice concerning how to combine them into a single number. The two classic alternatives are RAROC and EVA. The former is the ratio between profit and capital at risk:

$$\mathrm{RAROC} = \frac{\mathrm{Profit}}{\mathrm{CaR}}$$

while the latter is obtained by deducting from the profit the cost of risk capital. It must be noted that the original EVA, developed by Stern, Stewart and Co. for nonfinancial companies, was defined as

$$\mathrm{EVA} = \mathrm{NOPAT} - \mathrm{WACC} \times \mathrm{Invested\ Capital}$$

where NOPAT stands for net operating profit after taxes and WACC is the weighted average cost of capital, which is then multiplied by the capital invested in the firm (or division). In the case of banks, it is usually applied in a variant, where only the cost of equity capital times capital at risk is deducted,[3] and EVA is calculated as

$$\mathrm{EVA} = \mathrm{Profit} - (k_e - r_f) \times \mathrm{CaR}$$

where k_e is the target return for equity capital and the deduction of the risk-free rate is motivated by the fact that capital at risk is only ideally allocated but not invested in the business unit or business area.

Choosing between the two measures is not necessary when supporting top-management decisions, since they basically provide different information. While RAROC measures return on capital and hence (in percentage) the efficiency of capital usage, EVA is a measure in dollar terms identifying how much value has been created in a single year by producing earnings in excess of shareholders' requests. Clearly, top managers are interested in how large this amount of excess earnings may be, but at the same time for their capital allocation choices they would still need the information concerning which return may be produced by one unit of extra capital. Let us consider the simplified case presented in Table 8-8. While business unit beta has a higher EVA, this is explained mainly by the fact that it is five times larger (in CaR terms) than business unit gamma,

TABLE 8-8   Comparison between RAROC and EVA

Business Unit	Profit	CaR	RAROC	EVA
Beta	180	1000	18%	180 − 150 = 30
Gamma	40	200	20%	40 − 30 = 10

Assuming $k_e - r_f = 15\%$.

---

3. Some banks consider a weighted average cost of capital limited to equity capital and to those debt instruments that comprise Tier 2 or Tier 3 regulatory capital, therefore calculating a weighted average cost of *regulatory* capital.

which has instead a higher RAROC. Assuming that past returns predicted future returns, managers might be more willing, all else being equal, to invest extra capital in gamma (even if its EVA is lower) than in beta.

In any case, there has been some debate concerning which measure is more suitable to serve as a target for business unit managers. Zaik et al. (1996) claimed that RAROC may give the wrong suggestions to business unit decision makers when they are deciding whether to accept a new transaction or not. The argument is that business units with a low current RAROC may be willing to accept transactions offering a RAROC higher than their current one, even if RAROC of new transactions were lower than the cost of equity capital. Similarly, higher RAROC business units could refuse transactions whose expected returns are higher than the cost of equity capital but lower than their current RAROC, since if they accepted, their risk-adjusted performance would diminish. In short, business units oriented to RAROC maximization would consider current RAROC as the hurdle rate, rather than using the right hurdle rate based on shareholders' expected return. EVA, instead, suggests rejecting anything earning a return lower than $k_e - r_f$ and accepting any investment opportunity providing a higher return.

While this argument has some merits, a warning is required about its limitations and potentially counterproductive effects. First of all, we must note that a difference between RAROC and EVA in terms of the incentives for business unit managers would exist only when RAP is measured on utilized CaR. In fact, if all allocated CaR were charged to business units, then maximizing either RAROC or EVA would simply be equivalent to maximizing profits subject to a fixed CaR constraint, and no difference in behaviors could be observed. For instance, maximizing RAROC based on allocated CaR would mean maximizing a ratio where the denominator would be fixed (so that the ratio is maximized only by increasing profit).

Second, for business units whose current profitability is below the cost of capital, if EVA were the only measure, then all transactions with an expected return that is positive but below the cost of capital would be refused. The implicit idea is that the bank should either avoid asking shareholders for capital or give capital back to shareholders if it is unable to produce the desired return. This perspective may be fine for multiyear transactions. For instance, a 10-year loan should be refused if the expected return is insufficient (and no other business unit is willing to pay for the insufficient return, according to the transfer pricing mechanism described in Chapter 7). Yet, for a number of short-term transactions (e.g., a 3-month forward deal, a short-term loan) the real choice in practice is not between using capital at risk providing a return higher than the cost of capital or giving capital back to shareholders, but rather between using capital at risk to provide at least a positive return or leaving capital at risk unutilized (so that return would be zero). The more aggressive the cost of capital/target return that the CFO requires from business unit, the more selective the business unit may be. In the short term, this may potentially drive a reduction of business volumes, sometimes making it more difficult to cover the bank's fixed indirect costs. In this case therefore, the alternative of setting a challenging RAROC target promoting incremental change toward higher profitability may be more desirable. In practice, the choice of using EVA, RAROC, or both for setting performance targets should again be extremely pragmatic and should try to avoid potential pitfalls in incentive setting that might be created inadvertently. As always, the potential for these incentives is stronger when the RAP measure is conceived in theory or treated in practice as the only or largely the main indicator of the performance of a business unit, while the situation is different whenever it is considered as only one among other elements in a wider set of qualitative and quantitative variables taken into consideration.

8.7 Variants and Potential Extensions

When building a RAP measure, there is a significant potential for each bank to develop tailor-made measures or refinements in order to improve its quality. There are therefore a number of potential variants in how the measures are defined and how they are implemented in practice. We simply want to point out briefly here a few aspects that a risk manager and a CFO may consider when designing the risk-adjusted performance measurement system.

8.7.1 Differentiated Target Returns

When evaluating RAROC and EVA measures, a critical issue is whether or not the expected return on different business units (in the case of RAROC) or the target return/cost of capital used for EVA calculation should be the same for all business units. The rationale for that may be that different businesses generate a different portion of systematic risk and hence contribute in a different manner to determining the bank's cost of equity capital. Hence, businesses with lower systematic risk ("low-beta" businesses) should be assigned a lower cost of capital.

Although this topic is thoroughly discussed in the next chapter, dealing with target setting and the links between capital allocation and the planning process, it is useful here to anticipate that a bank using different target returns should then also calculate EVA according to different k_e values for each business unit. At the same time, RAROC may be evaluated in differential terms, i.e., by comparing ex post RAROC with the individual target RAROC of each business unit, rather than by simply considering its absolute level.

8.7.2 Alternative RAP Measures

Many banks use return-on-capital measures that appear to be different from RAROC. Sometimes this is only due to different terminology: Measures very similar to RAROC may have been given a different name when they were introduced in the bank and have maintained that name through time. Sometimes, instead, they can represent real variants. A potential example is what some banks call RARORAC (risk-adjusted return on risk-adjusted capital), which is equal to EVA divided by capital at risk. It is quite evident that if the capital used in the numerator and the denominator is the same, this measure is nothing more than RAROC minus the RAROC target $k_e - r_f$:

$$\text{RARORAC}_1 = \frac{\text{EVA}}{\text{CaR}} = \frac{\text{Profit} - (k_e - r_f)\text{CaR}}{\text{CaR}} = \frac{\text{Profit}}{\text{CaR}} - (k_e - r_f) = \text{RAROC} - (k_e - r_f)$$

If instead the two values of capital are different (e.g., EVA is calculated on utilized CaR while the denominator is represented by allocated CaR), then the measure could be used to mix the two elements into a single number, providing business units an incentive to be efficient both in using and in requiring capital at risk:

$$\text{RARORAC}_2 = \frac{\text{EVA}}{\text{Allocated CaR}} = \frac{\text{Profit} - (k_e - r_f)\text{Utilized CaR}}{\text{Allocated CaR}}$$

Of course, if a measure mixing both data is required, it is up to the bank to decide whether this solution is better than the one based on setting a penalty for allocated but unutilized capital, described in Section 8.4. Still, RARORAC is an example of the potential variants a bank might try to develop.

8.7.3 Expected Shortfall and Performance Measurement

In Chapter 3 we introduced the concept of expected shortfall (ES), which can be defined in a simplified way as the average loss in the worst $x\%$ of possible outcomes. In theory, different business units might have similar CaR values but different ES, if, for instance, the return distribution for one business is close to a Gaussian distribution whereas return distribution for the second comprises some catastrophic losses in the left tail of the return distribution. As a consequence, ES supporters claim that risk control, RAP measurement, and capital allocation should be based on ES rather than on CaR. An argument to support this view is that ES is a coherent measure (i.e., it has a number of desirable properties, including subadditivity) while VaR is not subadditive (i.e., it is possible in extreme cases for the VaR of a portfolio to be larger than the sum of the VaR values of its components).

While it is difficult to argue against the conceptual importance of ES, its application in practice is far from easy. Since ES depends only on data on the left tail of the distribution, properly estimating it requires more time and effort, especially if the risk manager does not need to measure it on a simple position but rather on a complex portfolio. While, in theory, measures such as a sort of "return on expected shortfall" may be built, they are unlikely to replace measures such as RAROC or EVA in the short term. Moreover, an issue for future research is whether ES and CaR should be considered substitutes or could instead be integrated into a single RAP measure. Integration could be achieved, for instance, by charging, in the numerator of the usual RAROC measure, the cost of acquiring external protection against extreme losses, as if the bank decided to pay a premium to transfer extreme losses beyond CaR to a reinsurance company. If it were possible to ask for realistic quotes for this protection from reinsurers, the expected-shortfall concept could relatively easily be integrated into the traditional risk-adjusted performance measurement system.

8.7.4 Operational Risk, Business Risk, and Performance Measurement

Operational risk and business risk, which are discussed in Chapter 5, may explain a non-trivial share of the bank's capital at risk; but their inclusion in risk-adjusted performance measures is not always obvious. Let us consider operational risk first. In this case a few larger banks claim they already consider operational risk capital as a component of risk-adjusted performance measurement. In order to understand whether it is possible and useful to do that, we must again consider the purpose that has to be attained.

If the aim is to provide top managers with useful information about a business area, then it is possible to estimate in the best possible way the contribution of the business area to the overall operational risk capital and to combine it with the market or credit risk capital the business unit had always been attributed. It would be wise to present to top managers a report with and without operational risk capital. In fact:

- The operational risk capital model may not be as developed (and tested) as the market and credit risk models.
- Data for a single business unit may be insufficient, especially if the unit is exposed mostly to low-frequency, high-impact events rather than to high-frequency, low-impact events. Given the entirely different set of data, the relative performance of units may be modified by the inclusion of operational risk without sufficient empirical evidence.
- Efforts to aggregate market or/and credit risk with operational risk at the business unit level will face the same problems as for bankwide risk aggregation and the relative ranking of different business units may prove to be sensitive to the approach and assumptions adopted.

As a consequence, while these problems should not prevent one from trying to measure operational risk capital at the macro-business unit level and trying to integrate it into top managers' profitability reports, substantial caution should be taken, at least until data-shortage and risk-integration methodological problems have found a satisfactory solution.

Let us now consider the objective of evaluating the business unit manager. In the case of operational risk, the main objectives to be pursued should be to improve operational risk management and — especially early on — building a reliable database of internal-loss events. This implies that the bank should first of all try to provide the business unit manager substantial incentives to reduce the exposure to operational risk and to cooperate in the process of collecting loss data. These objectives might be more easily obtained by including in the business unit managers' evaluation scorecard (1) the evolution of some key operational risk indicators defined for operational risk measurement and (2) audit reports on the quality of loss data reporting. If, instead, the bank chooses formally to insert operational risk capital of the business unit into risk-adjusted performance measurement calculations, it would be advisable to take into consideration the evolution of key risk indicators when allocating an operational risk capital component to the individual business line. In fact, while operational risk measurement requires building a large historical loss sample for each business line in order to better capture potential loss events, as the database becomes larger operational risk capital estimates might become less volatile from year to year if they were not also linked to the evolution of key risk indicators. Potentially, very stable estimates — which may be desirable from different perspectives — could be a problem if operational risk capital is considered in business unit managers' performance evaluation, since they may fail to provide sufficient incentives to improve operational risk management practices and reduce business unit exposure to future loss events.

Moreover, since business unit managers' performance evaluation must be fair and perceived as such, the difference between business units exposed mainly to relatively frequent but less severe loss events, as opposed to those that are exposed to rare but potentially very severe events, is particularly important here. In fact, while for the former a carefully designed internal-loss database could offer a substantial support to operational risk measurement, the latter would require integration of internal data with external data and scenario analysis. This implies that for the latter, operational risk capital estimates may be unavoidably more questionable and subjective, so perceived fairness may be at risk. Moreover, if the business unit manager knew he was being measured based on operational risk capital estimates as well, his or her contribution to risk mapping first and to scenario analysis and construction later may be biased. This is why even those banks that are introducing a formal quantified operational risk charge in their business performance evaluation are apparently doing that only in those businesses exposed to high-frequency, low-impact loss events only, rather than extending this solution to all the businesses.

A partially similar problem is the inclusion or exclusion of business risk capital from risk-adjusted performance measurement. Again, if we consider first the purpose of supporting top managers' evaluation of the businesses (rather than managers' evaluation), then including business risk is certainly important. Attention should be paid in making clear to profitability report readers that a business risk measure may not be as precise as a market or credit risk measure, due both to the methodological issues in deriving such a measure (already discussed in Chapter 5) and to the intrinsic impossibility of back-testing the capital-at-risk estimate.

If instead we consider the inclusion of business risk capital in business unit managers' evaluation, we should question again whether this would provide the right incentives to the manager. Apart from a few specific cases, the answer would often be negative. First of all, business risk measures need to be built based on long series of data, which implies that in the short term (e.g., one year) the impact of managerial action on the business risk capital measure is going to be extremely limited. If business risk capital estimates were relatively stable, then assigning to the manager a RAROC target or a simple profit target would make little difference (perhaps the profit target would even be perceived to be more clearly linked to the manager's effort and would hence represent a fairer measure). Second, since business risk capital measures have to be derived mostly from internal accounting data, there might be incentives to smooth income volatility or to alter slightly the allocation of costs over time or even to constrain potential growth in booming market phases in order to produce a more stable earnings time series and hence to reduce estimated business risk capital. All these incentives clearly have little to do with good management practices, and some banks may prefer to eliminate them entirely by simply avoiding linking business unit manager evaluation to a business risk capital estimate. At present, of course, the limited development of business risk measurement methodologies represents a clear constraint on extending the internal use of business risk capital estimates. When best-practice methodologies become common among banks, a wider application in internal processes might become possible and desirable.

8.8 Risk-Adjusted Performances and Managers' Performance Evaluation

In this chapter we have seen that one of the aims of RAP measures is to serve as targets in a management-by-objectives framework, which should be able to influence business unit manager behaviors in the right direction. In practice, their hopefully positive effects (and sometimes even their negative and unpredicted side effects) may be stronger or weaker, depending on whether RAP measures represent the only or the main criteria for evaluating performance or are just a part of a more complex performance evaluation mechanism. In practice, the bank has to decide whether performance evaluation should be based on financial performance only, as measured by a single RAP measure, as opposed to being based on a more qualitative judgment on a diversified scorecard of different elements.

Of course, issues of this kind are widely debated even outside the field of finance. Banks may adopt different approaches on this point, provided that organizational mechanisms are designed in a consistent way. For instance, a bank may adopt a more aggressive strategy based on making RAROC or EVA the cornerstone of performance evaluation of business unit managers, giving them maximum responsibility over decisions within their unit and using CaR limits to ensure that the bank's overall risk remains within acceptable boundaries. In this case, which could even be applied in the trading room at the individual trader level, the interdependencies between different profit centers should be minimized or should be managed through internal market mechanisms. For instance, discretional intervention by the head of the trading room or subjective authorization to exceed limits should be minimized. Internal transfer prices should be left entirely to a (reasonably fierce) negotiation between the involved parties, and substantial controls could be activated so as to avoid the profit-maximizing behavior of one unit from damaging others inside the bank. The advantages of this approach may be that the bank can link bonuses and financial performance in a stronger way and hence attract the best traders, who can be expected to obtain the best from a similar performance evaluation and compensation system. Other banks may opt for an entirely different approach, in which a RAP measure (or perhaps more than one RAP measure) may play a role, but in which other quantitative and qualitative elements are considered in performance evaluation and in which internal cooperation rather than competition is favored. These differences tend to form different cultures inside each financial institution, and in any case they require internal consistency of all organizational mechanisms in order to achieve desired results.

A framework that might be useful for addressing these issues has been developed within transaction cost economics. This approach was originally proposed by Williamson (1975, 1981) and was extended, among others, by Ouchi (1979, 1980) and Barney and Ouchi (1985). In order to explain why firms exist and when organizations might be better than pure market mechanisms in handling transactions among individuals, these authors stress the importance of performance ambiguity, i.e., the difficulty of clearly evaluating (1) the performance of a different individual offering a service or a good or (2) the value associated with that performance. Ideally, when performance ambiguity is very low, transactions could be managed through pure market mechanisms, while firms may typically arise when performance ambiguity is higher.

Barney and Ouchi (1985) also discuss the different mechanisms through which transactions can be handled and performance evaluated within an organization, and they distinguish among quasi-markets, bureaucracies, and clans. *Quasi-markets* are basically equivalent to the divisional structure, and they represent a case in which transactions are managed mostly through internal transfer prices (or "quasi-prices"). In quasi-markets, the financial performance of different units may be considered a reasonable measure of the true performance, since performance ambiguity is not too high. When performances become instead more difficult to evaluate since performance ambiguity is higher, transactions can be handled through either bureaucracies or clans. *Bureaucracies* are based on the imposition of rules and on controlling the compliance of individuals to stated rules. *Clans*, in contrast, are based on the presence of shared values and on the trust that potential errors in evaluating performances in single periods would be corrected and repaid in subsequent periods, according to what Ouchi (1980) calls *serial equity*. Therefore, performance evaluation has to be fair on average and through time, rather than in any single period (as in a "quasi-market" mechanism, which would be based on "spot equity," which requires immediate and exact compensation for each individual's performance).

Why is this relevant for a bank that is introducing risk-adjusted performances? The reason is that, on one hand, RAP can be considered a tool for reducing performance ambiguity. Measuring profit only, with no relationship to the risk being taken, clearly represents a situation in which financial performance alone cannot be considered a clean indicator of the contribution of a business unit to the whole bank. Improving performance measurement may be the way to make it possible to move the banks (or some divisions of the bank at least, e.g., the trading and sales division) closer to quasi-market mechanisms. In such a situation, risk-adjusted performances could be the main driver for bonus allocation. A more objective performance measurement and a stronger link between performance and bonuses might help attract the best traders to the bank and then further improve its performance. Therefore, the more aggressive bank, which was described earlier, would try to manage its portfolio of business units through a quasi-market mechanism.

However, there are two risks inherent in this model. First, the bank has to make sure that performance ambiguity is really sufficiently low. This means that the RAP measure must really be able to capture the value created by a certain business unit. It must therefore be possible to evaluate results within a relatively short time horizon, such as one year. This may be fine for trading, at least as long as there is a reliable market price for most of the instruments. Some doubts may still be raised, for instance, about the performance evaluation for trading desks of illiquid long-dated exotic interest rate contracts. At the same time, it may be more difficult for other business units, such as those in which building and maintaining a reputation through time is particularly important but for which there may be volatility in year-to-year results (e.g., IPO advisory), so short-term performances may be unlikely to capture the hidden value of creating a reputation or retaining customer relationships.

A well-known example of a bank totally centering the evaluation and compensation system on individual profits as opposed to teamwork and customer satisfaction was Bankers Trust in the late 1980s and early '90s (see Rogers 1993). Many think this excess of transaction-oriented attitude paved the way for the problems that emerged in 1994 when Procter and Gamble and other customers claimed that the bank had sold them complex derivatives under unfair conditions and without sufficiently explaining the real value and risks of the deals. This litigation generated both direct and reputational losses that strongly deteriorated the competitive position and financial performance of the bank, which was eventually acquired by Deutsche Bank in 1998 (Jorion 2002).

Second, all resources should be managed through a quasi-market. For instance, even human resources will be managed in this way. Therefore, there is no incentive for the head of currency trading to let brilliant young trader grow and move toward a different business unit. If maximizing trading profit were the only criterion, competition would exist on internal resources as well. This may mean that clever traders only have the chance to grow by leaving the bank, that turnover would be higher, and that it would be common to favor people coming from outside against insiders if the former are assumed to be more capable of raising short-term profits. In the mid-1990s I had a sequence of interviews (under the assurance of total anonymity) with different people in two top U.S. financial institutions. The main problems experienced by the most aggressive bank were (1) tough internal competition and consequent frequent conflicts, (2) significant turnover, with the loss of brilliant young traders, who were forced to leave the bank if they wanted either to grow faster or to change business units, and (3) the risk of predatory behavior by a few business unit managers or single traders versus key customers of the bank, in the quest for a product specialist to maximize their short-term performance independent of potential long-term impacts on the quality of the customer relationship.

The other bank, while obviously giving significant importance to RAP measures, was trying to maintain a different internal culture, by stressing the importance of potentially lifelong involvement of most personnel with the bank and the need to favor the growth of key young people across different units. For instance, the head of a trading desk allowing a brilliant young trader to leave the team would have had lower targets to reach for the subsequent year. Bonuses were allocated to larger teams rather than to individuals, and their division was left to the heads of the team, trying to favor expectations for "serial equity" through time rather than "spot equity." In short, while the bank was still an aggressive player on the market, internal mechanisms were a blend of quasi-market and clan mechanisms, as was also evident from the fact that most top managers had spent almost all their working life within that bank. This bank had a different structure of risk control systems, such as VaR limits, and a different style in managing those limits, and evaluated performances on a number of different aspects, including RAP among others.

Of course, even the second model has pitfalls: The bank may be unable to attract talented people from outside (unless they are hired when they are young), since the bank may be perceived as unwilling to provide good career opportunites to outsiders; the more qualitative evaluation may help underperformers hide for a longer time; business unit managers may be too conservative and prudent.

Although these models are markedly different, making a number of intermediate states of nature possible, they both need the internal consistency of the organizational mechanisms that have been designed. Defining both the risk control policies that were discussed in Chapter 7 and RAP measures for business unit managers is difficult precisely because not only does it require solving technical problems (e.g., how to link daily VaR for market risk to a yearly equivalent, how to measure diversification effects for VaR), but it also requires guaranteeing an internal fit among organizational processes, organization structure, and organizational culture, which is not easy to attain, maintain, or sometimes (e.g., after a merge) even re-create entirely.

8.9 Summary

Together with risk control, which is discussed in Chapter 7, risk-adjusted performance (RAP) measurement is the key area in which VaR measures can provide a fundamental contribution to a bank's decision processes. A risk-adjusted performance measure is a profitability measure combining the profit produced by a business and its capital at risk. RAP measures can be built either to support top-management decisions concerning a business or as a target performance measure for the head of a business unit (whose bonus may also depend on achieving the target RAP measure). This difference is important because while measures designed to support decisions should essentially be precise and theoretically correct, when a RAP measure is used as a performance target for an organizational unit, fairness is more relevant than precision, and the key issue is whether or not the target measure is able to produce desired behaviors. After briefly discussing the potential role of transfer prices, cost allocation, and the difference between capital allocation and investment in RAP measures, the chapter analyzed the main key choices in building a RAP measure.

The first decision is whether the measure of capital at risk to be used in the RAP measure should be represented by allocated capital (i.e., the ex ante annualized VaR limit assigned to the unit) or utilized capital (i.e., the ex post annualized actual VaR). While, in order to support top managers' decisions, measures based on utilized CaR may provide a better picture of the business potential profitability, when using a RAP measure as a performance target for a business unit the choice is more complex. In short, if fairness is to be preserved, the choice among allocated CaR, utilized CaR, and a mixture of the two should depend on the business unit's influence on the capital allocation the unit is granted by the bank's headquarters.

The second decision is whether the CaR measure should be the stand-alone CaR of the business or a measure of "diversified" CaR that takes into account the contribution of the business to the risk of the bank as a whole (which depends on the correlations between the business and the rest of the bank's portfolio and the overall business mix of the bank). When providing information to top managers, measures based on diversified CaR can be particularly relevant, since they help top managers assess the interaction of a business with a bank's portfolio. However, since diversified CaR measures are influenced by changes in correlations and business mix, they may be perceived as unfair as target measures if correlations were unstable or the business mix changed substantially; hence, stand-alone CaR could be preferred for this purpose.

The third choice is related to using a measure based on a ratio of profits to capital at risk (such as RAROC, risk-adjusted return on capital) or on the difference between profits and the cost of capital at risk (such as the bank-specific variant of EVA). In reality, the two different measures tend to provide complementary information and should not be viewed as rigid alternatives.

Finally, we discussed the role of RAP measures in performance evaluation and compensation since we must remember that even if RAP measures represent a substantial improvement in profitability measurement, they do not necessarily represent the only parameter to be used to evaluate the performance of an organization or a business unit. Therefore, the choice of the philosophy of the evaluation and compensation system, which has a relevant impact on organizational unit behavior and internal coordination mechanisms, should be carefully studied. Large banks with the same available risk measurement technology might make different decisions on this issue, and at the same time the behavioral consequences of the apparently technical decisions concerning the design of a RAP measure should always be monitored with care.

8.10   Further Reading

A general reference for the discussion of risk-adjusted performance measurement issue is Matten (2000); see also Bessis (2002). The measures of diversified CaR are discussed in Merton and Perold (1993), Garman (1996, 1997), Saita (1999a), and Matten (2000). The pros and cons of EVA versus RAROC have been debated in Zaik et al. (1996) and also, in a different framework, by Stoughton and Zechner (2000). For the application of EVA to banks, see Uyemura, Kantor, and Pettit (1996).

CHAPTER ◆ 9

Risk-Adjusted Performance Targets, Capital Allocation, and the Budgeting Process

After considering risk control through VaR-based limits and risk-adjusted performance measurement, we can now discuss the final step of the capital allocation process. While capital allocation has sometimes been addressed in more theoretical settings by a number of important papers (Froot and Stein 1998; Perold 1999; Stoughton and Zechner 1999, 2000; Denault 2001), in practice it represents an organizational process that is deeply intertwined with the strategy formation process. Just like corporate strategy, it can alternate between periods of sharp radical changes and periods of incremental changes. The former may lead to an abrupt reallocation of capital and other resources to new businesses that are perceived to offer the potential for higher risk-adjusted return. The latter may imply marginal (but sometimes repeated) capital reallocations deriving from the bank's learning process about which businesses appear to be able to deliver superior performances to shareholders. As a consequence, reallocations should always be driven by future expected performances. But past performances may also still play a role. In fact, a capital reallocation may derive from a strategic decision that has little to do with past numbers and is based largely on a forecast (think about a decision concerning an acquisition or the choice to expand geographically or to enter into a new product niche). But sometimes, instead, a capital reallocation may, at least in part, be the reaction to the satisfactory or unsatisfactory performances of certain existing business units.

For these reasons, we devote this chapter to two main topics. The first is the definition of performance targets for the different business units. Performance targets are important because the ability to reach or not reach these targets can influence top managers' perceptions about business unit profitability. Therefore, understanding the ways in which a cost of equity capital for the bank could be derived and how it could be translated into a return target for the different business units is relevant for the "learning-based" capital allocation process (Sections 9.1 and 9.2). The second main topic is the capital allocation process and, in particular, its links with the planning and budgeting process, which is discussed in Section 9.3 and illustrated in Section 9.4 (through the Unicredit Group case study).

9.1 From the Bank's Cost of Equity Capital to Performance Targets for the Bank

The first issue is to determine how a target return for the bank can be defined. We discuss first how to estimate the bank's cost of equity capital and then how to translate that into a return target for the bank.

9.1.1 Estimating the Cost of Equity Capital

The starting point in determining performance targets is to understand the return that shareholders would require from the bank as a whole, i.e., the bank's cost of equity capital. The classic solution to derive a cost of equity capital for the whole bank is to resort to the Capital Asset Pricing Model (CAPM), according to which the expected return on a risky asset, $E(r_i)$, should be

$$E(r_i) = r_f + \beta_i[E(r_m) - r_f] = r_f + \rho_{i,m}\frac{\sigma_i}{\sigma_m}[E(r_m) - r_f]$$

where r_f is the risk-free rate, $E(r_m)$ is the expected return on the market portfolio, and β_i is the beta of the risky asset (i.e., the bank's stock), equal to the correlation between stock and market portfolio returns ($\rho_{i,m}$) times the ratio between the volatility of stock returns σ_i and the volatility of market portfolio returns σ_m. Therefore, the target return on capital k_e that can be used as a target for RAROC or that can enter into EVA calculation could be set equal (as a first approximation) to $E(r_i)$ in the CAPM equation. Given the difficulty in practice of identifying the market portfolio (which in theory would comprise all risky assets available to investors), a broad stock market index is usually adopted as a proxy, and the component $E(r_m) - r_f$ is approximated by the long-term historical average excess return of the market index r_{mkt} over the risk-free rate, i.e., $r_{mkt} - r_f$ (typical values are around 5% for the United States and the UK and slightly lower, around 4%, for continental Europe; see for instance Matten 2000; Damodaran 2001).

While the limitations of the traditional version of the CAPM are well known (just consider Fama and French 1992, 1993), for most banks its simplicity still represents a remarkable advantage, and the usual problems are then the choice of the risk-free rate and the estimation of the bank's beta. As far as the risk-free rate is concerned, the typical alternatives are the yields of either a long-term Treasury bond or a short-term (1-year) Treasury bill. The estimate of the bank's stock beta can be made in different ways. One of the most common is to calculate *historical beta*, by computing β_i as $\rho_{i,mkt}\sigma_i/\sigma_{mkt}$ through a sample of historical returns of the bank's stock and of the market index (used again as a substitute for the market portfolio). Historical betas, which can also easily be obtained from market information providers, can be corrected to take into account changes in fundamental characteristics of the firm (e.g., its leverage or the volatility of its earnings) that may have an impact on beta. If the bank is not listed, the analyst should resort to solutions such as *bottom-up betas* (i.e., reconstructing betas as a weighted average of the betas of the different businesses the bank is in, based on betas of listed mono-business competitors) or *accounting betas* (i.e., estimating correlations and volatilities by using changes in accounting earnings for the bank and the stock market rather than returns, since they would not be available for the bank). Bottom-up betas and accounting betas suffer from the same problems already described in Chapter 5 when discussing alternative solutions for business risk measurement: Bottom-up betas may often be hard to determine due to the absence of mono-business competitors (even if some bank equity reports provide some useful insights about analysts' views on the betas of different banking businesses), while the quality of accounting betas depends on the quality of the accounting data, which may be conditioned by earning-smoothing practices, changes in accounting treatment of relevant items, and infrequent data (which are at best quarterly). Therefore, the choice of which method to use to estimate betas will depend on the bank's evaluation of the different pros and cons of alternative solutions as well as on data availability.

9.1.2 Defining the Target Rate of Return

The bank's cost of equity does not necessarily represent the target return of capital for the bank. In fact, by providing a return equal to the bank's cost of equity, the bank would not create value for its shareholders, but simply maintain it. As a consequence, top managers may decide to set a higher and more challenging target return as the starting point of the target negotiation process with the business units.

When doing so, however, potential consequences on business unit returns should be considered. In particular, if business units were evaluated based on EVA, and EVA were calculated on utilized CaR only (rather than on allocated capital), a higher target return might suggest to business unit managers to refuse more investment opportunities. In fact, even those whose expected return is equal to or greater than the cost of equity capital for the bank but lower than the higher target return on capital set by the bank would produce a negative EVA and may then be rejected. Potentially, this may lead to lower utilized capital and hence a lower return for the bank as a whole.

Moreover, even if the target return were set equal to the cost of equity capital, this would not represent the target RAROC for the bank as a whole. In fact (apart from the effect of taxes), we must take into consideration the following.

1. Total capital at risk (over which RAROC may be calculated) may be lower than total available capital for the bank, and this implies that remuneration for excess capital has to be accounted for.
2. While the cost of equity capital is the remuneration shareholders require on the market capitalization of the bank, return targets are often expressed in terms of return over the book value of equity.

As far as the first issue is concerned, let us assume, for instance, that total available capital for the bank is 500 and total allocated capital is 450, where 50 is a capital buffer that top managers consider necessary to protect against risks that are not perfectly measured or to preserve the bank from default in stress scenarios. If this were the case, if the profit target required to satisfy shareholder expectations were, say, 50, or 10% of total capital, the target return on allocated capital should be equal to $50/450 = 11.1\%$, since unallocated capital will not produce profits. Further corrections may be required to account for taxes (shareholders would require a return net of taxes, while the bank should define a pretax return target for business units) and for the difference between utilized and allocated capital at the business unit level, if utilized capital is used for performance evaluation (if 20% of allocated capital were unused, target performances on utilized capital should be raised further).

The second problem can be clarified by considering the difference between the cost of equity capital measured, for instance, by the CAPM equation and ROE (return on equity, i.e., the ratio between the net profit and the book value of equity). If we consider a bank whose market capitalization is 1500 with a cost of equity capital equal to 10%, the minimum profit would be 150 = 10% × 1500. If the book value of equity of the bank is 1000, the required ROE would be 150/1000 = 15%. In practice, if the price-to-book-value ratio (P/BV), defined as the ratio between the market capitalization of the bank and its book value of equity, is 1.5, then the target ROE would be equal to the cost of equity capital (10%) times the P/BV ratio (1.5) (see also Matten 2000). This correction may or may not be necessary, depending on whether the bank is defining targets through a capital-at-risk measure based on market capitalization at risk (MCaR) or book capital at risk (BCaR).

In fact, in the former case there would be no need to account for the difference between the book value of equity and market capitalization. It would be sufficient to increase target returns to account for unallocated capital. If BCaR were used, instead, target performance should be corrected on aggregate based on the bank's P/BV ratio. The difference between the two methods is illustrated in Table 9-1 with an example.

It must be noted that the choice of either BCaR or MCaR as the driver for allocating target profits to the different business units may have an impact on individual business unit targets, especially for those units exposed mainly to business risk and for which, as discussed in Chapter 5, the difference between BCaR and MCaR could be material. The potential effect can be illustrated through a simplified example based on Figure 9-1, which reports BCaR and MCaR values for the three different business units of Bank Gamma and for the bank as a whole (under a set of assumptions on correlations among different risks).

Differences between BCaR and MCaR have been assumed to exist for credit risk (assuming that loan portfolio VaR would change by moving from a non-mark-to-market to a mark-to-market approach) and for business risk (where we have assumed that MCaR is 20 times larger than BCaR). In both cases, total CaR is lower than available capital (i.e., BCaR is lower than book value of capital and MCaR is lower than capitalization). According to the target returns on either BCaR or MCaR calculated in Table 9-1, target profit requested of the different business units would change markedly, obviously increasing target profits for those units that face a higher business risk (see Figure 9-2).

TABLE 9-1   Target Setting Based on Book Capital at Risk versus Market Capitalization at Risk

Setting Targets Based on Market Capitalization at Risk		Setting Targets Based on Book Capital at Risk	
Capitalization	1700	Book value of equity	1000
Market capitalization at risk (MCaR)	1460.62	Book capital at risk (BCaR)	880.10
Unallocated CaR/MCaR	16.4%	Unallocated CaR/BCaR	12.6%
Target return for shareholders (on market capitalization)	10%	Target return for shareholders (on market capitalization)	10%
Required return on MCaR [10% × (1 + 16.4%)]	11.64%	Target return for shareholders (on book value of equity) [10% × 1.7]	17%
		Required return on BCaR [17% × (1 + 12.6%)]	19.14%

Book Capital at Risk

	Market Risk	Credit Risk	Operational Risk	Business Risk	Total After Inter-BU Diversification
Trading	100		150	5	149.10
Lending		600	250		513.59
Asset management			300	50	225.41
			Total CaR		888.10
			Book capital		1000	+12.60%

Market Capitalization at Risk

	Market Risk	Credit Risk	Operational Risk	Business Risk	Total After Inter-BU Diversification
Trading	100		150	100	179.11
Lending		720	250		544.27
Asset management			300	1000	737.23
			Total CaR		1460.62
			Book capital		1700	+16.39%

FIGURE 9-1   Example of differences between BCaR and MCaR for Bank Gamma.

(A) Driver = book CaR

Target return for shareholders	10.0%
Target return on book capital	17.0%
Target return on book CaR	19.1%

(B) Driver = capitalization at risk

Target return for shareholders	10.0%
Target return on CaR	11.6%

Book Capital at Risk	Total After Inter-BU Diversification	Target Earnings
Trading/ALM	149.10	28.54
Lending	513.59	98.31
Asset mgmt	225.41	43.15
Total Car	888.10	170
Book capital	1000.00	

Market

Capitalization at Risk	Total After Inter-BU Diversification	Target Earnings
Trading/ALM	179.11	20.85 (↓)
Lending	544.27	63.85 (↓)
Asset mgmt	737.23	85.81 (↑)
Total CaR	1460.62	170
Capitalization	1700.00	

FIGURE 9-2   Example of the impact of using BCaR rather than MCaR on the definition of target profit.

While the numbers in the example are meant to support the intuition behind the effect of different drivers, in order to check whether or not the difference is material, reliable capital-at-risk measures for business risk would be needed. We only want to make the point that choosing either MCaR or BCaR as the driver for target profit allocation is relevant because it may affect target profits required of business units with different exposures to business risk. Implicitly, by simply setting the target return on (book) capital to P/BV times the return on the market capitalization estimated through the CAPM, the bank would be assuming that all businesses are participating in the same way to produce that P/BV ratio, whereas this may not be the case from an analyst's viewpoint. Of course, we are not claiming that the definition of profit targets in most banks is the result of a purely technical process that starts from a strict CAPM-compliant definition of target returns and then mechanically derives target profits by following the right-hand side of Table 9-1. For instance, target profits depend largely on past profits achieved by the business unit and on a forward-looking evaluation of the market's potential growth in the future as well as on a number of other quantitative and qualitative elements that should be — and typically are — taken into consideration in the planning and budgeting process. Still, the simplified scheme in Table 9-1, with some variations, can be used to define ex post which is the return that should have been produced by each unit in order to provide the right contribution to the bank's overall results, or it can be used to define the cost of capital at risk in ex post EVA calculations. If this is the case, the way in which the target cost of capital is defined could affect top managers' perceptions about which business areas/units are over- or underperforming, which may still be relevant from a capital allocation viewpoint.

9.2   Should Business Units' Target Returns Be Different?

The next logical step is to move from the bank's target return on total allocated CaR to assigning target returns to individual business units. Apparently, it could be as simple as taking the target (pretax) RAROC for the bank and assigning it to each single business unit, with no correction. The argument to support this choice would be that even if different business units have different risks, this is taken into consideration when calculating CaR for the business units. Riskier business units would be assigned higher CaR, and then requiring the same return on different amounts of capital at risk would imply asking higher profits of riskier business units.

Unfortunately, the solution is not that simple. The conceptual problem is that while shareholders should in theory require being compensated for systematic risk only, CaR for each business unit is not based on systematic risk, but considers total risk. At best, it may take into account diversification benefits within the bank, but it would still consider a component of idiosyncratic risk at the bank level.

Therefore, it is highly uncertain that applying the same target return on different CaR levels would guarantee that each business unit is producing a return consistent with its contribution to systematic risk (Bessis 2002). In other words, the problem derives from the need to combine the shareholders' perspective (which requires a given return based on both the leverage of the bank and the mix of its businesses, which may have different exposures to systematic risk, but should, according to portfolio theory, be concerned with systematic risk only) and the debt holders' and supervisors' perspectives (since rating agencies as well as supervisors are concerned with the amount of capital needed to prevent the bank from default and therefore interested in idiosyncratic risk as well, with the ability in the case of supervisors to impose a minimum-capital constraint).

While in practice no clear way has been found to reconcile these two views, trying to consider both of them when assessing results and setting targets is important. There are at least two issues worth being discussed in more detail. The first is the potential risk of favoring high-risk businesses if the side effects of increasing their weight on the bank's beta are neglected. The second issue is how divisional betas for banks' macro-business units could be derived if the bank were willing to adopt a differentiated cost-of-equity-capital approach. In short, the two main points we would like to make are the following.

1. With flat return targets set for all units, those with higher systematic risk may find it easier to exceed the target returns' hurdle. Therefore, before simply increasing capital allocation to those units that have achieved a higher RAROC in the past, the bank should check the potential effects in terms of increased cost of equity capital for the bank as a whole.
2. It is conceptually possible and useful to calculate different betas for the different businesses of the bank. But when setting profit targets, the target returns obtained through those betas should be more consistently applied to the share of the market capitalization that derives from each of the businesses (as is estimated by bank analysts using a sum-of-parts valuation), whereas applying them to CaR values may be more problematic.

9.2.1 Potential Effects of a Single Hurdle Rate

By defining a flat target RAROC (or by calculating EVA applying the same cost of equity capital) for all businesses, the bank implicitly affirms that the units that are going to produce the highest RAROC will be considered as the best performers. From an ex ante perspective, then, businesses with the higher expected RAROC would be allocated a higher share of the bank's capital at risk. Nevertheless, by doing so, the bank may favor high-risk businesses relative to low-risk businesses, and this might increase the cost of the bank's equity capital. As a consequence, the increase in RAROC would not necessarily create extra value, since target return required by shareholders would grow as well.

The potential interaction between the riskiness of the business and the cost of equity capital was illustrated first by Crouhy, Turnbull, and Wakeman (1999), who describe the problem considering a mono-business bank investing in a risky asset whose expected return $E(r_A)$ is consistent with the CAPM equation, i.e.,

$$E(r_A) = r_f + \rho \frac{\sigma_A}{\sigma_M}[E(r_M) - r_f] = r_f + \beta_A[E(r_M) - r_f]$$

where r_f is the risk-free return, σ_A and σ_M represent return volatilities of the risky asset and the market portfolio, respectively, ρ is the return correlation between asset and market portfolio returns, $E(r_M)$ is the market portfolio's expected return, and β_A is the beta of the risky asset. In equilibrium, an increase in σ_A should imply an increase in expected return. Crouhy, Turnbull, and Wakeman (1999) also assume that while the investment is financed by debt, equity capital is maintained to cover potential losses up to a given confidence level (so as to keep probability of default constant). The numerical results are reported in Table 9-2.

The example in Table 9-2 shows how RAROC increases as σ_A increases, even if the probability of default is kept constant. Hence, according to Crouhy, Turnbull, and Wakeman (1999) riskier investments may be privileged if the bank defined a hurdle rate equal for all business units. In order to avoid this risk, they suggest adopting as the hurdle rate the *adjusted* RAROC, given by

$$\text{Adjusted RAROC} = \frac{\text{RAROC} - r_f}{\beta_E}$$

TABLE 9-2   RAROC and Asset Volatility

Risk-free rate, r_f	5.13%
Market portfolio expected return, $E(r_M)$	12%
Market portfolio expected excess return, $E(r_M) - r_f$	6.87%
Market portfolio return volatility, σ_M	15%
Correlation among asset and market portfolio returns, ρ	0.25
Time horizon	1 year

(1) Asset return volatility (σ_A)	(2) Expected return on the asset (%) $E(r_A)$	(3) CaR (for each dollar invested in the risky asset)	(4) RAROC (%)	(5) Adjusted RAROC (%)
5%	5.70	0.1063	10.46	6.88
10%	6.27	0.2032	10.71	6.88
20%	7.42	0.3716	11.25	6.88
40%	9.71	0.6207	12.48	6.88

Source: Crouhy, Turnbull, and Wakeman (1999).

where β_E is the bank's stock equity beta, which here simply depends on β_A and leverage. The criteria for accepting an investment should then be that the adjusted RAROC be greater than the market portfolio expected return:

$$\frac{\text{RAROC} - r_f}{\beta_E} > E(R_M) - r_f$$

Adjusted RAROC (see the last column of Table 9-2) does not depend on σ_A (since higher σ_A implies a simultaneous increase for RAROC and β_E) and in this case is consistent with the equity market risk premium, since the asset return is aligned with the CAPM equation.

In reality, even if we did not use a different version RAROC, the key relevant message by Crouhy, Turnbull, and Wakeman (1999) is that different businesses may contribute in a different way to the bank's equity beta. The criteria to accept an investment could in fact be easily restated as

$$\text{RAROC} - r_f > \beta_E[E(R_M) - r_f]$$

This logic could also be applied to different business units by considering different betas for each business. Of course this would then require the ability to estimate them.

9.2.2 *Estimating Betas for Different Businesses*

Defining different target rates of returns for different businesses would require estimating divisional betas for the bank. Traditionally, there are two main methods to determine divisional betas (Damodaran 2001):

1. Bottom-up estimates, based on publicly available betas of listed mono-business players (also known as the pure-play approach)
2. Accounting betas

TABLE 9-3   Beta Estimates for Different Businesses within Banking Groups

Variables	Parameter Estimates (standard error in parentheses)	
	Base Model	**Country of Domicile and Leverage Effects**
Adj-R^2 (F-Stat)	87.9% (466***)	89.1% (441***)
k_0 — Europe dummy		−0.56*** (0.13)
k_1 — Leverage effect		70.2*** (16.4)
β_1 — Commercial banking	1.21** (0.14)	1.36** (0.13)
β_2 — Retail banking	1.23** (0.09)	1.02** (0.09)
β_3 — Asset management	1.67** (0.11)	1.44** (0.11)
β_4 — Life insurance	0.94** (0.09)	0.87** (0.11)
β_5 — P&C insurance	1.05** (0.12)	0.93** (0.16)
β_6 — Equity investment banking	4.34** (0.85)	3.85** (0.93)
β_7 — Fixed-income investment banking	1.50* (0.70)	1.41* (0.57)

* Significant at a >10% confidence level
** Significant at a >5% confidence level
*** Significant at a >1% confidence level
Source: Wilson 2003.

In the first case, stand-alone business competitors should be identified. But, again, this is extremely difficult for all businesses in the case of large diversified groups, even if bottom-up estimates can be used as a check for those businesses for which listed mono-business competitors exist. Accounting betas, despite their limitations, which have already been described in Section 9.1, may then represent one of the few available solutions.

However, an alternative approach has been proposed by Wilson (2003), who strongly advocates the need for a differentiated beta for different businesses. Wilson suggests that businesses' beta could be derived through a regression from listed banks' betas, provided that earnings deriving from different businesses (or allocated capital, if available) could be used as a proxy for the weights to be assigned to industries for the same bank. According to the simpler of four different models tested in his paper, industry betas $\hat{\beta}_i$ can be estimated from observed levered betas of firms $l = 1, 2, \ldots, n$ at time t through the relationship

$$\beta_t^l = \sum_{i=1}^n \omega_{i,t}^l \hat{\beta}_i + \varepsilon_t^l$$

where $\omega_{i,t}$ represents the weight for each bank of industry i (estimated based on the percentage of earnings deriving from the industry) and ε is the error term of the regression. Different equations are also proposed to account for differences in banks' leverage and country. For instance, the equation that Wilson (2003) suggests in order to consider leverage and country of domicile is

$$\beta_t^l = (1 + k_1 p^*) \sum_{i=1}^n \omega_{i,t}^l \hat{\beta}_i^{(1+k_0 d)} + \varepsilon_t^l$$

where k_1 and p^* respectively represent the leverage parameter to be estimated and the three-year cumulative probability of default based on the observed credit rating of the bank and d and k_0 represent, respectively, the dummy variable and the constant term to be considered for continental European companies. Wilson (2003) finds that implied beta derived from this regression for different business areas could vary substantially, with much lower values for insurance and retail banking and much higher values for equity investment banking (see Table 9-3), and he concludes that failing to consider this differentiation in divisional betas may imply misperceptions in different business areas' profitability and hence also in top-management decisions.

9.2.3 Applying Different Costs of Capital: Identifying the Driver

If a bank decided to adopt different betas and hence different return targets for the different businesses, there is still the problem of identifying the proper driver to which the different costs of equity capital or return targets should be applied. Apparently, the simpler solution would clearly be to use estimated CaR for each division. But the theoretical problem in this case is that while the different cost of capital/target return estimated based on the CAPM would assume that the investor requires a return based on systematic risk only, CaR for different business units considers idiosyncratic risk as well, and it could then be questioned whether the component CaR of a business unit can serve as the right driver.

A potential alternative, when proper data are available, would be to apply different target returns to the share of the value of the firm that can be attributed to each business, according to external analysts' reports or to internal estimates developed by the planning department and that replicate analysts' methodologies. In fact, banks are sometimes evaluated by analysts (even if practices differ between the United States and Europe) through the sum-of-parts method, i.e., by adding separate evaluations for different businesses (which can be valued, for instance, through different P/E multiples). In Table 9-4, an example is presented, based on a real case, whose data have been slightly modified, simplified, and rescaled for confidentiality, though it still represents a realistic application of the sum-of-parts method by an equity analyst.

When these data are available or can be calculated internally by replicating analysts' evaluations, then the relative value of the different divisions can be used as the relevant driver. Problems in this case may derive from the potential uncertainty in how analysts (and ultimately investors) would decompose the value of the bank, which may potentially lead to discussions with the business unit managers involved in the process. The potential variations through time and across analysts of the decomposition of the value of the bank may also be an issue. Using an internal estimate derived by the planning department could

TABLE 9-4   Example of Sum-of-Parts Valuation for a European Banking Group

Division	Profit	P/E	Value
Retail banking	668.4	10.6	7,057.6
Consumer credit	191.2	11.2	2,150.8
Trading	361.2	9.2	3,318.0
Asset management and private banking	207.6	13.2	2,738.8
Wholesale banking	64.8	23.0	1,490.8
Total	1,493.2	11.2	16,756.0

solve this problem but might, at least apparently, introduce some subjectivity and discretionary power that business unit managers may dislike.

Given the pros and cons of the two alternative solutions, a bank might therefore choose either (1) to set targets in terms of absolute profits based on different costs of capital applied to business unit estimated values or (2) to set targets based on allocated CaR (possibly based on an MCaR framework rather than a BCaR one) or (3) to set targets in a more subjective way by taking into consideration results from both (1) and (2). Given that the process of setting targets also has to consider the real potential market perspectives of different businesses, adopting a combined approach often appears a reasonable way to proceed, unless a better synthesis can be found. While important contributions such as that of Froot and Stein (1998) have in fact addressed in a very clear theoretical framework the interaction between systematic risk and bank-specific idiosyncratic risk in banks' decisions about capital budgeting, capital structure and risk management, extensions to the more realistic framework of a bank's day-to-day decision-making process are still missing. Therefore, managing the business mix at the bank level and orienting the decision-making processes of business unit leaders through careful target setting unavoidably requires a considerable amount of human judgment.

9.3   Capital Allocation and the Planning and Budgeting Process

When VaR limits are defined for the first time in a bank for the different business units, the first capital allocation is being made. In a number of banks, initial VaR limits have basically been defined by measuring current VaR and adding some buffer (e.g., by setting a VaR limit of 120 to a desk whose average VaR was 90). The critical issue is how and through which process this initial capital allocation can be modified through time. Reallocation may be the result of a significant strategic choice (e.g., an acquisition or a merger, or the decision to enter into a certain business) adopted by the board or by top managers with an ad hoc process, but it may also be one of the outputs of the periodic strategic planning and budgeting process inside the bank or even of infra-annual decisions of a risk committee. While it is difficult to discuss in general terms the ad hoc reallocation process that are defined as a part of major strategic decisions, we can briefly analyze the links between the strategic planning and capital allocation. In any case, this discussion should not obscure that this is only one of the possible ways in which capital reallocation can occur and that relatively smaller and less complex financial institutions (including some top wholesale investment banks with only a limited number of risk-taking legal entities around the globe and a wider number of local subsidiaries that do not undertake risk directly) might have a much faster planning and budgeting process than large banking groups and handle capital allocation in an entirely different way.

Generally, capital reallocation is far from being frictionless. While reallocating capital among trading desks is relatively easy, reallocating capital among large legal entities may not be. Simply profitably increasing the capital allocated to credit risk is much more complex than increasing exposure to market risks, since new customers willing to pay a proper risk-adjusted rate on loans must be searched for and subtracted from competitors. Similarly, reducing credit risk exposure requires more time and caution than simply offsetting one exposure with an opposite one on the foreign exchange market. As a consequence, most capital reallocation decisions represent incremental movements toward a desired long-term objective rather than sharp reoptimizations, since the bank could not be considered a typical asset management portfolio. We should also consider realistically that, since business units are typically run by managers with a desire for growth and an aversion to downsizing the business units they are in charge of, capital reallocation might also be a process implying some political component, as it is unavoidable in decisional processes in large organizations (see Pfeffer 1992). As a consequence, we must honestly admit that the way in which the capital allocation process is usually structured (along with a crucial issue such as its degree of centralization or decentralization) reflects not only the distribution of relevant information among the bank's corporate center and the business units (e.g., their relative ability to define reasonable target returns for the business units or to consider potential synergies and interdependencies among different units), but also, up to a certain extent, the distribution of power among the different players inside the bank.

9.3.1   Why Should Capital Allocation Be Linked to the Planning Process?

If we consider whether the capital reallocation process should be a part of the planning and budgeting process, there are a number of reasons to link them strictly. First, in a large complex organization the planning process represents a crucial way to integrate business unit and top management expectations on the growth and profitability of different businesses. Especially for large diversified groups, which comprise many different divisions (from commercial banking to investment banking to insurance) and are present in a number of countries, a careful planning process is also important to check capital needs in terms of both regulatory capital and economic capital, to define priorities for growth at the group level, to identify proper risk-adjusted targets for the different divisions and legal entities, and to understand which capital management plans may be needed at the group level (from defining core capital-raising strategies in the medium term to identifying opportunities for saving regulatory capital). It would then be natural to consider the economic capital reallocation process as a part of the periodic planning and budgeting cycle.

Second, since the planning and budgeting process allows corporate headquarters to negotiate the profit targets for future periods with all business units, it would seem strange to negotiate the amount of capital at risk (which is generally a key resource for reaching those profit targets) separately. Third, if the planning and budgeting process is sufficiently participative (i.e., its outcomes are not the result of the views either only of corporate headquarters or only of top business units, as may happen if the organizational power of the two is completely unbalanced), then business unit responsibility in reaching the targets and efficiently using all allocated capital should be higher. This may also have a positive impact on avoiding large amounts of unutilized capital, as discussed in Chapter 8.

9.3.2   Why Should Capital Allocation Not Be Linked to the Planning Process?

At the same time, there are reasons why linking capital allocation only to the planning process might be dangerous. In short, the risks derive from the quality of the planning process itself. If the planning process were unable to produce good strategic decisions, then even the capital reallocation process might be weak and inconclusive. At best, the overall process may support capital management plans at corporate headquarters levels without really helping to optimize the risk–return profile of the bank by efficiently real-locating existing capital to those businesses that most deserve it.

There has always been a wide debate in the strategic management literature about the positive or negative role of the strategic planning process in the strategic decision-making process (see for instance Ansoff 1991, 1994; Goold 1992; Mintzberg 1990b, 1994). Opponents of the strategic planning process typically claim that a strategic planning process tends to become a number-crunching exercise that has little to do with real strategy making. Strategic options are usually limited, projects whose results are more easily quantifiable tend to be favored, and decisions are made at the end of the process even when the necessary information is still insufficient. According to this view, the success of firms with a complex planning process would be motivated by the fact that, luckily, not all strategic decisions are made during the strategic planning process.

While entering into the debate between supporters and opponents of the strategic planning process is outside the scope of this book, recalling this debate may be useful for two reasons. First, even in a bank where the capital allocation process and the planning and budgeting process are strictly linked (and we have seen that there may be reasons to do so), one should carefully check which processes could be designed to facilitate (1) faster reallocation when needed and (2) a higher usage rate of available capital. For instance, if strategic plan forecasts about the economic outlook for the year appear to be wrong in March, how could a reallocation of risk-taking capacity take place to reduce potential capital excesses in some business units? Of course, this is a relevant role for group risk committees, which could be used not only to handle problems of risk peaks or shortage of capital at risk in a fast and efficient way, but also to make infra-annual decisions about improving the efficiency of capital allocation. It may then be useful to allow for flexibility in capital allocation whenever possible, even when the main revisions are linked to the planning process.

Second, the strategic planning debate should stimulate a continual assessment of the process to avoid making it a purely formal, backward-looking exercise. An example might help describe the problem. In some banks wishing to integrate the capital allocation process in their planning and budgeting process, negotiation of profit targets and allocated capital has been linked through the target RAROC set by top managers. For instance, after the planning department and the business unit manager agreed over a profit target equal to 100 for the next year, a consistent capital allocation is defined based on the RAROC target set by the planning department. For instance, given a 20% RAROC target (i.e., 1 USD of profit for each 5 USD of capital at risk), a profit target of 100 would be consistent with a capital allocation of 500 (i.e., 100/20%). The advantage of this way of linking profit targets and allocated capital is that (1) the allocation is consistent with top managers' desired risk-adjusted profitability and (2) the process is quick and simple, since capital allocation is just a simple final step following the classic negotiation of the profit target. But at the same time, such a process could hardly produce a forward-looking, optimizing capital allocation. In fact, future profit targets are frequently largely dependent on a previous year ex post result, with the consequence that, all else being equal, business units with the highest profits in year 1 would be assigned higher profit targets in year 2 and hence more capital at risk. Allocating capital based mostly on past performances can of course be quite dangerous. No investment manager would systematically overweight asset classes that overperformed in the past; he would rather look for those that have chances to overperform in the future.

In summary, the planning and budgeting process can play a relevant role in the capital allocation process, provided that:

1. Capital allocation can and should occur, even independent of the annual planning process (in a number of cases, substantial reallocations may derive from strategic choices made outside the planning process and may force substantial plan revisions).
2. The planning process should be designed and periodically checked so as to avoid making capital allocation a purely mechanical exercise. If this were the case, the planning and budgeting process could still maintain an important role in coordinating capital management decisions, but it would be unlikely to support substantial and anticipatory changes in capital allocation.
3. Especially for those business units that might be faster in reallocating capital internally (e.g., trading and capital markets divisions), this flexibility must be safeguarded by allowing for infra-annual reallocation of capital, without linking it too strictly to the planning process alone. Group risk committees could be given the role of checking the consistency of proposed changes.

9.4   Case Study: Capital Allocation Process at UniCredit Group (by Elio Berti, head of Capital Allocation, CFO Department, UniCredit)

9.4.1   UniCredit Group Capital Allocation Process and Criteria

In UniCredit Group the consolidated shareholders' equity, i.e., the capital, plays a crucial role in the main corporate governance processes that drive strategic decisions. The Group's capital, in fact, is considered one of the main key factors of the planning process, because on one hand it represents the shareholders' investment, on which they have expected return, and on the other hand it is a scarce resource subject to external constraints set by supervisors. Hence, the capital allocation process is finalized to support maximizing the creation of shareholder value through planning, allocating, and managing the Group's capital in the most efficient way to compose the best banking group business mix that should realize a return (dividends and capital gain) higher than expectations (cost of equity).

To optimize the business mix and the creation of shareholder value, capital allocation is supported by an internally developed multiperiod risk-adjusted performance measurement (RAPM) methodology that allows the measuring of strategy effectiveness. The UniCredit Group capital allocation framework considers two different capital definitions: risk or invested capital represents shareholder investment, whose expected return is the cost of equity; capital at risk is the part of the risk capital that faces the risk that could be taken (allocated capital) or that has been taken (absorbed capital) to achieve profitability and value creation targets.

The invested capital is important for assigning shareholder value-creation targets and for measuring value-creation performance (EVA calculation). The capital at risk, in contrast, is important for linking the analysis of the value creation with the risk-adjusted performance measurement (through risk-adjusted return on risk-adjusted capital, RARORAC). The capital at risk depends on the propensity for risk and on the capitalization target level defined to grant the Group's target credit rating. For these reasons, it is measured considering both economic capital (i.e., the real part of the invested capital at risk measured via a probabilistic model for a given confidence interval) and core Tier 1 regulatory capital (the part of regulatory capital represented by shareholder equity).

Economic and regulatory capital are two different ways to represent group exposure. They differ on the categories of risk, on the definitions of risk factors, and on measurement approaches. Economic capital should be the true exposure measurement, but, of course, controlling regulatory capital according to Capital Adequacy Directive (CAD) is equally necessary. Given the two definitions of capital at risk, economic and regulatory, the capital allocation process follows a "double-headed" approach. Allocated capital, at every level of the Group's organization, is in fact the maximum of economic and regulatory (Core Tier 1) capital. The same applies to absorbed capital, even though allocated capital is calculated during the budget and the strategic planning processes and absorbed capital is calculated during the control process.

When economic capitalizing is greater than regulatory capital, the "double-headed" approach allows allocating the real capital at risk, which the supervisory rules are unable to measure. When regulatory capital is greater than economic capital, it allows allocating capital with respect to the supervisory limits, considering their inefficiency and cost. The level of regulatory capital allocation derives from the definition of a core Tier 1 ratio target in line with minimum regulatory capital requirements and with the average capitalization level of European Banking Groups with a credit rating equal to the Group's targeted credit rating.

The risk categories considered in computing Bank for International Settlements (BIS I) regulatory capital and the subsequent allocation are credit risk, market risk, and other requirements (e.g., securitization first losses). Economic capital represents the real risk exposure of the business mix portfolio. It is measured by stochastic models that adopt a confidence interval consistent with the capitalization target level and the regulatory capital.

The measurement of economic capital is derived by integrating the main risk categories faced: credit risk, trading and banking book market risk, operational risk, and business risk (represented by fee margin volatility). At UniCredit Group, the risk integration model is still under development. Therefore, at present, economic capital data for the Group and its business units are incomplete and unavailable. Where data on economic capital are not available, they are assumed equal to those for regulatory capital.

9.4.2 Setting of Value-Creation and Capital Allocation Targets within Planning and Control Processes

In UniCredit Group, the Capital Allocation unit, belonging to CFO Department, contributed (and is still contributing) to improving the traditional planning and control processes, because it synthesizes the issues concerning P/L statements, balance sheet, and risk and capital measurements in order to achieve value-creation targets. The process is usually based on a three-year strategic plan followed by yearly budgets, and a number of functions are involved and contribute inputs to the process (see Table 9-5).

Although the Group is large and has a complex divisional and geographical structure (see Figure 9-3), meaning a lot of actors are involved, the process, coordinated by the group planning function at the holding level as the business mix portfolio owner, provides for strong participation of the business units, since an iterative top-down/bottom-up process is followed.

A concrete example is represented by the budget on a yearly basis. At the beginning of the process, in fact, the preliminary phase at the holding level consists of proposing

TABLE 9-5   Role of Different Functions in the Strategic Planning and Capital Allocation Process

Units, Functions, or Legal Entities Involved	Inputs	Time
Group top management	Approval of capitalization target levels, capital allocation policies, and cost of equity per unit	Yearly
Group capital allocation	Definition of capitalization target levels, capital allocation policies, and cost of equity per unit; value target (TSR) and business portfolio composition through an efficient capital allocation setting	Yearly
Group planning	Formalization of strategies, P&L data, and profitability drivers	Yearly for the budget, monthly for ex post control
Finance area	Active balance sheet management initiatives to be included in the budget or plan	Yearly (or on demand when needed)
Business development	External growth strategies	On demand
Divisions and legal entities (planning and capital management functions)	Growth and market forecasts, profitability drivers, details on current and expected regulatory and economic capital	Yearly for budget, monthly (partially) for control, on demand when needed
Accounting	P&L statement and balance sheet results	Quarterly
Risk management	Details about economic capital per risk class and legal entity	Yearly for budget, monthly for ex post control, on demand when needed

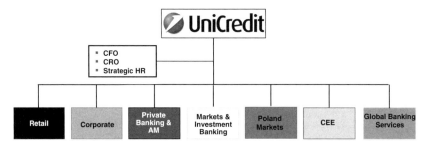

FIGURE 9-3   Unicredit Group's organizational structure.

for Board approval the Group's capitalization target levels, in terms of regulatory and economic capital. Targets are set to reflect risk propensity, the target UniCredit Group credit rating, and regulatory constraints. In this phase the Group cost of equity per unit (k_e) is also approved, where k_e represents shareholder expected return on the capital invested in the Group and it is one figure for the whole Group. This preliminary phase prepares and initializes the following stages of the process.

- At the holding level, top-down targets are prepared. Scenario and market potential analyses are elaborated, including indications related to the optimized business mix and information useful for setting challenging and negotiable value-creation paths and capital allocation targets for business unit leaders, considering and measuring

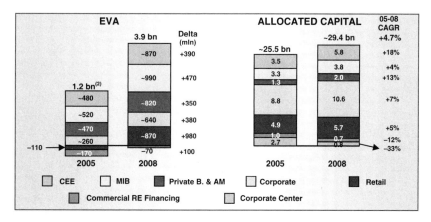

FIGURE 9-4   Target profitability and allocated capital for Unicredit divisions (2005–2008).

risk-adjusted performance potentialities evaluating the strategic impact on Group fair value and on total shareholder return (TSR).

- During the bottom-up phase, business units elaborate their strategic assumptions, and then an iterative process begins in which the underlying rationales of the business evolution are intensively analyzed. Each profitability driver and related risks are linked to define the most efficient capital allocation comparing the bottom-up results with the top-down indicators. The results are the final and agreed EVA, RARORAC, and capital allocation targets for the Group and its business units.

- In the process that leads to a revised capital allocation it is obviously necessary to consider that the existing capital allocation could generally be modified in an incremental way, but not radically altered, unless strategies for external growth based on acquisitions are considered. Of course, the Capital Allocation Unit is also involved in evaluating the impact of external growth strategies, while its contribution to the reallocation process is to suggest incremental changes to the capital allocation to existing business units in order to improve the risk–return profile for the group, where return is measured through a TSR measure over a multiperiod horizon.

- Suggested incremental changes in capital allocation also take into consideration the potential implications in terms of the bank's cost of capital. Therefore, business units producing a lower risk-adjusted return are not necessarily penalized in the optimal suggested capital allocation if they contribute to reducing the bank's cost of capital due to their lower systematic risk. Similarly, on an ex-post basis, while EVA is currently calculated by adopting the same k_e for all business units, the evaluation of the contribution of each business unit also takes into account its contribution to the bank's cost of capital, and risk-adjusted profitability targets are set in an incremental way (see, for instance, Figure 9-4, which presents data from the three-year strategic plan) rather than by mechanically imposing the same risk-adjusted return on all business units.

9.5 Summary

Optimizing the allocation of capital at risk across a bank's businesses is one of the final objectives pursued by a bank when developing a risk management system. Yet allocating capital is not as simple as optimizing the asset allocation for a managed portfolio. It also requires defining how the process of capital allocation should work. In practice, banks alternate periods of sharp changes and substantial reallocations, which can occur as a consequence of a new, ad hoc strategic plan, with periods of regular growth, during which incremental capital reallocations can occur mostly, but not exclusively, as a part of the planning process.

In order to discuss the relationship between risk-adjusted performance measures, the budgeting process and capital continuous reallocation, it is first necessary to discuss how risk-adjusted profitability targets are defined. This topic is important first of all because it represents the way in which VaR-based RAP measures enter into the budgeting process, and secondly because the comparison between targets and ex post performance can sometimes influence top managers' perceptions about which businesses should be allowed to grow, thereby indirectly affecting capital allocation. Defining risk-adjusted profitability targets requires estimating the cost of equity capital for the bank and then translating it into a target return on capital at risk. The chapter points out that choosing to adopt a book-capital- or a market-capitalization-based measure of capital at risk could affect the relative allocation of profit targets among units, especially for those that are mainly exposed to business risk. Moreover, when defining divisional risk-adjusted profitability targets, an open issue is whether the target should be the same for all businesses or should consider the contribution of each business to the systematic risk of the bank as measured by the beta of the business. While using a single target return rate may have shortcomings, estimating different divisional betas and translating them into a profit target is far from easy.

A second relevant issue is whether and to what extent the capital allocation process and the budgeting and planning process should be linked. The positive or negative role of the planning process in a corporation's strategy-making process has been widely debated in the management literature, and the pros and cons that they had pointed out can be applied largely to banks as well. On one hand, linking capital allocation and the budgeting and planning process can pave the way for a continuous incremental improvement of the capital allocation (which typically requires of a bank gradual and constant changes, since the business mix cannot easily be modified). On the other hand, the planning process should continually be checked to avoid having capital allocation become a purely mechanical exercise with no substantial impact on a bank's capital allocation. In any case, substantial reallocations often derive from ad hoc strategic decisions that do not represent the outcome of the periodic planning process. The Unicredit Group case clearly shows the different units in a capital allocation process and the typical incremental process that is applied to improve the overall bank's business mix gradually.

9.6   Further Reading

Capital allocation has been discussed from a theoretical point of view in many finance papers. Froot and Stein (1998) derived a model in which capital budgeting and capital structure decisions are integrated and that takes into account both systematic and idiosyncratic risks of the bank, integrating both into the decision process. Denault (2001) has defined conditions for guaranteeing a coherent capital allocation process, while Stoughton and Zechner (1999, 2000) have discussed the role of RAROC and EVA and their ability to orient capital allocation decisions.

Methodologies for calculating the cost of equity capital are illustrated in many corporate finance books (see Damodaran 2001). The application to banks for defining target returns on capital is discussed by Matten (2000). Crouhy, Turnbull, and Wakeman (1999) and Wilson (2003) critically discuss the adoption of a single RAROC target.

As far as the allocation process is concerned, a few selected readings outside the field of finance can provide interesting insights about the strategy formation process that can also be applied to the capital allocation process. Mintzberg (1990a) provides a great picture of the different schools of thought on strategy formation. Literature from the "learning school" emphasizing how strategy may change incrementally as an effect of a corporate learning process, e.g., as a reaction to the fact that some business units may overperform their targets while others do the opposite, may be relevant (see Quinn 1980; Mintzberg and Waters 1985), as well as the idea that firms may alternate between phases of incremental change and phases of radical changes, proposed by the so-called quantum view (Miller and Friesen 1984).

Final Remarks

Value at risk is a risk management tool that is not exempt from limitations, including, for instance, the fact that the size of losses beyond VaR is not taken into consideration, and its nonsubadditivity, i.e., the fact that in certain circumstances the VaR of a portfolio can be higher than the sum of the individual VaR values of its constituents. Nevertheless, VaR can be an extremely important tool for improving the quality of a bank's risk management processes, since it is potentially able to compare different risks under a similar metric, to support bank decisions concerning the optimal amount of capital the bank should hold, and to help the bank understand better its profitability in risk-adjusted terms.

Developing a risk management system is in any case a complex task that requires coordinated investments in many different areas: methodologies, databases and information technology infrastructure, internal processes, people, and risk management culture. Developing state-of-the-art methodologies can, of course, be important, and efforts to check and improve their effectiveness should be constant. At the same time, budget constraints and data availability always require accepting some compromises. Databases and IT infrastructure are particularly important since the former are a key condition for developing and applying sophisticated methodologies, while the IT infrastructure must ensure that data used by the risk management system are consistent, aligned with front and middle office data, and properly stored to allow subsequent analyses, while risk management outputs must be readily available wherever necessary throughout the bank.

Throughout the book we have stressed that efforts to improve risk measurement methodologies have to be coupled with at least equal efforts to improve risk management processes. Sophisticated measures and methodologies could have only a minor effect if they are not properly translated into improved risk control policies, risk-adjusted evaluation of the contribution of each business, and a careful capital allocation process supported by a reliable picture of the risk–return impact of the potential alternative allocations. Developing these processes requires having people who combine a clear understanding of risk measurement methodologies with remarkable experience and an attention to organizational issues. Risk management teams of some large international banks apparently try explicitly to merge people with very different expertise and skills.

Finally, it is important to invest in the risk management culture of the bank. A bank in which most decision makers clearly understand the benefits and the contribution that can derive from the bank's efforts in developing the risk measurement system is the bank most likely to obtain the highest return from its risk management investments. The current widespread application of VaR-based measures makes them a key tool not only for risk managers or a small group of specialists, but for most top managers, for external analysts, and for many other people in different staff functions and business lines. Hence, a better and more critical understanding of the benefits and potential limitations of VaR-based risk management processes is a condition enabling a bank to improve over time not only its measurement tools, but also the quality of its decisions.

Selected Free Risk Management–Related Websites

The interest in risk management is now so large and widespread that it is possible to find a large amount of risk management papers and resources on the Internet. While it may be almost impossible to list all websites with at least some relevant risk management, useful information, I wanted to provide a list of personal favorites. Most of them may be already well known to risk management specialists, who will certainly be able to find a few relevant sites I may have omitted or who may disagree with my choice. However, I hope this list can provide a useful starting point for nonspecialists and, perhaps, suggest one or two more sites to some of the specialists. A large number of risk management–related websites are linked to software companies offering various market, credit, or operational risk management tools, or to consulting companies offering advisory services for risk management projects, or to companies offering executive training courses. I have excluded these cases from my list, with a very few exceptions for certain websites that contained working papers that are also on my reference list. Of course, my selection and the definition of the dividing line about whether there was enough free documentation available was subjective, and some will disagree. In any case, to avoid any misunderstanding I must make it clear that I do not personally favor the companies whose sites are listed over those whose websites are not included, nor I have direct professional links or interests in the listed sites (I even avoided listing the website of the research center where I serve as a vice director). Consulting company and software vendor websites can very easily be found simply by searching via any common browser, so their exclusion here in order to remain impartial should not represent a problem.

Type of Website/ Organization	Website/ Organization Name	Web Address	Comments
General risk management resources	Gloriamundi	www.gloriamundi.org	Gloriamundi is probably the richest source for free papers among all the fields of risk management, from highly technical papers on market, credit, or operational risk to simple conference presentation slides, together with book reviews. The energy and passion of Barry Schachter, who launched the website, have been the key drivers of the development of the extremely comprehensive set of papers that can be found there, and a newsletter pointing out new additions to the huge paper database can easily be acquired by registering on the site. This is the first website that many practitioners typically suggest to people interested in learning more on specific topics or willing to find the latest academic or industry research, after not yet published in finance journals or which may not reach the form of a final paper in the future.
	Defaultrisk	www.defaultrisk.com	This website is run by Greg Gupton, one of the coauthors of J.P. Morgan's CreditMetrics Technical Document. Unlike Gloriamundi.org, it is devoted to credit risk only, and it provides a large number of freely downloadable papers. It also has a section on the most prolific credit risk authors, which can help you find, in a fast and easy way, some of the most important contributions by leading academics and industry experts in the credit risk field.
	RiskMetrics	www.riskmetrics.com	In this website all the old technical documents concerning RiskMetrics™ and CreditMetrics™ can easily be retrieved, along with a number of other publications (such as the RiskMetrics Monitor) that have been included in this book's reference list. Although RiskMetrics is a competitor of other software firms that have not been included in this list, its website could not be excluded, both for historical reasons (RiskMetrics™ and CreditMetrics™ technical documents were important in the 1990s in spreading the risk management culture to a number of smaller banks) and for the quality of risk management papers that can still be found on the website.
	Groupe de Recherche Opérationnelle	http://gro.creditlyonnais. fr/content/fr/home_ presentation.htm	The website of the Groupe de Recherche Opérationnelle (historically from Credit Lyonnais, now in Calyon group) offers a number of research papers (some in English, some in French) concerning asset and liability management, market, credit, and operational risks, and copulas. Although the website clearly is not as general or rich as Gloriamundi and Defaultrisk and hosts only papers produced internally, the papers on operational risk are particularly interesting and deal with important issues such as correlation across risks and the integration of internal and external-loss databases.

Type of Website/ Organization	Website/ Organization Name	Web Address	Comments
General finance resources	Social Sciences Research Network	www.ssrn.com	The Social Sciences Research Network is the best source for working papers in a number of fields, including finance. Finance papers can be searched by keyword, author, or title in the Financial Economics Network section. Although, unlike Gloriamundi, the website deals with all of the different areas of research in finance and is not devoted to risk management papers, it can still represent a way to find useful working papers for the risk management profession.
	University Research Centers		Another potential source for interesting working papers is represented by university research center websites, especially those that have a significant number of researchers working on risk management topics. Relevant examples include the Salomon Center at the Stern School of Business at New York University (http://w4.stern.nyu.edu/salomon/; see in particular the Credit and Debt Market and the Financial Econometrics sections) and by Wharton's Financial Institutions Center (http://fic.wharton.upenn.edu/fic/papers.html).
Regulatory authorities	Bank for International Settlements	www.bis.org	The Bank of International Settlement's website obviously needs no presentation. In the Basel Committee section, both the final version of the Basel II Accord and subsequent consultative or final documents concerning capital requirements and international prudential supervision can be easily found. The site also contains a Joint Forum section. The Joint Forum was established in 1996 under the aegis of the Basel Committee on Banking Supervision (BCBS), the International Organization of Securities Commissions (IOSCO), and the International Association of Insurance Supervisors (IAIS) to deal with issues common to the banking, securities, and insurance sectors, including the regulation of financial conglomerates, and it has authored, for instance, the 2003 risk integration survey discussed in Chapter 6. The Joint Forum section is http://www.bis.org/bcbs/jointforum.htm. Moreover, the website has interesting sections on BIS and Basel Committee working papers. A section on comment letters sent by the Basel Committee to other organizations (including the IASB) may also be of interest as far as the discussion on IAS/IFRS implementation is concerned.
	Federal Reserve Board of Governors	www.federalreserve.gov	This website is important both for technical publications concerning risk measurement and risk management and for learning about the evolution of Basel II Accord implementation in the United State, which has stimulated a very intense debate. The website section devoted to Basel II and that reports the evolution of U.S. rule making is http://www.federalreserve.gov/generalinfo/basel2/default.htm.

Type of Website/ Organization	Website/ Organization Name	Web Address	Comments
Regulatory authorities (cont.)	Federal Reserve Board of Governors (cont.)	www.federalreserve.gov (cont.)	As far as risk management research is concerned, all Federal Reserve publications can be searched through at the website http://www.frbsf.org/publications/fedinprint/index.html, which is hosted by the Federal Reserve Bank of San Francisco. Of course, it may also be possible for the interested researcher simply to bookmark some Federal Reserve Bank economists' personal websites (e.g., Til Schuermann's page at the Federal Reserve Bank of New York and Patrick de Fontnouvelle's page at the Federal Reserve Bank of Boston, to mention just two authors that were cited more than once in this book) in order to check regularly for new publications.
	European Commission	ec.europa.eu	The European Commission's website is relevant as far as European regulation is concerned. Risk managers should be interested particularly in the section on Internal markets/Financial services (http://ec.europa.eu/internal_market/finances/index_en.htm). One section is also devoted entirely to the adoption of the Capital Requirements Directive (CRD) and the subsequent amendment proposals (http://ec.europa.eu/internal_market/bank/regcapital/index_en.htm). Thus, this website is crucial for following the evolution of approved regulation in the European Union.
	Committee of European Banking Supervisors (CEBS)	www.c-ebs.org	As is clearly explained on its website, the Committee of European Banking Supervisors (CEBS) gives advice to the European Commission on banking policy issues and promotes cooperation and convergence of supervisory practice across the European Union. Consequently, the committee is also strictly involved in fostering a common implementation of the Capital Requirements Directive (CRD), publications from CEBS include, for instance, surveys on Basel II effects in European countries and guidelines issued for the validation of bank risk measurement systems.
Accounting	International Accounting Standards Board	www.iasb.org	The official website of the International Accounting Standards Board enables one to understand the agenda of the IASB and of the International Financial Reporting Interpretations Committee in renewing and harmonizing international accounting standards. Exposure drafts, discussion papers, and invitations to comment on the preliminary versions of new standards and interpretations of existing standards can be accessed at the website.
	Financial Accounting Standards Board	www.fasb.org	This website offers similar information related to the activity of the Financial Accounting Standards Board. (similar to the analogous website for the IASB).

Type of Website/ Organization	Website/ Organization Name	Web Address	Comments
Accounting (cont.)	IASPLUS	www.iasplus.com	In this website, which is run by a consultancy firm, a lot of up-to-date information concerning the evolution of accounting standards in all major countries can easily be found. The site offers extensive documentation and provides a useful picture of the accounting standards integration process.
Risk management associations (often partially free websites with large members' sections)	GARP	www.garp.com	GARP is the Global Association of Risk Professionals. GARP's website, however, is devoted mainly to members, but some suggested articles can be freely downloaded from the Library section.
	PRMIA	www.prmia.org	PRMIA is the Professional Risk Managers' International Association (PRMIA). All website resources are currently devoted to members only.
Insurance company regulation and risk management	Committee of European Insurance and Occupational Pensions Supervisors (CEIOPS)	www.ceiops.org	CEIOPS provides advice to the European Commission on the drafting of implementation measures for framework directives and regulations on insurance and occupational pensions and on establishing supervisory standards, recommendations, and guidelines to enhance convergent and effective application of the regulations and to facilitate cooperation between national supervisors, with a role that is equal to the one played by CEBS (Committee of European Banking Supervisors) and CESR (Committee of European Securities Regulators), respectively, in the banking and capital markets sectors. CEIOPS' role is particularly important in the "Solvency II" project, aimed at redefining minimum regulatory capital requirements for insurance companies according to a three-pillar framework similar to the Basel II framework.
	Society of Actuaries	www.soa.org	The Society of Actuaries has free papers and documents concerning mainly risk management from actuaries' viewpoint. Therefore, it can provide useful insights about how to approach common problems (e.g., the development of risk integration, the application of economic capital concepts) and offers technical papers on specific insurance issues that are relevant to financial risk managers of financial conglomerates. Some documents are also currently available on the website of the old Society of Actuaries' Risk Management Task Force (http://rmtf.soa.org/rmtf.html). The website also comprises some "specialty guides" on topics such as economic capital (http://rmtf.soa.org/rmtf_ecca.html) and enterprise risk management (see http://www.soa.org/ccm/content/research-publications/library-publications/specialty-guides/specialty-guides/).

Type of Website/ Organization	Website/ Organization Name	Web Address	Comments
Insurance company regulation and risk management (cont.)	Casualty Actuarial Society	http://www.casact.org	The comments made for the Society of Actuaries' website apply here as well. The site also comprises proceedings from previous CAS conferences. Recently, the Casualty Actuarial Society has developed a joint risk management section together with the Society of Actuaries, but access to this section requires an annual fee.
	Comitè Europeenne des Assurance	www.cea.assur.org	As the website of the European Insurance and Reinsurance Federation, the website offers publications and position papers from the association, including, for instance, a simple presentation of the Solvency II project.
General finance links	*Journal of Finance*'s list of finance-related sites	http://fisher.osu.edu/fin/journal/jofsites.htm	This website contains a lengthy list of links to finance journals, research centers, institutional and personal websites with downloadable working papers, finance associations, and software and consulting companies. Although the links span all finance subfields, many are of interest for risk management purposes.

References

Acharya, V. V., S. T. Bharath, and A. Srinivasan (2003), "Understanding the Recovery Rate of Defaulted Securities," *Center for Economic Policy Research Discussion Papers*, no. 4098 (available at www.cepr.org).

Aguais, S. D., L. R. Forest, Jr., E. Y. L. Wong, and D. Diaz-Ledesma (2004), "Point-in-Time Versus Through-the-Cycle Ratings," in M. Ong (ed.), *The Basel Handbook. A Guide for Financial Practitioners*, Risk Publications, London, 183–209.

Alexander, C. (2001), *Market Models: A Guide to Financial Data Analysis*, J. Wiley & Sons, Chichester, UK.

Alexander, C., and J. Pezier (2003), "On the Aggregation of Market and Credit Risks," *ISMA Centre Discussion Papers in Finance 2003–13*, University of Reading, Reading UK, October.

Altman, E. I. (1968), "Financial Ratios, Discriminant Analysis and the Prediction of Corporate Bankruptcy," *Journal of Finance, 23*, 589–609.

Altman, E. I. (1989), "Measuring Corporate Bond Mortality and Performance," *Journal of Finance, 44*, 909–922.

Altman, E. I. (1998), "The Importance and Subtlety of Credit Rating Migration," *Journal of Banking and Finance, 22*, 1231–1247.

Altman, E. I., and V. Kishore (1996), "Almost Everything You Wanted to Know About Recoveries on Defaulted Bonds," *Financial Analysts Journal, 52*, 57–64.

Altman, E. I., and H. J. Suggitt (2000), "Default Rates in the Syndicated Bank Loan Market: A Mortality Analysis," *Journal of Banking and Finance, 24*, 229–253.

Altman, E. I., A. Resti, and A. Sironi (2005), "Loss Given Default: A Review of the Literature," in Altman, E. I., A. Resti, and A. Sironi (eds.), *Recovery Risk: The Next Challenge in Credit Risk Management*, Risk Books, London, pp. 41–59.

Altman, E. I., B. Brady, A. Resti, and A. Sironi (2005), "The Link Between Default and Recovery Rates: Theory, Empirical Evidence, and Implications," *Journal of Business, 78*, 2203–2228.

Anders, U., and G. J. van der Brink (2004), "Implementing a Basel II Scenario-Based AMA for Operational Risk," in M. K. Ong (ed.), *The Basel Handbook: A Guide for Financial Practitioners*, Risk Publications, London, pp. 343–369.

245

Ansoff, I. (1991), "Critique of Henry Mintzberg's 'The Design School: Reconsidering the Basic Premises of Strategic Management'," *Strategic Management Journal*, *12*, 449–461.

Ansoff, I. (1994), "Comment on Henry Mintzberg's 'Rethinking Strategic Planning'," *Long-Range Planning*, *27*, 31–32.

Artzner, P., F. Delbaen, J. M. Eber, and D. Heath (1999), "Coherent Measures of Risk," *Mathematical Finance*, *9*, 203–228.

Asarnow, E., and D. Edwards (1995), "Measuring Loss on Defaulted Bank Loans: A 24-Year Study," *Journal of Commercial Lending*, *77*, 11–23.

Asarnow, E., and J. Marker (1995), "Historical Performance of the U.S. Corporate Loan Market: 1988–1993," *Journal of Commercial Lending*, *10*, 13–32.

Bangia, A., F. Diebold, A. Kronimus, C. Schaegen, and T. Schuermann (2002), "Ratings Migrations and the Business Cycle, with Application to Credit Portfolio Stress Testing," *Journal of Banking and Finance*, *26*, 445–474.

Barney, J. B., and W. G. Ouchi (1985), "Information Cost and the Governance of Economic Transactions," in R. D. Nacamulli and A. Rugiadini (eds.), *Organization and Markets*. Il Mulino, 347–372.

Barone-Adesi, G., K. Giannopoulos, and L. Vosper (1999), "VaR without Correlations for Nonlinear Portfolios," *Journal of Futures Markets*, *19*, 583–602.

Basel Committee on Banking Supervision (1996), "Supervisory Framework for the Use of 'Backtesting' in Conjunction with the Internal Models Approach for Market Risk," Bank for International Settlements, Basel, Switzerland.

Basel Committee on Banking Supervision (2005a), "An Explanatory Note on the Basel II Risk Weight Functions," Bank for International Settlements, Basel, Switzerland.

Basel Committee on Banking Supervision (2005b), "Studies on the Validation of Internal Rating Systems," Working Paper No. 14, Bank for International Settlements, Basel, Switzerland.

Basel Committee on Banking Supervision (2006a), "International Convergence of Capital Measurement and Capital Standards. A Revised Framework — Comprehensive Version," Bank for International Settlements, Basel, Switzerland.

Basel Committee on Banking Supervision (2006b), "Results of the Fifth Quantitative Impact Study (QIS5)," Bank for International Settlements, Basel, Switzerland.

Basel Committee on Banking Supervision (2006c), "Sound Credit Risk Assessment and Valuation of Loans," Bank for International Settlements, Basel, Switzerland.

Baud, N., A. Frachot, and T. Roncalli (2002), "Internal Data, External Data and Consortium Data for Operational Risk Measurement: How to Pool Data Properly," working paper, Credit Lyonnais, Group de Recherce Opérationnelle, Paris, France.

Beaver, W. (1967), "Financial Ratios as Predictors of Failures," *Empirical Research in Accounting: Selected Studies — 1966*, supplement to *Journal of Accounting Research*, *4*, 71–111.

Belkin, B., S. Suchower, and L. Forest (1998a), "The Effect of Systematic Credit Risk on Loan Portfolio Value-at-Risk and Loan Pricing," *CreditMetrics Monitor*, First Quarter, 17–28.

Belkin, B., S. Suchower, and L. Forest (1998b), "A One-Parameter Representation of Credit Risk and Transition Matrices," *CreditMetrics Monitor*, Third Quarter, 46–56.

Berger, A. N., R. J. Herring, and G. P. Szëgo (1995), "The Role of Capital in Financial Institutions," *Journal of Banking and Finance*, *19*, 393–430.

Berkowitz, J. (2000), "A Coherent Framework for Stress Testing," *Journal of Risk*, *2*, 1–11.

Berkowitz, J. (2001), "Testing Density Forecasts, with Applications for Risk Management," *Journal of Business and Economics Statistics*, *19*, 465–474.

Bessis, J. (2002), *Risk Management in Banking*, 2nd ed., John Wiley & Sons, Chichester, UK.

Black, F., and J. C. Cox (1976), "Valuing Corporate Securities: Some Effects of Bond Indenture Provisions," *Journal of Finance*, *31*, 351–368.

Black, F., and M. Scholes (1973), "The Pricing of Options and Corporate Liabilities," *Journal of Political Economy*, *81*, 637–654.

Board of Governors of the Federal Reserve Systems (2005), "Advance Notice of Proposed Rulemaking for Proposed Revisions for Current Risk-Based Capital Rules," mimeo (available at http://www.federalreserve.gov/generalinfo/basel2/default.htm).

Board of Governors of the Federal Reserve Systems (2006), "Risk-Based Capital Standards: Advanced Capital Adequacy Framework," Joint notice of proposed rulemaking, mimeo (available at http://www.federalreserve.gov/generalinfo/basel2/default.htm).

Bollerslev, T. (1986), "Generalized Autoregressive Conditional Heteroskedasticity," *Journal of Econometrics*, *31*, 307–327.

Boudoukh, J., M. Richardson, and R. Whitelaw (1998), "The Best of Both Worlds," *Risk*, *11*, 64–67.

Boyle, P. (1977), "Options: A Monte Carlo Approach," *Journal of Financial Economics*, *4*, 323–338.

Brewer, E., D. Fortier, and C. Pavel (1988), "Bank Risk from Nonbank Activities," *Economic Perspectives*, July–August, 14–26.

Britten-Jones, M., and S. Schaefer (1999), "Nonlinear Value at Risk," *European Finance Review*, *2*, 161–187.

Carey, M. (1998), "Credit Risk in Private Debt Portfolios," *Journal of Finance*, *53*, 1363–1387.

Carey, M., and R. M. Stulz (2005), *The Risks of Financial Institutions*, mimeo, June.

Carroll, R. B., T. Perry, H. Yang, and A. Ho (2001), "A New Approach to Component VaR," *Journal of Risk*, *3*, 57–67.

Carty, L. V., and D. Lieberman (1998), "Historical Default Rates of Corporate Bond Issuers, 1920–1996," in S. Das (ed.), *Credit Derivatives: Trading and Management of Credit and Default Risk*, John Wiley & Sons, Singapore, 317–348.

Chapelle, A., Y. Crama, G. Hübner, and J.-P. Peters (2004), "Basel II and Operational Risk: Implications for Risk Measurement and Management in the Financial Sector," *National Bank of Belgium Working Papers*, No. 51, May.

Cherubini, U., E. Luciano, and W. Vecchiato (2004), *Copula Methods in Finance*, J. Wiley & Sons, Chichester.

Christoffersen, P. F. (2003), *Elements of Financial Risk Management*, Elsevier Science, Academic Press, San Diego, CA.

Citigroup (2005), *Annual Report*, Citigroup, New York.

Commission of the European Communities (2004), Commission Regulation (EC) No. 2086/2004, *Official Journal of the European Union*, Brussels, Belgium.

Committee of European Banking Supervisors (2006), "Guidelines on the Implementation, Validation and Assessment of Advanced Measurement (AMA) and Internal Ratings Based (IRB) Approaches" (available at http://www.c-ebs.org).

Committee on the Global Financial System (2000), "Stress Testing by Large Financial Institutions: Current Practice and Aggregation Issues," Bank for International Settlement, Basel, Switzerland.

Credit Suisse Financial Products (1997), "CreditRisk+. A Credit Risk Management Framework," Technical Document, London, United Kingdom.

Crouhy, M. and D. Galai (1994), "The Interaction Between the Financial and Investment Decisions of the Firm: The Case of Issuing Warrants in a Levered Firm," *Journal of Banking and Finance*, *18*, 861–880.

Crouhy, M., D. Galai, and R. Mark (2000), "A Comparative Analysis of Current Credit Risk Models," *Journal of Banking and Finance*, *24*, 59–117.

Crouhy, M., D. Galai, and R. Mark (2001), *Risk Management*, McGraw-Hill, New York.

Crouhy, M., S. M. Turnbull, and L. M. Wakeman (1999), "Measuring Risk-Adjusted Performance," *Journal of Risk*, *2*, 5–35.

Cummins, D. J., C. M. Lewis, and R. Wei (2004), "The Market Value Impact of Operational Risk Events in U.S. Banks and Insurers," Wharton School Working paper, December, Philadelphia, PA.

Damodaran, A. (2001), *Corporate Finance. Theory and Practice*, 2nd ed., John Wiley & Sons, New York.

De Laurentis, G. (2005), "Corporate Banker's Role and Credit Risk Management," in G. De Laurentis (ed.), *Strategy and Organization of Corporate Banking*, Springer-Verlag, Berlin, 107–137.

de Fontnouvelle, P., V. Dejesus-Rueff, J. Jordan, and E. Rosengren (2003), "Capital and Risk: New Evidence on Implications of Large Operational Losses," Working Paper, Federal Reserve Bank of Boston.

de Fontnouvelle, P., E. Rosengren, and J. Jordan (2004), "Implications of Alternative Operational Risk Modeling Techniques," Working Paper, Federal Reserve Bank of Boston.

de Servigny, A., and O. Renault (2004), *Measuring and Managing Credit Risk*, J. Wiley & Sons, New York.

Denault, M. (2001), "Coherent Allocation of Risk Capital," *Journal of Risk*, *4*, 1–34.

Dhaene, J., S. Vanduffel, and Q. Tang (2004), "Solvency Capital, Risk Measures and Comonotonicity: A Review," Working Paper, University of Leuven, Leuven, Belgium.

Dhaene, J., S. Vanduffel, M. Goovaerts, R. Olieslagers, and R. Koch (2003), "On the Computation of the Capital Multiplier in the Fortis Credit Economic Capital Model," *Belgian Actuarial Bulletin*, *3*(1), 50–57.

Dimakos, X. K., and K. Aas (2003), "Integrated Risk Modeling," Working Paper, Norwegian Computing Center, December, Oslo, Norway.

Dimakos, X. K., K. Aas, and A. Øksendal (2005), "Risk Capital Aggregation," Working Paper, Norwegian Computing Center, December, Oslo, Norway.

Dinwoodie, C. M. (2002), "The A to Z of Standard & Poor's Ratings," in M. K. Ong (ed.), *Credit Ratings. Methodologies, Rationale and Default Risk*, Risk Publications, London, 7–16.

Eccles, R. (1983), "Control with Fairness in Transfer Pricing," *Harvard Business Review*, *61*, 149–161.

Embrechts, P. (ed.) (2000), *Extremes and Integrated Risk Management*, Risk Publications, London.

Embrechts, P., C. Klüppelberg, and T. Mikosch (1997), *Modeling Extremal Events*. Springer-Verlag, Berlin.

Embrechts, P., A. J. McNeil, and D. Straumann (1999), "Correlation and Dependence in Risk Management: Properties and Pitfalls," Working Paper, Department of Mathematics, ETH, Zurich.

Engle, R. F. (1982), "Autoregressive Conditional Heteroscedasticity with Estimates of the Variance of United Kingdom Inflation," *Econometrica*, *50*, 987–1007.

Fama, E., and K. French (1992), "The Cross Section of Expected Stock Returns," *Journal of Finance*, *47*, 427–465.

Fama, E., and K. French (1993), "Common Risk Factors in the Returns on Stocks and Bonds," *Journal of Financial Economics*, *33*, 3–56.

Financial Accounting Standards Board (1975), "Statement of Financial Accounting Standards No. 5. Accounting for Contingencies," Financial Accounting Standards Board, Norwalk, CT.

Financial Accounting Standards Board (1993), "Statement of Financial Accounting Standards No. 114. Accounting By Creditors for Impairment of a Loan," Financial Accounting Standards Board, Norwalk, CT.

Fisher, R. (1936), "The Use of Multiple Measurements in Taxonomic Problems," *Annals of Eugenics*, *7*, 179–188.

Flannery, M. J. (1998), "Using Market Information in Prudential Bank Supervision: A Review of the U.S. Empirical Evidence," *Journal of Money, Credit and Banking*, *30*, 273–305.

Frachot, M., O. Moudoulaud, and T. Roncalli (2004), "Loss Distribution Approach in Practice," in M. K. Ong (ed.), *The Basel Handbook*: *A Guide for Financial Practitioners*, Risk Publications, London, pp. 369–396.

Frachot, A., T. Roncalli, and E. Salomon (2005), "Correlation and Diversification Effects in Operational Risk Modeling," in E. Davis (ed.), *Operational Risk: Practical Approaches to Implementation*, Risk Publications, London, pp. 23–37.

Fritz, S., and D. Hosemann (2000), "Restructuring the Credit Process: Behavior Scoring for German Corporates," *International Journal of Intelligent Systems in Accounting, Finance and Management*, *9*, 9–21.

Fritz, S., M. Luxenburger, and T. Miehe (2004), "Implementation of an IRB-Compliant Rating System," in M. Ong (ed.), *The Basel Handbook*: *A Guide for Financial Practitioners*, Risk Publications, London, pp. 85–136.

Garman, M. (1996), "Improving on VaR," *Risk*, *9*, May, 61–63.

Garman, M. (1997), "Taking VaR to Pieces," *Risk*, *10*, October, 70–71.

Geske, R. (1977), "The Valuation of Corporate Liabilities as Compound Options," *Journal of Financial and Quantitative Analysis*, *12*, 541–552.

Giudici, P. (2004), "Integration of Qualitative and Quantitative Operational Risk Data: A Bayesian Approach," in M. Cruz (ed.), *Operational Risk Modeling and Analysis*, Risk Publications, London, pp. 131–138.

Glantz, M. (1994), *Loan Risk Management*, Probus, Chicago.

Glasserman, P. (2003), *Monte Carlo Methods in Financial Engineering*, Springer-Verlag, New York.

Goold, M. (1992), "Design, Learning and Planning: A Further Observation on the Design School Debate," *Strategic Management Journal*, *13*, 169–170.

Goovaerts, M. J., E. Van den Borre, and R. J. A. Laeven (2005), "Managing Economic and Virtual Economic Capital Within Financial Conglomerates," *North American Actuarial Journal 9*(3), 77–89.

Gordy, M. B. (2000), "A Comparative Analysis of Credit Risk Models," *Journal of Banking and Finance*, *24*, 119–149.

Gordy, M. B. (2003), "A Risk-Factor Model Foundation for Ratings-Based Bank Capital Rules," *Journal of Financial Intermediation*, *12*, 199–232.

Grossman, R. J., W. T. Brennan, and J. Vento (1998), "Syndicated Bank Loan Recovery Study, *CreditMetrics Monitor*," J.P. Morgan, First Quarter, 29–36.

Gupton, G. M. (2005), "Estimating Recovery Risk by Means of a Quantitative Model: LossCalc," in E. I. Altman, A. Resti, and A. Sironi (eds.), *Recovery Risk. The Next Challenge in Credit Risk Management*, Risk Books, London, pp. 61–86.

Gupton, G. M., C. C. Finger, and M. Bhatia (1997), *CreditMetrics^{TM} Technical Document*. J.P. Morgan, New York, April.

Haas, M., and T. Kaiser (2004), "Tackling the Insufficiency of Loss Data for the Quantification of Operational Risk," in M. Cruz (ed.), *Operational Risk Modeling and Analysis*, Risk Publications, London, pp. 13–24.

Hall, C. (2002), "Economic Capital: Towards an Integrated Risk Framework," *Risk*, October, 33–38.

Hallerbach, W. G. (2002), "Decomposing Portfolio Value at Risk: A General Analysis," *Journal of Risk*, 5, 1–18.

Hallerbach, W. G. (2004), "Capital Allocation, Portfolio Enhancement and Performance Measurement: A Unified Approach," in G. Szëgo (ed.), *Risk Measures for the 21st Century*, John Wiley & Sons, New York, pp. 435–450.

Haubenstock, M. (2004), "Constructing an Operational Event Database," in M. K. Ong (ed.), *The Basel Handbook: A Guide for Financial Practitioners*, Risk Publications, London, pp. 429–466.

Henrard, L., and R. Olieslagers (2004), "Risk Management of a Financial Conglomerate," Financial Forum/Bank — en Financiewezen, no. 1.

Holton, G. (2003), *Value-at-Risk: Theory and Practice*, Elsevier Science, Academic Press, San Diego, CA.

Hu, Y. T., and W. Perraudin (2002), "The Dependence of Recovery Rates and Defaults," mimeo, Birkbeck College, London.

Huisman, R., K. Kroedijk, C. Kool, and F. Palm (2001), "Tail-Index Estimates in Small Samples," *Journal of Business and Economic Statistics*, 19, 208–216.

Hull, J. (2005), *Options, Futures and Other Derivatives*, 6th ed., Prentice Hall International, New York.

Hull, J., and A. White (1998), "Incorporating Volatility Updating into the Historical Simulation Method for VaR," *Journal of Risk*, 1, 5–19.

IACPM-ISDA (2006), "Convergence of Credit Risk Capital Models," Working Paper (available at www.iacpm.org).

J.P. Morgan (1996), *RiskMetrics^{TM} Technical Document*, 4th ed., J.P. Morgan, New York (available at www.riskmetrics.com).

J.P. Morgan Chase (2004), "The J.P. Morgan Chase Operational Risk Environment," in M. Cruz (ed.), *Operational Risk Modeling and Analysis*, Risk Publications, London, pp. 295–328.

Joint Forum (2003), *Trends in Risk Integration and Aggregation*, Bank for International Settlements, Basel, Switzerland.

Jorion, P. (2002), "Fallacies About the Effects of Market Risk Management Systems," *Financial Stability Review*, December, 115–127.

Kim, J. (1999), "A Way to Condition Transition Matrix on Wind," *CreditMetrics Monitor*, May, 1–12.

Koylouglu, H. U., and A. Hickman (1998), "Reconciliable Differences," *Risk*, 11, 56–62.

Kühn, R., and P. Neu (2004), "Adequate Capital and Stress Testing for Operational Risk," in M. Cruz (ed.), *Operational Risk Modeling and Analysis*, Risk Publications, London, pp. 273–289.

Kuritzkes, A. (2002), "Operational Risk Capital: A Problem of Definition," *Journal of Risk Finance*, Fall, 1–10.

Kuritzkes, A., T. Schuermann, and S. M. Weiner (2001), *Study on the Risk Profile and Capital Adequacy of Financial Conglomerates*, Oliver, Wyman & Co. (available at www.dnb.nl/publicaties/pdf/study_risk_profile.pdf).

Kuritzkes, A., T. Schuermann, and S. M. Weiner (2002), *Risk Measurement, Risk Management and Capital Adequacy in Financial Conglomerates*, Wharton Financial Institutions Center Working Papers Series, no. 03-02, Philadelphia, PA.

Leippold, M., and P. Vanini (2005), "The Quantification of Operational Risk," *Journal of Risk*, 8, 59–85.

Litterman, R. (1997a), "Hot Spot and Hedges I," *Risk*, 10, March, 42–45.

Litterman, R. (1997b), "Hot Spot and Hedges II," *Risk*, 10, May, 38–42.

Matten, C. (2000), *Managing Bank Capital. Capital Allocation and Performance Measurement*, John Wiley & Sons, New York.

Merton, R. C. (1974), "On the Pricing of Corporate Debt: The Risk Structure of Interest Rates," *Journal of Finance*, 29, 449–470.

Merton, R. C., and A. F. Perold (1993), "Theory of Risk Capital in Financial Firms," *Journal of Applied Corporate Finance*, 6, 16–32.

Miller, D., and P. H. Friesen (1984), *Organizations: A Quantum View*, Prentice Hall, Englewood Cliffs, NJ.

Mintzberg, H. (1979), *The Structuring of Organizations*, Prentice Hall, Englewood Cliffs, NJ.

Mintzberg, H. (1990a), "Strategy Formation: Schools of Thought," in J. W. Fredrickson (ed.), *Perspectives on Strategic Management*, Harper Business, New York.

Mintzberg, H. (1990b), "The Design School: Reconsidering the Basic Premises of Strategic Management," *Strategic Management Journal*, 11, 171–195.

Mintzberg, H. (1994), *The Rise and Fall of Strategic Planning*, Prentice Hall International, New York.

Mintzberg, H., and J. Waters (1985), "Of Strategies, Deliberate and Emergent," *Strategic Management Journal*, 6, 257–272.

Moscadelli, M. (2004), "The Modeling of Operational Risk: Experience with the Analysis of the Data Collected by the Basel Committee," *Temi di discussione del servizio studi*, Banca d'Italia, no. 517, July.

Nelsen, R. B. (1999), *An Introduction to Copulas*, Springer-Verlag, New York.

Nickell, P., W. Perraudin, and S. Varotto (2000), "Stability of Rating Transitions," *Journal of Banking and Finance*, 24, 203–227.

Ouchi, W. G. (1979), "A Conceptual Framework for the Design of Organizational Control Mechanisms," *Management Science*, 25, 833–848.

Ouchi, W. G. (1980), "Markets, Bureaucracies, and Clans," *Administrative Science Quarterly*, 25, 129–141.

Perold, A. (1999), "Capital Allocation in Financial Firms," Working Paper, Harvard University, Graduate School of Business Administration, Cambridge, MA.

Perry, J., P. de Fontnouvelle (2005), "Measuring Reputational Risk: The Market Reaction to Operational Loss Announcements," Working Paper, Federal Reserve Bank of Boston.

Persaud, A. (2000), "Sending the Herd Off the Cliff Edge: The Disturbing Interaction Between Herding and Market-Sensitive Risk Management Practices," *Journal of Risk Finance*, 2, 59–65.

Pezier, J. (2003), "Application-Based Financial Risk Aggregation Models," ISMA Centre Discussion Papers in Finance 2003–11, September, University of Reading, Reading, UK.

Pfeffer, J. (1992), "Understanding Power in Organizations," *California Management Review*, 34, 29–50.

Pritsker, M. (1997), "Evaluating Value at Risk Methodologies: Accuracy vs. Computational Time," *Journal of Financial Services Research*, *12*, 201–241.

Pritsker, M. (2001), "The Hidden Dangers of Historical Simulations," *Finance and Economics Discussion Series 2001-27*, Board of Governors of the Federal Reserve System, Washington, DC.

Quinn, J. B. (1980), *Strategies for Change: Logical Incrementalism.* Irwin, Homewood, Illinois, IL.

Resti, A., and A. Sironi (2005), "Defining LGD: The Basel II Perspective," in E. I. Altman A. Resti, and A. Sironi (eds.), *Recovery Risk. The Next Challenge in Credit Risk Management*, Risk Books, London, pp. 25–39.

Rogers, D. (1993), *The Future of American Banking*, McGraw-Hill, New York.

Rosenberg, J. V., and T. Schuermann (2004), "A General Approach to Integrated Risk Management with Skewed, Fat-Tailed Risks," *Federal Reserve Bank of New York Staff Report*, no. 185, May.

Rutter Associates (2006), "Excerpts from 2004 Rutter Associates Survey of Credit Portfolio Management Practice," available at http://www.rutterassociates.com.

Saita, F. (1999a), "Allocation of Risk Capital in Financial Institutions," *Financial Management*, *28*, 95–111.

Saita, F. (1999b), "Controlling Trading Risk with VaR Limits," Newfin Research Center Working Paper, December, Milan.

Saita, F. (2004), "Risk Capital Aggregation: The Risk Manager's Perspective," Newfin Research Center Working Papers, November, Milan.

Saunders, A. (1994), *Financial Institutions Management. A Modern Perspective.* Irwin, Burr Ridge, IL.

Saunders, A., and L. Allen (2002), *Credit Risk Measurement: New Approaches to Value at Risk and Other Paradigms*, 2nd ed., J. Wiley & Sons, New York.

Saunders, A., and I. Walter (1993), *Universal Banking in the U.S.?* Oxford University Press, New York.

Scandizzo, S. (2005), "Risk Mapping and Key Risk Indicators in Operational Risk Management," *Economic Notes*, *34*, 231–256.

Schuermann, T. (2005), "What Do We Know About Loss Given Default?" in E. I. Altman, A. Resti, and A. Sironi (eds.), *Recovery Risk. The Next Challenge in Credit Risk Management*, Risk Books, London, pp. 3–24.

Sironi, A. (2001), "An Analysis of European Banks Subordinated Debt Issues and Its Implications for a Mandatory Subordinated Debt Policy," *Journal of Financial Services Research*, *20*, 233–266.

Sironi, A. (2003), "Testing for Market Discipline in the European Banking Industry: Evidence from Subordinated Debt Issues," *Journal of Money, Credit and Banking*, *35*, 443–472.

Sironi, A., and A. Resti (2007), *Risk Management and Shareholder Value in Banking*, John Wiley, New York.

Sklar, A. (1959), "Fonctions de répartition à *n* dimensions et leurs marges," *Publications de l'Institut de Statistique de L'Université de Paris*, *8*, 229–231.

Society of Actuaries (2004), "Specialty Guide on Economic Capital," mimeo (available at http://rmtf.soa.org/rmtf_ecca.html).

Standard & Poor's (2006), "Corporate Ratings Criteria," Working Paper, New York.

Stoughton, N., and J. Zechner (1999), "Optimal Capital Allocation Using RAROC and EVA," Working Paper (available at http://www.ssrn.com).

Stoughton, N., and J. Zechner (2000), "The Dynamics of Capital Allocation," Working Paper (available at http://www.ssrn.com).

Strassberger, M. (2004), "Risk Capital Allocation in Trading Divisions of Financial Institutions," Working Paper, Friedrich Schiller University of Jena, Germany.

Tasche, D. (2006), "Validation of Internal Rating Systems and PD Estimates," Working
Paper, May, Frankfurt am Main, Germany.

Treacy, W. F., and M. S. Carey (2000), "Credit Risk, Rating Systems at Large U.S. Banks,"
Journal of Banking and Finance, 24, Frankfort am Main, Gemany, 167–201.

Uyemura, D. G., C. C. Kantor, and J. M. Pettit (1996), "EVA for Banks: Value Creation,
Risk Management, and Profitability Measurement," *Journal of Applied Corporate
Finance*, 9, 94–113.

Vasicek, O. A. (1984), "Credit Valuation," Working Paper, KMV Corporation, San
Francesco, CA.

Vazza, D., D. Aurora, and R. Schneck (2006), "Annual 2005 Global Corporate Default
Study and Rating Transitions," Standard & Poor's, Global Fixed Income Research,
January, New York.

Venter, G. G. (2003), *Capital Allocation: An Opinionated Survey*, CAS Forum Summer
2003 (available at http://www.casact.org/pubs/forum/03sforum/03sf279.pdf).

Vojta, G. J. (1973), *Bank Capital Adequacy*, Citicorp, New York [reprinted in T. M.
Havrilesky, and J. T. Boorman (eds.) (1976), *Current Perspectives in Banking*, AHM,
Arlington Heights, IL].

Wang, S. (2002), *A Set of New Methods and Tools for Enterprise Risk Capital Management and Portfolio Optimization*, CAS Forum Summer 2002 (available at www.casact.
org/pubs/forum/02sforum/02sf043.pdf).

Ward, L. S., and D. H. Lee (2002), *Practical Application of the Risk-Adjusted Return on
Capital Framework*, CAS Forum Summer 2002 (available at www.casact.org/pubs/
forum/02sforum/02sftoc.pdf).

Watson, R. D. (1974), "Insuring Some Progress in the Bank Capital Hassle," *Federal
Reserve Bank of Philadelphia Business Review*, July–August, 3–18.

Williamson, O. (1975), *Markets and Hierarchies: Analysis and Antitrust Implications*,
Free Press, New York.

Williamson, O. (1981), "The Economics of Organization: The Transaction Cost Approach,"
American Journal of Sociology, 87, 548–577.

Wilson, T. (1997a), "Portfolio Credit Risk I," *Risk*, September, 111–117.

Wilson, T. (1997b), "Portfolio Credit Risk II," *Risk*, October, 56–61.

Wilson, T. (2003), "Overcoming the Hurdle," *Risk*, July, 79–83.

Zaik, E., J. Walter, G. Kelling, and C. James (1996), "RAROC at Bank of America: From
Theory to Practice," *Journal of Applied Corporate Finance*, 9, 83–93.

Zangari, P. (1996), "How Accurate Is the Delta-Gamma Methodology?" *RiskMetric*^{TM}
Monitor, J.P. Morgan-Reuters, Third Quarter, 12–29.

Zangari, P. (1997), "Streamlining the Market Risk Measurement Process," *RiskMetrics*^{TM}
Monitor, J.P. Morgan-Reuters, First Quarter, 3–22.

Index